Matrix of Meanings
of the Book of Changes

Matrix of Meanings
of the Book of Changes

DCB

© and translation 2024 by Daniel C. Bernardo

All rights reserved under International
and Pan-American Copyright Conventions.

ISBN:978-1-7390445-9-6

Preface

This book is aimed at those who already know the *Book of Changes* and wish to better understand its original message. The Chinese characters or sinograms that were used to write the *YiJing*, have multiple meanings that cannot be fully covered when translated into a Western language, because inevitably their range of meanings is truncated. Although these limitations of *YiJing* translations cannot be avoided, this book offers English-speaking readers a tool that will allow them to understand more deeply the many possible meanings that the *YiJing* sentences suggest.

This *YiJing* translation includes: **The Judgment** (*GuaCi*), **The Image** (*DaXiang*) and the comments assigned to the lines of the hexagrams (*YaoCi*), but instead of adding our own interpretation to them, we offer tables of meanings of the sinograms, which allow readers to take our translation only as a point of reference. Readers will thus be able, by combining the multiple meanings of the sinograms in different ways, to better appreciate the subtle nuances of meaning of the *YiJing* sentences, as well as forming alternative readings of the texts.

We display each *YiJing* sentence in a table, or matrix of meanings, which is read from top to bottom, just as traditional Chinese texts. Each line of the table shows the meaning of a sinogram, and is divided into four columns: the first shows the sinogram; the second its pronunciation, using the *PinYin* romanization system; the third its number in Mathews' Chinese-English dictionary and the fourth its range of meanings.

In preparing this book we follow the classical interpretation of the *YiJing* text, as it has been read from the *Han* to the *Qing* dynasty. The original text used for this translation is the *Zhouyi Zhezhong*, "Balanced Commentaries on the

ZhouYi," published in 1715 under the patronage of the *Qing* dynasty. It is the same text used by Richard Wilhelm and many other Sinologists as the basis of their translations.

PinYin uses four tones to indicate the pronunciation of each syllable, indicating them either with different accents or with numbers, as in this book. The appendix on *PinYin Pronunciation* has more information on this topic.

Because this book is not aimed at those who are just starting out with the *Book of Changes*, but rather at those who are already familiar with it, we do not indicate how to consult the *YiJing* nor do we add any other additional material, except for a *Concordance* that allows readers to study the repetitions of different sinograms throughout the book, according to their corresponding number in Mathews' dictionary.

THE 64 HEXAGRAMS

1 乾 *qian* – The Creative / Activity / Dynamic Force

THE JUDGMENT

Outstanding success. The determination is favorable.

乾	qian2	3233	Spirit power, creative, force, dynamic, strong, vigor, constant, heaven, heavenly generative principle (male), father, sovereign, power above the human, *yang* power, active, vigorous appearance.
元	yuan2	7707	Outstanding, greatest, sublime, supreme, greatest, very great, grand; source, beginning, cause, first or paramount, fundamentality; head, chief; used as a superlative.
亨	heng1	2099	Success, prevalence, smooth progress, growth, consummate, triumph; pervade; offering, sacrifice.
利	li4	3867	Favorable, lucky, advantageous, profitable, beneficial, furthering, harvesting; sharp, sharp witted.
貞	zhen1	0346	Perseverance, persistence, determination, steadiness, firmness; straight, correct, verified, certain; pure, loyal. Its original meaning was "to determine an uncertain matter through divination".

THE IMAGE

Heaven action is strong and dynamic.
Thus the noble never ceases to strengthen himself.

天	tian1	6361	Heaven, firmament, the sky, cosmos; celestial, divine, power above the human.
行	xing2	2754	Move, go, advance, act, do.
健	jian4	0854	Constant, tenacious, continuous; strong, healthy, dynamic.
君	jun1	1715	Noble, prince, aristocrat, lord, chief, gentleman; honorable, a highly principled person, superior man. Most times, this character appears alongside another one, forming the word *JunZi*, whose original meaning was "son of a prince or ruler": 君子.

1   MATRIX OF MEANINGS OF THE BOOK OF CHANGES

子	zi3	6939	Child, son or daughter, offspring; suffix; bride, wife; gentleman, officer, master, prince; young lady; the first of the *Earthly Branches*.
以	yi3	2932	Thus, in that way, by means of, with, for; instrument, medium, method, use (of), way (to).
自	zi4	6960	From, origin, source, cause, reason; oneself, yourself.
彊	qiang2	0668	Strong, stubborn, uncompromising, violent, fierce, demanding, coercive, dominant.
不	bu4	5379	No, not, negative prefix; without, none, nothing, will not, need not, will not be.
息	xi1	2495	Rest, pause; breathe, breathing-spell, take breath, enjoy the rest, well-being, prosper.

Nine at the beginning

    Submerged dragon. Do not act.

潛	qian2	0918	Submerged, hidden (below water); to secret oneself, concealed, to retire.
龍	long2	4258	Dragon, powerful force that surges from the waters, associated with rain, floods, heaven, the trigram ☰ and the hexagram 1.
勿	wu4	7208	Do not, no. Negative imperative.
用	yong4	7567	Use, apply, put to use, apply the oracle to real world situations; hereby, thereby.

Nine in the second place

    Dragon in the field. It is favorable to see the great man.

見	jian4	0860	See, observe, look at, to be seen; cause to appear; be exposed to, display, reveal; interview, visit or call on, meet.
龍	long2	4258	Dragon, powerful force that surges from the waters, associated with rain, floods, heaven, the trigram ☰ and the hexagram 1.
在	zai4	6657	Be at, at, in, on, within, be present; to lie in, depend upon, involved with; be living, dwell, located in.
田	tian2	6362	Field, cultivated land; hunt. The character is the picture of a cultivated field, divided in four sectors.
利	li4	3867	Favorable, lucky, advantageous, profitable, beneficial, furthering, harvesting; sharp, sharp witted.

The Creative (II)

見	jian4	0860	See, observe, look at, to be seen; cause to appear; be exposed to, display, reveal; interview, visit or call on, meet.
大	da4	5943	Big, great, tall; excessive, arrogant; spread out and reach everywhere.
人	ren2	3097	Man, person(s); people; others; human being, individual.

Nine in the third place

The noble is diligent without pause throughout the day.
At night he is cautious, as if in danger. No defect.

君	jun1	1715	Noble, prince, aristocrat, lord, chief, gentleman; honorable, a highly principled person, superior man. Most times, this character appears alongside another one, forming the word *JunZi*, whose original meaning was "son of a prince or ruler": 君子.
子	zi3	6939	Child, son or daughter, offspring; suffix; bride, wife; gentleman, officer, master, prince; young lady; the first of the *Earthly Branches*.
終	zhong1	1500	End, finish, complete; for ever; end of a cycle; carried to conclusion, consummation, closure; death. The original meaning was: tied-off end of a thread.
日	ri4	3124	Sun, day, daylight, daytime; daily.
乾	qian2	3233	Spirit power, creative, force, dynamic, strong, vigor, constant, heaven, heavenly generative principle (male), father, sovereign, power above the human, *yang* power, active, vigorous appearance. Its duplication is usually interpreted as "diligent, vigorous", although some say it means "sad and fearful".
乾	qian2	3233	
夕	xi4	2485	Nightfall, evening, twilight, dark. Ancient representations in oracular bone, show clearly the crescent moon.
惕	ti4	6263	Wary, cautious, alert, alarmed; fear, respect, to stand in awe of.
若	ruo4	3126	Like, just as, to be like; agree, conform to; approve; concordant; compliant.
厲	li4	3906	Danger, threat; oppressive, cruel, wicked, brutal, harsh; sickness, malevolent devil; grind, polish, sharpen; discipline.
无	wu2	7173	No, not, negative; without, does not possess, not have.
咎	jiu4	1192	Fault, blame, mistake, wrong; inauspicious; misfortune, bad luck, calamity; reproach, censure.

Nine in the fourth place

> He hesitates before jumping over the chasm. No defect.

或	huo4	2402	Perhaps, possibly, if, by chance; doubtful, uncertain; some, someone, something, sometime.
躍	yue4	7504	Leap, jump; shamanic dance of flight, a rite of passage.
在	zai4	6657	Be at, at, in, on, within, be present; to lie in, depend upon, involved with; be living, dwell, located in.
淵	yuan1	7723	A deep, an abyss, deep waters, a chasm with a whirlpool in its depths.
无	wu2	7173	No, not, negative; without, does not possess, not have.
咎	jiu4	1192	Fault, blame, mistake, wrong; inauspicious; misfortune, bad luck, calamity; reproach, censure.

Nine in the fifth place

> Dragon flying in the sky. It is favorable to see the great man.

飛	fei1	1850	Fly, flying, soaring; go quickly.
龍	long2	4258	Dragon, powerful force that surges from the waters, associated with rain, floods, heaven, the trigram ☰ and the hexagram 1.
在	zai4	6657	Be at, at, in, on, within, be present; to lie in, depend upon, involved with; be living, dwell, located in.
天	tian1	6361	Heaven, firmament, the sky, cosmos; celestial, divine, power above the human.
利	li4	3867	Favorable, lucky, advantageous, profitable, beneficial, furthering, harvesting; sharp, sharp witted.
見	jian4	0860	See, observe, look at, to be seen; cause to appear; be exposed to, display, reveal; interview, visit or call on, meet.
大	da4	5943	Big, great, tall; excessive, arrogant; spread out and reach everywhere.
人	ren2	3097	Man, person(s); people; others; human being, individual.

Nine at the top

> Arrogant dragon. There will be occasion for repentance.

亢	kang4	3273	Arrogant, haughty, overbearing, excessive, unbending; protect, defend, obstruct; gully (Kunst).
龍	long2	4258	Dragon, powerful force that surges from the waters, associated with rain, floods, heaven, the trigram ☰ and the hexagram 1.

The Creative (13) 1

有	you3	7533	Have, possession, there be, there is.
悔	hui3	2336	Repent, regret, contrition; trouble. This word indicates both an objective situation and a subjective reaction to such circumstance.

When all the lines are nines

A group of dragons without heads. Auspicious.

見	jian4	0860	See, observe, look at, to be seen; cause to appear; be exposed to, display, reveal; interview, visit or call on, meet.
羣	qun2	1737	Group, herd, flock, crowd, host, multitude, congregation.
龍	long2	4258	Dragon, powerful force that surges from the waters, associated with rain, floods, heaven, the trigram ☰ and the hexagram 1.
无	wu2	7173	No, not, negative; without, does not possess, not have.
首	shou3	5839	Head; foremost, first; leader, chief.
吉	ji2	0476	Good fortune, auspicious, promising, fortunate, lucky, advantageous, happiness, good auspices. It is the only single character meaning good luck in the *YiJing*.

2 坤 *kun* – The Receptive

THE JUDGMENT

The Receptive. Outstanding success favorable for the determination of a mare. If the noble takes the lead he goes astray, but if he follows, he finds a master. It is favorable to find friends in the west and south, avoid friends in the east and north. A quiet determination is auspicious.

坤	kun1	3684	Earth, receptive; compliance; matter, field; feminine, mother.
元	yuan2	7707	Outstanding, greatest, sublime, supreme, greatest, very great, grand; source, beginning, cause, first or paramount, fundamentality; head, chief; used as a superlative.
亨	heng1	2099	Success, prevalence, smooth progress, growth, consummate, triumph; pervade; offering, sacrifice.
利	li4	3867	Favorable, lucky, advantageous, profitable, beneficial, furthering, harvesting; sharp, sharp witted.
牝	pin4	5280	Female (used for farm animals and birds), female sexual organs, cow.
馬	ma3	4310	Horse.
之	zhi1	0935	Personal pronoun, he she, it; this, that, these, etc.; often used as a possessive.
貞	zhen1	0346	Perseverance, persistence, determination, steadiness, firmness; straight, correct, verified, certain; pure, loyal. Its original meaning was "to determine an uncertain matter through divination".
君	jun1	1715	Noble, prince, aristocrat, lord, chief, gentleman; honorable, a highly principled person, superior man. Most times, this character appears alongside another one, forming the word *JunZi*, whose original meaning was "son of a prince or ruler": 君子.
子	zi3	6939	Child, son or daughter, offspring; suffix; bride, wife; gentleman, officer, master, prince; young lady; the first of the *Earthly Branches*.
有	you3	7533	Have, possession, there be, there is.

The Receptive (15)

攸	you1	7519	Goal, direction, destination, objective; distant, far away; a place; that which, whereby, thereby, for which; mark of the passive voice.
往	wang3	7050	Go, to go to, go forward, go towards; depart, bygone, former. 攸往: have a place to go; have a goal.
先	xian1	2702	Before, first, foremost, in front, lead.
迷	mi2	4450	Lose the way, go astray; miss, error; delude, infatuation.
後	hou4	2143	Later, behind, rear, afterward, come after; follow; descendants, successor.
得	de2	6161	Get, obtain, gain; reach, achieve; can; attain the desired thing.
主	zhu3	1336	Master, lord, chief; host, innkeeper.
利	li4	3867	Favorable, lucky, advantageous, profitable, beneficial, furthering, harvesting; sharp, sharp witted.
西	xi1	2460	The West, western. Related to the autumn.
南	nan2	4620	The South. The region associated with Summer, fire, work in community and vegetation.
得	de2	6161	Get, obtain, gain; reach, achieve; can; attain the desired thing.
朋	peng2	5054	Friend, companion, pair, equal, comrade; a string of cowries (small shiny shells used as coins in ancient China).
東	dong1	6605	The East.
北	bei3	4974	The North. The character depicts two persons standing, back to back. In China, the north has traditionally been considered the "back side". Maps shown the south on top and compasses pointed south.
喪	sang4	5429	Lose, let drop, disappear, destroy, perish, mourning, burial.
朋	peng2	5054	Friend, companion, pair, equal, comrade; a string of cowries (small shiny shells used as coins in ancient China).
安	an1	0026	Quiet, at peace, calm; tranquility, safety, security; settled, comfort, contentment.
貞	zhen1	0346	Perseverance, persistence, determination, steadiness, firmness; straight, correct, verified, certain; pure, loyal. Its original meaning was "to determine an uncertain matter through divination".
吉	ji2	0476	Good fortune, auspicious, promising, fortunate, lucky, advantageous, happiness, good auspices. It is the only single character meaning good luck in the *YiJing*.

The Image

> The Earth condition is receptive obedience. Thus the noble, who has a munificent character, sustains all living creatures.

地	di4	6198	Earth, soil, ground.
勢	shi4	5799	Power, capacity, potency, force, authority, influence; aspect, circumstances, condition.
坤	kun1	3684	Earth, receptive; compliance; matter, field; feminine, mother.
君	jun1	1715	Noble, prince, aristocrat, lord, chief, gentleman; honorable, a highly principled person, superior man. Most times, this character appears alongside another one, forming the word *JunZi*, whose original meaning was "son of a prince or ruler": 君子.
子	zi3	6939	Child, son or daughter, offspring; suffix; bride, wife; gentleman, officer, master, prince; young lady; the first of the *Earthly Branches*.
以	yi3	2932	Thus, in that way, by means of, with, for; instrument, medium, method, use (of), way (to).
厚	hou4	2147	Munificent, generous, liberal; ample, tolerant; substantial, thick, large.
德	de2	6162	Virtue, spiritual power, moral integrity; quality, nature, aptitude, ability, character.
載	zai4	6653	Transport, carry, load, bear; contain, sustain; load a vessel or cart, conveyance.
物	wu4	7209	Thing/s, being/s, creature/s; substance, the physical world, all living things; others.

Six at the beginning

> Walking on hoarfrost one reaches hard ice.

履	lu3	3893	Step on, treading, track, walk or follow a trail or way; footwear, shoes; conduct, behavior; ceremonies.
霜	shuang1	5919	Frost, hoarfrost. 履霜: *a)* the coming winter; signs of decay; *b)* an approaching marriage; *c)* ceremonial walking on hoarfrost for the autumnal sacrifices.
堅	jian1	0825	Solid, firm, strong, hard, resolute, obstinate; durable, hardened, solidified.
冰	bing1	5283	Ice.
至	zhi4	0982	Arrive, culminate, reach the highest point, utmost, superlative.

The Receptive (17) 2

Six in the second place

Right, square and large, inexperienced.
But nothing will not be favorable.

直	zhi2	1006	Straight, direct, outspoken, honorable.
方	fang1	1802	Square, squarely, directly, straightforward, honest; a place, a region; on all sides; direction, trend, method; suddenly, quick, definite; take a place, occupy; sacrifice to the spirits of the four quarters.
大	da4	5943	Big, great, tall; excessive, arrogant; spread out and reach everywhere.
不	bu4	5379	No, not, negative prefix; without, none, nothing, will not, need not, will not be.
習	xi2	2499	Double, duplicate; repeated, repeatedly; practice, exercise, rehearsal, learning; to practice flying (young birds learning to fly flapping its wings).
无	wu2	7173	No, not, negative; without, does not possess, not have.
不	bu4	5379	No, not, negative prefix; without, none, nothing, will not, need not, will not be.
利	li4	3867	Favorable, lucky, advantageous, profitable, beneficial, furthering, harvesting; sharp, sharp witted.

Six in the third place

Hidden brilliance; can be determined. If you're still in the service of a King you will not have achievements, but will carry to conclusion.

含	han2	2017	Hidden, hold in the mouth; contain, restrain, tolerate.
章	zhang1	0182	Brilliance, splendor, refinement, distinction; ornament, emblem of distinction, jade tablet; amulet. Its short form, with the jade radical means "jade baton".
可	ke3	3381	Can, able, may; permit, allow; satisfactory, proper, suitable.
貞	zhen1	0346	Perseverance, persistence, determination, steadiness, firmness; straight, correct, verified, certain; pure, loyal. Its original meaning was "to determine an uncertain matter through divination".
或	huo4	2402	Perhaps, possibly, if, by chance; doubtful, uncertain; some, someone, something, sometime.
從	cong2	6919	Follow (somebody or a way or doctrine), adhere, obey, pursue; follower attendant; attend to business; from, by, since, whence, through.

王	wang2	7037	King, prince, sovereign, ruler.
事	shi4	5787	Serve, service; affairs, business, matters.
无	wu2	7173	No, not, negative; without, does not possess, not have.
成	cheng2	0379	Accomplish, achieve, finish, complete a task, fulfill; completed, perfect, fully developed, mature; peace making.
有	you3	7533	Have, possession, there be, there is.
終	zhong1	1500	End, finish, complete; for ever; end of a cycle; carried to conclusion, consummation, closure; death. The original meaning was: tied-off end of a thread.

Six in the fourth place

A tied up bag. No defect, no praise.

括	kuo4	3519	Tie, tied up, closed; bring together; include, embrace.
囊	nang2	4627	Sack, bag, pouch.
无	wu2	7173	No, not, negative; without, does not possess, not have.
咎	jiu4	1192	Fault, blame, mistake, wrong; inauspicious; misfortune, bad luck, calamity; reproach, censure.
无	wu2	7173	No, not, negative; without, does not possess, not have.
譽	yu4	7617	Fame, renown, reputation, honor, honored, praised.

Six in the fifth place

Yellow lower garment. There will be outstanding happiness.

黃	huang2	2297	Yellow, yellow-brown; color of the soil in central China. In the *YiJing* the yellow color is always favorable, it is the color of the middle and the moderation and it was the imperial color since the *Han* dynasty.
裳	chang2	5671	Lower garment, skirt, clothing, garment used from the waist down worn by both men and women; ceremonial garment.
元	yuan2	7707	Outstanding, greatest, sublime, supreme, greatest, very great, grand; source, beginning, cause, first or paramount, fundamentality; head, chief; used as a superlative.
吉	ji2	0476	Good fortune, auspicious, promising, fortunate, lucky, advantageous, happiness, good auspices. It is the only single character meaning good luck in the *YiJing*.

THE RECEPTIVE (19) 2

Six at the top
Dragons fight in the open country. His blood is black and yellow.

龍	long2	4258	Dragon, powerful force that surges from the waters, associated with rain, floods, heaven, the trigram ☰ and the hexagram 1.
戰	zhan4	0147	Battle, struggle, fight, war, combat; hostilities.
于	yu2	7592	At, to, in, into, on, from, by, go, go to, move towards, proceed, be.
野	ye3	7314	Meadow, open country, countryside, fields, wilderness.
其	qi2	0525	Their, his, its, the; this, that. A demonstrative and possessive pronoun.
血	xue4	2901	Blood, bleeding. Its ancient form shows a sacrificial vessel with its content.
玄	xuan2	2881	Black, dark, blue-black; deep, profound. Originally meant a dyed thread of rope.
黃	huang2	2297	Yellow, yellow-brown; color of the soil in central China. In the *YiJing* the yellow color is always favorable, it is the color of the middle and the moderation and it was the imperial color since the *Han* dynasty.

When all the lines are sixes
Long term determination is favorable.

利	li4	3867	Favorable, lucky, advantageous, profitable, beneficial, furthering, harvesting; sharp, sharp witted.
永	yong3	7589	For a long time, constant, permanent, everlasting; prolong; distant, far reaching.
貞	zhen1	0346	Perseverance, persistence, determination, steadiness, firmness; straight, correct, verified, certain; pure, loyal. Its original meaning was "to determine an uncertain matter through divination".

3 屯 *zhun* – Difficulties at the Beginning

The Judgment

The initial difficulty. Outstanding success. Favorable determination. It should not be pursued any goal. It is favorable to appoint officials.

屯	zhun1	6592	Difficult; to sprout, begin to grow; assemble, accumulate, hoard; a camp, to garrison soldiers, a village, massed, bunched.
元	yuan2	7707	Outstanding, greatest, sublime, supreme, greatest, very great, grand; source, beginning, cause, first or paramount, fundamentality; head, chief; used as a superlative.
亨	heng1	2099	Success, prevalence, smooth progress, growth, consummate, triumph; pervade; offering, sacrifice.
利	li4	3867	Favorable, lucky, advantageous, profitable, beneficial, furthering, harvesting; sharp, sharp witted.
貞	zhen1	0346	Perseverance, persistence, determination, steadiness, firmness; straight, correct, verified, certain; pure, loyal. Its original meaning was "to determine an uncertain matter through divination".
勿	wu4	7208	Do not, no. Negative imperative.
用	yong4	7567	Use, apply, put to use, apply the oracle to real world situations; hereby, thereby.
有	you3	7533	Have, possession, there be, there is.
攸	you1	7519	Goal, direction, destination, objective; distant, far away; a place; that which, whereby, thereby, for which; mark of the passive voice.
往	wang3	7050	Go, to go to, go forward, go towards; depart, bygone, former. 攸往: have a place to go; have a goal.
利	li4	3867	Favorable, lucky, advantageous, profitable, beneficial, furthering, harvesting; sharp, sharp witted.
建	jian4	0853	Establish, found, appoint, confirm a position.
侯	hou2	2135	Feudal lord, (vassal) prince, marquis; officer, governor, chief; skilled archer.

Difficulties at the Beginning (21)   3

The Image

Clouds and Thunder: The image of Difficulties at the Beginning. Thus the noble adjusts his measures of government.

雲	yun2	7750	Clouds.
雷	lei2	4236	Thunder, shock, terrifying, arousing power surging from the earth.
屯	zhun1	6592	Difficult; to sprout, begin to grow; assemble, accumulate, hoard; a camp, to garrison soldiers, a village, massed, bunched.
君	jun1	1715	Noble, prince, aristocrat, lord, chief, gentleman; honorable, a highly principled person, superior man. Most times, this character appears alongside another one, forming the word *JunZi*, whose original meaning was "son of a prince or ruler": 君子.
子	zi3	6939	Child, son or daughter, offspring; suffix; bride, wife; gentleman, officer, master, prince; young lady; the first of the *Earthly Branches*.
以	yi3	2932	Thus, in that way, by means of, with, for; instrument, medium, method, use (of), way (to).
經	jing1	1123	Classic works; canon, regulate. Literally indicates the warp of a fabric, pass through; the original meaning was "warp in a loom".
綸	lun2	4252	Woof, silk threads, to twist or bend silk; classify, coordinate, adjust.

Nine at the beginning

Looking to overcome an obstacle. It is favorable to maintain the determination. It is favorable to appoint assistants.

磐	pan2	4904	Boulder, large rock; stable, immovable.
桓	huan2	2236	Hesitation; around, surrounding, turn around, turn back. 磐桓: "hindrance, large rock" and hesitation; turning around temporarily when facing an obstacle.
利	li4	3867	Favorable, lucky, advantageous, profitable, beneficial, furthering, harvesting; sharp, sharp witted.
居	ju1	1535	Remain; rest (in); abides, dwell; to occupy a position or place; overbearing, arrogant.
貞	zhen1	0346	Perseverance, persistence, determination, steadiness, firmness; straight, correct, verified, certain; pure, loyal. Its original meaning was "to determine an uncertain matter through divination".

利	li4	3867	Favorable, lucky, advantageous, profitable, beneficial, furthering, harvesting; sharp, sharp witted.
建	jian4	0853	Establish, found, appoint, confirm a position.
侯	hou2	2135	Feudal lord, (vassal) prince, marquis; officer, governor, chief; skilled archer.

Six in the second place

Difficulties impeding progress. Horse and cart separate. It's not a villain, but a pretender. The girl has determination and does not plight her troth. After ten years she will pledge herself.

屯	zhun1	6592	Difficult; to sprout, begin to grow; assemble, accumulate, hoard; a camp, to garrison soldiers, a village, massed, bunched.
如	ru2	3137	Thus, in this way, as, like, similar to, if (conditional).
邅	zhan1	8010	Move or proceed with difficulty; turn around, unable to advance; quit.
如	ru2	3137	Thus, in this way, as, like, similar to, if (conditional).
乘	cheng2	0398	A team of four horses. Riding horses was not practiced until the fifth century BC in China. When the *ZhouYi* was written, horses were used only for drawing chariots and carriages.
馬	ma3	4310	Horse.
班	ban1	4889	Divide, scatter, distribute, classify, arrayed, ordered, dispose according to rank.
如	ru2	3137	Thus, in this way, as, like, similar to, if (conditional).
匪	fei3	1820	No, strong negative.
寇	kou4	3444	Bandit, invader, enemy, robber, violent people, outcasts, plunderers.
婚	hun1	2360	Marriage, take a wife; bridegroom, ally.
媾	gou4	3426	Marriage, a second marriage, mating, match, families united by marriage; suitor, groom; allying, friendship, favor.
女	nu3	4776	Maiden, woman, lady, girl, feminine.
子	zi3	6939	Child, son or daughter, offspring; suffix; bride, wife; gentleman, officer, master, prince; young lady; the first of the *Earthly Branches*.

Difficulties at the Beginning (23)

貞	zhen1	0346	Perseverance, persistence, determination, steadiness, firmness; straight, correct, verified, certain; pure, loyal. Its original meaning was "to determine an uncertain matter through divination".
不	bu4	5379	No, not, negative prefix; without, none, nothing, will not, need not, will not be.
字	zi4	6942	Conceive, pregnant; pledge, betrothal; breed; nurture, nourish, suckle.
十	shi2	5807	Ten; complete, perfect, whole.
年	nian2	4711	Year(s), season(s), harvest(s).
乃	nai3	4612	Then, and, also, thereupon, as it turned out, namely, after all, only then; really, indeed.
字	zi4	6942	Conceive, pregnant; pledge, betrothal; breed; nurture, nourish, suckle.

Six in the third place

Chasing the deer without forester, astray in the depths of the forest.
The noble sees the signs and desists.
If he went forward, he would regret it.

即	ji2	0495	Approach, come to; promptly.
鹿	lu4	4203	Deer (mature male with antlers).
无	wu2	7173	No, not, negative; without, does not possess, not have.
虞	yu2	7648	Gamekeeper, forester. Take precautions, to provide against; foresee; anxious, not at ease.
惟	wei2	7066	Think; namely, it is; only; alone. Initial particle, often unstranslatable.
入	ru4	3152	Enter, go into (this is the meaning used in the *YiJing*); to make to enter; put into; bring in, present; encroach.
于	yu2	7592	At, to, in, into, on, from, by, go, go to, move towards, proceed, be.
林	lin2	4022	Woods, forest, grove, copse.
中	zhong1	1504	Center, inner, in the inside, put in the center, hit (target); balanced, central, middle, correct.
君	jun1	1715	Noble, prince, aristocrat, lord, chief, gentleman; honorable, a highly principled person, superior man. Most times, this character appears alongside another one, forming the word *JunZi*, whose original meaning was "son of a prince or ruler": 君子.

子	zi3	6939	Child, son or daughter, offspring; suffix; bride, wife; gentleman, officer, master, prince; young lady; the first of the *Earthly Branches*.
幾	ji1	0409	Almost; imminent, nearly; occasion; minutiae, first subtle signs; approaches.
不	bu4	5379	No, not, negative prefix; without, none, nothing, will not, need not, will not be.
如	ru2	3137	Thus, in this way, as, like, similar to, if (conditional).
舍	she3	5699	Quit, abandon, let go, leave, put down, set aside, put away, store; stop, rest in, halt, resting place, encampment.
往	wang3	7050	Go, to go to, go forward, go towards; depart, bygone, former.
吝	lin4	4040	Humiliation, regret, shame, distress, grief, sorrow; miserly, niggardly. It is a warning of trouble.

Six in the fourth place

Horse and cart separate. Look for the union. Advance brings happiness. Everything will be auspicious and without blemish.

乘	cheng2	0398	A team of four horses. Riding horses was not practiced until the fifth century BC in China. When the *ZhouYi* was written, horses were used only for drawing chariots and carriages.
馬	ma3	4310	Horse.
班	ban1	4889	Divide, scatter, distribute, classify, arrayed, ordered, dispose according to rank.
如	ru2	3137	Thus, in this way, as, like, similar to, if (conditional).
求	qiu2	1217	Seek, strive; ask, implore, beg, pray; desire.
婚	hun1	2360	Marriage, take a wife; bridegroom, ally.
媾	gou4	3426	Marriage, a second marriage, mating, match, families united by marriage; suitor, groom; allying, friendship, favor.
往	wang3	7050	Go, to go to, go forward, go towards; depart, bygone, former.
吉	ji2	0476	Good fortune, auspicious, promising, fortunate, lucky, advantageous, happiness, good auspices. It is the only single character meaning good luck in the *YiJing*.
无	wu2	7173	No, not, negative; without, does not possess, not have.

Difficulties at the Beginning (25)

不	bu4	5379	No, not, negative prefix; without, none, nothing, will not, need not, will not be.
利	li4	3867	Favorable, lucky, advantageous, profitable, beneficial, furthering, harvesting; sharp, sharp witted.

Nine in the fifth place

Difficulties with their wealth. Determination in small matters is auspicious. Determination in major ways brings misfortune.

屯	zhun1	6592	Difficult; to sprout, begin to grow; assemble, accumulate, hoard; a camp, to garrison soldiers, a village, massed, bunched.
其	qi2	0525	Their, his, its, the; this, that. A demonstrative and possessive pronoun.
膏	gao1	3296	Fat, grease, far meat; richness, favors, dispensing favors.
小	xiao3	2605	Small, insignificant, common, humble, mediocre; diminish, belittle.
貞	zhen1	0346	Perseverance, persistence, determination, steadiness, firmness; straight, correct, verified, certain; pure, loyal. Its original meaning was "to determine an uncertain matter through divination".
吉	ji2	0476	Good fortune, auspicious, promising, fortunate, lucky, advantageous, happiness, good auspices. It is the only single character meaning good luck in the *YiJing*.
大	da4	5943	Big, great, tall; excessive, arrogant; spread out and reach everywhere.
貞	zhen1	0346	Perseverance, persistence, determination, steadiness, firmness; straight, correct, verified, certain; pure, loyal. Its original meaning was "to determine an uncertain matter through divination".
凶	xiong1	2808	Misfortune, pitfall, ominous, bad, unlucky, disastrous, trouble, accident.

Six at the top

Horse and cart separate. Tears of blood are spilled.

乘	cheng2	0398	A team of four horses. Riding horses was not practiced until the fifth century BC in China. When the *ZhouYi* was written, horses were used only for drawing chariots and carriages.
馬	ma3	4310	Horse.
班	ban1	4889	Divide, scatter, distribute, classify, arrayed, ordered, dispose according to rank.

如	ru2	3137	Thus, in this way, as, like, similar to, if (conditional).
泣	qi4	0563	Weep, tears, sob, to weep silent tears, broken heart.
血	xue4	2901	Blood, bleeding. Its ancient form shows a sacrificial vessel with its content.
漣	lian2	4012	Flowing water, ripples raised on water by wind, in streams, dripping (as tears).
如	ru2	3137	Thus, in this way, as, like, similar to, if (conditional).

4 蒙 *meng* – Youthful Folly

THE JUDGMENT

The Youthful Folly is successful. It is not I who seek the young fool, the young fool seeks me. At the first oracle I inform, but a second or third time is troublesome; and I do not instruct the annoying. The determination is favorable.

蒙	meng2	4437	Ignorant, immaturity, inexpert, youthful folly; go with covered eyes against; cover, hidden, in darkness, deception, conceal, cheat.
亨	heng1	2099	Success, prevalence, smooth progress, growth, consummate, triumph; pervade; offering, sacrifice.
匪	fei3	1820	No, strong negative.
我	wo3	4778	We, us, I, my, mine, our.
求	qiu2	1217	Seek, strive; ask, implore, beg, pray; desire.
童	tong2	6626	Youth, boy, young person (boy or girl); page, pupil; servant; a virgin, pure, undefiled; young animal without horns (esp. calf or lamb).
蒙	meng2	4437	Ignorant, immaturity, inexpert, youthful folly; go with covered eyes against; cover, hidden, in darkness, deception, conceal, cheat.
童	tong2	6626	Youth, boy, young person (boy or girl); page, pupil; servant; a virgin, pure, undefiled; young animal without horns (esp. calf or lamb).
蒙	meng2	4437	Ignorant, immaturity, inexpert, youthful folly; go with covered eyes against; cover, hidden, in darkness, deception, conceal, cheat.
求	qiu2	1217	Seek, strive; ask, implore, beg, pray; desire.
我	wo3	4778	We, us, I, my, mine, our.
初	chu1	1390	At first, beginning, initial, incipient, in the early stages.
筮	shi4	5763	Divination by yarrow (*Achillea millefolium*) stalks, consult the oracle.
告	gao4	3287	Inform, announce, report, proclaim.
再	zai4	6658	Twice, second, again, repeated.

三	san1	5415	Three, thrice, third time or place.
瀆	du2	6515	Importune, harass, insult, molest, abuse, annoy, disrespect; canal, ditch, drain.
瀆	du2	6515	Importune, harass, insult, molest, abuse, annoy, disrespect; canal, ditch, drain.
則	ze2	6746	Then, thus, accordingly, consequently, and so, in that case; law, rule, pattern; follow a law.
不	bu4	5379	No, not, negative prefix; without, none, nothing, will not, need not, will not be.
告	gao4	3287	Inform, announce, report, proclaim.
利	li4	3867	Favorable, lucky, advantageous, profitable, beneficial, furthering, harvesting; sharp, sharp witted.
貞	zhen1	0346	Perseverance, persistence, determination, steadiness, firmness; straight, correct, verified, certain; pure, loyal. Its original meaning was "to determine an uncertain matter through divination".

THE IMAGE

Under the Mountain flows a spring: The image of the Youthful folly. Thus the noble makes his actions resolute and nourishes his virtue.

山	shan1	5630	Mountain, hill, peak.
下	xia4	2520	Below, down, descend.
出	chu1	1409	Go out, came out, appear, departure; arise, emerge; bring out, take out, expel, leave, get rid of; produce, beget.
泉	quan2	1674	Spring, fountain.
蒙	meng2	4437	Ignorant, immaturity, inexpert, youthful folly; go with covered eyes against; cover, hidden, in darkness, deception, conceal, cheat.
君	jun1	1715	Noble, prince, aristocrat, lord, chief, gentleman; honorable, a highly principled person, superior man. Most times, this character appears alongside another one, forming the word *JunZi*, whose original meaning was "son of a prince or ruler": 君子.
子	zi3	6939	Child, son or daughter, offspring; suffix; bride, wife; gentleman, officer, master, prince; young lady; the first of the *Earthly Branches*.

Youthful Folly

以	yi3	2932	Thus, in that way, by means of, with, for; instrument, medium, method, use (of), way (to).
果	guo3	3732	Fruit (of a plant), come to fruition, realization, result, effect; bring to result, reach the conclusion; determined, courageous, go to the bitter end.
行	xing2	2754	Move, go, advance, act, do.
育	yu4	7687	Give birth; rear, breed, raise, nurture, nourish, bring up, educate.
德	de2	6162	Virtue, spiritual power, moral integrity; quality, nature, aptitude, ability, character.

Six at the beginning

To develop the foolish man it will be favorable to discipline him. The fetters must be removed, otherwise there will be regret.

發	fa1	1768	Develop, expand, open, manifest, send out, emit, arouse.
蒙	meng2	4437	Ignorant, immaturity, inexpert, youthful folly; go with covered eyes against; cover, hidden, in darkness, deception, conceal, cheat.
利	li4	3867	Favorable, lucky, advantageous, profitable, beneficial, furthering, harvesting; sharp, sharp witted.
用	yong4	7567	Use, apply, put to use, apply the oracle to real world situations; hereby, thereby.
刑	xing2	2755	Punishment, discipline, sanction.
人	ren2	3097	Man, person(s); people; others; human being, individual.
用	yong4	7567	Use, apply, put to use, apply the oracle to real world situations; hereby, thereby.
說	tuo1	5939	Remove, take off, come off, let loose.
桎	zhi4	0993	Fetters, leg shackles, handcuffs; restrain movement.
梏	gu4	3484	Handcuffs (wooden), shackles, manacles.
以	yi3	2932	Thus, in that way, by means of, with, for; instrument, medium, method, use (of), way (to).
往	wang3	7050	Go, to go to, go forward, go towards; depart, bygone, former.
吝	lin4	4040	Humiliation, regret, shame, distress, grief, sorrow; miserly, niggardly. It is a warning of trouble.

Matrix of Meanings of the Book of Changes

Nine in the second place

Supporting the Youthful Folly is auspicious. To take a wife is auspicious. A son can take care of the family.

包	bao1	4937	Bundle, wrap, reed mat for wrapping; kitchen, butchering room; contain, support, take responsibility over.
蒙	meng2	4437	Ignorant, immaturity, inexpert, youthful folly; go with covered eyes against; cover, hidden, in darkness, deception, conceal, cheat.
吉	ji2	0476	Good fortune, auspicious, promising, fortunate, lucky, advantageous, happiness, good auspices. It is the only single character meaning good luck in the *YiJing*.
納	na4	4607	Bring in, convey to, hand to, present; take, receive, let in.
婦	fu4	1963	Woman, lady, wife, married woman.
吉	ji2	0476	Good fortune, auspicious, promising, fortunate, lucky, advantageous, happiness, good auspices. It is the only single character meaning good luck in the *YiJing*.
子	zi3	6939	Child, son or daughter, offspring; suffix; bride, wife; gentleman, officer, master, prince; young lady; the first of the *Earthly Branches*.
克	ke4	3320	Can, able, carry, sustain; conquest, dominate, prevail.
家	jia1	0594	Family, household, clan; home, to keep a home.

Six in the third place

Do not marry a girl who when she sees a man of metal, loses her self-possession. No place is favorable.

勿	wu4	7208	Do not, no. Negative imperative.
用	yong4	7567	Use, apply, put to use, apply the oracle to real world situations; hereby, thereby.
取	qu3	1615	Take, take a wife, obtain, lay hold of, grasp.
女	nu3	4776	Maiden, woman, lady, girl, feminine.
見	jian4	0860	See, observe, look at, to be seen; cause to appear; be exposed to, display, reveal; interview, visit or call on, meet.
金	jin1	1057	Metal, bronze, gold, golden; money, riches.
夫	fu1	1908	Man, male adult, husband; this, that, those.
不	bu4	5379	No, not, negative prefix; without, none, nothing, will not, need not, will not be.
有	you3	7533	Have, possession, there be, there is.

Youthful Folly (31) 4

躬	gong1	3704	Oneself, (own) body, person.
无	wu2	7173	No, not, negative; without, does not possess, not have.
攸	you1	7519	Goal, direction, destination, objective; distant, far away; a place; that which, whereby, thereby, for which; mark of the passive voice.
利	li4	3867	Favorable, lucky, advantageous, profitable, beneficial, furthering, harvesting; sharp, sharp witted.

Six in the fourth place

> Trapped by his folly he will suffer shame.

困	kun4	3688	Oppression, obstruction; besieged, surrounded; entangled; distress, exhaustion, anxiety.
蒙	meng2	4437	Ignorant, immaturity, inexpert, youthful folly; go with covered eyes against; cover, hidden, in darkness, deception, conceal, cheat.
吝	lin4	4040	Humiliation, regret, shame, distress, grief, sorrow; miserly, niggardly. It is a warning of trouble.

Six in the fifth place

> Children's folly is auspicious.

童	tong2	6626	Youth, boy, young person (boy or girl); page, pupil; servant; a virgin, pure, undefiled; young animal without horns (esp. calf or lamb).
蒙	meng2	4437	Ignorant, immaturity, inexpert, youthful folly; go with covered eyes against; cover, hidden, in darkness, deception, conceal, cheat.
吉	ji2	0476	Good fortune, auspicious, promising, fortunate, lucky, advantageous, happiness, good auspices. It is the only single character meaning good luck in the *YiJing*.

Nine at the top

> Punishing Youthful Folly. It is not favorable to act like a bandit [committing abuses], but it is favorable to defend oneself against bandits [abuses].

擊	ji1	0481	Strike, repel, beat, attack.
蒙	meng2	4437	Ignorant, immaturity, inexpert, youthful folly; go with covered eyes against; cover, hidden, in darkness, deception, conceal, cheat.
不	bu4	5379	No, not, negative prefix; without, none, nothing, will not, need not, will not be.

利	li4	3867	Favorable, lucky, advantageous, profitable, beneficial, furthering, harvesting; sharp, sharp witted.
爲	wei2	7059	Act, do, accomplish, make, to be; act for, stand for, support, help; become.
寇	kou4	3444	Bandit, invader, enemy, robber, violent people, outcasts, plunderers.
利	li4	3867	Favorable, lucky, advantageous, profitable, beneficial, furthering, harvesting; sharp, sharp witted.
禦	yu4	7665	Defend against, fight off, resist, withstand, hold out against, hinder.
寇	kou4	3444	Bandit, invader, enemy, robber, violent people, outcasts, plunderers.

5 需 *xu* – Waiting

THE JUDGMENT

Waiting. With brilliance and sincerity you will succeed.
The determination is favorable. It is favorable to cross the great river.

需	xu1	2844	Wait, serve; tarry, stop; get wet. From 雨, "rain" and 而: "stopped by rain, waiting it out".
有	you3	7533	Have, possession, there be, there is.
孚	fu2	1936	Truth; reliable, sincere; to inspire confidence in others; capture, prisoner, plunder.
光	guang1	3583	Light, illumination, brilliance, glory, honor.
亨	heng1	2099	Success, prevalence, smooth progress, growth, consummate, triumph; pervade; offering, sacrifice.
貞	zhen1	0346	Perseverance, persistence, determination, steadiness, firmness; straight, correct, verified, certain; pure, loyal. Its original meaning was "to determine an uncertain matter through divination".
吉	ji2	0476	Good fortune, auspicious, promising, fortunate, lucky, advantageous, happiness, good auspices. It is the only single character meaning good luck in the *YiJing*.
利	li4	3867	Favorable, lucky, advantageous, profitable, beneficial, furthering, harvesting; sharp, sharp witted.
涉	she4	5707	Cross, wade across (a river, stream), ford, pass through or over.
大	da4	5943	Big, great, tall; excessive, arrogant; spread out and reach everywhere.
川	chuan1	1439	River, flowing water; flood.

THE IMAGE

Clouds ascend to Heaven: The image of waiting.
Thus the noble drinks, eats and parties.

雲	yun2	7750	Clouds.
上	shang4	5669	Up, above, on, over, upwards, top, rise; higher, superior; first, best.

5 — Matrix of Meanings of the Book of Changes

於	yu2	7643	On, in, at, by, from; with reference to; interjection.
天	tian1	6361	Heaven, firmament, the sky, cosmos; celestial, divine, power above the human.
需	xu1	2844	Wait, serve; tarry, stop; get wet. From 雨, "rain" and 而: "stopped by rain, waiting it out".
君	jun1	1715	Noble, prince, aristocrat, lord, chief, gentleman; honorable, a highly principled person, superior man. Most times, this character appears alongside another one, forming the word *JunZi*, whose original meaning was "son of a prince or ruler": 君子.
子	zi3	6939	Child, son or daughter, offspring; suffix; bride, wife; gentleman, officer, master, prince; young lady; the first of the *Earthly Branches*.
以	yi3	2932	Thus, in that way, by means of, with, for; instrument, medium, method, use (of), way (to).
飲	yin3	7454	Drink; swallow; give to drink. 飲食: drink and eat; eating together.
食	shi2	5810	Eat, feed, ingest; food, give food to; nourishment; salary of an officer, livelihood; eclipse (eating of Sun or Moon).
宴	yan4	7364	Rest, repose; feast, banquet; leisure, pleasure. 宴樂: peace and happiness; to feast.
樂	le4	4129	Music, joyous, happy.

Nine at the beginning

Waiting in the suburbs. It is favorable to have perseverance. No defect.

需	xu1	2844	Wait, serve; tarry, stop; get wet. From 雨, "rain" and 而: "stopped by rain, waiting it out".
于	yu2	7592	At, to, in, into, on, from, by, go, go to, move towards, proceed, be.
郊	jiao1	0714	Countryside, suburbs, outskirts, frontier; suburban altar and sacrifice.
利	li4	3867	Favorable, lucky, advantageous, profitable, beneficial, furthering, harvesting; sharp, sharp witted.
用	yong4	7567	Use, apply, put to use, apply the oracle to real world situations; hereby, thereby.
恆	heng2	2107	Duration, persistence, endurance, steadiness, continuity; for a long time.

WAITING (35) 5

无	wu2	7173	No, not, negative; without, does not possess, not have.
咎	jiu4	1192	Fault, blame, mistake, wrong; inauspicious; misfortune, bad luck, calamity; reproach, censure.

Nine in the second place

> Waiting in the sand. They say little things.
> Finally there will be good fortune.

需	xu1	2844	Wait, serve; tarry, stop; get wet. From 雨, "rain" and 而: "stopped by rain, waiting it out".
于	yu2	7592	At, to, in, into, on, from, by, go, go to, move towards, proceed, be.
沙	sha1	5606	Sand, gravel, sandbank, beach.
小	xiao3	2605	Small, insignificant, common, humble, mediocre; diminish, belittle.
有	you3	7533	Have, possession, there be, there is.
言	yan2	7334	Talk, speech, words, sayings; big flute.
終	zhong1	1500	End, finish, complete; for ever; end of a cycle; carried to conclusion, consummation, closure; death. The original meaning was: tied-off end of a thread.
吉	ji2	0476	Good fortune, auspicious, promising, fortunate, lucky, advantageous, happiness, good auspices. It is the only single character meaning good luck in the *YiJing*.

Nine in the third place

> Waiting in the mud attracts bandits.

需	xu1	2844	Wait, serve; tarry, stop; get wet. From 雨, "rain" and 而: "stopped by rain, waiting it out".
于	yu2	7592	At, to, in, into, on, from, by, go, go to, move towards, proceed, be.
泥	ni2	4660	Mud, sludge; mire, an area of wet, soggy ground, to be mired; to paste, to plaster; impeded, obstructed.
致	zhi4	0984	Bring about, cause; involve, induce; present, offer, hand over; send, transmit; extend, apply; carry on to the limit.
寇	kou4	3444	Bandit, invader, enemy, robber, violent people, outcasts, plunderers.
至	zhi4	0982	Arrive, culminate, reach the highest point, utmost, superlative.

5   MATRIX OF MEANINGS OF THE BOOK OF CHANGES

Six in the fourth place

> Waiting in blood. Outside the pit!

需	xu1	2844	Wait, serve; tarry, stop; get wet. From 雨, "rain" and 而: "stopped by rain, waiting it out".
于	yu2	7592	At, to, in, into, on, from, by, go, go to, move towards, proceed, be.
血	xue4	2901	Blood, bleeding. Its ancient form shows a sacrificial vessel with its content.
出	chu1	1409	Go out, came out, appear, departure; arise, emerge; bring out, take out, expel, leave, get rid of; produce, beget.
自	zi4	6960	From, origin, source, cause, reason; oneself, yourself.
穴	xue2	2899	Pit, cave, den, hole, underground dwellings.

Nine in the fifth place

> Waiting with wine and food. The determination is favorable.

需	xu1	2844	Wait, serve; tarry, stop; get wet. From 雨, "rain" and 而: "stopped by rain, waiting it out".
于	yu2	7592	At, to, in, into, on, from, by, go, go to, move towards, proceed, be.
酒	jiu3	1208	Drink, wine, liquor, spirits.
食	shi2	5810	Eat, feed, ingest; food, give food to; nourishment; salary of an officer, livelihood; eclipse (eating of Sun or Moon).
貞	zhen1	0346	Perseverance, persistence, determination, steadiness, firmness; straight, correct, verified, certain; pure, loyal. Its original meaning was "to determine an uncertain matter through divination".
吉	ji2	0476	Good fortune, auspicious, promising, fortunate, lucky, advantageous, happiness, good auspices. It is the only single character meaning good luck in the *YiJing*.

Six at the top

> One falls into the cave. Three uninvited guests arrive.
> Treat them with respect and in the end there will be good fortune.

入	ru4	3152	Enter, go into (this is the meaning used in the *YiJing*); to make to enter; put into; bring in, present; encroach.
于	yu2	7592	At, to, in, into, on, from, by, go, go to, move towards, proceed, be.
穴	xue2	2899	Pit, cave, den, hole, underground dwellings.

Waiting (37)

有	you3	7533	Have, possession, there be, there is.
不	bu4	5379	No, not, negative prefix; without, none, nothing, will not, need not, will not be.
速	su4	5505	Invitation, invite; rapid, quick, urge on, hurried.
之	zhi1	0935	Personal pronoun, he she, it; this, that, these, etc.; often used as a possessive.
客	ke4	3324	Guest, visitor; stranger, traveler, traveler from afar.
三	san1	5415	Three, thrice, third time or place.
人	ren2	3097	Man, person(s); people; others; human being, individual.
來	lai2	3768	Come, arrive, return, bring.
敬	jing4	1138	Respect, take care of, careful; honor; a present; reverent attention to; good manners.
之	zhi1	0935	Personal pronoun, he she, it; this, that, these, etc.; often used as a possessive.
終	zhong1	1500	End, finish, complete; for ever; end of a cycle; carried to conclusion, consummation, closure; death. The original meaning was: tied-off end of a thread.
吉	ji2	0476	Good fortune, auspicious, promising, fortunate, lucky, advantageous, happiness, good auspices. It is the only single character meaning good luck in the *YiJing*.

6 訟 *song* – Conflict

The Judgment

Conflict. You are sincere but you are hold back. Cautiously stopped halfway brings good fortune. Going to the end is ominous.

It is advantageous to see the great man.

It is not favorable to cross the great river.

訟	song4	5558	Conflict, litigation, dispute, to demand justice, accusation.
有	you3	7533	Have, possession, there be, there is.
孚	fu2	1936	Truth; reliable, sincere; to inspire confidence in others; capture, prisoner, plunder.
窒	zhi4	0994	Obstruct, block, restrain; block-headed; frightened.
惕	ti4	6263	Wary, cautious, alert, alarmed; fear, respect, to stand in awe of.
中	zhong1	1504	Center, inner, in the inside, put in the center, hit (target); balanced, central, middle, correct.
吉	ji2	0476	Good fortune, auspicious, promising, fortunate, lucky, advantageous, happiness, good auspices. It is the only single character meaning good luck in the *YiJing*.
終	zhong1	1500	End, finish, complete; for ever; end of a cycle; carried to conclusion, consummation, closure; death. The original meaning was: tied-off end of a thread.
凶	xiong1	2808	Misfortune, pitfall, ominous, bad, unlucky, disastrous, trouble, accident.
利	li4	3867	Favorable, lucky, advantageous, profitable, beneficial, furthering, harvesting; sharp, sharp witted.
見	jian4	0860	See, observe, look at, to be seen; cause to appear; be exposed to, display, reveal; interview, visit or call on, meet.
大	da4	5943	Big, great, tall; excessive, arrogant; spread out and reach everywhere.
人	ren2	3097	Man, person(s); people; others; human being, individual.
不	bu4	5379	No, not, negative prefix; without, none, nothing, will not, need not, will not be.

Conflict (39) 6

利	li4	3867	Favorable, lucky, advantageous, profitable, beneficial, furthering, harvesting; sharp, sharp witted.
涉	she4	5707	Cross, wade across (a river, stream), ford, pass through or over.
大	da4	5943	Big, great, tall; excessive, arrogant; spread out and reach everywhere.
川	chuan1	1439	River, flowing water; flood.

The Image

> Heaven and Water move in opposite directions:
> The image of Conflict.
> Thus the noble, in all his tasks, plans well before starting.

天	tian1	6361	Heaven, firmament, the sky, cosmos; celestial, divine, power above the human.
與	yu3	7615	With, and; associate with, together with, participate in, be present at; help; give.
水	shui3	5922	Water, river, stream, flood, liquid, fluid.
違	wei2	7093	Oppose, go against; disobey, disregard, refuse; go away, leave; deviate from; error; perverse.
行	xing2	2754	Move, go, advance, act, do.
訟	song4	5558	Conflict, litigation, dispute, to demand justice, accusation.
君	jun1	1715	Noble, prince, aristocrat, lord, chief, gentleman; honorable, a highly principled person, superior man. Most times, this character appears alongside another one, forming the word *JunZi*, whose original meaning was "son of a prince or ruler": 君子.
子	zi3	6939	Child, son or daughter, offspring; suffix; bride, wife; gentleman, officer, master, prince; young lady; the first of the *Earthly Branches*.
以	yi3	2932	Thus, in that way, by means of, with, for; instrument, medium, method, use (of), way (to).
作	zuo4	6780	Act, do, make, work, perform; rise, stand up, get to work; project, undertaking, ceremony, to sacrifice.
事	shi4	5787	Serve, service; affairs, business, matters.
謀	mou2	4578	Plan, scheme; consult, appraise, deliberate.
始	shi3	5772	Begin, beginning, start, first.

Six at the beginning

> If one does not perpetuate the affair, there will be some gossip, but eventually it will be auspicious.

不	bu4	5379	No, not, negative prefix; without, none, nothing, will not, need not, will not be.
永	yong3	7589	For a long time, constant, permanent, everlasting; prolong; distant, far reaching.
所	suo3	5465	That which, place, location, residence, dwelling; reason, a cause, whereby; function, position, role; habitual focus or object.
事	shi4	5787	Serve, service; affairs, business, matters.
小	xiao3	2605	Small, insignificant, common, humble, mediocre; diminish, belittle.
有	you3	7533	Have, possession, there be, there is.
言	yan2	7334	Talk, speech, words, sayings; big flute.
終	zhong1	1500	End, finish, complete; for ever; end of a cycle; carried to conclusion, consummation, closure; death. The original meaning was: tied-off end of a thread.
吉	ji2	0476	Good fortune, auspicious, promising, fortunate, lucky, advantageous, happiness, good auspices. It is the only single character meaning good luck in the *YiJing*.

Nine in the second place

> One cannot succeed in the suit and escapes back to his home. The inhabitants of his city, three hundred families, will not suffer misfortune.

不	bu4	5379	No, not, negative prefix; without, none, nothing, will not, need not, will not be.
克	ke4	3320	Can, able, carry, sustain; conquest, dominate, prevail.
訟	song4	5558	Conflict, litigation, dispute, to demand justice, accusation.
歸	gui1	3617	Send in marriage, marriage of a woman, go as a bride to the new home; return to, revert to, to send back.
而	er2	1756	And, then, but, nevertheless, also, only. Join and contrasts two words.
逋	bu1	5373	Flee, escape, run away.
其	qi2	0525	Their, his, its, the; this, that. A demonstrative and possessive pronoun.

CONFLICT (41)

邑	yi4	3037	City, town; walled or fortified city, seat of the of government for a district.
人	ren2	3097	Man, person(s); people; others; human being, individual.
三	san1	5415	Three, thrice, third time or place.
百	bai3	4976	Hundred, hundredth, a hundred times, numerous, many.
戶	hu4	2180	Door, inner door, the house entrance door; household, family.
无	wu2	7173	No, not, negative; without, does not possess, not have.
眚	sheng3	5741	Disaster, calamity, serious mistake; offense by mishap or fault; cloudy eyes, disease of the eye, new moon, eclipse, meanings that indicate blindness or lack of light, a mistake due to ignorance or an error of judgment.

Six in the third place

Subsisting on old virtue. Determination in front of danger. There will be good fortune in the end. If you are in the service of a King you will not be able to complete your work.

食	shi2	5810	Eat, feed, ingest; food, give food to; nourishment; salary of an officer, livelihood; eclipse (eating of Sun or Moon).
舊	jiu4	1205	Ancient, old; past, long ago, for a long time; obsolete. It is used for people, places and things.
德	de2	6162	Virtue, spiritual power, moral integrity; quality, nature, aptitude, ability, character.
貞	zhen1	0346	Perseverance, persistence, determination, steadiness, firmness; straight, correct, verified, certain; pure, loyal. Its original meaning was "to determine an uncertain matter through divination".
厲	li4	3906	Danger, threat; oppressive, cruel, wicked, brutal, harsh; sickness, malevolent devil; grind, polish, sharpen; discipline.
終	zhong1	1500	End, finish, complete; for ever; end of a cycle; carried to conclusion, consummation, closure; death. The original meaning was: tied-off end of a thread.
吉	ji2	0476	Good fortune, auspicious, promising, fortunate, lucky, advantageous, happiness, good auspices. It is the only single character meaning good luck in the *YiJing*.
或	huo4	2402	Perhaps, possibly, if, by chance; doubtful, uncertain; some, someone, something, sometime.

從	cong2	6919	Follow (somebody or a way or doctrine), adhere, obey, pursue; follower attendant; attend to business; from, by, since, whence, through.
王	wang2	7037	King, prince, sovereign, ruler.
事	shi4	5787	Serve, service; affairs, business, matters.
无	wu2	7173	No, not, negative; without, does not possess, not have.
成	cheng2	0379	Accomplish, achieve, finish, complete a task, fulfill; completed, perfect, fully developed, mature; peace making.

Nine in the fourth place

One cannot win the fight. Turns back and accepts
the Heaven command. Changes his attitude and finds peace.
The determination is auspicious.

不	bu4	5379	No, not, negative prefix; without, none, nothing, will not, need not, will not be.
克	ke4	3320	Can, able, carry, sustain; conquest, dominate, prevail.
訟	song4	5558	Conflict, litigation, dispute, to demand justice, accusation.
復	fu4	1992	Return, turn back; repeat, restore, revert, recommence.
即	ji2	0495	Approach, come to; promptly.
命	ming4	4537	Heaven's will; command(s), fate, destiny; will; investiture; birth and death as limits of life.
渝	yu2	7635	Change, to change one's mind or attitude, retract, amend; fail, change for worse.
安	an1	0026	Quiet, at peace, calm; tranquility, safety, security; settled, comfort, contentment.
貞	zhen1	0346	Perseverance, persistence, determination, steadiness, firmness; straight, correct, verified, certain; pure, loyal. Its original meaning was "to determine an uncertain matter through divination".
吉	ji2	0476	Good fortune, auspicious, promising, fortunate, lucky, advantageous, happiness, good auspices. It is the only single character meaning good luck in the *YiJing*.

Nine in the fifth place

Litigating. Outstanding fortune.

訟	song4	5558	Conflict, litigation, dispute, to demand justice, accusation.

Conflict (43)

元	yuan2	7707	Outstanding, greatest, sublime, supreme, greatest, very great, grand; source, beginning, cause, first or paramount, fundamentality; head, chief; used as a superlative.
吉	ji2	0476	Good fortune, auspicious, promising, fortunate, lucky, advantageous, happiness, good auspices. It is the only single character meaning good luck in the *YiJing*.

Nine at the top

If you get rewarded with a leather belt,
by late morning it will have been snatched away three times.

或	huo4	2402	Perhaps, possibly, if, by chance; doubtful, uncertain; some, someone, something, sometime.
錫	xi1	2505	Bestow (a reward), confer (honor, employment, rights or dignity), gift.
之	zhi1	0935	Personal pronoun, he she, it; this, that, these, etc.; often used as a possessive.
鞶	pan2	8005	Large belt, belt with a pocket or pouch, rawhide belt.
帶	dai4	6005	Belt, large belt; band or ribbon worn about the waist that serves as a purse; girdle.
終	zhong1	1500	End, finish, complete; for ever; end of a cycle; carried to conclusion, consummation, closure; death. The original meaning was: tied-off end of a thread.
朝	zhao1	0233	The dawn, early morning. It also means royal audience, because the king attended to the business of state early in the morning.
三	san1	5415	Three, thrice, third time or place.
褫	chi3	1028	Take off, strip off (rank), deprive off, tear off; undress (by force).
之	zhi1	0935	Personal pronoun, he she, it; this, that, these, etc.; often used as a possessive.

7 師 *shi* – The Army

THE JUDGMENT

The Army. The determination brings good fortune for a strong man. No defect.

師	shi1	5760	Army, troops, militias; multitude; master, leader; take as a master, imitate, follow a role model or norm.
貞	zhen1	0346	Perseverance, persistence, determination, steadiness, firmness; straight, correct, verified, certain; pure, loyal. Its original meaning was "to determine an uncertain matter through divination".
丈	zhang4	0200	Strong, mature, a married man; responsible; respectable; a gentleman. One to be respected.
人	ren2	3097	Man, person(s); people; others; human being, individual.
吉	ji2	0476	Good fortune, auspicious, promising, fortunate, lucky, advantageous, happiness, good auspices. It is the only single character meaning good luck in the *YiJing*.
无	wu2	7173	No, not, negative; without, does not possess, not have.
咎	jiu4	1192	Fault, blame, mistake, wrong; inauspicious; misfortune, bad luck, calamity; reproach, censure.

THE IMAGE

The Earth contains Water inside it: The image of The Army. Thus the noble takes care of and increases the crowd.

地	di4	6198	Earth, soil, ground.
中	zhong1	1504	Center, inner, in the inside, put in the center, hit (target); balanced, central, middle, correct.
有	you3	7533	Have, possession, there be, there is.
水	shui3	5922	Water, river, stream, flood, liquid, fluid.

師	shi1	5760	Army, troops, militias; multitude; master, leader; take as a master, imitate, follow a role model or norm.
君	jun1	1715	Noble, prince, aristocrat, lord, chief, gentleman; honorable, a highly principled person, superior man. Most times, this character appears alongside another one, forming the word *JunZi*, whose original meaning was "son of a prince or ruler": 君子.
子	zi3	6939	Child, son or daughter, offspring; suffix; bride, wife; gentleman, officer, master, prince; young lady; the first of the *Earthly Branches*.
以	yi3	2932	Thus, in that way, by means of, with, for; instrument, medium, method, use (of), way (to).
容	rong2	7560	Generosity, tolerance; contain, hold, embrace, admit; support, endure. 容民: Contain or tolerate people.
民	min2	4508	People, the masses, citizenry, the common people, crowd.
畜	chu4	1412	Accumulate, nurture, support, cultivate, domesticate.
眾	zhong4	1517	Multitude, all, the whole of, majority.

Six at the beginning

>The Army should set forward in orderly rows.
>If discipline is bad there will be misfortune.

師	shi1	5760	Army, troops, militias; multitude; master, leader; take as a master, imitate, follow a role model or norm.
出	chu1	1409	Go out, came out, appear, departure; arise, emerge; bring out, take out, expel, leave, get rid of; produce, beget.
以	yi3	2932	Thus, in that way, by means of, with, for; instrument, medium, method, use (of), way (to).
律	lu4	4297	Law, rule, discipline, follow a model; ranks; standard bamboo tuning pitch pipes.
否	fou3	1902	Standstill, stagnation, obstruction, stoppage, dead end; bad, wrong.
臧	zang1	6704	Good, right; generous; command.
凶	xiong1	2808	Misfortune, pitfall, ominous, bad, unlucky, disastrous, trouble, accident.

Nine in the second place

> In the midst of The Army. Good fortune. No defect.
> The King gives rewards and promotions thrice.

在	zai4	6657	Be at, at, in, on, within, be present; to lie in, depend upon, involved with; be living, dwell, located in.
師	shi1	5760	Army, troops, militias; multitude; master, leader; take as a master, imitate, follow a role model or norm.
中	zhong1	1504	Center, inner, in the inside, put in the center, hit (target); balanced, central, middle, correct.
吉	ji2	0476	Good fortune, auspicious, promising, fortunate, lucky, advantageous, happiness, good auspices. It is the only single character meaning good luck in the *YiJing*.
无	wu2	7173	No, not, negative; without, does not possess, not have.
咎	jiu4	1192	Fault, blame, mistake, wrong; inauspicious; misfortune, bad luck, calamity; reproach, censure.
王	wang2	7037	King, prince, sovereign, ruler.
三	san1	5415	Three, thrice, third time or place.
錫	xi1	2505	Bestow (a reward), confer (honor, employment, rights or dignity), gift.
命	ming4	4537	Heaven's will; command(s), fate, destiny; will; investiture; birth and death as limits of life.

Six in the third place

> Perhaps The Army carries corpses in the carriage. Ominous.

師	shi1	5760	Army, troops, militias; multitude; master, leader; take as a master, imitate, follow a role model or norm.
或	huo4	2402	Perhaps, possibly, if, by chance; doubtful, uncertain; some, someone, something, sometime.
輿	yu2	7618	Wagon, cart, chariot, carriage; carrier, transport, transportation; carry on the shoulders; contain, hold.
尸	shi1	5756	Corpse; one who impersonates the death (usually a child) at a sacrifice; lie as a corpse, sit motionless.
凶	xiong1	2808	Misfortune, pitfall, ominous, bad, unlucky, disastrous, trouble, accident.

Six in the fourth place

> The Army camps on the left. No defect.

師	shi1	5760	Army, troops, militias; multitude; master, leader; take as a master, imitate, follow a role model or norm.

The Army (47) 7

左	zuo3	6774	Left side, to the left; the left bank of a river, the East; help, assist, support.
次	ci4	6980	Camp, take a position, to stop at a place, halt; lodge, hostel, lodging place, hut; hard-going; put in order, sequel, next in order, second, second rate.
无	wu2	7173	No, not, negative; without, does not possess, not have.
咎	jiu4	1192	Fault, blame, mistake, wrong; inauspicious; misfortune, bad luck, calamity; reproach, censure.

Six in the fifth place

There is game in the field. It is favorable to capture them for questioning. No defect. The eldest son should lead The Army, if the younger brother leads, the carriages will be used to carry corpses. The determination is ominous.

田	tian2	6362	Field, cultivated land; hunt. The character is the picture of a cultivated field, divided in four sectors.
有	you3	7533	Have, possession, there be, there is.
禽	qin2	1100	Game, animals, birds, prey; quarry, captives, capture. It may be a deer, but it is not its specific meaning.
利	li4	3867	Favorable, lucky, advantageous, profitable, beneficial, furthering, harvesting; sharp, sharp witted.
執	zhi2	0996	Catch, hold, size, capture; keep, retain; direct, control, manage.
言	yan2	7334	Talk, speech, words, sayings; big flute.
无	wu2	7173	No, not, negative; without, does not possess, not have.
咎	jiu4	1192	Fault, blame, mistake, wrong; inauspicious; misfortune, bad luck, calamity; reproach, censure.
長	zhang3	0213	Eldest, grown-up, senior, superior, leader, chief, maturity, tenured. Long, long lasting; tall.
子	zi3	6939	Child, son or daughter, offspring; suffix; bride, wife; gentleman, officer, master, prince; young lady; the first of the *Earthly Branches*.
帥	shuai4	5909	Lead (an army), commander, leader, officer; direct, arrange, govern; follow the lead, obey, imitate.
師	shi1	5760	Army, troops, militias; multitude; master, leader; take as a master, imitate, follow a role model or norm.
弟	di4	6201	Younger brother, junior, respectful towards elder brothers.

子	zi3	6939	Child, son or daughter, offspring; suffix; bride, wife; gentleman, officer, master, prince; young lady; the first of the *Earthly Branches*.
輿	yu2	7618	Wagon, cart, chariot, carriage; carrier, transport, transportation; carry on the shoulders; contain, hold.
尸	shi1	5756	Corpse; one who impersonates the death (usually a child) at a sacrifice; lie as a corpse, sit motionless.
貞	zhen1	0346	Perseverance, persistence, determination, steadiness, firmness; straight, correct, verified, certain; pure, loyal. Its original meaning was "to determine an uncertain matter through divination".
凶	xiong1	2808	Misfortune, pitfall, ominous, bad, unlucky, disastrous, trouble, accident.

Six at the top

The great King has the mandate to found a state and inherit the house. Small men should not be used.

大	da4	5943	Big, great, tall; excessive, arrogant; spread out and reach everywhere.
君	jun1	1715	Noble, prince, aristocrat, lord, chief, gentleman; honorable, a highly principled person, superior man. Most times, this character appears alongside another one, forming the word *JunZi*, whose original meaning was "son of a prince or ruler": 君子.
有	you3	7533	Have, possession, there be, there is.
命	ming4	4537	Heaven's will; command(s), fate, destiny; will; investiture; birth and death as limits of life.
開	kai1	3204	Open, establish, found, initiate, start.
國	guo2	3738	State, country, nation, kingdom, a dynasty; capital city.
承	cheng2	0386	Inherit, receive; to present, support, assist, bear, serve.
家	jia1	0594	Family, household, clan; home, to keep a home.
小	xiao3	2605	Small, insignificant, common, humble, mediocre; diminish, belittle.
人	ren2	3097	Man, person(s); people; others; human being, individual.
勿	wu4	7208	Do not, no. Negative imperative.
用	yong4	7567	Use, apply, put to use, apply the oracle to real world situations; hereby, thereby.

8 比 *bi* – Union

THE JUDGMENT

Union brings happiness. Look deep and divine to see if you have great long-term determination; if so there will be no defect.
They will come from the lands without peace.
Those who arrive late will have misfortune.

比	bi3	5077	Union, go together with, assemble, associate with, combine, ally with, pair; compare.
吉	ji2	0476	Good fortune, auspicious, promising, fortunate, lucky, advantageous, happiness, good auspices. It is the only single character meaning good luck in the *YiJing*.
原	yuan2	7725	Source, spring; original, beginning; repeat, again, trace to the source.
筮	shi4	5763	Divination by yarrow (*Achillea millefolium*) stalks, consult the oracle.
元	yuan2	7707	Outstanding, greatest, sublime, supreme, greatest, very great, grand; source, beginning, cause, first or paramount, fundamentality; head, chief; used as a superlative.
永	yong3	7589	For a long time, constant, permanent, everlasting; prolong; distant, far reaching.
貞	zhen1	0346	Perseverance, persistence, determination, steadiness, firmness; straight, correct, verified, certain; pure, loyal. Its original meaning was "to determine an uncertain matter through divination".
无	wu2	7173	No, not, negative; without, does not possess, not have.
咎	jiu4	1192	Fault, blame, mistake, wrong; inauspicious; misfortune, bad luck, calamity; reproach, censure.
不	bu4	5379	No, not, negative prefix; without, none, nothing, will not, need not, will not be.
寧	ning2	4725	Peace, peaceful, rest, serenity, at ease, body and mind at ease.
方	fang1	1802	Square, squarely, directly, straightforward, honest; a place, a region; on all sides; direction, trend, method; suddenly, quick, definite; take a place, occupy; sacrifice to the spirits of the four quarters.

來	lai2	3768	Come, arrive, return, bring.
後	hou4	2143	Later, behind, rear, afterward, come after; follow; descendants, successor.
夫	fu1	1908	Those, this, that; man, male adult, husband.
凶	xiong1	2808	Misfortune, pitfall, ominous, bad, unlucky, disastrous, trouble, accident.

The Image

On Earth there is Water: The image of Union. So the kings of old established ten thousand different states and kept close relations with all the feudal lords.

地	di4	6198	Earth, soil, ground.
上	shang4	5669	Up, above, on, over, upwards, top, rise; higher, superior; first, best.
有	you3	7533	Have, possession, there be, there is.
水	shui3	5922	Water, river, stream, flood, liquid, fluid.
比	bi3	5077	Union, go together with, assemble, associate with, combine, ally with, pair; compare.
先	xian1	2702	Before, first, foremost, in front, lead.
王	wang2	7037	King, prince, sovereign, ruler.
以	yi3	2932	Thus, in that way, by means of, with, for; instrument, medium, method, use (of), way (to).
建	jian4	0853	Establish, found, appoint, confirm a position.
萬	wan4	7030	Literally: ten thousands, e.g. many, countless.
國	guo2	3738	State, country, nation, kingdom, a dynasty; capital city.
親	qin1	1107	Parents, relatives, near, intimate, love, to be fond of, to relate, attach to.
諸	zhu1	1362	Many, all them, every, each one, several, numerous.
侯	hou2	2135	Feudal lord, (vassal) prince, marquis; officer, governor, chief; skilled archer.

Six at the beginning

If there is sincerity, the Union will be without defect.
Full of sincerity as a full earthenware vessel.
Finally, through others, the happiness will come.

Union (51) 8

有	you3	7533	Have, possession, there be, there is.
孚	fu2	1936	Truth; reliable, sincere; to inspire confidence in others; capture, prisoner, plunder.
比	bi3	5077	Union, go together with, assemble, associate with, combine, ally with, pair; compare.
之	zhi1	0935	Personal pronoun, he she, it; this, that, these, etc.; often used as a possessive.
无	wu2	7173	No, not, negative; without, does not possess, not have.
咎	jiu4	1192	Fault, blame, mistake, wrong; inauspicious; misfortune, bad luck, calamity; reproach, censure.
有	you3	7533	Have, possession, there be, there is.
孚	fu2	1936	Truth; reliable, sincere; to inspire confidence in others; capture, prisoner, plunder.
盈	ying2	7474	Fill, full, satisfied; overfill, overflowing.
缶	fou3	1905	Pot, earthen vessel.
終	zhong1	1500	End, finish, complete; for ever; end of a cycle; carried to conclusion, consummation, closure; death. The original meaning was: tied-off end of a thread.
來	lai2	3768	Come, arrive, return, bring.
有	you3	7533	Have, possession, there be, there is.
它	tuo1	6439	Another, other; danger, calamity, obstacle.
吉	ji2	0476	Good fortune, auspicious, promising, fortunate, lucky, advantageous, happiness, good auspices. It is the only single character meaning good luck in the *YiJing*.

Six in the second place

Union from the inside. The determination is fortunate.

比	bi3	5077	Union, go together with, assemble, associate with, combine, ally with, pair; compare.
之	zhi1	0935	Personal pronoun, he she, it; this, that, these, etc.; often used as a possessive.
自	zi4	6960	From, origin, source, cause, reason; oneself, yourself.
內	nei4	4766	Inside, inner, interior; to bring in, enter.
貞	zhen1	0346	Perseverance, persistence, determination, steadiness, firmness; straight, correct, verified, certain; pure, loyal. Its original meaning was "to determine an uncertain matter through divination".

| 吉 | ji2 | 0476 | Good fortune, auspicious, promising, fortunate, lucky, advantageous, happiness, good auspices. It is the only single character meaning good luck in the *YiJing*. |

Six in the third place

> Union with worthless people.

比	bi3	5077	Union, go together with, assemble, associate with, combine, ally with, pair; compare.
之	zhi1	0935	Personal pronoun, he she, it; this, that, these, etc.; often used as a possessive.
匪	fei3	1820	No, strong negative.
人	ren2	3097	Man, person(s); people; others; human being, individual.

Six in the fourth place

Union with people on the outside. Determination brings good fortune.

外	wai4	7001	Outside, beyond, external, foreign, unfamiliar, extraordinary, barbarian.
比	bi3	5077	Union, go together with, assemble, associate with, combine, ally with, pair; compare.
之	zhi1	0935	Personal pronoun, he she, it; this, that, these, etc.; often used as a possessive.
貞	zhen1	0346	Perseverance, persistence, determination, steadiness, firmness; straight, correct, verified, certain; pure, loyal. Its original meaning was "to determine an uncertain matter through divination".
吉	ji2	0476	Good fortune, auspicious, promising, fortunate, lucky, advantageous, happiness, good auspices. It is the only single character meaning good luck in the *YiJing*.

Nine in the fifth place

> Noticeable Union. The King uses beaters for hunting prey on three sides, and lets go the animals that run off in front of him. The inhabitants of the district are not wary. Good fortune.

顯	xian3	2692	Manifest, display, make clear; bright, clear, illustrious, conspicuous; girth.
比	bi3	5077	Union, go together with, assemble, associate with, combine, ally with, pair; compare.
王	wang2	7037	King, prince, sovereign, ruler.

用	yong4	7567	Use, apply, put to use, apply the oracle to real world situations; hereby, thereby.
三	san1	5415	Three, thrice, third time or place.
驅	qu1	1602	Beaters, mounted game flushers; drive horses; chase, expel, to drive away.
失	shi1	5806	Lose, let go, neglect, an omission; fail, err; lose control.
前	qian2	0919	Ahead, front, foremost, forward, formerly, before, ancient, come before in time, anterior.
禽	qin2	1100	Game, animals, birds, prey; quarry, captives, capture. It may be a deer, but it is not its specific meaning.
邑	yi4	3037	City, town; walled or fortified city, seat of the of government for a district.
人	ren2	3097	Man, person(s); people; others; human being, individual.
不	bu4	5379	No, not, negative prefix; without, none, nothing, will not, need not, will not be.
誡	jie4	0628	Warn, admonish, compel, coerce; to be on guard, to be frightened, to mistrust.
吉	ji2	0476	Good fortune, auspicious, promising, fortunate, lucky, advantageous, happiness, good auspices. It is the only single character meaning good luck in the *YiJing*.

Six at the top

Union without a leader. Misfortune.

比	bi3	5077	Union, go together with, assemble, associate with, combine, ally with, pair; compare.
之	zhi1	0935	Personal pronoun, he she, it; this, that, these, etc.; often used as a possessive.
无	wu2	7173	No, not, negative; without, does not possess, not have.
首	shou3	5839	Head; foremost, first; leader, chief.
凶	xiong1	2808	Misfortune, pitfall, ominous, bad, unlucky, disastrous, trouble, accident.

9 小畜 *xiao xu* – Little Domestication

THE JUDGMENT

Little Domestication is successful.
Dense clouds, no rain from our western borders.

小	xiao3	2605	Small, insignificant, common, humble, mediocre; diminish, belittle.
畜	chu4	1412	Accumulate, nurture, support, cultivate, domesticate.
亨	heng1	2099	Success, prevalence, smooth progress, growth, consummate, triumph; pervade; offering, sacrifice.
密	mi4	4464	Dense, thick, intimate, confidential; hidden, secret; silent.
雲	yun2	7750	Clouds.
不	bu4	5379	No, not, negative prefix; without, none, nothing, will not, need not, will not be.
雨	yu3	7662	Rain, shower, sudden downpour.
自	zi4	6960	From, origin, source, cause, reason; oneself, yourself.
我	wo3	4778	We, us, I, my, mine, our.
西	xi1	2460	The West, western. Related to the autumn.
郊	jiao1	0714	Countryside, suburbs, outskirts, frontier; suburban altar and sacrifice.

THE IMAGE

The Wind crosses the Heaven: The image of Little Domestication.
Thus the noble refines the outward manifestation of his virtue.

風	feng1	1890	Wind, breath, air; manners, atmosphere.
行	xing2	2754	Move, go, advance, act, do.
天	tian1	6361	Heaven, firmament, the sky, cosmos; celestial, divine, power above the human.

Little Domestication (55)

上	shang4	5669	Up, above, on, over, upwards, top, rise; higher, superior; first, best.
小	xiao3	2605	Small, insignificant, common, humble, mediocre; diminish, belittle.
畜	chu4	1412	Accumulate, nurture, support, cultivate, domesticate.
君	jun1	1715	Noble, prince, aristocrat, lord, chief, gentleman; honorable, a highly principled person, superior man. Most times, this character appears alongside another one, forming the word *JunZi*, whose original meaning was "son of a prince or ruler": 君子.
子	zi3	6939	Child, son or daughter, offspring; suffix; bride; wife; gentleman, officer, master, prince; young lady; the first of the *Earthly Branches*.
以	yi3	2932	Thus, in that way, by means of, with, for; instrument, medium, method, use (of), way (to).
懿	yi4	2999	Excellent, good, esteemed, admirable, beautiful, virtuous; restrain, concentrate, discipline, improve.
文	wen2	7129	Elegant, refined, ornate, stylish; civil, polite, urbane; literary, artistic, cultural pursuits.<
德	de2	6162	Virtue, spiritual power, moral integrity; quality, nature, aptitude, ability, character.

Nine at the beginning

Returns to his own way. How could it be wrong? Good fortune.

復	fu4	1992	Return, turn back; repeat, restore, revert, recommence.
自	zi4	6960	From, origin, source, cause, reason; oneself, yourself.
道	dao4	6136	Road, course, path, way, method; show the way, lead, explain.
何	he2	2109	What? how? why? what is? for that reason, therefore.
其	qi2	0525	Their, his, its, the; this, that. A demonstrative and possessive pronoun.
咎	jiu4	1192	Fault, blame, mistake, wrong; inauspicious; misfortune, bad luck, calamity; reproach, censure.
吉	ji2	0476	Good fortune, auspicious, promising, fortunate, lucky, advantageous, happiness, good auspices. It is the only single character meaning good luck in the *YiJing*.

Nine in the second place

> Led to return. Good fortune.

牽	qian1	0881	Lead by hand, lead; haul, drag; to drag into an affair, to connect.
復	fu4	1992	Return, turn back; repeat, restore, revert, recommence.
吉	ji2	0476	Good fortune, auspicious, promising, fortunate, lucky, advantageous, happiness, good auspices. It is the only single character meaning good luck in the *YiJing*.

Nine in the third place

> Rays are removed from the carriage wheels.
> Man and wife avert his eyes from each other.

輿	yu2	7618	Wagon, cart, chariot, carriage; carrier, transport, transportation; carry on the shoulders; contain, hold.
說	tuo1	5939	Remove, take off, come off, let loose.
輻	fu2	1980	The spokes of a wheel.
夫	fu1	1908	Man, male adult, husband; this, that, those.
妻	qi1	0555	Wife, consort. A legal wife (first wife).
反	fan3	1781	Turn, reverse, come back, return.
目	mu4	4596	Eye/s, look, see.

Six in the fourth place

> If you are sincere, blood disappears and concerns are cast aside.
> No defect.

有	you3	7533	Have, possession, there be, there is.
孚	fu2	1936	Truth; reliable, sincere; to inspire confidence in others; capture, prisoner, plunder.
血	xue4	2901	Blood, bleeding. Its ancient form shows a sacrificial vessel with its content.
去	qu4	1594	Go away, leave, depart; remove, put away, eliminate, reject.
惕	ti4	6263	Wary, cautious, alert, alarmed; fear, respect, to stand in awe of.
出	chu1	1409	Go out, came out, appear, departure; arise, emerge; bring out, take out, expel, leave, get rid of; produce, beget.
无	wu2	7173	No, not, negative; without, does not possess, not have.
咎	jiu4	1192	Fault, blame, mistake, wrong; inauspicious; misfortune, bad luck, calamity; reproach, censure.

LITTLE DOMESTICATION (57) 9

Nine in the fifth place

> If you are sincere with your neighbors the alliance
> will bring prosperity for all.

有	you3	7533	Have, possession, there be, there is.
孚	fu2	1936	Truth; reliable, sincere; to inspire confidence in others; capture, prisoner, plunder.
攣	luan2	4300	Attach, link, bind, tie together; connect, continue.
如	ru2	3137	Thus, in this way, as, like, similar to, if (conditional).
富	fu4	1952	Rich, wealth, treasure, abundance, prosperity, to enrich.
以	yi3	2932	Thus, in that way, by means of, with, for; instrument, medium, method, use (of), way (to).
其	qi2	0525	Their, his, its, the; this, that. A demonstrative and possessive pronoun.
鄰	lin2	4033	Neighbor, neighborhood, extended family, associate, assistant.

Nine at the top

> The rain fell and he could rest. His spiritual power brings him
> recognition. The determination is dangerous for a wife.
> The moon is almost full. Enterprises are unfortunate.

既	ji4	0453	Already, consummated, completed, finished; to be done with, get done.
雨	yu3	7662	Rain, shower, sudden downpour.
既	ji4	0453	Already, consummated, completed, finished; to be done with, get done.
處	chu3	1407	Rest, stop, stay; dwell in a place for a while.
尚	shang4	5670	High, ascend, admirable, superior, surpass, respected, esteemed, reward; still, yet an besides, in addition to.
德	de2	6162	Virtue, spiritual power, moral integrity; quality, nature, aptitude, ability, character.
載	zai4	6653	Transport, carry, load, bear; contain, sustain; load a vessel or cart, conveyance.
婦	fu4	1963	Woman, lady, wife, married woman.
貞	zhen1	0346	Perseverance, persistence, determination, steadiness, firmness; straight, correct, verified, certain; pure, loyal. Its original meaning was "to determine an uncertain matter through divination".

厲	li4	3906	Danger, threat; oppressive, cruel, wicked, brutal, harsh; sickness, malevolent devil; grind, polish, sharpen; discipline.
月	yue4	7696	The Moon, lunar month.
幾	ji1	0409	Almost; imminent, nearly; occasion; minutiae, first subtle signs; approaches.
望	wang4	7043	Full Moon; the 15th day of the lunar calendary; hope; expect; look forward to.
君	jun1	1715	Noble, prince, aristocrat, lord, chief, gentleman; honorable, a highly principled person, superior man. Most times, this character appears alongside another one, forming the word *JunZi*, whose original meaning was "son of a prince or ruler": 君子.
子	zi3	6939	Child, son or daughter, offspring; suffix; bride, wife; gentleman, officer, master, prince; young lady; the first of the *Earthly Branches*.
征	zheng1	0352	Punishing expedition ("to correct"), to reduce to submission, attack, punish; to levy taxes; comes, brings.
凶	xiong1	2808	Misfortune, pitfall, ominous, bad, unlucky, disastrous, trouble, accident.

10 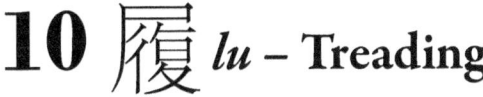 *lu* – Treading

THE JUDGMENT

Treading the tiger's tail. The man is not bitten. Success.

履	lu3	3893	Step on, treading, track, walk or follow a trail or way; footwear, shoes; conduct, behavior; ceremonies.
虎	hu3	2161	Tiger. Emblem of bravery and cruelty: strong, wild, extreme.
尾	wei3	7109	Tail, rear, back, behind, the end; last.
不	bu4	5379	No, not, negative prefix; without, none, nothing, will not, need not, will not be.
咥	die2	2456	Bite, cleave, split, gnaw, damage.
人	ren2	3097	Man, person(s); people; others; human being, individual.
亨	heng1	2099	Success, prevalence, smooth progress, growth, consummate, triumph; pervade; offering, sacrifice.

THE IMAGE

Above Heaven, down the Lake: The image of Treading.
Thus the noble distinguishes between high and low
and makes certain the will of the people.

上	shang4	5669	Up, above, on, over, upwards, top, rise; higher, superior; first, best.
天	tian1	6361	Heaven, firmament, the sky, cosmos; celestial, divine, power above the human.
下	xia4	2520	Below, down, descend.
澤	ze2	0277	Marsh, pool, pond, lake; flat body of water and the vapors rising from it; enrich, fertilize, benefit; moist, moisten; glossy, polished.
履	lu3	3893	Step on, treading, track, walk or follow a trail or way; footwear, shoes; conduct, behavior; ceremonies.
君	jun1	1715	Noble, prince, aristocrat, lord, chief, gentleman; honorable, a highly principled person, superior man. Most times, this character appears alongside another one, forming the word *JunZi*, whose original meaning was "son of a prince or ruler": 君子.

子	zi3	6939	Child, son or daughter, offspring; suffix; bride, wife; gentleman, officer, master, prince; young lady; the first of the *Earthly Branches*.
以	yi3	2932	Thus, in that way, by means of, with, for; instrument, medium, method, use (of), way (to).
辨	bian4	5240	Discriminate, distinguish, discern, identify; divide, distribute; frame that divides a bed from its stand.
上	shang4	5669	Up, above, on, over, upwards, top, rise; higher, superior; first, best.
下	xia4	2520	Below, down, descend.
定	ding4	6393	Settle, establish, put in place, make certain, fix, resolve, decide; settled, certain; quiet.
民	min2	4508	People, the masses, citizenry, the common people, crowd.
志	zhi4	0971	Purpose, will, determination, goal; keep the mind on target; treaty; annals.

Nine at the beginning

Simple treading. Advance without defect.

素	su4	5490	Simple, plain, unadorned; white, white silk.
履	lu3	3893	Step on, treading, track, walk or follow a trail or way; footwear, shoes; conduct, behavior; ceremonies.
往	wang3	7050	Go, to go to, go forward, go towards; depart, bygone, former.
无	wu2	7173	No, not, negative; without, does not possess, not have.
咎	jiu4	1192	Fault, blame, mistake, wrong; inauspicious; misfortune, bad luck, calamity; reproach, censure.

Nine in the second place

Treading a smooth and easy way.
The determination of a lonely man brings good fortune.

履	lu3	3893	Step on, treading, track, walk or follow a trail or way; footwear, shoes; conduct, behavior; ceremonies.
道	dao4	6136	Road, course, path, way, method; show the way, lead, explain.
坦	tan3	6057	Level, smooth, flat; smooth appearance, a ease, in peace, satisfied. Appearing duplicated intensifies its meaning.
坦	tan3	6057	Level, smooth, flat; smooth appearance, a ease, in peace, satisfied. Appearing duplicated intensifies its meaning.

TREADING (61) 10

幽	you1	7505	Dark, obscure; solitary, secluded, hidden from view; secret, difficult to understand.
人	ren2	3097	Man, person(s); people; others; human being, individual.
貞	zhen1	0346	Perseverance, persistence, determination, steadiness, firmness; straight, correct, verified, certain; pure, loyal. Its original meaning was "to determine an uncertain matter through divination".
吉	ji2	0476	Good fortune, auspicious, promising, fortunate, lucky, advantageous, happiness, good auspices. It is the only single character meaning good luck in the *YiJing*.

Six in the third place

A one-eyed man can see, a lame can tread.
The tiger bites the one who treads on his tail. Misfortune.
A warrior acts as [if he were] a great lord.

眇	miao3	4476	Weak-sighted, one-eyed, having one eye smaller than the other.
能	neng2	4648	Able, skill, power, talent, ability, expertise.
視	shi4	5789	See, look, inspect, observe, regard.
跛	bo3	5317	Lame, limping, crippled.
能	neng2	4648	Able, skill, power, talent, ability, expertise.
履	lu3	3893	Step on, treading, track, walk or follow a trail or way; footwear, shoes; conduct, behavior; ceremonies. Appearing duplicated intensifies its meaning.
履	lu3	3893	
虎	hu3	2161	Tiger. Emblem of bravery and cruelty: strong, wild, extreme.
尾	wei3	7109	Tail, rear, back, behind, the end; last.
咥	die2	2456	Bite, cleave, split, gnaw, damage.
人	ren2	3097	Man, person(s); people; others; human being, individual.
凶	xiong1	2808	Misfortune, pitfall, ominous, bad, unlucky, disastrous, trouble, accident.
武	wu3	7195	Martial, military; warlike, warrior.
人	ren2	3097	Man, person(s); people; others; human being, individual.
爲	wei2	7059	Act, do, accomplish, make, to be; act for, stand for, support, help; become.
于	yu2	7592	At, to, in, into, on, from, by, go, go to, move towards, proceed, be.

| 大 | da4 | 5943 | Big, great, tall; excessive, arrogant; spread out and reach everywhere. |
| 君 | jun1 | 1715 | Noble, prince, aristocrat, lord, chief, gentleman; honorable, a highly principled person, superior man. Most times, this character appears alongside another one, forming the word *JunZi*, whose original meaning was "son of a prince or ruler": 君子. |

Nine in the fourth place

Steps on the tiger's tail with great caution.
At the end there will be good fortune.

履	lu3	3893	Step on, treading, track, walk or follow a trail or way; footwear, shoes; conduct, behavior; ceremonies.
虎	hu3	2161	Tiger. Emblem of bravery and cruelty: strong, wild, extreme.
尾	wei3	7109	Tail, rear, back, behind, the end; last.
愬	su4	5494	Fear, caution, panicky appearance; appeal, plead, accuse, complain.
愬	su4	5494	Fear, caution, panicky appearance; appeal, plead, accuse, complain.
終	zhong1	1500	End, finish, complete; for ever; end of a cycle; carried to conclusion, consummation, closure; death. The original meaning was: tied-off end of a thread.
吉	ji2	0476	Good fortune, auspicious, promising, fortunate, lucky, advantageous, happiness, good auspices. It is the only single character meaning good luck in the *YiJing*.

Nine in the fifth place

Resolute treading. The determination is dangerous.

夬	guai4	3535	Breakthrough, make a breach, split, cut off, pull off; resolute, decisive.
履	lu3	3893	Step on, treading, track, walk or follow a trail or way; footwear, shoes; conduct, behavior; ceremonies.
貞	zhen1	0346	Perseverance, persistence, determination, steadiness, firmness; straight, correct, verified, certain; pure, loyal. Its original meaning was "to determine an uncertain matter through divination".
厲	li4	3906	Danger, threat; oppressive, cruel, wicked, brutal, harsh; sickness, malevolent devil; grind, polish, sharpen; discipline.

TREADING (63) 10

Nine at the top

> Watch the trodden path and examine the omens.
> The cycle starts back. Great good fortune

視	shi4	5789	See, look, inspect, observe, regard.
履	lu3	3893	Step on, treading, track, walk or follow a trail or way; footwear, shoes; conduct, behavior; ceremonies.
考	kao3	3299	Examine, inspect; deceased ancestor or father, old.
祥	xiang2	2577	Omen of good luck, auspicious, good presage.
其	qi2	0525	Their, his, its, the; this, that. A demonstrative and possessive pronoun.
旋	xuan2	2894	Return, revolve, move in orbit, spin, come full circle, make a circuit.
元	yuan2	7707	Outstanding, greatest, sublime, supreme, greatest, very great, grand; source, beginning, cause, first or paramount, fundamentality; head, chief; used as a superlative.
吉	ji2	0476	Good fortune, auspicious, promising, fortunate, lucky, advantageous, happiness, good auspices. It is the only single character meaning good luck in the *YiJing*.

11 泰 *tai* – Harmony / Great

THE JUDGMENT

Harmony. The petty depart and the great is coming.
Good fortune and success.

泰	tai4	6023	Great, extensive, exalted, superior, prosperous, successful; liberal; extreme, excessive, arrogant; influential, spread out and reach everywhere, permeate, pervade; peace, quiet.
小	xiao3	2605	Small, insignificant, common, humble, mediocre; diminish, belittle.
往	wang3	7050	Go, to go to, go forward, go towards; depart, bygone, former.
大	da4	5943	Big, great, tall; excessive, arrogant; spread out and reach everywhere.
來	lai2	3768	Come, arrive, return, bring.
吉	ji2	0476	Good fortune, auspicious, promising, fortunate, lucky, advantageous, happiness, good auspices. It is the only single character meaning good luck in the *YiJing*.
亨	heng1	2099	Success, prevalence, smooth progress, growth, consummate, triumph; pervade; offering, sacrifice.

THE IMAGE

Heaven and Earth are closely related: The image of Harmony.
Thus the sovereign regulates and completes the course
of Heaven and Earth, and assists Heaven and Earth in the right way;
thereby helping the people.

天	tian1	6361	Heaven, firmament, the sky, cosmos; celestial, divine, power above the human.
地	di4	6198	Earth, soil, ground.

HARMONY

交	jiao1	0702	Union, relation, meeting; exchange, do business; share; contact; have relations with; to hand in or over.
泰	tai4	6023	Great, extensive, exalted, superior, prosperous, successful; liberal; extreme, excessive, arrogant; influential, spread out and reach everywhere, permeate, pervade; peace, quiet.
后	hou4	2144	Sovereign, lord, prince; empress; descendants, heirs.
以	yi3	2932	Thus, in that way, by means of, with, for; instrument, medium, method, use (of), way (to).
裁	cai2	6664	Regulate, divide, cut out.
成	cheng2	0379	Accomplish, achieve, finish, complete a task, fulfill; completed, perfect, fully developed, mature; peace making.
天	tian1	6361	Heaven, firmament, the sky, cosmos; celestial, divine, power above the human.
地	di4	6198	Earth, soil, ground.
之	zhi1	0935	Personal pronoun, he she, it; this, that, these, etc.; often used as a possessive.
道	dao4	6136	Road, course, path, way, method; show the way, lead, explain.
輔	fu3	1945	Jaws, cheeks, cheek bone; protect, help, support.
相	xiang1	2562	Each other, mutual, reciprocal, cooperative; look to, look at, assist, aid.
天	tian1	6361	Heaven, firmament, the sky, cosmos; celestial, divine, power above the human.
地	di4	6198	Earth, soil, ground.
之	zhi1	0935	Personal pronoun, he she, it; this, that, these, etc.; often used as a possessive.
宜	yi2	2993	Right, proper, sacrifice to the deity of the soil.
以	yi3	2932	Thus, in that way, by means of, with, for; instrument, medium, method, use (of), way (to).
左	zuo3	6774	Left side, to the left; the left bank of a river, the East; help, assist, support.
右	you4	7541	Right, the right hand, on the right, make things right. 左右: help, assist, support; control; influence.
民	min2	4508	People, the masses, citizenry, the common people, crowd.

Nine at the beginning

When reeds are pulled, they pull up others of the same kind together with them. Enterprises bring good fortune.

拔	ba2	4848	Pull up, pull out, uproot, pluck up.
茅	mao2	4364	Reeds, cogon grass, white grass, used for wrapping offerings.
茹	ru2	3139	Interlaced roots, roots, shoots.
以	yi3	2932	Thus, in that way, by means of, with, for; instrument, medium, method, use (of), way (to).
其	qi2	0525	Their, his, its, the; this, that. A demonstrative and possessive pronoun.
彙	hui4	2349	Category, class; group, bunch; roots.
征	zheng1	0352	Punishing expedition ("to correct"), to reduce to submission, attack, punish; to levy taxes; comes, brings.
吉	ji2	0476	Good fortune, auspicious, promising, fortunate, lucky, advantageous, happiness, good auspices. It is the only single character meaning good luck in the *YiJing*.

Nine in the second place

Bear with the uneducated, wade the river, do not neglect the distant. Thus factions disappear. One get honors if stays in the middle path.

包	bao1	4937	Bundle, wrap, reed mat for wrapping; kitchen, butchering room; contain, support, take responsibility over.
荒	huang1	2271	Barren, dried-out, waste; wild, wed covered, uncultured, uncultivated, neglected; hollow.
用	yong4	7567	Use, apply, put to use, apply the oracle to real world situations; hereby, thereby.
馮	ping2	1895	Ford, wade, cross a stream (shallow or frozen) without a boat.
河	he2	2111	River, stream, He (Yellow) river.
不	bu4	5379	No, not, negative prefix; without, none, nothing, will not, need not, will not be.
遐	xia2	2517	Far, distant; disappear in the distance, travel far away; remote in time.
遺	yi2	2995	Leave behind, reject, abandon, neglect, lose through carelessness.
朋	peng2	5054	Friend, companion, pair, equal, comrade; a string of cowries (small shiny shells used as coins in ancient China).

亡	wang2	7034	Go away, disappear, exile; fail; destroy, perish, not have, not exist.
得	de2	6161	Get, obtain, gain; reach, achieve; can; attain the desired thing.
尚	shang4	5670	High, ascend, admirable, superior, surpass, respected, esteemed, reward; still, yet an besides, in addition to.
于	yu2	7592	At, to, in, into, on, from, by, go, go to, move towards, proceed, be.
中	zhong1	1504	Center, inner, in the inside, put in the center, hit (target); balanced, central, middle, correct.
行	xing2	2754	Move, go, advance, act, do.

Nine in the third place

There are no plains without slopes. There is no going forth without a return. Fortitude under trying conditions. No defect. Do not regret this truth. Enjoy the happiness you still possess.

无	wu2	7173	No, not, negative; without, does not possess, not have.
平	ping2	5303	A plain, level, equal, even; equalize, harmonize, regulate, pacify; peace.
不	bu4	5379	No, not, negative prefix; without, none, nothing, will not, need not, will not be.
陂	pi2	5345	Slope, incline, slanting; river bank, embankment, dyke.
无	wu2	7173	No, not, negative; without, does not possess, not have.
往	wang3	7050	Go, to go to, go forward, go towards; depart, bygone, former.
不	bu4	5379	No, not, negative prefix; without, none, nothing, will not, need not, will not be.
復	fu4	1992	Return, turn back; repeat, restore, revert, recommence.
艱	jian1	0834	Hardship, distressing, difficult, laborious.
貞	zhen1	0346	Perseverance, persistence, determination, steadiness, firmness; straight, correct, verified, certain; pure, loyal. Its original meaning was "to determine an uncertain matter through divination".
无	wu2	7173	No, not, negative; without, does not possess, not have.
咎	jiu4	1192	Fault, blame, mistake, wrong; inauspicious; misfortune, bad luck, calamity; reproach, censure.
勿	wu4	7208	Do not, no. Negative imperative.

恤	xu4	2862	Worry, care about, fear, sorrow, pity.
其	qi2	0525	Their, his, its, the; this, that. A demonstrative and possessive pronoun.
孚	fu2	1936	Truth; reliable, sincere; to inspire confidence in others; capture, prisoner, plunder.
于	yu2	7592	At, to, in, into, on, from, by, go, go to, move towards, proceed, be.
食	shi2	5810	Eat, feed, ingest; food, give food to; nourishment; salary of an officer, livelihood; eclipse (eating of Sun or Moon).
有	you3	7533	Have, possession, there be, there is.
福	fu2	1978	Happiness, good fortune, blessings.

Six in the fourth place

Flapping, fluttering.
Not using his own rich resources to deal with his neighbors.
Without having to ask gets confidence.

翩	pian1	5249	Flutter, fly to and from, flap the wings. Appearing duplicated intensifies its meaning.
翩	pian1	5249	
不	bu4	5379	No, not, negative prefix; without, none, nothing, will not, need not, will not be.
富	fu4	1952	Rich, wealth, treasure, abundance, prosperity, to enrich.
以	yi3	2932	Thus, in that way, by means of, with, for; instrument, medium, method, use (of), way (to).
其	qi2	0525	Their, his, its, the; this, that. A demonstrative and possessive pronoun.
鄰	lin2	4033	Neighbor, neighborhood, extended family, associate, assistant.
不	bu4	5379	No, not, negative prefix; without, none, nothing, will not, need not, will not be.
戒	jie4	0627	Warn, caution, limit, on guard, wary.
以	yi3	2932	Thus, in that way, by means of, with, for; instrument, medium, method, use (of), way (to).
孚	fu2	1936	Truth; reliable, sincere; to inspire confidence in others; capture, prisoner, plunder.

Harmony

Six in the fifth place

> The sovereign *Yi* gives his daughter in marriage.
> This brings happiness and great fortune.

帝	di4	6204	Sovereign, emperor, god.
乙	yi3	3017	*Yi*, name of the penultimate *Shang* Emperor; cyclic character: second stem.
歸	gui1	3617	Send in marriage, marriage of a woman, go as a bride to the new home; return to, revert to, to send back.
妹	mei4	4410	Younger sister, maiden, daughter, daughter of a secondary wife; virgin.
以	yi3	2932	Thus, in that way, by means of, with, for; instrument, medium, method, use (of), way (to).
祉	zhi3	0942	Blessings, happiness, gratification, good luck, prosperity.
元	yuan2	7707	Outstanding, greatest, sublime, supreme, greatest, very great, grand; source, beginning, cause, first or paramount, fundamentality; head, chief; used as a superlative.
吉	ji2	0476	Good fortune, auspicious, promising, fortunate, lucky, advantageous, happiness, good auspices. It is the only single character meaning good luck in the *YiJing*.

Six at the top

> The wall falls back into the pit. Do not use the army now!
> Proclaim your commands only in your own town.
> The determination brings humiliation.

城	cheng2	0380	City walls; battlements, place fortified for defense; city, citadel.
復	fu4	1992	Return, turn back; repeat, restore, revert, recommence.
于	yu2	7592	At, to, in, into, on, from, by, go, go to, move towards, proceed, be.
隍	huang2	2295	Dry moat around the city walls.
勿	wu4	7208	Do not, no. Negative imperative.
用	yong4	7567	Use, apply, put to use, apply the oracle to real world situations; hereby, thereby.
師	shi1	5760	Army, troops, militias; multitude; master, leader; take as a master, imitate, follow a role model or norm.
自	zi4	6960	From, origin, source, cause, reason; oneself, yourself.
邑	yi4	3037	City, town; walled or fortified city, seat of the of government for a district.

告	gao4	3287	Inform, announce, report, proclaim.
命	ming4	4537	Heaven's will; command(s), fate, destiny; will; investiture; birth and death as limits of life.
貞	zhen1	0346	Perseverance, persistence, determination, steadiness, firmness; straight, correct, verified, certain; pure, loyal. Its original meaning was "to determine an uncertain matter through divination".
吝	lin4	4040	Humiliation, regret, shame, distress, grief, sorrow; miserly, niggardly. It is a warning of trouble.

12 否 *pi* – Standstill / Stagnation

The Judgment

Standstill. Worthless people are unfavorable to the determination of the noble. The great is going away, the petty is coming.

否	pi3	1902	Standstill, stagnation, obstruction, stoppage, dead end; bad, wrong.
之	zhi1	0935	Personal pronoun, he she, it; this, that, these, etc.; often used as a possessive.
匪	fei3	1820	No, strong negative.
人	ren2	3097	Man, person(s); people; others; human being, individual.
不	bu4	5379	No, not, negative prefix; without, none, nothing, will not, need not, will not be.
利	li4	3867	Favorable, lucky, advantageous, profitable, beneficial, furthering, harvesting; sharp, sharp witted.
君	jun1	1715	Noble, prince, aristocrat, lord, chief, gentleman; honorable, a highly principled person, superior man. Most times, this character appears alongside another one, forming the word *JunZi*, whose original meaning was "son of a prince or ruler": 君子.
子	zi3	6939	Child, son or daughter, offspring; suffix; bride, wife; gentleman, officer, master, prince; young lady; the first of the *Earthly Branches*.
貞	zhen1	0346	Perseverance, persistence, determination, steadiness, firmness; straight, correct, verified, certain; pure, loyal. Its original meaning was "to determine an uncertain matter through divination".
大	da4	5943	Big, great, tall; excessive, arrogant; spread out and reach everywhere.
往	wang3	7050	Go, to go to, go forward, go towards; depart, bygone, former.
小	xiao3	2605	Small, insignificant, common, humble, mediocre; diminish, belittle.
來	lai2	3768	Come, arrive, return, bring.

The Image

Heaven and Earth are not related: The image of Standstill.
Thus the noble, restrains the manifestation of his virtue, and avoids the calamities. He does not accept receiving rank or salary.

天	tian1	6361	Heaven, firmament, the sky, cosmos; celestial, divine, power above the human.
地	di4	6198	Earth, soil, ground.
不	bu4	5379	No, not, negative prefix; without, none, nothing, will not, need not, will not be.
交	jiao1	0702	Union, relation, meeting; exchange, do business; share; contact; have relations with; to hand in or over.
否	pi3	1902	Standstill, stagnation, obstruction, stoppage, dead end; bad, wrong.
君	jun1	1715	Noble, prince, aristocrat, lord, chief, gentleman; honorable, a highly principled person, superior man. Most times, this character appears alongside another one, forming the word *JunZi*, whose original meaning was "son of a prince or ruler": 君子.
子	zi3	6939	Child, son or daughter, offspring; suffix; bride, wife; gentleman, officer, master, prince; young lady; the first of the *Earthly Branches*.
以	yi3	2932	Thus, in that way, by means of, with, for; instrument, medium, method, use (of), way (to).
儉	jian3	0848	Thrift, temperate, restricted, frugal, meager; poor harvest.
德	de2	6162	Virtue, spiritual power, moral integrity; quality, nature, aptitude, ability, character.
辟	bi4	5172	Escape, avoid, go away from; ward off; keep away. It also means expel, punish and apply the laws.
難	nan2	4625	Difficult, arduous, trouble, hardship, calamity, complication.
不	bu4	5379	No, not, negative prefix; without, none, nothing, will not, need not, will not be.
可	ke3	3381	Can, able, may; permit, allow; satisfactory, proper, suitable.
榮	rong2	7582	Honor, glory; flourish, luxuriant, prosper.
以	yi3	2932	Thus, in that way, by means of, with, for; instrument, medium, method, use (of), way (to).
祿	lu4	4196	Prosperity, revenue, salary, favors, official recognition, blessings.

Standstill (73) 12

Six at the beginning

When reeds are pulled, they pull up others of the same kind together with them. The determination brings good fortune and success.

拔	ba2	4848	Pull up, pull out, uproot, pluck up.
茅	mao2	4364	Reeds, cogon grass, white grass, used for wrapping offerings.
茹	ru2	3139	Interlaced roots, roots, shoots.
以	yi3	2932	Thus, in that way, by means of, with, for; instrument, medium, method, use (of), way (to).
其	qi2	0525	Their, his, its, the; this, that. A demonstrative and possessive pronoun.
彙	hui4	2349	Category, class; group, bunch; roots.
貞	zhen1	0346	Perseverance, persistence, determination, steadiness, firmness; straight, correct, verified, certain; pure, loyal. Its original meaning was "to determine an uncertain matter through divination".
吉	ji2	0476	Good fortune, auspicious, promising, fortunate, lucky, advantageous, happiness, good auspices. It is the only single character meaning good luck in the *YiJing*.
亨	heng1	2099	Success, prevalence, smooth progress, growth, consummate, triumph; pervade; offering, sacrifice.

Six in the second place

They support and tolerate. Good fortune for the petty.
By accepting the Standstill the great man will have success.

包	bao1	4937	Bundle, wrap, reed mat for wrapping; kitchen, butchering room; contain, support, take responsibility over.
承	cheng2	0386	Support; assist, bear, serve.
小	xiao3	2605	Small, insignificant, common, humble, mediocre; diminish, belittle.
人	ren2	3097	Man, person(s); people; others; human being, individual.
吉	ji2	0476	Good fortune, auspicious, promising, fortunate, lucky, advantageous, happiness, good auspices. It is the only single character meaning good luck in the *YiJing*.
大	da4	5943	Big, great, tall; excessive, arrogant; spread out and reach everywhere.
人	ren2	3097	Man, person(s); people; others; human being, individual.

| 否 | pi3 | 1902 | Standstill, stagnation, obstruction, stoppage, dead end; bad, wrong. |
| 亨 | heng1 | 2099 | Success, prevalence, smooth progress, growth, consummate, triumph; pervade; offering, sacrifice. |

Six in the third place

They bear the shame.

| 包 | bao1 | 4937 | Bundle, wrap, reed mat for wrapping; kitchen, butchering room; contain, support, take responsibility over. |
| 羞 | xiu1 | 2797 | Shame, disgrace; inferior, unworthy; a prepared offering, prepared meat, sacrifice, offerings. |

Nine in the fourth place

Who follows the commands of Heaven will have no defect.
His comrades will share the blessings.

有	you3	7533	Have, possession, there be, there is.
命	ming4	4537	Heaven's will; command(s), fate, destiny; will; investiture; birth and death as limits of life.
无	wu2	7173	No, not, negative; without, does not possess, not have.
咎	jiu4	1192	Fault, blame, mistake, wrong; inauspicious; misfortune, bad luck, calamity; reproach, censure.
疇	chou2	1322	Comrades, mates, class, category; plowed field, arable land.
離	li2	3902	Brightness, radiance, attach, cling; name of a bird. The modern meaning is leave, separate.
祉	zhi3	0942	Blessings, happiness, gratification, good luck, prosperity.

Nine in the fifth place

The Standstill is stopping. Good fortune for the great man. It can fail!
It can fail! Tie it to a luxuriant mulberry tree.

休	xiu1	2786	Stop, rest, relax, quiet; happy, glad; resign, cease; good, fine; benefit, blessings, luck.
否	pi3	1902	Standstill, stagnation, obstruction, stoppage, dead end; bad, wrong.
大	da4	5943	Big, great, tall; excessive, arrogant; spread out and reach everywhere.
人	ren2	3097	Man, person(s); people; others; human being, individual.
吉	ji2	0476	Good fortune, auspicious, promising, fortunate, lucky, advantageous, happiness, good auspices. It is the only single character meaning good luck in the *YiJing*.

其	qi2	0525	Their, his, its, the; this, that. A demonstrative and possessive pronoun.
亡	wang2	7034	Go away, disappear, exile; fail; destroy, perish, not have, not exist.
其	qi2	0525	Their, his, its, the; this, that. A demonstrative and possessive pronoun.
亡	wang2	7034	Go away, disappear, exile; fail; destroy, perish, not have, not exist.
繫	xi4	2458	Tie, attach, bind, connect, tether, restrain; suspend, hang from a cord; keep in mind.
于	yu2	7592	At, to, in, into, on, from, by, go, go to, move towards, proceed, be.
苞	bao1	4941	Dense, massive, luxuriant, thick-leafed, shrubbery, bushy.
桑	sang1	5424	Mulberry tree. Tree from the *Moraceae* family. Its leaves are the food source of the silkworm which produces the silk.

Nine at the top

The Standstill is overthrown. First Standstill, afterwards joy.

傾	qing1	1161	To collapse, overturn, upset, overthrown, subvert, bend, exhaust, incline the head; short time *(Kunst)*.
否	pi3	1902	Standstill, stagnation, obstruction, stoppage, dead end; bad, wrong.
先	xian1	2702	Before, first, foremost, in front, lead.
否	pi3	1902	Standstill, stagnation, obstruction, stoppage, dead end; bad, wrong.
後	hou4	2143	Later, behind, rear, afterward, come after; follow; descendants, successor.
喜	xi3	2434	Pleasure, joy, happiness, gratification, delight.

13 同人 *tong ren* – Fellowship

THE JUDGMENT

Fellowship in the fields. Success. It is advantageous to cross the great river. The determination brings good fortune for the noble.

同	tong2	6615	Gather people, assemble, join, partake in; identical, together, fellowship; in agreement, identical, identified.
人	ren2	3097	Man, person(s); people; others; human being, individual.
于	yu2	7592	At, to, in, into, on, from, by, go, go to, move towards, proceed, be.
野	ye3	7314	Meadow, open country, countryside, fields, wilderness.
亨	heng1	2099	Success, prevalence, smooth progress, growth, consummate, triumph; pervade; offering, sacrifice.
利	li4	3867	Favorable, lucky, advantageous, profitable, beneficial, furthering, harvesting; sharp, sharp witted.
涉	she4	5707	Cross, wade across (a river, stream), ford, pass through or over.
大	da4	5943	Big, great, tall; excessive, arrogant; spread out and reach everywhere.
川	chuan1	1439	River, flowing water; flood.
利	li4	3867	Favorable, lucky, advantageous, profitable, beneficial, furthering, harvesting; sharp, sharp witted.
君	jun1	1715	Noble, prince, aristocrat, lord, chief, gentleman; honorable, a highly principled person, superior man. Most times, this character appears alongside another one, forming the word *JunZi*, whose original meaning was "son of a prince or ruler": 君子.
子	zi3	6939	Child, son or daughter, offspring; suffix; bride, wife; gentleman, officer, master, prince; young lady; the first of the *Earthly Branches*.
貞	zhen1	0346	Perseverance, persistence, determination, steadiness, firmness; straight, correct, verified, certain; pure, loyal. Its original meaning was "to determine an uncertain matter through divination".

Fellowship (77) 13

The Image

> Heaven and Fire: The image of the Fellowship.
> Thus the noble organizes the clans and discriminates among things.

天	tian1	6361	Heaven, firmament, the sky, cosmos; celestial, divine, power above the human.
與	yu3	7615	With, and; associate with, together with, participate in, be present at; help; give.
火	huo3	2395	Fire, flame.
同	tong2	6615	Gather people, assemble, join, partake in; identical, together, fellowship; in agreement, identical, identified.
人	ren2	3097	Man, person(s); people; others; human being, individual.
君	jun1	1715	Noble, prince, aristocrat, lord, chief, gentleman; honorable, a highly principled person, superior man. Most times, this character appears alongside another one, forming the word *JunZi*, whose original meaning was "son of a prince or ruler": 君子.
子	zi3	6939	Child, son or daughter, offspring; suffix; bride, wife; gentleman, officer, master, prince; young lady; the first of the *Earthly Branches*.
以	yi3	2932	Thus, in that way, by means of, with, for; instrument, medium, method, use (of), way (to).
類	lei4	4244	Class, category, group, kind; discriminate, categorize.
族	zu2	6830	Clan, kin, extended family; group of families; tribe.
辨	bian4	5240	Discriminate, distinguish, discern, identify; divide, distribute; frame that divides a bed from its stand.
物	wu4	7209	Thing/s, being/s, creature/s; substance, the physical world, all living things; others.

Nine at the beginning

> Fellowship in the front door. No defect.

同	tong2	6615	Gather people, assemble, join, partake in; identical, together, fellowship; in agreement, identical, identified.
人	ren2	3097	Man, person(s); people; others; human being, individual.
于	yu2	7592	At, to, in, into, on, from, by, go, go to, move towards, proceed, be.
門	men2	4418	Gate, door. This is the external door, separating courtyard and street, meanwhile 戶 is the inner door, the entrance door.

无	wu2	7173	No, not, negative; without, does not possess, not have.
咎	jiu4	1192	Fault, blame, mistake, wrong; inauspicious; misfortune, bad luck, calamity; reproach, censure.

Six in the second place

Fellowship in the clan. Shame.

同	tong2	6615	Gather people, assemble, join, partake in; identical, together, fellowship; in agreement, identical, identified.
人	ren2	3097	Man, person(s); people; others; human being, individual.
于	yu2	7592	At, to, in, into, on, from, by, go, go to, move towards, proceed, be.
宗	zong1	6896	Clan, kin, sect, faction, school; ancestor; ancestral temple; ancestral hall.
吝	lin4	4040	Humiliation, regret, shame, distress, grief, sorrow; miserly, niggardly. It is a warning of trouble.

Nine in the third place

He hides weapons in the bush and climbs the high hill, but for three years he will not rise.

伏	fu2	1964	Hide away, conceal; crouch, hide, lie hidden, place an ambush.
戎	rong2	3181	Weapons, arms; war chariot; violence, attack.
于	yu2	7592	At, to, in, into, on, from, by, go, go to, move towards, proceed, be.
莽	mang3	4354	Thicket, weeds, underbrush, luxuriant grass.
升	sheng1	5745	Climb, push upwards, rise, go up, arise.
其	qi2	0525	Their, his, its, the; this, that. A demonstrative and possessive pronoun.
高	gao1	3290	High, elevated, exalted, eminent, lofty, illustrious, higher.
陵	ling2	4067	Hill, mound (the meanings it seems to have in the *YiJing*); tumulus, barrow; ascend a hill, ascend; transgress, overstep the limits, invade, encroach upon, usurp.
三	san1	5415	Three, thrice, third time or place.
歲	sui4	5538	Years, seasons, harvests.
不	bu4	5379	No, not, negative prefix; without, none, nothing, will not, need not, will not be.
興	xing1	2753	Rise up, be aroused; lift, raise, start, begin, prosper, flourish, be elated.

Fellowship (79) 13

Nine in the fourth place

He climbs to his wall but he cannot attack. Good fortune.

乘	cheng2	0398	Mount, ascend, climb up.
其	qi2	0525	Their, his, its, the; this, that. A demonstrative and possessive pronoun.
墉	yong1	7578	Wall, a fortified wall, defensive wall.
弗	fu2	1981	Not (not able or not willing to), negative.
克	ke4	3320	Can, able, carry, sustain; conquest, dominate, prevail.
攻	gong1	3699	Attack, assault, take the offensive; criticize; work at.
吉	ji2	0476	Good fortune, auspicious, promising, fortunate, lucky, advantageous, happiness, good auspices. It is the only single character meaning good luck in the *YiJing*.

Nine in the fifth place

The men in Fellowship first weep and mourn, but then laugh. Great armies come across.

同	tong2	6615	Gather people, assemble, join, partake in; identical, together, fellowship; in agreement, identical, identified.
人	ren2	3097	Man, person(s); people; others; human being, individual.
先	xian1	2702	Before, first, foremost, in front, lead.
號	hao4	2064	Weep; cry out, call out, scream, cry for help; signal, command.
咷	tao2	6152	Wail, weep, cry loudly, lament, moaning.
而	er2	1756	And, then, but, nevertheless, also, only. Join and contrasts two words.
後	hou4	2143	Later, behind, rear, afterward, come after; follow; descendants, successor.
笑	xiao4	2615	Laugh, smile, merriment, good humor.
大	da4	5943	Big, great, tall; excessive, arrogant; spread out and reach everywhere.
師	shi1	5760	Army, troops, militias; multitude; master, leader; take as a master, imitate, follow a role model or norm.
克	ke4	3320	Can, able, carry, sustain; conquest, dominate, prevail.
相	xiang1	2562	Each other, mutual, reciprocal, cooperative; look to, look at, assist, aid.
遇	yu4	7625	Meet, encounter, come across, happen.

Nine at the top

Fellowship in the field. No repentance.

同	tong2	6615	Gather people, assemble, join, partake in; identical, together, fellowship; in agreement, identical, identified.
人	ren2	3097	Man, person(s); people; others; human being, individual.
于	yu2	7592	At, to, in, into, on, from, by, go, go to, move towards, proceed, be.
郊	jiao1	0714	Countryside, suburbs, outskirts, frontier; suburban altar and sacrifice.
无	wu2	7173	No, not, negative; without, does not possess, not have.
悔	hui3	2336	Repent, regret, contrition; trouble. This word indicates both an objective situation and a subjective reaction to such circumstance.

14 大有 *da you* – Great Possession

The Judgment

Great Possession. Outstanding success.

大	da4	5943	Big, great, tall; excessive, arrogant; spread out and reach everywhere.
有	you3	7533	Have, possession, there be, there is.
元	yuan2	7707	Outstanding, greatest, sublime, supreme, greatest, very great, grand; source, beginning, cause, first or paramount, fundamentality; head, chief; used as a superlative.
亨	heng1	2099	Success, prevalence, smooth progress, growth, consummate, triumph; pervade; offering, sacrifice.

The Image

Fire at the top of Heaven: The image of Great Possession.
Thus the noble punishes evil and promotes good,
following the good will of Heaven.

火	huo3	2395	Fire, flame.
在	zai4	6657	Be at, at, in, on, within, be present; to lie in, depend upon, involved with; be living, dwell, located in.
天	tian1	6361	Heaven, firmament, the sky, cosmos; celestial, divine, power above the human.
上	shang4	5669	Up, above, on, over, upwards, top, rise; higher, superior; first, best.
大	da4	5943	Big, great, tall; excessive, arrogant; spread out and reach everywhere.
有	you3	7533	Have, possession, there be, there is.
君	jun1	1715	Noble, prince, aristocrat, lord, chief, gentleman; honorable, a highly principled person, superior man. Most times, this character appears alongside another one, forming the word *JunZi*, whose original meaning was "son of a prince or ruler": 君子.

子	zi3	6939	Child, son or daughter, offspring; suffix; bride, wife; gentleman, officer, master, prince; young lady; the first of the *Earthly Branches*.
以	yi3	2932	Thus, in that way, by means of, with, for; instrument, medium, method, use (of), way (to).
遏	e4	4812	Curb, repress, check, stop, suppress; cease.
惡	e4	4809	Evil, bad; ugly; wrong, fault, bad; hate.
揚	yang2	7259	Display, make known, announce, extol; scatter, spread; lift, raise; stir.
善	shan4	5657	Good, virtuous; perfect, improve.
順	shun4	5935	Follow, obey, yield, agree, submissive, docile.
天	tian1	6361	Heaven, firmament, the sky, cosmos; celestial, divine, power above the human.
休	xiu1	2786	Stop, rest, relax, quiet; happy, glad; resign, cease; good, fine; benefit, blessings, luck.
命	ming4	4537	Heaven's will; command(s), fate, destiny; will; investiture; birth and death as limits of life.

Nine at the beginning

No relationship with harmful things. No defect.
There will be hardship but no defect.

无	wu2	7173	No, not, negative; without, does not possess, not have.
交	jiao1	0702	Union, relation, meeting; exchange, do business; share; contact; have relations with; to hand in or over.
害	hai4	2015	Harm, harmful; injure; to suffer a disease or harm, to injury, hurt, frighten or destroy.
匪	fei3	1820	No, strong negative.
咎	jiu4	1192	Fault, blame, mistake, wrong; inauspicious; misfortune, bad luck, calamity; reproach, censure.
艱	jian1	0834	Hardship, distressing, difficult, laborious.
則	ze2	6746	Then, thus, accordingly, consequently, and so, in that case; law, rule, pattern; follow a law.
无	wu2	7173	No, not, negative; without, does not possess, not have.
咎	jiu4	1192	Fault, blame, mistake, wrong; inauspicious; misfortune, bad luck, calamity; reproach, censure.

Nine in the second place

A great carriage for carrying things. One has a goal. No defect.

| 大 | da4 | 5943 | Big, great, tall; excessive, arrogant; spread out and reach everywhere. |

Great Possession (83)

車	che1	0280	Chariot, wagon, cart, carriage.
以	yi3	2932	Thus, in that way, by means of, with, for; instrument, medium, method, use (of), way (to).
載	zai4	6653	Transport, carry, load, bear; contain, sustain; load a vessel or cart, conveyance.
有	you3	7533	Have, possession, there be, there is.
攸	you1	7519	Goal, direction, destination, objective; distant, far away; a place; that which, whereby, thereby, for which; mark of the passive voice.
往	wang3	7050	Go, to go to, go forward, go towards; depart, bygone, former. 攸往: have a place to go; have a goal.
无	wu2	7173	No, not, negative; without, does not possess, not have.
咎	jiu4	1192	Fault, blame, mistake, wrong; inauspicious; misfortune, bad luck, calamity; reproach, censure.

Nine in the third place

A prince presents his offerings to the Son of Heaven.
A petty man is not able to do so.

公	gong1	3701	Prince, feudal lord, duke, noble of rank (the nobiliary titles, from high to low, were: duke, marquis, count, viscount, baron); public, impartial, with justice, fair.
用	yong4	7567	Use, apply, put to use, apply the oracle to real world situations; hereby, thereby.
亨	heng1	2099	Success, prevalence, smooth progress, growth, consummate, triumph; pervade; offering, sacrifice.
于	yu2	7592	At, to, in, into, on, from, by, go, go to, move towards, proceed, be.
天	tian1	6361	Heaven, firmament, the sky, cosmos; celestial, divine, power above the human.
子	zi3	6939	Child, son or daughter, offspring; suffix; bride, wife; gentleman, officer, master, prince; young lady; the first of the *Earthly Branches*.
小	xiao3	2605	Small, insignificant, common, humble, mediocre; diminish, belittle.
人	ren2	3097	Man, person(s); people; others; human being, individual.
弗	fu2	1981	Not (not able or not willing to), negative.
克	ke4	3320	Can, able, carry, sustain; conquest, dominate, prevail.

Nine in the fourth place
He is not arrogant. No defect.

匪	fei3	1820	No, strong negative.
其	qi2	0525	Their, his, its, the; this, that. A demonstrative and possessive pronoun.
彭	peng2	5060	Forceful, overbearing, fullness, plenitude, an overwhelming sound.
无	wu2	7173	No, not, negative; without, does not possess, not have.
咎	jiu4	1192	Fault, blame, mistake, wrong; inauspicious; misfortune, bad luck, calamity; reproach, censure.

Six in the fifth place
His sincerity will gain trust and respect from others. Good fortune.

厥	jue2	1680	Their, his, its.
孚	fu2	1936	Truth; reliable, sincere; to inspire confidence in others; capture, prisoner, plunder.
交	jiao1	0702	Union, relation, meeting; exchange, do business; share; contact; have relations with; to hand in or over.
如	ru2	3137	Thus, in this way, as, like, similar to, if (conditional).
威	wei1	7051	Dignity, respect; awesome, majestic; impress, terrify; the mother of one's husband.
如	ru2	3137	Thus, in this way, as, like, similar to, if (conditional).
吉	ji2	0476	Good fortune, auspicious, promising, fortunate, lucky, advantageous, happiness, good auspices. It is the only single character meaning good luck in the *YiJing*.

Nine at the top
He has the protection of Heaven. Good fortune.
Nothing that is not favorable.

自	zi4	6960	From, origin, source, cause, reason; oneself, yourself.
天	tian1	6361	Heaven, firmament, the sky, cosmos; celestial, divine, power above the human.
祐	you4	7543	Divine help, help, aid, protection, blessing. 天祐: protection or help from heaven.
之	zhi1	0935	Personal pronoun, he she, it; this, that, these, etc.; often used as a possessive.

Great Possession

吉	ji2	0476	Good fortune, auspicious, promising, fortunate, lucky, advantageous, happiness, good auspices. It is the only single character meaning good luck in the *YiJing*.
无	wu2	7173	No, not, negative; without, does not possess, not have.
不	bu4	5379	No, not, negative prefix; without, none, nothing, will not, need not, will not be.
利	li4	3867	Favorable, lucky, advantageous, profitable, beneficial, furthering, harvesting; sharp, sharp witted.

15 謙 *qian* – Modesty

The Judgment

Modesty. Success.
The noble carries things to completion.

謙	qian1	0885	Modest, humble, yielding, unassuming, reverent.
亨	heng1	2099	Success, prevalence, smooth progress, growth, consummate, triumph; pervade; offering, sacrifice.
君	jun1	1715	Noble, prince, aristocrat, lord, chief, gentleman; honorable, a highly principled person, superior man. Most times, this character appears alongside another one, forming the word *JunZi*, whose original meaning was "son of a prince or ruler": 君子.
子	zi3	6939	Child, son or daughter, offspring; suffix; bride, wife; gentleman, officer, master, prince; young lady; the first of the *Earthly Branches*.
有	you3	7533	Have, possession, there be, there is.
終	zhong1	1500	End, finish, complete; for ever; end of a cycle; carried to conclusion, consummation, closure; death. The original meaning was: tied-off end of a thread.

The Image

A Mountain in the middle of the Earth: The image of Modesty.
So the noble reduces what is excessive
and increases what is insufficient.
Weighs and distributes things evenly.

地	di4	6198	Earth, soil, ground.
中	zhong1	1504	Center, inner, in the inside, put in the center, hit (target); balanced, central, middle, correct.
有	you3	7533	Have, possession, there be, there is.
山	shan1	5630	Mountain, hill, peak.
謙	qian1	0885	Modest, humble, yielding, unassuming, reverent.

Modesty

君	jun1	1715	Noble, prince, aristocrat, lord, chief, gentleman; honorable, a highly principled person, superior man. Most times, this character appears alongside another one, forming the word *JunZi*, whose original meaning was "son of a prince or ruler": 君子.
子	zi3	6939	Child, son or daughter, offspring; suffix; bride, wife; gentleman, officer, master, prince; young lady; the first of the *Earthly Branches*.
以	yi3	2932	Thus, in that way, by means of, with, for; instrument, medium, method, use (of), way (to).
衰	shuai1	5908	Reduce, decrease, lessen; weaken, decline.
多	duo1	6416	Too much, many, numerous; excessive; often.
益	yi4	3052	Increase, augment; more; benefit, profit, advantage.
寡	gua3	3517	Little, few; alone, solitary, friendless, single standing, widow; unique; resourceless, inadequate.
稱	cheng1	0383	Evaluate, to weigh, assess, appraise.
物	wu4	7209	Thing/s, being/s, creature/s; substance, the physical world, all living things; others.
平	ping2	5303	A plain, level, equal, even; equalize, harmonize, regulate, pacify; peace.
施	shi1	5768	Expand, spread out, dispense, distribute, give, bestow.

Six at the beginning

An extremely modest noble can cross the great river. Good fortune.

謙	qian1	0885	Modest, humble, yielding, unassuming, reverent. Appearing duplicated intensifies its intensity.
謙	qian1	0885	
君	jun1	1715	Noble, prince, aristocrat, lord, chief, gentleman; honorable, a highly principled person, superior man. Most times, this character appears alongside another one, forming the word *JunZi*, whose original meaning was "son of a prince or ruler": 君子.
子	zi3	6939	Child, son or daughter, offspring; suffix; bride, wife; gentleman, officer, master, prince; young lady; the first of the *Earthly Branches*.
用	yong4	7567	Use, apply, put to use, apply the oracle to real world situations; hereby, thereby.
涉	she4	5707	Cross, wade across (a river, stream), ford, pass through or over.

大	da4	5943	Big, great, tall; excessive, arrogant; spread out and reach everywhere.
川	chuan1	1439	River, flowing water; flood.
吉	ji2	0476	Good fortune, auspicious, promising, fortunate, lucky, advantageous, happiness, good auspices. It is the only single character meaning good luck in the *YiJing*.

Six in the second place

Modesty expresses itself. The determination is fortunate.

鳴	ming2	4535	Cry of a bird or animal, a sound, to make sounds, distinctive sound, voice, express, proclaim.
謙	qian1	0885	Modest, humble, yielding, unassuming, reverent.
貞	zhen1	0346	Perseverance, persistence, determination, steadiness, firmness; straight, correct, verified, certain; pure, loyal. Its original meaning was "to determine an uncertain matter through divination".
吉	ji2	0476	Good fortune, auspicious, promising, fortunate, lucky, advantageous, happiness, good auspices. It is the only single character meaning good luck in the *YiJing*.

Nine in the third place

A noble meritorious for his modesty carries things to completion. Good fortune.

勞	lao2	3826	Toil, diligent work; deeds, achievements, merits.
謙	qian1	0885	Modest, humble, yielding, unassuming, reverent.
君	jun1	1715	Noble, prince, aristocrat, lord, chief, gentleman; honorable, a highly principled person, superior man. Most times, this character appears alongside another one, forming the word *JunZi*, whose original meaning was "son of a prince or ruler": 君子.
子	zi3	6939	Child, son or daughter, offspring; suffix; bride, wife; gentleman, officer, master, prince; young lady; the first of the *Earthly Branches*.
有	you3	7533	Have, possession, there be, there is.
終	zhong1	1500	End, finish, complete; for ever; end of a cycle; carried to conclusion, consummation, closure; death. The original meaning was: tied-off end of a thread.

MODESTY (89) 15

吉	ji2	0476	Good fortune, auspicious, promising, fortunate, lucky, advantageous, happiness, good auspices. It is the only single character meaning good luck in the *YiJing*.

Six in the fourth place

Nothing that is not favorable for manifested modesty.

无	wu2	7173	No, not, negative; without, does not possess, not have.
不	bu4	5379	No, not, negative prefix; without, none, nothing, will not, need not, will not be.
利	li4	3867	Favorable, lucky, advantageous, profitable, beneficial, furthering, harvesting; sharp, sharp witted.
撝	hui1	2356	Display, wave, fly a banner, signal; tear.
謙	qian1	0885	Modest, humble, yielding, unassuming, reverent.

Six in the fifth place

Without wealth can employ his neighbors.
It is advantageous to take the offensive. Nothing that is not favorable.

不	bu4	5379	No, not, negative prefix; without, none, nothing, will not, need not, will not be.
富	fu4	1952	Rich, wealth, treasure, abundance, prosperity, to enrich.
以	yi3	2932	Thus, in that way, by means of, with, for; instrument, medium, method, use (of), way (to).
其	qi2	0525	Their, his, its, the; this, that. A demonstrative and possessive pronoun.
鄰	lin2	4033	Neighbor, neighborhood, extended family, associate, assistant.
利	li4	3867	Favorable, lucky, advantageous, profitable, beneficial, furthering, harvesting; sharp, sharp witted.
用	yong4	7567	Use, apply, put to use, apply the oracle to real world situations; hereby, thereby.
侵	qin1	1108	Invade, encroach, appropriate, surprise attack, usurp. The ancient meaning was to approach gradually.
伐	fa1	1765	Attack, punish (rebels), submit; beat, cut down, fell.
无	wu2	7173	No, not, negative; without, does not possess, not have.
不	bu4	5379	No, not, negative prefix; without, none, nothing, will not, need not, will not be.
利	li4	3867	Favorable, lucky, advantageous, profitable, beneficial, furthering, harvesting; sharp, sharp witted.

15

Six at the top

Manifest Modesty.
It is favorable to launch armies to punish the capital city.

鳴	ming2	4535	Cry of a bird or animal, a sound, to make sounds, distinctive sound, voice, express, proclaim.
謙	qian1	0885	Modest, humble, yielding, unassuming, reverent.
利	li4	3867	Favorable, lucky, advantageous, profitable, beneficial, furthering, harvesting; sharp, sharp witted.
用	yong4	7567	Use, apply, put to use, apply the oracle to real world situations; hereby, thereby.
行	xing2	2754	Move, go, advance, act, do.
師	shi1	5760	Army, troops, militias; multitude; master, leader; take as a master, imitate, follow a role model or norm.
征	zheng1	0352	Punishing expedition ("to correct"), to reduce to submission, attack, punish; to levy taxes; comes, brings.
邑	yi4	3037	City, town; walled or fortified city, seat of the of government for a district.
國	guo2	3738	State, country, nation, kingdom, a dynasty; capital city.

16 豫 yu – Enthusiasm

The Judgment

> Enthusiasm. It is favorable to appoint officers
> and to set the army in motion.

豫	yu4	7603	Think beforehand, take precautions, anticipate, hesitate; joy, happy, amusement, recreation, enthusiasm, contentment, at ease.
利	li4	3867	Favorable, lucky, advantageous, profitable, beneficial, furthering, harvesting; sharp, sharp witted.
建	jian4	0853	Establish, found, appoint, confirm a position.
侯	hou2	2135	Feudal lord, (vassal) prince, marquis; officer, governor, chief; skilled archer.
行	xing2	2754	Move, go, advance, act, do.
師	shi1	5760	Army, troops, militias; multitude; master, leader; take as a master, imitate, follow a role model or norm.

The Image

> Thunder come out from the Earth: The image of Enthusiasm.
> So the kings of old made music to honor merit, and lavishly offered it
> to the Supreme Lord to be worthy of their dead ancestors.

雷	lei2	4236	Thunder, shock, terrifying, arousing power surging from the earth.
出	chu1	1409	Go out, came out, appear, departure; arise, emerge; bring out, take out, expel, leave, get rid of; produce, beget.
地	di4	6198	Earth, soil, ground.
奮	fen4	1874	Impetuous, aroused, excited, impulsive, spirited; determined.
豫	yu4	7603	Think beforehand, take precautions, anticipate, hesitate; joy, happy, amusement, recreation, enthusiasm, contentment, at ease.

先	xian1	2702	Before, first, foremost, in front, lead.
王	wang2	7037	King, prince, sovereign, ruler.
以	yi3	2932	Thus, in that way, by means of, with, for; instrument, medium, method, use (of), way (to).
作	zuo4	6780	Act, do, make, work, perform; rise, stand up, get to work; project, undertaking, ceremony, to sacrifice.
樂	le4	4129	Music, joyous, happy.
崇	chong2	1528	Extol, honor, reference, esteem; lofty, noble.
德	de2	6162	Virtue, spiritual power, moral integrity; quality, nature, aptitude, ability, character.
殷	yin1	7423	Great, ample, exalted, flourishing, abundant; a kind of sacrifice.
薦	jian4	0872	Offer in sacrifice, offering, worship.
之	zhi1	0935	Personal pronoun, he she, it; this, that, these, etc.; often used as a possessive.
上	shang4	5669	Up, above, on, over, upwards, top, rise; higher, superior; first, best.
帝	di4	6204	Sovereign, emperor, god.
以	yi3	2932	Thus, in that way, by means of, with, for; instrument, medium, method, use (of), way (to).
配	pei4	5019	Match, equal, pair, colleague, consort; worthy, to be qualified.
祖	zu3	6815	Ancestor, grandfather.
考	kao3	3299	Examine, inspect; deceased ancestor or father, old.

Six at the beginning

Manifest Enthusiasm is ominous.

鳴	ming2	4535	Cry of a bird or animal, a sound, to make sounds, distinctive sound, voice, express, proclaim.
豫	yu4	7603	Think beforehand, take precautions, anticipate, hesitate; joy, happy, amusement, recreation, enthusiasm, contentment, at ease.
凶	xiong1	2808	Misfortune, pitfall, ominous, bad, unlucky, disastrous, trouble, accident.

Enthusiasm (93)   16

Six in the second place

> Solid as a rock. His chance will come before the end of the day.
> The determination brings good fortune.

介	jie4	0629	Firm, solid; curb; limit, restriction, boundary; armour; protect, assist, depend on, support; great, important.
于	yu2	7592	At, to, in, into, on, from, by, go, go to, move towards, proceed, be.
石	shi2	5813	Rock, stone.
不	bu4	5379	No, not, negative prefix; without, none, nothing, will not, need not, will not be.
終	zhong1	1500	End, finish, complete; for ever; end of a cycle; carried to conclusion, consummation, closure; death. The original meaning was: tied-off end of a thread.
日	ri4	3124	Sun, day, daylight, daytime; daily.
貞	zhen1	0346	Perseverance, persistence, determination, steadiness, firmness; straight, correct, verified, certain; pure, loyal. Its original meaning was "to determine an uncertain matter through divination".
吉	ji2	0476	Good fortune, auspicious, promising, fortunate, lucky, advantageous, happiness, good auspices. It is the only single character meaning good luck in the *YiJing*.

Six in the third place

> Enthusiasm that looks upward brings repentance.
> Hesitation brings repentance.

盱	xu1	2819	Look upward, stare, lift the eyes and regard, wide-eyed, amazed.
豫	yu4	7603	Think beforehand, take precautions, anticipate, hesitate; joy, happy, amusement, recreation, enthusiasm, contentment, at ease.
悔	hui3	2336	Repent, regret, contrition; trouble. This word indicates both an objective situation and a subjective reaction to such circumstance.
遲	chi2	1024	Hesitation, delay, slow, dilatory, late, procrastinate.
有	you3	7533	Have, possession, there be, there is.
悔	hui3	2336	Repent, regret, contrition; trouble. This word indicates both an objective situation and a subjective reaction to such circumstance.

Nine in the fourth place

> Excitement causes great things. Do not hesitate.
> Friends are quick to join your side.

由	you2	7513	Source, cause, reason; proceed from.
豫	yu4	7603	Think beforehand, take precautions, anticipate, hesitate; joy, happy, amusement, recreation, enthusiasm, contentment, at ease.
大	da4	5943	Big, great, tall; excessive, arrogant; spread out and reach everywhere.
有	you3	7533	Have, possession, there be, there is.
得	de2	6161	Get, obtain, gain; reach, achieve; can; attain the desired thing.
勿	wu4	7208	Do not, no. Negative imperative.
疑	yi2	2940	Doubt, mistrust, suspect, hesitate.
朋	peng2	5054	Friend, companion, pair, equal, comrade; a string of cowries (small shiny shells used as coins in ancient China).
盍	he2	2119	United, joined, assemble, gather; why not?
簪	zan1	6679	Hairpin, hair clasp, wear in the hair; skewer; loan for *zhen*, quick, rapid.

Six in the fifth place

> Determination. Persistently ill but not dying.

貞	zhen1	0346	Perseverance, persistence, determination, steadiness, firmness; straight, correct, verified, certain; pure, loyal. Its original meaning was "to determine an uncertain matter through divination".
疾	ji2	0492	Ill, harm, defect, stress; hurry; hate.
恆	heng2	2107	Duration, persistence, endurance, steadiness, continuity; for a long time.
不	bu4	5379	No, not, negative prefix; without, none, nothing, will not, need not, will not be.
死	si3	5589	Die, death, doomed.

Six at the top

> Confused Enthusiasm.
> But if one changes course after it is over, there will be no defect.

冥	ming2	4528	Dark, darkness, obscured; benighted, confused, ignorant, blind; deep, the underworld.

豫	yu4	7603	Think beforehand, take precautions, anticipate, hesitate; joy, happy, amusement, recreation, enthusiasm, contentment, at ease.
成	cheng2	0379	Accomplish, achieve, finish, complete a task, fulfill; completed, perfect, fully developed, mature; peace making.
有	you3	7533	Have, possession, there be, there is.
渝	yu2	7635	Change, to change one's mind or attitude, retract, amend; fail, change for worse.
无	wu2	7173	No, not, negative; without, does not possess, not have.
咎	jiu4	1192	Fault, blame, mistake, wrong; inauspicious; misfortune, bad luck, calamity; reproach, censure.

17 隨 sui – Following

The Judgment

Following has outstanding success.
The determination is favorable. No defect.

隨	sui2	5523	Follow, pursue; conform to, respond, follow a way or religion; subsequently, in the course of time; listen to, submit; marrow, flesh.
元	yuan2	7707	Outstanding, greatest, sublime, supreme, greatest, very great, grand; source, beginning, cause, first or paramount, fundamentality; head, chief; used as a superlative.
亨	heng1	2099	Success, prevalence, smooth progress, growth, consummate, triumph; pervade; offering, sacrifice.
利	li4	3867	Favorable, lucky, advantageous, profitable, beneficial, furthering, harvesting; sharp, sharp witted.
貞	zhen1	0346	Perseverance, persistence, determination, steadiness, firmness; straight, correct, verified, certain; pure, loyal. Its original meaning was "to determine an uncertain matter through divination".
无	wu2	7173	No, not, negative; without, does not possess, not have.
咎	jiu4	1192	Fault, blame, mistake, wrong; inauspicious; misfortune, bad luck, calamity; reproach, censure.

The Image

Thunder is in the middle of the Lake: The image of Following.
Thus the noble, at dusk, enters and rests in peace.

澤	ze2	0277	Marsh, pool, pond, lake; flat body of water and the vapors rising from it; enrich, fertilize, benefit; moist, moisten; glossy, polished.
中	zhong1	1504	Center, inner, in the inside, put in the center, hit (target); balanced, central, middle, correct.
有	you3	7533	Have, possession, there be, there is.
雷	lei2	4236	Thunder, shock, terrifying, arousing power surging from the earth.

隨	sui2	5523	Follow, pursue; conform to, respond, follow a way or religion; subsequently, in the course of time; listen to, submit; marrow, flesh.
君	jun1	1715	Noble, prince, aristocrat, lord, chief, gentleman; honorable, a highly principled person, superior man. Most times, this character appears alongside another one, forming the word *JunZi*, whose original meaning was "son of a prince or ruler": 君子.
子	zi3	6939	Child, son or daughter, offspring; suffix; bride, wife; gentleman, officer, master, prince; young lady; the first of the *Earthly Branches*.
以	yi3	2932	Thus, in that way, by means of, with, for; instrument, medium, method, use (of), way (to).
嚮	xiang4	2561	Getting towards, approach, face, near.
晦	hui4	2337	Dark, to get dark, obscure, twilight, shading; the last day of the lunar month; reticent.
入	ru4	3152	Enter, go into (this is the meaning used in the *YiJing*); to make to enter; put into; bring in, present; encroach.
宴	yan4	7364	Rest, repose; feast, banquet; leisure, pleasure. 宴息: rest and leisure.
息	xi1	2495	Rest, pause; breathe, breathing-spell, take breath, enjoy the rest, well-being, prosper.

Nine at the beginning

> The situation is changing. The determination is favorable.
> Going outside to find associates is worthwhile.

官	guan1	3552	Office, official, officer, public servant, official's residence, public charge.
有	you3	7533	Have, possession, there be, there is.
渝	yu2	7635	Change, to change one's mind or attitude, retract, amend; fail, change for worse.
貞	zhen1	0346	Perseverance, persistence, determination, steadiness, firmness; straight, correct, verified, certain; pure, loyal. Its original meaning was "to determine an uncertain matter through divination".
吉	ji2	0476	Good fortune, auspicious, promising, fortunate, lucky, advantageous, happiness, good auspices. It is the only single character meaning good luck in the *YiJing*.
出	chu1	1409	Go out, came out, appear, departure; arise, emerge; bring out, take out, expel, leave, get rid of; produce, beget.

門	men2	4418	Gate, door. This is the external door, separating courtyard and street, meanwhile 戶 is the inner door, the entrance door.
交	jiao1	0702	Union, relation, meeting; exchange, do business; share; contact; have relations with; to hand in or over.
有	you3	7533	Have, possession, there be, there is.
功	gong1	3698	Deeds, accomplishments, merits, good result, praiseworthy.

Six in the second place

He clings to the boy and lets go the strong man.

係	xi4	2424	Cling to, attach to, bind to, (en)tangled, involved, relation.
小	xiao3	2605	Small, insignificant, common, humble, mediocre; diminish, belittle.
子	zi3	6939	Child, son or daughter, offspring; suffix; bride, wife; gentleman, officer, master, prince; young lady; the first of the *Earthly Branches*.
失	shi1	5806	Lose, let go, neglect, an omission; fail, err; lose control.
丈	zhang4	0200	Strong, mature, a married man; responsible; respectable; a gentleman. One to be respected.
夫	fu1	1908	Man, male adult, husband; this, that, those.

Six in the third place

He is involved with the strong man and lets go the boy.
By Following one gets what one seeks for.
The determination is favorable.

係	xi4	2424	Cling to, attach to, bind to, (en)tangled, involved, relation.
丈	zhang4	0200	Strong, mature, a married man; responsible; respectable; a gentleman. One to be respected.
夫	fu1	1908	Man, male adult, husband; this, that, those.
失	shi1	5806	Lose, let go, neglect, an omission; fail, err; lose control.
小	xiao3	2605	Small, insignificant, common, humble, mediocre; diminish, belittle.
子	zi3	6939	Child, son or daughter, offspring; suffix; bride, wife; gentleman, officer, master, prince; young lady; the first of the *Earthly Branches*.

Following (99) 17

隨	sui2	5523	Follow, pursue; conform to, respond, follow a way or religion; subsequently, in the course of time; listen to, submit; marrow, flesh.
有	you3	7533	Have, possession, there be, there is.
求	qiu2	1217	Seek, strive; ask, implore, beg, pray; desire.
得	de2	6161	Get, obtain, gain; reach, achieve; can; attain the desired thing.
利	li4	3867	Favorable, lucky, advantageous, profitable, beneficial, furthering, harvesting; sharp, sharp witted.
居	ju1	1535	Remain; rest (in); abides, dwell; to occupy a position or place; overbearing, arrogant.
貞	zhen1	0346	Perseverance, persistence, determination, steadiness, firmness; straight, correct, verified, certain; pure, loyal. Its original meaning was "to determine an uncertain matter through divination".

Nine in the fourth place

By Following there will be a catch. The determination is ominous.
He is truthful and bright on the way.
How could there be defect in this?

隨	sui2	5523	Follow, pursue; conform to, respond, follow a way or religion; subsequently, in the course of time; listen to, submit; marrow, flesh.
有	you3	7533	Have, possession, there be, there is.
獲	huo4	2412	Catch (in hunt), seize, get, obtain, hit the mark, find; succeed. What is caught, gotten or found may be a thing, a person, an opportunity, an idea or perception.
貞	zhen1	0346	Perseverance, persistence, determination, steadiness, firmness; straight, correct, verified, certain; pure, loyal. Its original meaning was "to determine an uncertain matter through divination".
凶	xiong1	2808	Misfortune, pitfall, ominous, bad, unlucky, disastrous, trouble, accident.
有	you3	7533	Have, possession, there be, there is.
孚	fu2	1936	Truth; reliable, sincere; to inspire confidence in others; capture, prisoner, plunder.
在	zai4	6657	Be at, at, in, on, within, be present; to lie in, depend upon, involved with; be living, dwell, located in.

MATRIX OF MEANINGS OF THE BOOK OF CHANGES

道	dao4	6136	Road, course, path, way, method; show the way, lead, explain.
以	yi3	2932	Thus, in that way, by means of, with, for; instrument, medium, method, use (of), way (to).
明	ming2	4534	Light, brightness, clarity, clear; enlightenment, discernment; seeing, perception; agreement, contract.
何	he2	2109	What? how? why? what is? for that reason, therefore.
咎	jiu4	1192	Fault, blame, mistake, wrong; inauspicious; misfortune, bad luck, calamity; reproach, censure.

Nine in the fifth place

Sincerity leads to excellence. Good fortune.

孚	fu2	1936	Truth; reliable, sincere; to inspire confidence in others; capture, prisoner, plunder.
于	yu2	7592	At, to, in, into, on, from, by, go, go to, move towards, proceed, be.
嘉	jia1	0592	Good, excellent, joyful; commendations, approbation; admirable, praiseworthy.
吉	ji2	0476	Good fortune, auspicious, promising, fortunate, lucky, advantageous, happiness, good auspices. It is the only single character meaning good luck in the *YiJing*.

Six at the top

Strong ties between those who follow the same path. The King makes an offering in the Western Mountain.

拘	ju1	1542	Grasp, seize, arrest, catch; to embrace (a person or an idea), to hold in the arms.
係	xi4	2424	Cling to, attach to, bind to, (en)tangled, involved, relation.
之	zhi1	0935	Personal pronoun, he she, it; this, that, these, etc.; often used as a possessive.
乃	nai3	4612	Then, and, also, thereupon, as it turned out, namely, after all, only then; really, indeed.
從	cong2	6919	Follow (somebody or a way or doctrine), adhere, obey, pursue; follower attendant; attend to business; from, by, since, whence, through.
維	wei2	7067	Tie up, bound, bind together; guiding rope of a net; guiding principle, rule; but only.
之	zhi1	0935	Personal pronoun, he she, it; this, that, these, etc.; often used as a possessive.

王	wang2	7037	King, prince, sovereign, ruler.
用	yong4	7567	Use, apply, put to use, apply the oracle to real world situations; hereby, thereby.
亨	heng1	2099	Success, prevalence, smooth progress, growth, consummate, triumph; pervade; offering, sacrifice.
于	yu2	7592	At, to, in, into, on, from, by, go, go to, move towards, proceed, be.
西	xi1	2460	The West, western. Related to the autumn.
山	shan1	5630	Mountain, hill, peak.

18 蠱 *gu* – Correcting Decay

THE JUDGMENT

Correcting Decay has outstanding success.
It is favorable to cross the great river.
Before the first day three days.
After the first day three days.

蠱	gu3	3475	Decay, corruption, poisonous worms in the food or the stomach, spoiled grain (infected with insects), poison, evil influence, seduction, madness, insanity, curse, spell.
元	yuan2	7707	Outstanding, greatest, sublime, supreme, greatest, very great, grand; source, beginning, cause, first or paramount, fundamentality; head, chief; used as a superlative.
亨	heng1	2099	Success, prevalence, smooth progress, growth, consummate, triumph; pervade; offering, sacrifice.
利	li4	3867	Favorable, lucky, advantageous, profitable, beneficial, furthering, harvesting; sharp, sharp witted.
涉	she4	5707	Cross, wade across (a river, stream), ford, pass through or over.
大	da4	5943	Big, great, tall; excessive, arrogant; spread out and reach everywhere.
川	chuan1	1439	River, flowing water; flood.
先	xian1	2702	Before, first, foremost, in front, lead.
甲	jia3	0610	First day of the ten day week; the day to issue new commands; cyclical character; shell, buff coat. Cyclical character; the first of the Ten Celestial Stems, first heavenly branch.
三	san1	5415	Three, thrice, third time or place.
日	ri4	3124	Sun, day, daylight, daytime; daily.
後	hou4	2143	Later, behind, rear, afterward, come after; follow; descendants, successor.

Correcting Decay (103) **18**

甲	jia3	0610	First day of the ten day week; the day to issue new commands; cyclical character; shell, buff coat. Cyclical character; the first of the Ten Celestial Stems, first heavenly branch.
三	san1	5415	Three, thrice, third time or place.
日	ri4	3124	Sun, day, daylight, daytime; daily.

The Image

Under the Mountain is the Wind: The image of corruption.
Thus the noble puts in motion the people
and cultivates their moral values.

山	shan1	5630	Mountain, hill, peak.
下	xia4	2520	Below, down, descend.
有	you3	7533	Have, possession, there be, there is.
風	feng1	1890	Wind, breath, air; manners, atmosphere.
蠱	gu3	3475	Decay, corruption, poisonous worms in the food or the stomach, spoiled grain (infected with insects), poison, evil influence, seduction, madness, insanity, curse, spell.
君	jun1	1715	Noble, prince, aristocrat, lord, chief, gentleman; honorable, a highly principled person, superior man. Most times, this character appears alongside another one, forming the word *JunZi*, whose original meaning was "son of a prince or ruler": 君子.
子	zi3	6939	Child, son or daughter, offspring; suffix; bride, wife; gentleman, officer, master, prince; young lady; the first of the *Earthly Branches*.
以	yi3	2932	Thus, in that way, by means of, with, for; instrument, medium, method, use (of), way (to).
振	zhen4	0313	Excite, shake, quake (Kunst), arouse action; save help; arrange, to marshall troops; to restore order.
民	min2	4508	People, the masses, citizenry, the common people, crowd.
育	yu4	7687	Give birth; rear, breed, raise, nurture, nourish, bring up, educate.
德	de2	6162	Virtue, spiritual power, moral integrity; quality, nature, aptitude, ability, character.

Six at the beginning

Correcting the decay left by his father. Since there is a son the father will have no defect. Danger. Good fortune in the end.

幹	gan4	3235	Manage, attend to business; correct, straighten, rectify; stem, framework, skeleton; the trunk of tree or of the body; body, substance.
父	fu4	1933	Father, progenitor; elder, ruler of the family, patriarchal.
之	zhi1	0935	Personal pronoun, he she, it; this, that, these, etc.; often used as a possessive.
蠱	gu3	3475	Decay, corruption, poisonous worms in the food or the stomach, spoiled grain (infected with insects), poison, evil influence, seduction, madness, insanity, curse, spell.
有	you3	7533	Have, possession, there be, there is.
子	zi3	6939	Child, son or daughter, offspring; suffix; bride, wife; gentleman, officer, master, prince; young lady; the first of the *Earthly Branches*.
考	kao3	3299	Examine, inspect; deceased ancestor or father, old.
无	wu2	7173	No, not, negative; without, does not possess, not have.
咎	jiu4	1192	Fault, blame, mistake, wrong; inauspicious; misfortune, bad luck, calamity; reproach, censure.
厲	li4	3906	Danger, threat; oppressive, cruel, wicked, brutal, harsh; sickness, malevolent devil; grind, polish, sharpen; discipline.
終	zhong1	1500	End, finish, complete; for ever; end of a cycle; carried to conclusion, consummation, closure; death. The original meaning was: tied-off end of a thread.
吉	ji2	0476	Good fortune, auspicious, promising, fortunate, lucky, advantageous, happiness, good auspices. It is the only single character meaning good luck in the *YiJing*.

Nine in the second place

Correcting the decay left by his mother. One shouldn't be too hard.

幹	gan4	3235	Manage, attend to business; correct, straighten, rectify; stem, framework, skeleton; the trunk of tree or of the body; body, substance.
母	mu3	4582	Mother; female elder; grandmother.

之	zhi1	0935	Personal pronoun, he she, it; this, that, these, etc.; often used as a possessive.
蠱	gu3	3475	Decay, corruption, poisonous worms in the food or the stomach, spoiled grain (infected with insects), poison, evil influence, seduction, madness, insanity, curse, spell.
不	bu4	5379	No, not, negative prefix; without, none, nothing, will not, need not, will not be.
可	ke3	3381	Can, able, may; permit, allow; satisfactory, proper, suitable.
貞	zhen1	0346	Perseverance, persistence, determination, steadiness, firmness; straight, correct, verified, certain; pure, loyal. Its original meaning was "to determine an uncertain matter through divination".

Nine in the third place

Correcting the decay left by his father.
There will be some regrets, but no great defect.

幹	gan4	3235	Manage, attend to business; correct, straighten, rectify; stem, framework, skeleton; the trunk of tree or of the body; body, substance.
父	fu4	1933	Father, progenitor; elder, ruler of the family, patriarchal.
之	zhi1	0935	Personal pronoun, he she, it; this, that, these, etc.; often used as a possessive.
蠱	gu3	3475	Decay, corruption, poisonous worms in the food or the stomach, spoiled grain (infected with insects), poison, evil influence, seduction, madness, insanity, curse, spell.
小	xiao3	2605	Small, insignificant, common, humble, mediocre; diminish, belittle.
有	you3	7533	Have, possession, there be, there is.
悔	hui3	2336	Repent, regret, contrition; trouble. This word indicates both an objective situation and a subjective reaction to such circumstance.
无	wu2	7173	No, not, negative; without, does not possess, not have.
大	da4	5943	Big, great, tall; excessive, arrogant; spread out and reach everywhere.
咎	jiu4	1192	Fault, blame, mistake, wrong; inauspicious; misfortune, bad luck, calamity; reproach, censure.

Six in the fourth place
Tolerating the decay left by his father. He will regret going this way.

裕	yu4	7667	Tolerating, indulgent, forgiving, liberal; ample, abundant, opulent; neglect, postpone.
父	fu4	1933	Father, progenitor; elder, ruler of the family, patriarchal.
之	zhi1	0935	Personal pronoun, he she, it; this, that, these, etc.; often used as a possessive.
蠱	gu3	3475	Decay, corruption, poisonous worms in the food or the stomach, spoiled grain (infected with insects), poison, evil influence, seduction, madness, insanity, curse, spell.
往	wang3	7050	Go, to go to, go forward, go towards; depart, bygone, former.
見	jian4	0860	See, observe, look at, to be seen; cause to appear; be exposed to, display, reveal; interview, visit or call on, meet.
吝	lin4	4040	Humiliation, regret, shame, distress, grief, sorrow; miserly, niggardly. It is a warning of trouble.

Six in the fifth place
Correcting the decay left by his father. You get praises.

幹	gan4	3235	Manage, attend to business; correct, straighten, rectify; stem, framework, skeleton; the trunk of tree or of the body; body, substance.
父	fu4	1933	Father, progenitor; elder, ruler of the family, patriarchal.
之	zhi1	0935	Personal pronoun, he she, it; this, that, these, etc.; often used as a possessive.
蠱	gu3	3475	Decay, corruption, poisonous worms in the food or the stomach, spoiled grain (infected with insects), poison, evil influence, seduction, madness, insanity, curse, spell.
用	yong4	7567	Use, apply, put to use, apply the oracle to real world situations; hereby, thereby.
譽	yu4	7617	Fame, renown, reputation, honor, honored, praised.

Nine at the top
Does not serve kings or lords. He seeks much higher goals.

不	bu4	5379	No, not, negative prefix; without, none, nothing, will not, need not, will not be.
事	shi4	5787	Serve, service; affairs, business, matters.
王	wang2	7037	King, prince, sovereign, ruler.

侯	hou2	2135	Feudal lord, (vassal) prince, marquis; officer, governor, chief; skilled archer.
高	gao1	3290	High, elevated, exalted, eminent, lofty, illustrious, higher.
尚	shang4	5670	High, ascend, admirable, superior, surpass, respected, esteemed, reward; still, yet an besides, in addition to.
其	qi2	0525	Their, his, its, the; this, that. A demonstrative and possessive pronoun.
事	shi4	5787	Serve, service; affairs, business, matters.

19 臨 *lin* – Approach / Leadership

THE JUDGMENT

Approach. Outstanding Success. The determination is favorable. On the eighth month there will be misfortune.

臨	lin2	4027	Approach, oversee, inspect, supervise (a sacrifice), ceremonial wailing; siege machine.
元	yuan2	7707	Outstanding, greatest, sublime, supreme, greatest, very great, grand; source, beginning, cause, first or paramount, fundamentality; head, chief; used as a superlative.
亨	heng1	2099	Success, prevalence, smooth progress, growth, consummate, triumph; pervade; offering, sacrifice.
利	li4	3867	Favorable, lucky, advantageous, profitable, beneficial, furthering, harvesting; sharp, sharp witted.
貞	zhen1	0346	Perseverance, persistence, determination, steadiness, firmness; straight, correct, verified, certain; pure, loyal. Its original meaning was "to determine an uncertain matter through divination".
至	zhi4	0982	Arrive, culminate, reach the highest point, utmost, superlative.
于	yu2	7592	At, to, in, into, on, from, by, go, go to, move towards, proceed, be.
八	ba1	4845	Eight, eighth, eight times.
月	yue4	7696	The Moon, lunar month.
有	you3	7533	Have, possession, there be, there is.
凶	xiong1	2808	Misfortune, pitfall, ominous, bad, unlucky, disastrous, trouble, accident.

THE IMAGE

Earth is above the Lake: The image of Approach.
Thus the noble is tireless in his efforts to educate,
and doesn't know boundaries in protecting and supporting them.

Approach (109)

澤	ze2	0277	Marsh, pool, pond, lake; flat body of water and the vapors rising from it; enrich, fertilize, benefit; moist, moisten; glossy, polished.
上	shang4	5669	Up, above, on, over, upwards, top, rise; higher, superior; first, best.
有	you3	7533	Have, possession, there be, there is.
地	di4	6198	Earth, soil, ground.
臨	lin2	4027	Approach, oversee, inspect, supervise (a sacrifice), ceremonial wailing; siege machine.
君	jun1	1715	Noble, prince, aristocrat, lord, chief, gentleman; honorable, a highly principled person, superior man. Most times, this character appears alongside another one, forming the word *JunZi*, whose original meaning was "son of a prince or ruler": 君子.
子	zi3	6939	Child, son or daughter, offspring; suffix; bride, wife; gentleman, officer, master, prince; young lady; the first of the *Earthly Branches*.
以	yi3	2932	Thus, in that way, by means of, with, for; instrument, medium, method, use (of), way (to).
教	jiao1	0719	*Teach instruct; teaching, instruction, doctrine.*
思	si1	5580	Think, consider, ponder; brood, reflect, plan.
無	wu2	7173	No, not, negative; without, does not possess, not have.
窮	qiong2	1247	Exhaust, worn out, impoverished; has gone too far, reduced to extremity; dead end.
容	rong2	7560	Generosity, tolerance; contain, hold, embrace, admit; support, endure. 容保民: tolerate and protect people.
保	bao3	4946	Preserve, protect, maintain, care for.
民	min2	4508	People, the masses, citizenry, the common people, crowd.
無	wu2	7173	No, not, negative; without, does not possess, not have.
疆	jiang1	0643	Limit, boundary, restriction.

Nine at the beginning

Joint approach. The determination is favorable.

咸	xian2	2666	Influence, wooing; joined, together, to unite, completely; reciprocity (Lynn); feelings (Shaughnessy).

臨	lin2	4027	Approach, oversee, inspect, supervise (a sacrifice), ceremonial wailing; siege machine.
貞	zhen1	0346	Perseverance, persistence, determination, steadiness, firmness; straight, correct, verified, certain; pure, loyal. Its original meaning was "to determine an uncertain matter through divination".
吉	ji2	0476	Good fortune, auspicious, promising, fortunate, lucky, advantageous, happiness, good auspices. It is the only single character meaning good luck in the *YiJing*.

Nine in the second place

Joint approach. Good fortune. Everything is favorable.

咸	xian2	2666	Influence, wooing; joined, together, to unite, completely; reciprocity (Lynn); feelings (Shaughnessy).
臨	lin2	4027	Approach, oversee, inspect, supervise (a sacrifice), ceremonial wailing; siege machine.
吉	ji2	0476	Good fortune, auspicious, promising, fortunate, lucky, advantageous, happiness, good auspices. It is the only single character meaning good luck in the *YiJing*.
无	wu2	7173	No, not, negative; without, does not possess, not have.
不	bu4	5379	No, not, negative prefix; without, none, nothing, will not, need not, will not be.
利	li4	3867	Favorable, lucky, advantageous, profitable, beneficial, furthering, harvesting; sharp, sharp witted.

Six in the third place

Sweet approach. No goal is favorable.
If he become anxious about it, there will be no defect.

甘	gan1	3223	Sweet, pleasant, happy, enjoy.
臨	lin2	4027	Approach, oversee, inspect, supervise (a sacrifice), ceremonial wailing; siege machine.
无	wu2	7173	No, not, negative; without, does not possess, not have.
攸	you1	7519	Goal, direction, destination, objective; distant, far away; a place; that which, whereby, thereby, for which; mark of the passive voice.
利	li4	3867	Favorable, lucky, advantageous, profitable, beneficial, furthering, harvesting; sharp, sharp witted.

Approach (III)

既	ji4	0453	Already, consummated, completed, finished; to be done with, get done.
憂	you1	7508	Grieved, sad, mournful; grief, melancholy.
之	zhi1	0935	Personal pronoun, he she, it; this, that, these, etc.; often used as a possessive.
无	wu2	7173	No, not, negative; without, does not possess, not have.
咎	jiu4	1192	Fault, blame, mistake, wrong; inauspicious; misfortune, bad luck, calamity; reproach, censure.

Six in the fourth place

Approach reaches its climax. No defect.

至	zhi4	0982	Arrive, culminate, reach the highest point, utmost, superlative.
臨	lin2	4027	Approach, oversee, inspect, supervise (a sacrifice), ceremonial wailing; siege machine.
无	wu2	7173	No, not, negative; without, does not possess, not have.
咎	jiu4	1192	Fault, blame, mistake, wrong; inauspicious; misfortune, bad luck, calamity; reproach, censure.

Six in the fifth place

Wise approach. It is fitting for a lord. Good fortune.

知	zhi1	0932	Wise (19), knows (54); understand; informed.
臨	lin2	4027	Approach, oversee, inspect, supervise (a sacrifice), ceremonial wailing; siege machine.
大	da4	5943	Big, great, tall; excessive, arrogant; spread out and reach everywhere.
君	jun1	1715	Noble, prince, aristocrat, lord, chief, gentleman; honorable, a highly principled person, superior man. Most times, this character appears alongside another one, forming the word *JunZi*, whose original meaning was "son of a prince or ruler": 君子.
之	zhi1	0935	Personal pronoun, he she, it; this, that, these, etc.; often used as a possessive.
宜	yi2	2993	Right, proper, sacrifice to the deity of the soil.
吉	ji2	0476	Good fortune, auspicious, promising, fortunate, lucky, advantageous, happiness, good auspices. It is the only single character meaning good luck in the *YiJing*.

19

Six at the top

    Sincere and generous approach. Good fortune. No defect.

敦	dun1	6571	Earnest, generous, authentic, honest, sincere; staunch, strong, thick, solid.
臨	lin2	4027	Approach, oversee, inspect, supervise (a sacrifice), ceremonial wailing; siege machine.
吉	ji2	0476	Good fortune, auspicious, promising, fortunate, lucky, advantageous, happiness, good auspices. It is the only single character meaning good luck in the *YiJing*.
无	wu2	7173	No, not, negative; without, does not possess, not have.
咎	jiu4	1192	Fault, blame, mistake, wrong; inauspicious; misfortune, bad luck, calamity; reproach, censure.

20 觀 *guan* – Contemplation

THE JUDGMENT

Contemplation. The ablution was done but not yet the offering. His dignified appearance inspires confidence.

觀	guan1	3575	Contempla/te/tion, look at, observe, watch; regard, examine, evaluate; scenery, sight, aspect.
盥	guan4	3569	Ablution, hand washing, cleansing before a sacred ceremony.
而	er2	1756	And, then, but, nevertheless, also, only. Join and contrasts two words.
不	bu4	5379	No, not, negative prefix; without, none, nothing, will not, need not, will not be.
薦	jian4	0872	Offer in sacrifice, offering, worship.
有	you3	7533	Have, possession, there be, there is.
孚	fu2	1936	Truth; reliable, sincere; to inspire confidence in others; capture, prisoner, plunder.
顒	yong2	8008	Great, dignified, solemn, imposing majestic; a big head.
若	ruo4	3126	Like, just as, to be like; agree, conform to; approve; concordant; compliant.

THE IMAGE

The Wind moves upon the Earth: The image of Contemplation. Thus the Ancient Kings inspected all regions looking at the people and giving instruction.

風	feng1	1890	Wind, breath, air; manners, atmosphere.
行	xing2	2754	Move, go, advance, act, do.
地	di4	6198	Earth, soil, ground.
上	shang4	5669	Up, above, on, over, upwards, top, rise; higher, superior; first, best.
觀	guan1	3575	Contempla/te/tion, look at, observe, watch; regard, examine, evaluate; scenery, sight, aspect.

先	xian1	2702	Before, first, foremost, in front, lead.
王	wang2	7037	King, prince, sovereign, ruler.
以	yi3	2932	Thus, in that way, by means of, with, for; instrument, medium, method, use (of), way (to).
省	xing3	5744	Visit, inspect, study, go and visit, inspection visit; examine oneself; frugal, to save, to reduce.
方	fang1	1802	Square, squarely, directly, straightforward, honest; a place, a region; on all sides; direction, trend, method; suddenly, quick, definite; take a place, occupy; sacrifice to the spirits of the four quarters.
觀	guan1	3575	Contempla/te/tion, look at, observe, watch; regard, examine, evaluate; scenery, sight, aspect.
民	min2	4508	People, the masses, citizenry, the common people, crowd.
設	she4	5711	Found, establish, arrange, set up.
教	jiao4	0719	*Teach instruct; teaching, instruction, doctrine.*

Six at the beginning

Childish contemplation. No defect for the small man.
For the noble is humiliating.

童	tong2	6626	Youth, boy, young person (boy or girl); page, pupil; servant; a virgin, pure, undefiled; young animal without horns (esp. calf or lamb).
觀	guan1	3575	Contempla/te/tion, look at, observe, watch; regard, examine, evaluate; scenery, sight, aspect.
小	xiao3	2605	Small, insignificant, common, humble, mediocre; diminish, belittle.
人	ren2	3097	Man, person(s); people; others; human being, individual.
无	wu2	7173	No, not, negative; without, does not possess, not have.
咎	jiu4	1192	Fault, blame, mistake, wrong; inauspicious; misfortune, bad luck, calamity; reproach, censure.
君	jun1	1715	Noble, prince, aristocrat, lord, chief, gentleman; honorable, a highly principled person, superior man. Most times, this character appears alongside another one, forming the word *JunZi*, whose original meaning was "son of a prince or ruler": 君子.
子	zi3	6939	Child, son or daughter, offspring; suffix; bride, wife; gentleman, officer, master, prince; young lady; the first of the *Earthly Branches*.
吝	lin4	4040	Humiliation, regret, shame, distress, grief, sorrow; miserly, niggardly. It is a warning of trouble.

Contemplation

Six in the second place

Furtive contemplation. The determination is favorable for a woman.

闚	kui1	3649	Peek, observe furtively; to pry, spy.
觀	guan1	3575	Contempla/te/tion, look at, observe, watch; regard, examine, evaluate; scenery, sight, aspect.
利	li4	3867	Favorable, lucky, advantageous, profitable, beneficial, furthering, harvesting; sharp, sharp witted.
女	nu3	4776	Maiden, woman, lady, girl, feminine.
貞	zhen1	0346	Perseverance, persistence, determination, steadiness, firmness; straight, correct, verified, certain; pure, loyal. Its original meaning was "to determine an uncertain matter through divination".

Six in the third place

Looking at the progress and setbacks in my life.

觀	guan1	3575	Contempla/te/tion, look at, observe, watch; regard, examine, evaluate; scenery, sight, aspect.
我	wo3	4778	We, us, I, my, mine, our.
生	sheng1	5738	Live, give birth to, to be born living being; produce; sacrificial animal, victim.
進	jin4	1091	Advance, to urge forward, progress; present, introduce, recommend, propose.
退	tui4	6568	Retreat, withdraw, back up, retire; decline, refuse.

Six in the fourth place

Contemplation of the glory of the kingdom.
It is favorable to act as a guest of a King.

觀	guan1	3575	Contempla/te/tion, look at, observe, watch; regard, examine, evaluate; scenery, sight, aspect.
國	guo2	3738	State, country, nation, kingdom, a dynasty; capital city.
之	zhi1	0935	Personal pronoun, he she, it; this, that, these, etc.; often used as a possessive.
光	guang1	3583	Light, illumination, brilliance, glory, honor.
利	li4	3867	Favorable, lucky, advantageous, profitable, beneficial, furthering, harvesting; sharp, sharp witted.

用	yong4	7567	Use, apply, put to use, apply the oracle to real world situations; hereby, thereby.
賓	bin1	5259	Guest, visitor.
于	yu2	7592	At, to, in, into, on, from, by, go, go to, move towards, proceed, be.
王	wang2	7037	King, prince, sovereign, ruler.

Nine in the fifth place

Contemplation of my life. The noble has no defect.

觀	guan1	3575	Contempla/te/tion, look at, observe, watch; regard, examine, evaluate; scenery, sight, aspect.
我	wo3	4778	We, us, I, my, mine, our.
生	sheng1	5738	Live, give birth to, to be born living being; produce; sacrificial animal, victim.
君	jun1	1715	Noble, prince, aristocrat, lord, chief, gentleman; honorable, a highly principled person, superior man. Most times, this character appears alongside another one, forming the word *JunZi*, whose original meaning was "son of a prince or ruler": 君子.
子	zi3	6939	Child, son or daughter, offspring; suffix; bride, wife; gentleman, officer, master, prince; young lady; the first of the *Earthly Branches*.
无	wu2	7173	No, not, negative; without, does not possess, not have.
咎	jiu4	1192	Fault, blame, mistake, wrong; inauspicious; misfortune, bad luck, calamity; reproach, censure.

Nine at the top

Contemplation of his life. The noble has no defect.

觀	guan1	3575	Contempla/te/tion, look at, observe, watch; regard, examine, evaluate; scenery, sight, aspect.
其	qi2	0525	Their, his, its, the; this, that. A demonstrative and possessive pronoun.
生	sheng1	5738	Live, give birth to, to be born living being; produce; sacrificial animal, victim.
君	jun1	1715	Noble, prince, aristocrat, lord, chief, gentleman; honorable, a highly principled person, superior man. Most times, this character appears alongside another one, forming the word *JunZi*, whose original meaning was "son of a prince or ruler": 君子.

子	zi3	6939	Child, son or daughter, offspring; suffix; bride, wife; gentleman, officer, master, prince; young lady; the first of the *Earthly Branches*.
无	wu2	7173	No, not, negative; without, does not possess, not have.
咎	jiu4	1192	Fault, blame, mistake, wrong; inauspicious; misfortune, bad luck, calamity; reproach, censure.

21 噬嗑 *shi he* – Biting Through

The Judgment

Biting Through is successful. It is favorable to administer justice.

噬	shi4	5764	Bite, gnaw, snap at, chew.
嗑	he2	2120	Crunch, shut (the jaws), bite, chew; (to be) through.
亨	heng1	2099	Success, prevalence, smooth progress, growth, consummate, triumph; pervade; offering, sacrifice.
利	li4	3867	Favorable, lucky, advantageous, profitable, beneficial, furthering, harvesting; sharp, sharp witted.
用	yong4	7567	Use, apply, put to use, apply the oracle to real world situations; hereby, thereby.
獄	yu4	7685	Justice, litigation, lawsuit, criminal cases; prison, jail.

The Image

Thunder and Lightning: The image of Biting Through.
Thus the Ancient Kings applied punishments
with intelligence and enacted laws.

雷	lei2	4236	Thunder, shock, terrifying, arousing power surging from the earth.
電	dian4	6358	Lightning, sudden illumination, complete clarity.
噬	shi4	5764	Bite, gnaw, snap at, chew.
嗑	he2	2120	Crunch, shut (the jaws), bite, chew; (to be) through.
先	xian1	2702	Before, first, foremost, in front, lead.
王	wang2	7037	King, prince, sovereign, ruler.
以	yi3	2932	Thus, in that way, by means of, with, for; instrument, medium, method, use (of), way (to).
明	ming2	4534	Light, brightness, clarity, clear; enlightenment, discernment; seeing, perception; agreement, contract.
罰	fa2	1769	Penalty, fine, punish, penalize.

Biting Through (119) — 21

敕	chi4	1050	Imperial decree, compel obedience; ordain, dispose, correct, warn. An order from the highest authority.
法	fa3	1762	Law, statute; regulations, plan or method; model.

Nine at the beginning

His feet are trapped by fetters and his toes are mangled. No defect.

履	ju4	1572	Wear on feet, footwear, shoes; walk on, tread on.
校	xiao4	0706	Shackles, yoke; foot fetters; punitive restraint; imprison.
滅	mie4	4483	Submerge, destroy, extinguish, exterminate.
趾	zhi3	0944	Toes, feet, hoof, paw. Legs (of animals or furniture), footprints, tracks.
无	wu2	7173	No, not, negative; without, does not possess, not have.
咎	jiu4	1192	Fault, blame, mistake, wrong; inauspicious; misfortune, bad luck, calamity; reproach, censure.

Six in the second place

Biting Through tender flesh, the nose is destroyed. No defect.

噬	shi4	5764	Bite, gnaw, snap at, chew.
膚	fu1	1958	Skin, flesh; cut meat, tender meat.
滅	mie4	4483	Submerge, destroy, extinguish, exterminate.
鼻	bi2	5100	Nose.
无	wu2	7173	No, not, negative; without, does not possess, not have.
咎	jiu4	1192	Fault, blame, mistake, wrong; inauspicious; misfortune, bad luck, calamity; reproach, censure.

Six in the third place

Biting Through dried meat finds poison.
A little humiliation. No defect.

噬	shi4	5764	Bite, gnaw, snap at, chew.
腊	xi1	3763	Seasoned, dried and/or salted meat.
肉	rou4	3153	Meat, flesh, fleshy, full.
遇	yu4	7625	Meet, encounter, come across, happen.
毒	du2	6509	Poison, venom; hate, cruel, evil, hurtful, kill with poison, narcotics.

小	xiao3	2605	Small, insignificant, common, humble, mediocre; diminish, belittle.
吝	lin4	4040	Humiliation, regret, shame, distress, grief, sorrow; miserly, niggardly. It is a warning of trouble.
无	wu2	7173	No, not, negative; without, does not possess, not have.
咎	jiu4	1192	Fault, blame, mistake, wrong; inauspicious; misfortune, bad luck, calamity; reproach, censure.

Nine in the fourth place

Biting Through bone-dry meat he gets metal arrows.
Fortitude under trying conditions is favorable. Good fortune.

噬	shi4	5764	Bite, gnaw, snap at, chew.
乾	gan1	3233	Dry, dried, sun-dried, to make extremely dry, all gone, exhausted.
胏	zi3	6950	Slice of dried meat with bone.
得	de2	6161	Get, obtain, gain; reach, achieve; can; attain the desired thing.
金	jin1	1057	Metal, bronze, gold, golden; money, riches.
矢	shi3	5784	Arrow.
利	li4	3867	Favorable, lucky, advantageous, profitable, beneficial, furthering, harvesting; sharp, sharp witted.
艱	jian1	0834	Hardship, distressing, difficult, laborious.
貞	zhen1	0346	Perseverance, persistence, determination, steadiness, firmness; straight, correct, verified, certain; pure, loyal. Its original meaning was "to determine an uncertain matter through divination".
吉	ji2	0476	Good fortune, auspicious, promising, fortunate, lucky, advantageous, happiness, good auspices. It is the only single character meaning good luck in the *YiJing*.

Six in the fifth place

Biting Through dry meat he gets yellow metal.
The determination is dangerous. No defect.

噬	shi4	5764	Bite, gnaw, snap at, chew.
乾	gan1	3233	Dry, dried, sun-dried, to make extremely dry, all gone, exhausted.
肉	rou4	3153	Meat, flesh, fleshy, full.

得	de2	6161	Get, obtain, gain; reach, achieve; can; attain the desired thing.
黃	huang2	2297	Yellow, yellow-brown; color of the soil in central China. In the *YiJing* the yellow color is always favorable, it is the color of the middle and the moderation and it was the imperial color since the *Han* dynasty.
金	jin1	1057	Metal, bronze, gold, golden; money, riches.
貞	zhen1	0346	Perseverance, persistence, determination, steadiness, firmness; straight, correct, verified, certain; pure, loyal. Its original meaning was "to determine an uncertain matter through divination".
厲	li4	3906	Danger, threat; oppressive, cruel, wicked, brutal, harsh; sickness, malevolent devil; grind, polish, sharpen; discipline.
无	wu2	7173	No, not, negative; without, does not possess, not have.
咎	jiu4	1192	Fault, blame, mistake, wrong; inauspicious; misfortune, bad luck, calamity; reproach, censure.

Nine at the top

He carries a yoke that makes his ears disappear. Ominous.

何	he4	2109	What? how? why? what is? for that reason, therefore.
校	xiao4	0706	Shackles, yoke; foot fetters; punitive restraint; imprison.
滅	mie4	4483	Submerge, destroy, extinguish, exterminate.
耳	er3	1744	Ear/s, handle/s; that which is at the side (as handles).
凶	xiong1	2808	Misfortune, pitfall, ominous, bad, unlucky, disastrous, trouble, accident.

22 賁 *bi* – Elegance / Adornment

THE JUDGMENT

Elegance. Success. It is favorable to have a goal in minor matters.

賁	bi4	5027	Ornate, elegant, motley, brilliant; embellish, adorn.
亨	heng1	2099	Success, prevalence, smooth progress, growth, consummate, triumph; pervade; offering, sacrifice.
小	xiao3	2605	Small, insignificant, common, humble, mediocre; diminish, belittle.
利	li4	3867	Favorable, lucky, advantageous, profitable, beneficial, furthering, harvesting; sharp, sharp witted.
有	you3	7533	Have, possession, there be, there is.
攸	you1	7519	Goal, direction, destination, objective; distant, far away; a place; that which, whereby, thereby, for which; mark of the passive voice.
往	wang3	7050	Go, to go to, go forward, go towards; depart, bygone, former. 攸往: have a place to go; have a goal.

THE IMAGE

Fire at the foot of the Mountain: The image of Elegance.
Thus the noble regulates the crowds with enlightenment.
But he does not dare to decide criminal cases.

山	shan1	5630	Mountain, hill, peak.
下	xia4	2520	Below, down, descend.
有	you3	7533	Have, possession, there be, there is.
火	huo3	2395	Fire, flame.
賁	bi4	5027	Ornate, elegant, motley, brilliant; embellish, adorn.

Elegance

君	jun1	1715	Noble, prince, aristocrat, lord, chief, gentleman; honorable, a highly principled person, superior man. Most times, this character appears alongside another one, forming the word *JunZi*, whose original meaning was "son of a prince or ruler": 君子.
子	zi3	6939	Child, son or daughter, offspring; suffix; bride, wife; gentleman, officer, master, prince; young lady; the first of the *Earthly Branches*.
以	yi3	2932	Thus, in that way, by means of, with, for; instrument, medium, method, use (of), way (to).
明	ming2	4534	Light, brightness, clarity, clear; enlightenment, discernment; seeing, perception; agreement, contract.
庶	shu4	5874	Numerous, many, multitude, the masses; ample, abundant; many chances for.
政	zheng4	0355	Standard, law (civil, not criminal), regulation, government.
无	wu2	7173	No, not, negative; without, does not possess, not have.
敢	gan3	3229	Dare, venture, have the courage to try, bold, intrepid; rash, take offensive.
折	zhe2	0267	Sever, break; bend, destroy, execute; decide a cause, discriminate, judge.
獄	yu4	7685	Justice, litigation, lawsuit, criminal cases; prison, jail.

Nine at the beginning

He gives elegance to his feet, leaves the carriage and walks.

賁	bi4	5027	Ornate, elegant, motley, brilliant; embellish, adorn.
其	qi2	0525	Their, his, its, the; this, that. A demonstrative and possessive pronoun.
趾	zhi3	0944	Toes, feet, hoof, paw. Legs (of animals or furniture), footprints, tracks.
舍	she3	5699	Quit, abandon, let go, leave, put down, set aside, put away, store; stop, rest in, halt, resting place, encampment.
車	che1	0280	Chariot, wagon, cart, carriage.
而	er2	1756	And, then, but, nevertheless, also, only. Join and contrasts two words.
徒	tu2	6536	Walk, go on foot; foot soldier; follower, adherent; servant; common people, multitude.

Six in the second place
> He gives elegance to his beard.

賁	bi4	5027	Ornate, elegant, motley, brilliant; embellish, adorn.
其	qi2	0525	Their, his, its, the; this, that. A demonstrative and possessive pronoun.
須	xu1	2847	Beard, whiskers; wait, expect, require. Beard is the original meaning.

Nine in the third place
> Adorned with moisture. Long-term determination is fortunate.

賁	bi4	5027	Ornate, elegant, motley, brilliant; embellish, adorn.
如	ru2	3137	Thus, in this way, as, like, similar to, if (conditional).
濡	ru2	3149	Moist, soak, immerse, wet.
如	ru2	3137	Thus, in this way, as, like, similar to, if (conditional).
永	yong3	7589	For a long time, constant, permanent, everlasting; prolong; distant, far reaching.
貞	zhen1	0346	Perseverance, persistence, determination, steadiness, firmness; straight, correct, verified, certain; pure, loyal. Its original meaning was "to determine an uncertain matter through divination".
吉	ji2	0476	Good fortune, auspicious, promising, fortunate, lucky, advantageous, happiness, good auspices. It is the only single character meaning good luck in the *YiJing*.

Six in the fourth place
> Adorned in white. A white horse soaring.
> He is not a robber, but a suitor.

賁	bi4	5027	Ornate, elegant, motley, brilliant; embellish, adorn.
如	ru2	3137	Thus, in this way, as, like, similar to, if (conditional).
皤	po2	5351	White, silver, gray; white or silver haired; old, aged.
如	ru2	3137	Thus, in this way, as, like, similar to, if (conditional).
白	bai2	4975	White, simple, easy to understand, bare, pure; color of death an mourning.
馬	ma3	4310	Horse.
翰	han4	2042	Pheasant feather; wing, winged, in flight, soaring.
如	ru2	3137	Thus, in this way, as, like, similar to, if (conditional).
匪	fei3	1820	No, strong negative.

ELEGANCE (125) 22

寇	kou4	3444	Bandit, invader, enemy, robber, violent people, outcasts, plunderers.
婚	hun1	2360	Marriage, take a wife; bridegroom, ally.
媾	gou4	3426	Marriage, a second marriage, mating, match, families united by marriage; suitor, groom; allying, friendship, favor.

Six in the fifth place

Elegance in hills and gardens. The silk bundle is meager.
Humiliation, but good fortune at the end.

賁	bi4	5027	Ornate, elegant, motley, brilliant; embellish, adorn.
于	yu2	7592	At, to, in, into, on, from, by, go, go to, move towards, proceed, be.
丘	qiu1	1213	Hill, mound, small hill; great; waste, ruins.
園	yuan2	7731	Garden, park, enclosed garden. 丘園: garden in the hills, native forest, wild park.
束	shu4	5891	Roll, bundle; tie together, gather into a bundle; bind, restrain, control.
帛	bo2	4979	Silk, undyed silk.
戔	jian1	0866	Meager, small, insignificant, shabby; narrow, prejudiced.
戔	jian1	0866	Meager, small, insignificant, shabby; narrow, prejudiced.
吝	lin4	4040	Humiliation, regret, shame, distress, grief, sorrow; miserly, niggardly. It is a warning of trouble.
終	zhong1	1500	End, finish, complete; for ever; end of a cycle; carried to conclusion, consummation, closure; death. The original meaning was: tied-off end of a thread.
吉	ji2	0476	Good fortune, auspicious, promising, fortunate, lucky, advantageous, happiness, good auspices. It is the only single character meaning good luck in the *YiJing*.

Nine at the top

Simple elegance. No defect.

白	bai2	4975	White, simple, easy to understand, bare, pure; color of death an mourning.
賁	bi4	5027	Ornate, elegant, motley, brilliant; embellish, adorn.
无	wu2	7173	No, not, negative; without, does not possess, not have.
咎	jiu4	1192	Fault, blame, mistake, wrong; inauspicious; misfortune, bad luck, calamity; reproach, censure.

23 剝 *bo* – Splitting Apart

THE JUDGMENT

Splitting Apart. It is not favorable to go anywhere.

剝	bo1	5337	Flay, strip, peel; pluck, lay bare, strip (as clothes or badges of office); split, slice, crack.
不	bu4	5379	No, not, negative prefix; without, none, nothing, will not, need not, will not be.
利	li4	3867	Favorable, lucky, advantageous, profitable, beneficial, furthering, harvesting; sharp, sharp witted.
有	you3	7533	Have, possession, there be, there is.
攸	you1	7519	Goal, direction, destination, objective; distant, far away; a place; that which, whereby, thereby, for which; mark of the passive voice.
往	wang3	7050	Go, to go to, go forward, go towards; depart, bygone, former. 攸往: have a place to go; have a goal.

THE IMAGE

The Mountain lies on Earth: The image of Splitting Apart.
Thus by means of being munificent with those below them,
the superiors secure the peace and stability of their own position.

山	shan1	5630	Mountain, hill, peak.
附	fu4	1924	Lean on, rest; adjoin, join.
於	yu2	7643	On, in, at, by, from; with reference to; interjection.
地	di4	6198	Earth, soil, ground.
剝	bo1	5337	Flay, strip, peel; pluck, lay bare, strip (as clothes or badges of office); split, slice, crack.
上	shang4	5669	Up, above, on, over, upwards, top, rise; higher, superior; first, best.
以	yi3	2932	Thus, in that way, by means of, with, for; instrument, medium, method, use (of), way (to).
厚	hou4	2147	Munificent, generous, liberal; ample, tolerant; substantial, thick, large.

Splitting Apart (127) 23

下	xia4	2520	Below, down, descend.
安	an1	0026	Quiet, at peace, calm; tranquility, safety, security; settled, comfort, contentment.
宅	zhai2	0275	Position, residence, dwelling, place for settlement; inhabit; consolidate; good situation in life.

Six at the beginning

Splitting Apart the legs of the bed.
Determination leads to destruction. Ominous.

剝	bo1	5337	Flay, strip, peel; pluck, lay bare, strip (as clothes or badges of office); split, slice, crack.
牀	chuang2	1459	Bed, couch; platform, place to sleep. Rutt says "bed" means a platform on which other things rest, such as offerings before a spirit table".
以	yi3	2932	Thus, in that way, by means of, with, for; instrument, medium, method, use (of), way (to).
足	zu2	6824	Leg, foot, base, support.
蔑	mie4	4485	Destroy, extinguish; throw away, disregard, ignore, contempt, minute, worthless; not have, nothing.
貞	zhen1	0346	Perseverance, persistence, determination, steadiness, firmness; straight, correct, verified, certain; pure, loyal. Its original meaning was "to determine an uncertain matter through divination".
凶	xiong1	2808	Misfortune, pitfall, ominous, bad, unlucky, disastrous, trouble, accident.

Six in the second place

Splitting Apart the bed's frame.
Determination leads to destruction. Ominous.

剝	bo1	5337	Flay, strip, peel; pluck, lay bare, strip (as clothes or badges of office); split, slice, crack.
牀	chuang2	1459	Bed, couch; platform, place to sleep. Rutt says "bed" means a platform on which other things rest, such as offerings before a spirit table".
以	yi3	2932	Thus, in that way, by means of, with, for; instrument, medium, method, use (of), way (to).
辨	bian4	5240	Discriminate, distinguish, discern, identify; divide, distribute; frame that divides a bed from its stand.
蔑	mie4	4485	Destroy, extinguish; throw away, disregard, ignore, contempt, minute, worthless; not have, nothing.

貞	zhen1	0346	Perseverance, persistence, determination, steadiness, firmness; straight, correct, verified, certain; pure, loyal. Its original meaning was "to determine an uncertain matter through divination".
凶	xiong1	2808	Misfortune, pitfall, ominous, bad, unlucky, disastrous, trouble, accident.

Six in the third place

> Splitting Apart them. No defect.

剝	bo1	5337	Flay, strip, peel; pluck, lay bare, strip (as clothes or badges of office); split, slice, crack.
之	zhi1	0935	Personal pronoun, he she, it; this, that, these, etc.; often used as a possessive.
无	wu2	7173	No, not, negative; without, does not possess, not have.
咎	jiu4	1192	Fault, blame, mistake, wrong; inauspicious; misfortune, bad luck, calamity; reproach, censure.

Six in the fourth place

> The bed is peeled down to the skin. Ominous.

剝	bo1	5337	Flay, strip, peel; pluck, lay bare, strip (as clothes or badges of office); split, slice, crack.
牀	chuang2	1459	Bed, couch; platform, place to sleep. Rutt says "bed, means a platform on which other things rest, such as offerings before a spirit table".
以	yi3	2932	Thus, in that way, by means of, with, for; instrument, medium, method, use (of), way (to).
膚	fu1	1958	Skin, flesh; cut meat, tender meat.
凶	xiong1	2808	Misfortune, pitfall, ominous, bad, unlucky, disastrous, trouble, accident.

Six in the fifth place

> A string of fishes. Favors through the ladies of palace. Nothing that is not favorable.

貫	guan4	3566	String, string together, pass a string through, thread tightly together.
魚	yu2	7668	Fish, symbol of abundance. 貫魚: strung fish; "Gao says this symbolizes the organizing of palace women, who were called to the king in prescribed order" (Rutt).
以	yi3	2932	Thus, in that way, by means of, with, for; instrument, medium, method, use (of), way (to).

Splitting Apart (129) 23

宮	gong1	3705	House, palace, dwelling place, chambers, mansion, temple.
人	ren2	3097	Man, person(s); people; others; human being, individual.
寵	chong3	1534	Favor, kindness, grace, esteem, affection; receive or give gifts; win favor; to favor (a concubine); concubine.
无	wu2	7173	No, not, negative; without, does not possess, not have.
不	bu4	5379	No, not, negative prefix; without, none, nothing, will not, need not, will not be.
利	li4	3867	Favorable, lucky, advantageous, profitable, beneficial, furthering, harvesting; sharp, sharp witted.

Nine at the top

A large fruit still uneaten.
The noble gets a carriage, the petty man shelter is split apart.

碩	shuo4	5815	Large, great, stately, eminent, ripe, full grown, maturity.
果	guo3	3732	Fruit (of a plant), come to fruition, realization, result, effect; bring to result, reach the conclusion; determined, courageous, go to the bitter end.
不	bu4	5379	No, not, negative prefix; without, none, nothing, will not, need not, will not be.
食	shi2	5810	Eat, feed, ingest; food, give food to; nourishment; salary of an officer, livelihood; eclipse (eating of Sun or Moon).
君	jun1	1715	Noble, prince, aristocrat, lord, chief, gentleman; honorable, a highly principled person, superior man. Most times, this character appears alongside another one, forming the word *JunZi*, whose original meaning was "son of a prince or ruler": 君子.
子	zi3	6939	Child, son or daughter, offspring; suffix; bride, wife; gentleman, officer, master, prince; young lady; the first of the *Earthly Branches*.
得	de2	6161	Get, obtain, gain; reach, achieve; can; attain the desired thing.
輿	yu2	7618	Wagon, cart, chariot, carriage; carrier, transport, transportation; carry on the shoulders; contain, hold.
小	xiao3	2605	Small, insignificant, common, humble, mediocre; diminish, belittle.
人	ren2	3097	Man, person(s); people; others; human being, individual.
剝	bo1	5337	Flay, strip, peel; pluck, lay bare, strip (as clothes or badges of office); split, slice, crack.
廬	lu2	4158	Hut, hovel, shack, a thatched cottage; a rustic place to pass the night.

24 復 *fu* – Return

THE JUDGMENT

Return. Success. Exit and entry without harm. Friends come. No defect. Back and forth along the way. In seven days will return. It is favorable to have where to go.

復	fu4	1992	Return, turn back; repeat, restore, revert, recommence.
亨	heng1	2099	Success, prevalence, smooth progress, growth, consummate, triumph; pervade; offering, sacrifice.
出	chu1	1409	Go out, came out, appear, departure; arise, emerge; bring out, take out, expel, leave, get rid of; produce, beget.
入	ru4	3152	Enter, go into (this is the meaning used in the *YiJing*); to make to enter; put into; bring in, present; encroach.
无	wu2	7173	No, not, negative; without, does not possess, not have.
疾	ji2	0492	Ill, harm, defect, stress; hurry; hate.
朋	peng2	5054	Friend, companion, pair, equal, comrade; a string of cowries (small shiny shells used as coins in ancient China).
來	lai2	3768	Come, arrive, return, bring.
无	wu2	7173	No, not, negative; without, does not possess, not have.
咎	jiu4	1192	Fault, blame, mistake, wrong; inauspicious; misfortune, bad luck, calamity; reproach, censure.
反	fan3	1781	Turn, reverse, come back, return.
復	fu4	1992	Return, turn back; repeat, restore, revert, recommence.
其	qi2	0525	Their, his, its, the; this, that. A demonstrative and possessive pronoun.
道	dao4	6136	Road, course, path, way, method; show the way, lead, explain.
七	qi1	0579	Seven, seventh; seventh day when the moon reaches a major phase after the new moon.
日	ri4	3124	Sun, day, daylight, daytime; daily.

Return (131) 24

來	lai2	3768	Come, arrive, return, bring.
復	fu4	1992	Return, turn back; repeat, restore, revert, recommence.
利	li4	3867	Favorable, lucky, advantageous, profitable, beneficial, furthering, harvesting; sharp, sharp witted.
有	you3	7533	Have, possession, there be, there is.
攸	you1	7519	Goal, direction, destination, objective; distant, far away; a place; that which, whereby, thereby, for which; mark of the passive voice.
往	wang3	7050	Go, to go to, go forward, go towards; depart, bygone, former. 攸往: have a place to go; have a goal.

The Image

Thunder in the middle of Earth: The image of Return.
So on the day of the solstice, the Ancient Kings closed the border crossings. Merchants and travelers did not travel
and the ruler did not visit his dominions.

雷	lei2	4236	Thunder, shock, terrifying, arousing power surging from the earth.
在	zai4	6657	Be at, at, in, on, within, be present; to lie in, depend upon, involved with; be living, dwell, located in.
地	di4	6198	Earth, soil, ground.
中	zhong1	1504	Center, inner, in the inside, put in the center, hit (target); balanced, central, middle, correct.
復	fu4	1992	Return, turn back; repeat, restore, revert, recommence.
先	xian1	2702	Before, first, foremost, in front, lead.
王	wang2	7037	King, prince, sovereign, ruler.
以	yi3	2932	Thus, in that way, by means of, with, for; instrument, medium, method, use (of), way (to).
至	zhi4	0982	Arrive, culminate, reach the highest point, utmost, superlative.
日	ri4	3124	Sun, day, daylight, daytime; daily.
閉	bi4	5092	Close, shut, close the door.
關	guan1	3571	Passage, frontier pass; pass gates, barrier.
商	shang1	5673	Bargain, discuss, deliberate, negotiate, calculate; merchant, trader.

旅	lu3	4286	Wanderer, traveler; stranger; stay away from home; guest, to lodge; multitude, troops.
不	bu4	5379	No, not, negative prefix; without, none, nothing, will not, need not, will not be.
行	xing2	2754	Move, go, advance, act, do.
后	hou4	2144	Sovereign, lord, prince; empress; descendants, heirs.
不	bu4	5379	No, not, negative prefix; without, none, nothing, will not, need not, will not be.
省	xing3	5744	Visit, inspect, study, go and visit, inspection visit; examine oneself; frugal, to save, to reduce.
方	fang1	1802	Square, squarely, directly, straightforward, honest; a place, a region; on all sides; direction, trend, method; suddenly, quick, definite; take a place, occupy; sacrifice to the spirits of the four quarters.

Nine at the beginning

>Returning before going too far.
>There will be no need for repentance.
>Outstanding good fortune.

不	bu4	5379	No, not, negative prefix; without, none, nothing, will not, need not, will not be.
遠	yuan3	7734	Distance, far, remote; keep far from; leave.
復	fu4	1992	Return, turn back; repeat, restore, revert, recommence.
无	wu2	7173	No, not, negative; without, does not possess, not have.
祗	zhi1	0952	Respect, revere, take as a model. Most *YiJing* translations replace this character by 祇 in the two places where it appears in the *Zhouyi Zhezhong*. The usual meanings for 祇 are: "need" (24.1), and "only" (29.5).
悔	hui3	2336	Repent, regret, contrition; trouble. This word indicates both an objective situation and a subjective reaction to such circumstance.
元	yuan2	7707	Outstanding, greatest, sublime, supreme, greatest, very great, grand; source, beginning, cause, first or paramount, fundamentality; head, chief; used as a superlative.
吉	ji2	0476	Good fortune, auspicious, promising, fortunate, lucky, advantageous, happiness, good auspices. It is the only single character meaning good luck in the *YiJing*.

Return (133) 24

Six in the second place
Quiet return. Good fortune.

休	xiu1	2786	Stop, rest, relax, quiet; happy, glad; resign, cease; good, fine; benefit, blessings, luck.
復	fu4	1992	Return, turn back; repeat, restore, revert, recommence.
吉	ji2	0476	Good fortune, auspicious, promising, fortunate, lucky, advantageous, happiness, good auspices. It is the only single character meaning good luck in the *YiJing*.

Six in the third place
Repeated return. Danger. No defect.

頻	pin2	5275	Repeated, incessant, urgent, pressing; on the brink of.
復	fu4	1992	Return, turn back; repeat, restore, revert, recommence.
厲	li4	3906	Danger, threat; oppressive, cruel, wicked, brutal, harsh; sickness, malevolent devil; grind, polish, sharpen; discipline.
无	wu2	7173	No, not, negative; without, does not possess, not have.
咎	jiu4	1192	Fault, blame, mistake, wrong; inauspicious; misfortune, bad luck, calamity; reproach, censure.

Six in the fourth place
Returns alone by the middle of the road.

中	zhong1	1504	Center, inner, in the inside, put in the center, hit (target); balanced, central, middle, correct.
行	xing2	2754	Move, go, advance, act, do.
獨	du2	6512	Alone, single, solitary, only; isolated; meditative.
復	fu4	1992	Return, turn back; repeat, restore, revert, recommence.

Six in the fifth place
Earnest return. No repentance.

敦	dun1	6571	Earnest, generous, authentic, honest, sincere; staunch, strong, thick, solid.
復	fu4	1992	Return, turn back; repeat, restore, revert, recommence.
无	wu2	7173	No, not, negative; without, does not possess, not have.
悔	hui3	2336	Repent, regret, contrition; trouble. This word indicates both an objective situation and a subjective reaction to such circumstance.

Six at the top

The return goes astray. Ominous. Calamities and errors.
If he puts armies on the march, in the end will suffer a great defeat,
whose misfortune will extend to the ruler of the state.
For ten years he will not be able to attack.

迷	mi2	4450	Lose the way, go astray; miss, error; delude, infatuation.
復	fu4	1992	Return, turn back; repeat, restore, revert, recommence.
凶	xiong1	2808	Misfortune, pitfall, ominous, bad, unlucky, disastrous, trouble, accident.
有	you3	7533	Have, possession, there be, there is.
災	zai1	6652	Calamity, disaster, injury; misfortune from without (undeserved); calamities from Heaven, as floods, famines, pestilence, etc.
眚	sheng3	5741	Disaster, calamity, serious mistake; offense by mishap or fault; cloudy eyes, disease of the eye, new moon, eclipse, meanings that indicate blindness or lack of light, a mistake due to ignorance or an error of judgment.
用	yong4	7567	Use, apply, put to use, apply the oracle to real world situations; hereby, thereby.
行	xing2	2754	Move, go, advance, act, do.
師	shi1	5760	Army, troops, militias; multitude; master, leader; take as a master, imitate, follow a role model or norm.
終	zhong1	1500	End, finish, complete; for ever; end of a cycle; carried to conclusion, consummation, closure; death. The original meaning was: tied-off end of a thread.
有	you3	7533	Have, possession, there be, there is.
大	da4	5943	Big, great, tall; excessive, arrogant; spread out and reach everywhere.
敗	bai4	4866	Defeat, destruction, ruin, spoil.
以	yi3	2932	Thus, in that way, by means of, with, for; instrument, medium, method, use (of), way (to).
其	qi2	0525	Their, his, its, the; this, that. A demonstrative and possessive pronoun.
國	guo2	3738	State, country, nation, kingdom, a dynasty; capital city.
君	jun1	1715	Noble, prince, aristocrat, lord, chief, gentleman; honorable, a highly principled person, superior man. Most times, this character appears alongside another one, forming the word *JunZi*, whose original meaning was "son of a prince or ruler": 君子.

Return

凶	xiong1	2808	Misfortune, pitfall, ominous, bad, unlucky, disastrous, trouble, accident.
至	zhi4	0982	Arrive, culminate, reach the highest point, utmost, superlative.
于	yu2	7592	At, to, in, into, on, from, by, go, go to, move towards, proceed, be.
十	shi2	5807	Ten; complete, perfect, whole.
年	nian2	4711	Year(s), season(s), harvest(s).
不	bu4	5379	No, not, negative prefix; without, none, nothing, will not, need not, will not be.
克	ke4	3320	Can, able, carry, sustain; conquest, dominate, prevail.
征	zheng1	0352	Punishing expedition ("to correct"), to reduce to submission, attack, punish; to levy taxes; comes, brings.

25 无妄 *wu wang* – Innocence/ No expectations

THE JUDGMENT

Innocence. Outstanding success. The determination is favorable.
The one that is not honest has misfortune.
It is favorable to have a goal.

无	wu2	7173	No, not, negative; without, does not possess, not have.
妄	wang4	7035	Expect, look forward, hope (loan, see note below), presume, pretense; extravagant, foolish, absurd, wild, disorderly, lawless, reckless, rude; false, errancy.
元	yuan2	7707	Outstanding, greatest, sublime, supreme, greatest, very great, grand; source, beginning, cause, first or paramount, fundamentality; head, chief; used as a superlative.
亨	heng1	2099	Success, prevalence, smooth progress, growth, consummate, triumph; pervade; offering, sacrifice.
利	li4	3867	Favorable, lucky, advantageous, profitable, beneficial, furthering, harvesting; sharp, sharp witted.
贞	zhen1	0346	Perseverance, persistence, determination, steadiness, firmness; straight, correct, verified, certain; pure, loyal. Its original meaning was "to determine an uncertain matter through divination".
其	qi2	0525	Their, his, its, the; this, that. A demonstrative and possessive pronoun.
匪	fei3	1820	No, strong negative.
正	zheng4	0351	Correct, proper, upright, straight; regulate; chief, ruler; just, exactly.
有	you3	7533	Have, possession, there be, there is.
眚	sheng3	5741	Disaster, calamity, serious mistake; offense by mishap or fault; cloudy eyes, disease of the eye, new moon, eclipse, meanings that indicate blindness or lack of light, a mistake due to ignorance or an error of judgment.
不	bu4	5379	No, not, negative prefix; without, none, nothing, will not, need not, will not be.

INNOCENCE (137) 25

利	li4	3867	Favorable, lucky, advantageous, profitable, beneficial, furthering, harvesting; sharp, sharp witted.
有	you3	7533	Have, possession, there be, there is.
攸	you1	7519	Goal, direction, destination, objective; distant, far away; a place; that which, whereby, thereby, for which; mark of the passive voice.
往	wang3	7050	Go, to go to, go forward, go towards; depart, bygone, former. 攸往: have a place to go; have a goal.

THE IMAGE

Thunder moves under Heaven and all things partake of innocence. Thus the Ancient Kings, in excellent harmony with the seasons, nurtured all beings.

天	tian1	6361	Heaven, firmament, the sky, cosmos; celestial, divine, power above the human.
下	xia4	2520	Below, down, descend.
雷	lei2	4236	Thunder, shock, terrifying, arousing power surging from the earth.
行	xing2	2754	Move, go, advance, act, do.
物	wu4	7209	Thing/s, being/s, creature/s; substance, the physical world, all living things; others.
與	yu3	7615	With, and; associate with, together with, participate in, be present at; help; give.
无	wu2	7173	No, not, negative; without, does not possess, not have.
妄	wang4	7035	Expect, look forward, hope (loan, see note below), presume, pretense; extravagant, foolish, absurd, wild, disorderly, lawless, reckless, rude; false, errancy.
先	xian1	2702	Before, first, foremost, in front, lead.
王	wang2	7037	King, prince, sovereign, ruler.
以	yi3	2932	Thus, in that way, by means of, with, for; instrument, medium, method, use (of), way (to).
茂	mao4	4580	Flourishing, luxuriant; vigorous, healthy; beautiful, excellent.
對	dui4	6562	Harmony, correspond to, suitable, agreeing with; right, correct, proper.
時	shi2	5780	Time, season, epoch, period, opportune moment.

育	yu4	7687	Give birth; rear, breed, raise, nurture, nourish, bring up, educate.
萬	wan4	7030	Literally: ten thousands, e.g. many, countless.
物	wu4	7209	Thing/s, being/s, creature/s; substance, the physical world, all living things; others.

Nine at the beginning

Going forward with innocence brings good fortune.

无	wu2	7173	No, not, negative; without, does not possess, not have.
妄	wang4	7035	Expect, look forward, hope (loan, see note below), presume, pretense; extravagant, foolish, absurd, wild, disorderly, lawless, reckless, rude; false, errancy.
往	wang3	7050	Go, to go to, go forward, go towards; depart, bygone, former.
吉	ji2	0476	Good fortune, auspicious, promising, fortunate, lucky, advantageous, happiness, good auspices. It is the only single character meaning good luck in the *YiJing*.

Six in the second place

Harvests without plowing. The fields are ready for use without having been prepared. It is favorable to have a goal.

不	bu4	5379	No, not, negative prefix; without, none, nothing, will not, need not, will not be.
耕	geng1	3343	Plow, cultivate, till.
穫	huo4	2207	Harvest, cut grain, reap.
不	bu4	5379	No, not, negative prefix; without, none, nothing, will not, need not, will not be.
菑	zi1	6932	Clearing, breaking new ground for cultivation; land that has been under cultivation for one year, recently broken field.
畬	yu2	7606	Field in the 2nd or 3rd year of cultivation, plowed for such a span of time. 菑畬: farming; husbandry.
則	ze2	6746	Then, thus, accordingly, consequently, and so, in that case; law, rule, pattern; follow a law.
利	li4	3867	Favorable, lucky, advantageous, profitable, beneficial, furthering, harvesting; sharp, sharp witted.
有	you3	7533	Have, possession, there be, there is.

INNOCENCE

攸	you1	7519	Goal, direction, destination, objective; distant, far away; a place; that which, whereby, thereby, for which; mark of the passive voice.
往	wang3	7050	Go, to go to, go forward, go towards; depart, bygone, former. 攸往: have a place to go; have a goal.

Six in the third place

Unexpected disaster. The cow tied by someone, is the traveler's gain and the villager's misfortune.

无	wu2	7173	No, not, negative; without, does not possess, not have.
妄	wang4	7035	Expect, look forward, hope (loan, see note below), presume, pretense; extravagant, foolish, absurd, wild, disorderly, lawless, reckless, rude; false, errancy.
之	zhi1	0935	Personal pronoun, he she, it; this, that, these, etc.; often used as a possessive.
災	zai1	6652	Calamity, disaster, injury; misfortune from without (undeserved); calamities from Heaven, as floods, famines, pestilence, etc.
或	huo4	2402	Perhaps, possibly, if, by chance; doubtful, uncertain; some, someone, something, sometime.
繫	xi4	2458	Tie, attach, bind, connect, tether, restrain; suspend, hang from a cord; keep in mind.
之	zhi1	0935	Personal pronoun, he she, it; this, that, these, etc.; often used as a possessive.
牛	niu2	4737	Cow, bull, ox.
行	xing2	2754	Move, go, advance, act, do.
人	ren2	3097	Man, person(s); people; others; human being, individual.
之	zhi1	0935	Personal pronoun, he she, it; this, that, these, etc.; often used as a possessive.
得	de2	6161	Get, obtain, gain; reach, achieve; can; attain the desired thing.
邑	yi4	3037	City, town; walled or fortified city, seat of the of government for a district.
人	ren2	3097	Man, person(s); people; others; human being, individual.
之	zhi1	0935	Personal pronoun, he she, it; this, that, these, etc.; often used as a possessive.
災	zai1	6652	Calamity, disaster, injury; misfortune from without (undeserved); calamities from Heaven, as floods, famines, pestilence, etc.

Nine in the fourth place

   Can be determined. No defect.

可	ke3	3381	Can, able, may; permit, allow; satisfactory, proper, suitable.
貞	zhen1	0346	Perseverance, persistence, determination, steadiness, firmness; straight, correct, verified, certain; pure, loyal. Its original meaning was "to determine an uncertain matter through divination".
无	wu2	7173	No, not, negative; without, does not possess, not have.
咎	jiu4	1192	Fault, blame, mistake, wrong; inauspicious; misfortune, bad luck, calamity; reproach, censure.

Nine in the fifth place

   Unexpected illness. Do not take medicine and you will rejoice.

无	wu2	7173	No, not, negative; without, does not possess, not have.
妄	wang4	7035	Expect, look forward, hope (loan, see note below), presume, pretense; extravagant, foolish, absurd, wild, disorderly, lawless, reckless, rude; false, errancy.
之	zhi1	0935	Personal pronoun, he she, it; this, that, these, etc.; often used as a possessive.
疾	ji2	0492	Ill, harm, defect, stress; hurry; hate.
勿	wu4	7208	Do not, no. Negative imperative.
藥	yao4	7501	Medicinal plant, medicine, healing herbs; to take medicine, treat; peony.
有	you3	7533	Have, possession, there be, there is.
喜	xi3	2434	Pleasure, joy, happiness, gratification, delight.

Nine at the top

   Innocent action brings misfortune. No place is favorable.

无	wu2	7173	No, not, negative; without, does not possess, not have.
妄	wang4	7035	Expect, look forward, hope (loan, see note below), presume, pretense; extravagant, foolish, absurd, wild, disorderly, lawless, reckless, rude; false, errancy.
行	xing2	2754	Move, go, advance, act, do.
有	you3	7533	Have, possession, there be, there is.

INNOCENCE (141) 25

眚	sheng3	5741	Disaster, calamity, serious mistake; offense by mishap or fault; cloudy eyes, disease of the eye, new moon, eclipse, meanings that indicate blindness or lack of light, a mistake due to ignorance or an error of judgment.
无	wu2	7173	No, not, negative; without, does not possess, not have.
攸	you1	7519	Goal, direction, destination, objective; distant, far away; a place; that which, whereby, thereby, for which; mark of the passive voice.
利	li4	3867	Favorable, lucky, advantageous, profitable, beneficial, furthering, harvesting; sharp, sharp witted.

26 大畜 *da chu* – Great / Accumulation

The Judgment

    Great Accumulation. The determination is favorable.
    Not eating at home brings good fortune.
    It is favorable to cross the great river.

大	da4	5943	Big, great, tall; excessive, arrogant; spread out and reach everywhere.
畜	chu4	1412	Accumulate, nurture, support, cultivate, domesticate.
利	li4	3867	Favorable, lucky, advantageous, profitable, beneficial, furthering, harvesting; sharp, sharp witted.
貞	zhen1	0346	Perseverance, persistence, determination, steadiness, firmness; straight, correct, verified, certain; pure, loyal. Its original meaning was "to determine an uncertain matter through divination".
不	bu4	5379	No, not, negative prefix; without, none, nothing, will not, need not, will not be.
家	jia1	0594	Family, household, clan; home, to keep a home.
食	shi2	5810	Eat, feed, ingest; food, give food to; nourishment; salary of an officer, livelihood; eclipse (eating of Sun or Moon).
吉	ji2	0476	Good fortune, auspicious, promising, fortunate, lucky, advantageous, happiness, good auspices. It is the only single character meaning good luck in the *YiJing*.
利	li4	3867	Favorable, lucky, advantageous, profitable, beneficial, furthering, harvesting; sharp, sharp witted.
涉	she4	5707	Cross, wade across (a river, stream), ford, pass through or over.
大	da4	5943	Big, great, tall; excessive, arrogant; spread out and reach everywhere.
川	chuan1	1439	River, flowing water; flood.

Great Accumulation (143) 26

The Image

Heaven in the middle of the Mountain: Great Accumulation.
Thus, the noble is acquainted with many words and deeds
of the past and cultivates his character.

天	tian1	6361	Heaven, firmament, the sky, cosmos; celestial, divine, power above the human.
在	zai4	6657	Be at, at, in, on, within, be present; to lie in, depend upon, involved with; be living, dwell, located in.
山	shan1	5630	Mountain, hill, peak.
中	zhong1	1504	Center, inner, in the inside, put in the center, hit (target); balanced, central, middle, correct.
大	da4	5943	Big, great, tall; excessive, arrogant; spread out and reach everywhere.
畜	chu4	1412	Accumulate, nurture, support, cultivate, domesticate.
君	jun1	1715	Noble, prince, aristocrat, lord, chief, gentleman; honorable, a highly principled person, superior man. Most times, this character appears alongside another one, forming the word *JunZi*, whose original meaning was "son of a prince or ruler": 君子.
子	zi3	6939	Child, son or daughter, offspring; suffix; bride, wife; gentleman, officer, master, prince; young lady; the first of the *Earthly Branches*.
以	yi3	2932	Thus, in that way, by means of, with, for; instrument, medium, method, use (of), way (to).
多	duo1	6416	Too much, many, numerous; excessive; often.
識	shi2	5825	Record, remember, archive, annals; commemorate; know, learn, recognize, be acquainted with.
前	qian2	0919	Ancient, formerly, before, come before in time, anterior; ahead, front, foremost,
言	yan2	7334	Talk, speech, words, sayings; big flute.
往	wang3	7050	Go, to go to, go forward, go towards; depart, bygone, former.
行	xing2	2754	Move, go, advance, act, do.
以	yi3	2932	Thus, in that way, by means of, with, for; instrument, medium, method, use (of), way (to).
畜	chu4	1412	Accumulate, nurture, support, cultivate, domesticate.
其	qi2	0525	Their, his, its, the; this, that. A demonstrative and possessive pronoun.
德	de2	6162	Virtue, spiritual power, moral integrity; quality, nature, aptitude, ability, character.

Nine at the beginning
Danger. It is best to halt.

有	you3	7533	Have, possession, there be, there is.
厲	li4	3906	Danger, threat; oppressive, cruel, wicked, brutal, harsh; sickness, malevolent devil; grind, polish, sharpen; discipline.
利	li4	3867	Favorable, lucky, advantageous, profitable, beneficial, furthering, harvesting; sharp, sharp witted.
已	yi3	2930	Desist, stop, cease, completion, reach the culmination and stop.

Nine in the second place
The axle brackets are removed from the carriage.

輿	yu2	7618	Wagon, cart, chariot, carriage; carrier, transport, transportation; carry on the shoulders; contain, hold.
說	tuo1	5939	Remove, take off, come off, let loose.
輹	fu4	1997	Axletrees, axle-brace, two pieces of wood underneath a cart, which hold the axle firm on both sides.

Nine in the third place
Good horses that run one after another.
Fortitude under trying conditions. Alarm. Barricade and defend the carriages. It is favorable to have a goal.

良	liang2	3941	Good, fine, gorgeous, excellent; virtuous; natural.
馬	ma3	4310	Horse.
逐	zhu2	1383	Chase, run after, hunt; expel, push out; in order, in succession; one by one.
利	li4	3867	Favorable, lucky, advantageous, profitable, beneficial, furthering, harvesting; sharp, sharp witted.
艱	jian1	0834	Hardship, distressing, difficult, laborious.
貞	zhen1	0346	Perseverance, persistence, determination, steadiness, firmness; straight, correct, verified, certain; pure, loyal. Its original meaning was "to determine an uncertain matter through divination".
曰	yue1	7694	To say, says, said, tell, calling, called, appointed, speaking, say. It is a verbal prefix.
閑	xian2	2679	Defend, guard, protect, barricade, enclose; enclosure, stables, corral; discipline, train, restrain, forbid.
輿	yu2	7618	Wagon, cart, chariot, carriage; carrier, transport, transportation; carry on the shoulders; contain, hold.

Great Accumulation

衛	wei4	7089	Protect, guard, defend; good.
利	li4	3867	Favorable, lucky, advantageous, profitable, beneficial, furthering, harvesting; sharp, sharp witted.
有	you3	7533	Have, possession, there be, there is.
攸	you1	7519	Goal, direction, destination, objective; distant, far away; a place; that which, whereby, thereby, for which; mark of the passive voice.
往	wang3	7050	Go, to go to, go forward, go towards; depart, bygone, former. 攸往: have a place to go; have a goal.

Six in the fourth place

> The protective covering of the horns of the calf.
> Outstanding good fortune.

童	tong2	6626	Youth, boy, young person (boy or girl); page, pupil; servant; a virgin, pure, undefiled; young animal without horns (esp. calf or lamb).
牛	niu2	4737	Cow, bull, ox.
之	zhi1	0935	Personal pronoun, he she, it; this, that, these, etc.; often used as a possessive.
牿	gu4	8003	Pen, stable, enclosure; confinement; hobbled; headboard: wooden guard placed over the point of each horn to prevent beasts from causing injury.
元	yuan2	7707	Outstanding, greatest, sublime, supreme, greatest, very great, grand; source, beginning, cause, first or paramount, fundamentality; head, chief; used as a superlative.
吉	ji2	0476	Good fortune, auspicious, promising, fortunate, lucky, advantageous, happiness, good auspices. It is the only single character meaning good luck in the *YiJing*.

Six in the fifth place

> The tusks of a castrated pig. Good fortune.

豮	fen2	1873	Gelded (pig), castrated; to geld a pig.
豕	shi3	5766	Pig, boar, swine. Symbol of wealth and luck.
之	zhi1	0935	Personal pronoun, he she, it; this, that, these, etc.; often used as a possessive.
牙	ya2	7214	Tusks, fangs, teeth.
吉	ji2	0476	Good fortune, auspicious, promising, fortunate, lucky, advantageous, happiness, good auspices. It is the only single character meaning good luck in the *YiJing*.

Nine at the top

Attains the way of Heaven. Success.

何	he2	2109	What? how? why? what is? for that reason, therefore.
天	tian1	6361	Heaven, firmament, the sky, cosmos; celestial, divine, power above the human.
之	zhi1	0935	Personal pronoun, he she, it; this, that, these, etc.; often used as a possessive.
衢	qu2	1611	Main road, highway, thoroughfare; a point where many roads meet; crossroads.
亨	heng1	2099	Success, prevalence, smooth progress, growth, consummate, triumph; pervade; offering, sacrifice.

27 頤 *yi* – Nourishment / The Jaws

The Judgment

>Nourishment. Determination brings good fortune.
>Watch what you nourishes and what you are looking
>to fill your mouth with.

頤	yi2	2969	The jaws, the chin, the cheeks; nourish, feed.
貞	zhen1	0346	Perseverance, persistence, determination, steadiness, firmness; straight, correct, verified, certain; pure, loyal. Its original meaning was "to determine an uncertain matter through divination".
吉	ji2	0476	Good fortune, auspicious, promising, fortunate, lucky, advantageous, happiness, good auspices. It is the only single character meaning good luck in the *YiJing*.
觀	guan1	3575	Contempla/te/tion, look at, observe, watch; regard, examine, evaluate; scenery, sight, aspect.
頤	yi2	2969	The jaws, the chin, the cheeks; nourish, feed.
自	zi4	6960	From, origin, source, cause, reason; oneself, yourself.
求	qiu2	1217	Seek, strive; ask, implore, beg, pray; desire.
口	kou3	3434	Mouth, an opening, a hole.
實	shi2	5821	Contents, substance; actual, real; full, fill; solid, truthful, honest; fruit.

The Image

>Under the Mountain is the Thunder: The image of Nourishment.
>Thus the noble is careful with what he says, and restrained
>in his drinking and eating.

山	shan1	5630	Mountain, hill, peak.
下	xia4	2520	Below, down, descend.
有	you3	7533	Have, possession, there be, there is.

雷	lei2	4236	Thunder, shock, terrifying, arousing power surging from the earth.
頤	yi2	2969	The jaws, the chin, the cheeks; nourish, feed.
君	jun1	1715	Noble, prince, aristocrat, lord, chief, gentleman; honorable, a highly principled person, superior man. Most times, this character appears alongside another one, forming the word *JunZi*, whose original meaning was "son of a prince or ruler": 君子.
子	zi3	6939	Child, son or daughter, offspring; suffix; bride, wife; gentleman, officer, master, prince; young lady; the first of the *Earthly Branches*.
以	yi3	2932	Thus, in that way, by means of, with, for; instrument, medium, method, use (of), way (to).
愼	shen4	5734	Careful, cautious, circumspect.
言	yan2	7334	Talk, speech, words, sayings; big flute.
語	yu3	7651	Speak, to tell, conversation, discourse, words. 言語: spoken language; speech.
節	jie2	0795	Regulate, moderate, articulate, rule; moral integrity; degree, rank; regular division; juncture, circumstance; baton, token of authority. Knot, node, joint, in bamboo of other plants.
飲	yin3	7454	Drink; swallow; give to drink. 飲食: drink and eat; eating together.
食	shi2	5810	Eat, feed, ingest; food, give food to; nourishment; salary of an officer, livelihood; eclipse (eating of Sun or Moon).

Nine at the beginning

> You let your magic turtle go and look at me
> with your jaws hanging. Misfortune.

舍	she3	5699	Quit, abandon, let go, leave, put down, set aside, put away, store; stop, rest in, halt, resting place, encampment.
爾	er3	1754	Your, you.
靈	ling2	4071	Supernatural, numinous, spiritual, magic; sorcerer, diviner.
龜	gui1	3621	Turtle, symbol of longevity.
觀	guan1	3575	Contempla/te/tion, look at, observe, watch; regard, examine, evaluate; scenery, sight, aspect.
我	wo3	4778	We, us, I, my, mine, our.

NOURISHMENT (149) 27

朵	duo3	6419	Hang, hanging open, move (sc. the jaw, in chewing). 朵頤: the movement of the jaw in chewing.
頤	yi2	2969	The jaws, the chin, the cheeks; nourish, feed.
凶	xiong1	2808	Misfortune, pitfall, ominous, bad, unlucky, disastrous, trouble, accident.

Six in the second place

Forages in the summit. Turns away from the path and goes to the summit for Nourishment. Going forward brings misfortune.

顛	dian1	6337	Summit, peak, top, top of head; invert, upturn, topple, fall on the head; overthrow.
頤	yi2	2969	The jaws, the chin, the cheeks; nourish, feed.
拂	fu2	1986	To reject, discard, dismiss, abrupt dismissal; to turn away.
經	jing1	1123	Classic works; canon, regulate. Literally indicates the warp of a fabric, pass through; the original meaning was "warp in a loom".
于	yu2	7592	At, to, in, into, on, from, by, go, go to, move towards, proceed, be.
丘	qiu1	1213	Hill, mound, small hill; great; waste, ruins.
頤	yi2	2969	The jaws, the chin, the cheeks; nourish, feed.
征	zheng1	0352	Punishing expedition ("to correct"), to reduce to submission, attack, punish; to levy taxes; comes, brings.
凶	xiong1	2808	Misfortune, pitfall, ominous, bad, unlucky, disastrous, trouble, accident.

Six in the third place

Rejects Nourishment. The determination brings misfortune. Do not act for ten years. Nothing at all is favorable.

拂	fu2	1986	To reject, discard, dismiss, abrupt dismissal; to turn away.
頤	yi2	2969	The jaws, the chin, the cheeks; nourish, feed.
貞	zhen1	0346	Perseverance, persistence, determination, steadiness, firmness; straight, correct, verified, certain; pure, loyal. Its original meaning was "to determine an uncertain matter through divination".
凶	xiong1	2808	Misfortune, pitfall, ominous, bad, unlucky, disastrous, trouble, accident.

十	shi2	5807	Ten; complete, perfect, whole.
年	nian2	4711	Year(s), season(s), harvest(s).
勿	wu4	7208	Do not, no. Negative imperative.
用	yong4	7567	Use, apply, put to use, apply the oracle to real world situations; hereby, thereby.
无	wu2	7173	No, not, negative; without, does not possess, not have.
攸	you1	7519	Goal, direction, destination, objective; distant, far away; a place; that which, whereby, thereby, for which; mark of the passive voice.
利	li4	3867	Favorable, lucky, advantageous, profitable, beneficial, furthering, harvesting; sharp, sharp witted.

Six in the fourth place

Forages in the summit. Staring like a tiger, with greed and insatiable desire to chase. No defect.

顛	dian1	6337	Summit, peak, top, top of head; invert, upturn, topple, fall on the head; overthrow.
頤	yi2	2969	The jaws, the chin, the cheeks; nourish, feed.
吉	ji2	0476	Good fortune, auspicious, promising, fortunate, lucky, advantageous, happiness, good auspices. It is the only single character meaning good luck in the *YiJing*.
虎	hu3	2161	Tiger. Emblem of bravery and cruelty: strong, wild, extreme.
視	shi4	5789	See, look, inspect, observe, regard.
眈	dan1	6028	Glare, stare; look downwards; glare intensely; the glare of a tiger. Appearing duplicated means "eyeing gloatingly; looking at greedily".
眈	dan1	6028	
其	qi2	0525	Their, his, its, the; this, that. A demonstrative and possessive pronoun.
欲	yu4	7671	Desire, wish, expectation, longing; lust, passion.
逐	zhu2	1383	Chase, run after, hunt; expel, push out; in order, in succession; one by one.
逐	zhu2	1383	Chase, run after, hunt; expel, push out; in order, in succession; one by one.
无	wu2	7173	No, not, negative; without, does not possess, not have.
咎	jiu4	1192	Fault, blame, mistake, wrong; inauspicious; misfortune, bad luck, calamity; reproach, censure.

Nourishment (151) 27

Six in the fifth place

> Moving away from the path. The determination brings good fortune. He cannot cross the great river.

拂	fu2	1986	To reject, discard, dismiss, abrupt dismissal; to turn away.
經	jing1	1123	Classic works; canon, regulate. Literally indicates the warp of a fabric, pass through; the original meaning was "warp in a loom".
居	ju1	1535	Remain; rest (in); abides, dwell; to occupy a position or place; overbearing, arrogant.
貞	zhen1	0346	Perseverance, persistence, determination, steadiness, firmness; straight, correct, verified, certain; pure, loyal. Its original meaning was "to determine an uncertain matter through divination".
吉	ji2	0476	Good fortune, auspicious, promising, fortunate, lucky, advantageous, happiness, good auspices. It is the only single character meaning good luck in the *YiJing*.
不	bu4	5379	No, not, negative prefix; without, none, nothing, will not, need not, will not be.
可	ke3	3381	Can, able, may; permit, allow; satisfactory, proper, suitable.
涉	she4	5707	Cross, wade across (a river, stream), ford, pass through or over.
大	da4	5943	Big, great, tall; excessive, arrogant; spread out and reach everywhere.
川	chuan1	1439	River, flowing water; flood.

Nine at the top

> The source of Nourishment. Danger, but good fortune. It is favorable to cross the great river.

由	you2	7513	Source, cause, reason; proceed from.
頤	yi2	2969	The jaws, the chin, the cheeks; nourish, feed.
厲	li4	3906	Danger, threat; oppressive, cruel, wicked, brutal, harsh; sickness, malevolent devil; grind, polish, sharpen; discipline.
吉	ji2	0476	Good fortune, auspicious, promising, fortunate, lucky, advantageous, happiness, good auspices. It is the only single character meaning good luck in the *YiJing*.
利	li4	3867	Favorable, lucky, advantageous, profitable, beneficial, furthering, harvesting; sharp, sharp witted.

涉	she4	5707	Cross, wade across (a river, stream), ford, pass through or over.
大	da4	5943	Big, great, tall; excessive, arrogant; spread out and reach everywhere.
川	chuan1	1439	River, flowing water; flood.

28 大過 *da guo* – Great Excess

The Judgment

> Great Excess. The main beam sags.
> It is favorable to have a goal. Success.

大	da4	5943	Big, great, tall; excessive, arrogant; spread out and reach everywhere.
過	guo4	3730	Pass, pass through, go across, go beyond, excess, beyond the ordinary or proper limit; ; transgression, fault.
棟	dong4	6607	Ridgepole, main beam supporting house, ridge of a roof.
橈	nao2	3087	Sag, bend; bent wood; crooked; weak.
利	li4	3867	Favorable, lucky, advantageous, profitable, beneficial, furthering, harvesting; sharp, sharp witted.
有	you3	7533	Have, possession, there be, there is.
攸	you1	7519	Goal, direction, destination, objective; distant, far away; a place; that which, whereby, thereby, for which; mark of the passive voice.
往	wang3	7050	Go, to go to, go forward, go towards; depart, bygone, former. 攸往: have a place to go; have a goal.
亨	heng1	2099	Success, prevalence, smooth progress, growth, consummate, triumph; pervade; offering, sacrifice.

The Image

> The Lake covers the Trees: The image of Great Excess.
> Thus the noble remains alone without fear
> and can retreat from the world without regret.

澤	ze2	0277	Marsh, pool, pond, lake; flat body of water and the vapors rising from it; enrich, fertilize, benefit; moist, moisten; glossy, polished.
滅	mie4	4483	Submerge, destroy, extinguish, exterminate.
木	mu4	4593	Tree, wood, timber, wooden.

大	da4	5943	Big, great, tall; excessive, arrogant; spread out and reach everywhere.
過	guo4	3730	Pass, pass through, go across, go beyond, excess, beyond the ordinary or proper limit; ; transgression, fault.
君	jun1	1715	Noble, prince, aristocrat, lord, chief, gentleman; honorable, a highly principled person, superior man. Most times, this character appears alongside another one, forming the word *JunZi*, whose original meaning was "son of a prince or ruler": 君子.
子	zi3	6939	Child, son or daughter, offspring; suffix; bride, wife; gentleman, officer, master, prince; young lady; the first of the *Earthly Branches*.
以	yi3	2932	Thus, in that way, by means of, with, for; instrument, medium, method, use (of), way (to).
獨	du2	6512	Alone, single, solitary, only; isolated; meditative.
立	li4	3921	Stand up or erect; set up, establish; raise, ascend; keep the position or the course, resist, endure.
不	bu4	5379	No, not, negative prefix; without, none, nothing, will not, need not, will not be.
懼	ju4	1560	Fear, dread, alarm, apprehension.
遯	dun4	6586	Retreat, escape, evade, withdraw; hide away, skulk; young pig, piglet.
世	shi4	5790	Generation, epoch, age; world, worldly, society, vulgar.
无	wu2	7173	No, not, negative; without, does not possess, not have.
悶	men4	4420	Sad, depressed, sorrowful, melancholy.

Six at the beginning

Use a white reeds offering mat. No defect.

藉	jie4	0767	Offering mat, usually made of straw. Sacrifices or gifts to the gods or the dead ancestors were placed over it.
用	yong4	7567	Use, apply, put to use, apply the oracle to real world situations; hereby, thereby.
白	bai2	4975	White, simple, easy to understand, bare, pure; color of death an mourning.
茅	mao2	4364	Reeds, cogon grass, white grass, used for wrapping offerings.
无	wu2	7173	No, not, negative; without, does not possess, not have.
咎	jiu4	1192	Fault, blame, mistake, wrong; inauspicious; misfortune, bad luck, calamity; reproach, censure.

GREAT EXCESS (155) 28

Nine in the second place

New shoots grow from a withered willow. An old man gets a young wife. Nothing that is not favorable.

枯	ku1	3492	Withered, dry, dry wood, decayed, rotten.
楊	yang2	7261	Poplar, willow, aspen.
生	sheng1	5738	Live, give birth to, to be born living being; produce; sacrificial animal, victim.
稊	ti2	6252	Shoot, sprout, newly sprouted leaf, a new shoot from a dried stem.
老	lao3	3833	Old, aged.
夫	fu1	1908	Man, male adult, husband; this, that, those.
得	de2	6161	Get, obtain, gain; reach, achieve; can; attain the desired thing.
其	qi2	0525	Their, his, its, the; this, that. A demonstrative and possessive pronoun.
女	nu3	4776	Maiden, woman, lady, girl, feminine.
妻	qi1	0555	Wife, consort. A legal wife (first wife).
无	wu2	7173	No, not, negative; without, does not possess, not have.
不	bu4	5379	No, not, negative prefix; without, none, nothing, will not, need not, will not be.
利	li4	3867	Favorable, lucky, advantageous, profitable, beneficial, furthering, harvesting; sharp, sharp witted.

Nine in the third place

The main beam sags. Misfortune.

棟	dong4	6607	Ridgepole, main beam supporting house, ridge of a roof.
橈	nao2	3087	Sag, bend; bent wood; crooked; weak.
凶	xiong1	2808	Misfortune, pitfall, ominous, bad, unlucky, disastrous, trouble, accident.

Nine in the fourth place

The main beam bulges upward. Good fortune. If there is something else, it will be regretful.

棟	dong4	6607	Ridgepole, main beam supporting house, ridge of a roof.
隆	long2	4255	Bulge upward, rise above all others, high, ample, surpassing, plentiful, eminent, prosperous.

吉	ji2	0476	Good fortune, auspicious, promising, fortunate, lucky, advantageous, happiness, good auspices. It is the only single character meaning good luck in the Yi Jing.
有	you3	7533	Have, possession, there be, there is.
它	tuo1	6439	Another, other; danger, calamity, obstacle.
吝	lin4	4040	Humiliation, regret, shame, distress, grief, sorrow; miserly, niggardly. It is a warning of trouble.

Nine in the fifth place

A withered willow produces flowers.
An old woman gets a young husband. No failure nor praise.

枯	ku1	3492	Withered, dry, dry wood, decayed, rotten.
楊	yang2	7261	Poplar, willow, aspen.
生	sheng1	5738	Live, give birth to, to be born living being; produce; sacrificial animal, victim.
華	hua2	2217	Flowers, blossom, elegance.
老	lao3	3833	Old, aged.
婦	fu4	1963	Woman, lady, wife, married woman.
得	de2	6161	Get, obtain, gain; reach, achieve; can; attain the desired thing.
其	qi2	0525	Their, his, its, the; this, that. A demonstrative and possessive pronoun.
士	shi4	5776	Young man, bachelor, man, gentleman, warrior, soldier, officer.
夫	fu1	1908	Man, male adult, husband; this, that, those.
无	wu2	7173	No, not, negative; without, does not possess, not have.
咎	jiu4	1192	Fault, blame, mistake, wrong; inauspicious; misfortune, bad luck, calamity; reproach, censure.
无	wu2	7173	No, not, negative; without, does not possess, not have.
譽	yu4	7617	Fame, renown, reputation, honor, honored, praised.

Six at the top

Excess when fording the river. The water covers the top of the head.
Misfortune. No defect.

過	guo4	3730	Pass, pass through, go across, go beyond, excess, beyond the ordinary or proper limit; ; transgression, fault.

Great Excess (157) 28

涉	she4	5707	Cross, wade across (a river, stream), ford, pass through or over.
滅	mie4	4483	Submerge, destroy, extinguish, exterminate.
頂	ding3	6390	Top of the head, crown.
凶	xiong1	2808	Misfortune, pitfall, ominous, bad, unlucky, disastrous, trouble, accident.
无	wu2	7173	No, not, negative; without, does not possess, not have.
咎	jiu4	1192	Fault, blame, mistake, wrong; inauspicious; misfortune, bad luck, calamity; reproach, censure.

29 習坎 *xi kan* – The Pit Doubled / The Abysmal / Water

The Judgment

The Pit Doubled. If you follow the feeling in your heart
you will succeed. Moving forward brings rewards.

習	xi2	2499	Double, duplicate; repeated, repeatedly; practice, exercise, rehearsal, learning; to practice flying (young birds learning to fly flapping its wings).
坎	kan3	3245	Abyss, pit, hole, chasm, gorge, precipice; snare, trap; dangerous position, critical time.
有	you3	7533	Have, possession, there be, there is.
孚	fu2	1936	Truth; reliable, sincere; to inspire confidence in others; capture, prisoner, plunder.
維	wei2	7067	Tie up, bound, bind together; guiding rope of a net; guiding principle, rule; but only.
心	xin1	2735	Heart; conscience, moral nature; soul; core; mind; source of feelings, intentions, will.
亨	heng1	2099	Success, prevalence, smooth progress, growth, consummate, triumph; pervade; offering, sacrifice.
行	xing2	2754	Move, go, advance, act, do.
有	you3	7533	Have, possession, there be, there is.
尚	shang4	5670	High, ascend, admirable, superior, surpass, respected, esteemed, reward; still, yet an besides, in addition to.

The Image

The Water flows to reach the goal: The image of the Pit Doubled.
Thus the noble maintains constantly his virtuous conduct,
and practices the job of teaching.

水	shui3	5922	Water, river, stream, flood, liquid, fluid.
洊	jian4	0880	Continuous flow, repeated, for a second time; flowing water.

The Pit Doubled (159)

至	zhi4	0982	Arrive, culminate, reach the highest point, utmost, superlative.
習	xi2	2499	Double, duplicate; repeated, repeatedly; practice, exercise, rehearsal, learning; to practice flying (young birds learning to fly flapping its wings).
坎	kan3	3245	Abyss, pit, hole, chasm, gorge, precipice; snare, trap; dangerous position, critical time.
君	jun1	1715	Noble, prince, aristocrat, lord, chief, gentleman; honorable, a highly principled person, superior man. Most times, this character appears alongside another one, forming the word *JunZi*, whose original meaning was "son of a prince or ruler": 君子.
子	zi3	6939	Child, son or daughter, offspring; suffix; bride, wife; gentleman, officer, master, prince; young lady; the first of the *Earthly Branches*.
以	yi3	2932	Thus, in that way, by means of, with, for; instrument, medium, method, use (of), way (to).
常	chang2	0221	A regular task or duty; constant, always, lasting; perpetuate; frequent, regular, recurring; a rule or principle.
德	de2	6162	Virtue, spiritual power, moral integrity; quality, nature, aptitude, ability, character.
行	xing2	2754	Move, go, advance, act, do.
習	xi2	2499	Double, duplicate; repeated, repeatedly; practice, exercise, rehearsal, learning; to practice flying (young birds learning to fly flapping its wings).
教	jiao1	0719	*Teach instruct; teaching, instruction, doctrine.*
事	shi4	5787	Serve, service; affairs, business, matters.

Six at the beginning

The Pit Doubled. One falls into a pit at the bottom of the cave.
Misfortune.

習	xi2	2499	Double, duplicate; repeated, repeatedly; practice, exercise, rehearsal, learning; to practice flying (young birds learning to fly flapping its wings).
坎	kan3	3245	Abyss, pit, hole, chasm, gorge, precipice; snare, trap; dangerous position, critical time.
入	ru4	3152	Enter, go into (this is the meaning used in the *YiJing*); to make to enter; put into; bring in, present; encroach.
于	yu2	7592	At, to, in, into, on, from, by, go, go to, move towards, proceed, be.

Matrix of Meanings of the Book of Changes

坎	kan3	3245	Abyss, pit, hole, chasm, gorge, precipice; snare, trap; dangerous position, critical time.
窞	dan4	8002	Pit within a pit, recess or smaller pit in bottom of cave or cellar; pitfall, trap. 坎窞: cave, basement, cellar or underground vault, pit.
凶	xiong1	2808	Misfortune, pitfall, ominous, bad, unlucky, disastrous, trouble, accident.

Nine in the second place

> The Pit is dangerous. You can only get small gains.

坎	kan3	3245	Abyss, pit, hole, chasm, gorge, precipice; snare, trap; dangerous position, critical time.
有	you3	7533	Have, possession, there be, there is.
險	xian3	2689	Danger, a narrow pass, precipice, a perilous defile, steep, dangerous and challenging obstacle that must be confronted.
求	qiu2	1217	Seek, strive; ask, implore, beg, pray; desire.
小	xiao3	2605	Small, insignificant, common, humble, mediocre; diminish, belittle.
得	de2	6161	Get, obtain, gain; reach, achieve; can; attain the desired thing.

Six in the third place

> Coming to the Pit. Deep and dangerous Pit.
> Enter a pit in the cave. Do nothing.

來	lai2	3768	Come, arrive, return, bring.
之	zhi1	0935	Personal pronoun, he she, it; this, that, these, etc.; often used as a possessive.
坎	kan3	3245	Abyss, pit, hole, chasm, gorge, precipice; snare, trap; dangerous position, critical time. Appearing duplicated intensifies its meaning.
坎	kan3	3245	
險	xian3	2689	Danger, a narrow pass, precipice, a perilous defile, steep, dangerous and challenging obstacle that must be confronted.
且	qie3	0803	And; meanwhile; moreover; also; both; alternatively.
枕	zhen3	0308	Pillow, to use as a pillow; rest, resting place; stop, lean back on, soften, relax; a stake to tether cattle. Rutt, Kunst and Shaughnessy replace this character with 沉: deep; to sink; to perish.

The Pit Doubled (161)

入	ru4	3152	Enter, go into (this is the meaning used in the *YiJing*); to make to enter; put into; bring in, present; encroach.
于	yu2	7592	At, to, in, into, on, from, by, go, go to, move towards, proceed, be.
坎	kan3	3245	Abyss, pit, hole, chasm, gorge, precipice; snare, trap; dangerous position, critical time.
窞	dan4	8002	Pit within a pit, recess or smaller pit in bottom of cave or cellar; pitfall, trap. 坎窞: cave, basement, cellar or underground vault, pit.
勿	wu4	7208	Do not, no. Negative imperative.
用	yong4	7567	Use, apply, put to use, apply the oracle to real world situations; hereby, thereby.

Six in the fourth place

A jug of wine over a bowl of rice. Using clay pots, delivered jointly by the window. At the end it will be no defect.

樽	zun1	6886	Goblet, jug, wine-cup, flask, cup.
酒	jiu3	1208	Drink, wine, liquor, spirits.
簋	gui3	3633	Bowl, square basket of bamboo, tureen of rice, small or plain rice basket; a kind of vessel or basked used at sacrifices.
貳	er4	1752	Supplement, double, secondary, spare; repeat.
用	yong4	7567	Use, apply, put to use, apply the oracle to real world situations; hereby, thereby.
缶	fou3	1905	Pot, earthen vessel.
納	na4	4607	Bring in, convey to, hand to, present; take, receive, let in.
約	yue1	7493	Bind, lump together; cord, rope; restrain, restrict; bond, contract, covenant, an agreement.
自	zi4	6960	From, origin, source, cause, reason; oneself, yourself.
牖	you3	7507	Window, opening in wall or roof to let the light enter; to enlighten, to lead.
終	zhong1	1500	End, finish, complete; for ever; end of a cycle; carried to conclusion, consummation, closure; death. The original meaning was: tied-off end of a thread.
无	wu2	7173	No, not, negative; without, does not possess, not have.
咎	jiu4	1192	Fault, blame, mistake, wrong; inauspicious; misfortune, bad luck, calamity; reproach, censure.

Nine in the fifth place

The Pit does not overflow. Only is filled to the brim. No defect.

坎	kan3	3245	Abyss, pit, hole, chasm, gorge, precipice; snare, trap; dangerous position, critical time.
不	bu4	5379	No, not, negative prefix; without, none, nothing, will not, need not, will not be.
盈	ying2	7474	Fill, full, satisfied; overfill, overflowing.
祇	zhi1	0952	Respect, revere, take as a model. Most *YiJing* translations replace this character by 衹 in the two places where it appears in the *Zhouyi Zhezhong*. The usual meanings for 衹 are: "only" (29.5) and "need" (24.1).
既	ji4	0453	Already, consummated, completed, finished; to be done with, get done.
平	ping2	5303	A plain, level, equal, even; equalize, harmonize, regulate, pacify; peace.
无	wu2	7173	No, not, negative; without, does not possess, not have.
咎	jiu4	1192	Fault, blame, mistake, wrong; inauspicious; misfortune, bad luck, calamity; reproach, censure.

Six at the top

Tied with a braided rope and a black cord.
Abandoned in a thorny bush.
For three years you get nothing. Misfortune.

係	xi4	2424	Cling to, attach to, bind to, (en)tangled, involved, relation.
用	yong4	7567	Use, apply, put to use, apply the oracle to real world situations; hereby, thereby.
徽	hui1	2354	A three-fold (strong) cord.
纆	mo4	4387	Rope, stranded black cord.
寘	zhi4	0976	Put aside, abandon, to place.
于	yu2	7592	At, to, in, into, on, from, by, go, go to, move towards, proceed, be.
叢	cong2	6921	Thicket, thickly-growing, a clump of threes, hedge, grove; dense, crowded together.
棘	ji2	0486	Thorny shrubs, jujube (*Zizyphus jujuba*), thorns; harassing, painful, distress.
三	san1	5415	Three, thrice, third time or place.
歲	sui4	5538	Years, seasons, harvests.

The Pit Doubled (163) 29

不	bu4	5379	No, not, negative prefix; without, none, nothing, will not, need not, will not be.
得	de2	6161	Get, obtain, gain; reach, achieve; can; attain the desired thing.
凶	xiong1	2808	Misfortune, pitfall, ominous, bad, unlucky, disastrous, trouble, accident.

30 離 *li* – Clinging Light / Fire

The Judgment

*Clinging Light. The determination is favorable.
Taming a cow brings good fortune.*

離	li2	3902	Brightness, radiance, attach, cling; name of a bird. The modern meaning is leave, separate.
利	li4	3867	Favorable, lucky, advantageous, profitable, beneficial, furthering, harvesting; sharp, sharp witted.
貞	zhen1	0346	Perseverance, persistence, determination, steadiness, firmness; straight, correct, verified, certain; pure, loyal. Its original meaning was "to determine an uncertain matter through divination".
亨	heng1	2099	Success, prevalence, smooth progress, growth, consummate, triumph; pervade; offering, sacrifice.
畜	chu4	1412	Accumulate, nurture, support, cultivate, domesticate.
牝	pin4	5280	Female (used for farm animals and birds), female sexual organs, cow.
牛	niu2	4737	Cow, bull, ox.
吉	ji2	0476	Good fortune, auspicious, promising, fortunate, lucky, advantageous, happiness, good auspices. It is the only single character meaning good luck in the *YiJing*.

The Image

*Brightness duplicated: The image of Clinging Light.
Thus the great man maintains its clarity
illuminating the four cardinal points.*

明	ming2	4534	Light, brightness, clarity, clear; enlightenment, discernment; seeing, perception; agreement, contract.
兩	liang3	3953	Two, twice, two times, duplicated, double, again; pair, couple.
作	zuo4	6780	Act, do, make, work, perform; rise, stand up, get to work; project, undertaking, ceremony, to sacrifice.

Clinging Light (165) 30

離	li2	3902	Brightness, radiance, attach, cling; name of a bird. The modern meaning is leave, separate.
大	da4	5943	Big, great, tall; excessive, arrogant; spread out and reach everywhere.
人	ren2	3097	Man, person(s); people; others; human being, individual.
以	yi3	2932	Thus, in that way, by means of, with, for; instrument, medium, method, use (of), way (to).
繼	ji4	0452	Perpetuate, continue, carry on; consecutive, connected, line of succession; to follow.
明	ming2	4534	Light, brightness, clarity, clear; enlightenment, discernment; seeing, perception; agreement, contract.
照	zhao4	0238	Shine, illumine; enlighten; to look after.
于	yu2	7592	At, to, in, into, on, from, by, go, go to, move towards, proceed, be.
四	si4	5598	Four, four times, quadruple.
方	fang1	1802	Square, squarely, directly, straightforward, honest; a place, a region; on all sides; direction, trend, method; suddenly, quick, definite; take a place, occupy; sacrifice to the spirits of the four quarters.

Nine at the beginning

Walking with hesitant and cautious steps.
If you are respectful there will be no defect.

履	lu3	3893	Step on, treading, track, walk or follow a trail or way; footwear, shoes; conduct, behavior; ceremonies.
錯	cuo4	6793	Cautious, hesitant, scared; whetstone, grindstone, to polish; crisscrossed, crossed; confused, complicated; wrong, mistaken. The initial uncertainty leads to caution and gradual improvement.
然	ran2	3072	Thus, therefore, hence, in this way; yes, affirm, approve.
敬	jing4	1138	Respect, take care of, careful; honor; a present; reverent attention to; good manners.
之	zhi1	0935	Personal pronoun, he she, it; this, that, these, etc.; often used as a possessive.
无	wu2	7173	No, not, negative; without, does not possess, not have.
咎	jiu4	1192	Fault, blame, mistake, wrong; inauspicious; misfortune, bad luck, calamity; reproach, censure.

Six in the second place

> Yellow glow. Outstanding good fortune.

黃	huang2	2297	Yellow, yellow-brown; color of the soil in central China. In the *YiJing* the yellow color is always favorable, it is the color of the middle and the moderation and it was the imperial color since the *Han* dynasty.
離	li2	3902	Brightness, radiance, attach, cling; name of a bird. The modern meaning is leave, separate.
元	yuan2	7707	Outstanding, greatest, sublime, supreme, greatest, very great, grand; source, beginning, cause, first or paramount, fundamentality; head, chief; used as a superlative.
吉	ji2	0476	Good fortune, auspicious, promising, fortunate, lucky, advantageous, happiness, good auspices. It is the only single character meaning good luck in the *YiJing*.

Nine in the third place

> Under the light of the setting sun, he drums an earthenware pot or laments the approach of old age. Misfortune.

日	ri4	3124	Sun, day, daylight, daytime; daily.
昃	ze4	6755	Sun setting in the afternoon, the afternoon; to decline.
之	zhi1	0935	Personal pronoun, he she, it; this, that, these, etc.; often used as a possessive.
離	li2	3902	Brightness, radiance, attach, cling; name of a bird. The modern meaning is leave, separate.
不	bu4	5379	No, not, negative prefix; without, none, nothing, will not, need not, will not be.
鼓	gu3	3479	Drum, drumbeating.
缶	fou3	1905	Pot, earthen vessel.
而	er2	1756	And, then, but, nevertheless, also, only. Join and contrasts two words.
歌	ge1	3364	Sing, song, sad or mournful songs.
則	ze2	6746	Then, thus, accordingly, consequently, and so, in that case; law, rule, pattern; follow a law.
大	da4	5943	Big, great, tall; excessive, arrogant; spread out and reach everywhere.
耋	die2	6314	Old age (70 or more years), aged, old, infirm.
之	zhi1	0935	Personal pronoun, he she, it; this, that, these, etc.; often used as a possessive.

Clinging Light (167) 30

| 嗟 | jie1 | 0763 | Lament, sigh, interjection of regret or sorrow, alas, groan. |
| 凶 | xiong1 | 2808 | Misfortune, pitfall, ominous, bad, unlucky, disastrous, trouble, accident. |

Nine in the fourth place

Comes abruptly, as with fire and death and thus is discarded.

突	tu1	6540	Suddenly, abruptly; break through, bursting forth, abrupt attack.
如	ru2	3137	Thus, in this way, as, like, similar to, if (conditional).
其	qi2	0525	Their, his, its, the; this, that. A demonstrative and possessive pronoun.
來	lai2	3768	Come, arrive, return, bring.
如	ru2	3137	Thus, in this way, as, like, similar to, if (conditional).
焚	fen2	1866	Burn, set fire; destroy, overthrow.
如	ru2	3137	Thus, in this way, as, like, similar to, if (conditional).
死	si3	5589	Die, death, doomed.
如	ru2	3137	Thus, in this way, as, like, similar to, if (conditional).
棄	qi4	0550	Thrown away, abandoned, forgotten, discarded.
如	ru2	3137	Thus, in this way, as, like, similar to, if (conditional).

Six in the fifth place

Torrents of tears with sorrow and lamentations. Good fortune.

出	chu1	1409	Go out, came out, appear, departure; arise, emerge; bring out, take out, expel, leave, get rid of; produce, beget.
涕	ti4	6250	Tears, weep, snivel, mucus.
沱	tuo2	6442	Flowing, flow; water diverting into streams, running or streaming water; tears or rain falling heavily.
若	ruo4	3126	Like, just as, to be like; agree, conform to; approve; concordant; compliant.
戚	qi1	0575	Grieved, lamenting; distressed; mourn; pitiful.
嗟	jie1	0763	Lament, sigh, interjection of regret or sorrow, alas, groan.
若	ruo4	3126	Like, just as, to be like; agree, conform to; approve; concordant; compliant.
吉	ji2	0476	Good fortune, auspicious, promising, fortunate, lucky, advantageous, happiness, good auspices. It is the only single character meaning good luck in the *YiJing*.

Nine at the top

The King sends him to attack. It is worthwhile to execute the leaders and capture those that are not of the same evil sort. No defect.

王	wang2	7037	King, prince, sovereign, ruler.
用	yong4	7567	Use, apply, put to use, apply the oracle to real world situations; hereby, thereby.
出	chu1	1409	Go out, came out, appear, departure; arise, emerge; bring out, take out, expel, leave, get rid of; produce, beget.
征	zheng1	0352	Punishing expedition ("to correct"), to reduce to submission, attack, punish; to levy taxes; comes, brings.
有	you3	7533	Have, possession, there be, there is.
嘉	jia1	0592	Good, excellent, joyful; commendations, approbation; admirable, praiseworthy.
折	zhe2	0267	Sever, break; bend, destroy, execute; decide a cause, discriminate, judge.
首	shou3	5839	Head; foremost, first; leader, chief.
獲	huo4	2412	Catch (in hunt), seize, get, obtain, hit the mark, find; succeed. What is caught, gotten or found may be a thing, a person, an opportunity, an idea or perception.
匪	fei3	1820	No, strong negative.
其	qi2	0525	Their, his, its, the; this, that. A demonstrative and possessive pronoun.
醜	chou3	1327	Ugly (physically or morally); evil, vile; disgraceful, ominous; drunken, drunk; category, class; enemies. Possessed for an evil spirit.
无	wu2	7173	No, not, negative; without, does not possess, not have.
咎	jiu4	1192	Fault, blame, mistake, wrong; inauspicious; misfortune, bad luck, calamity; reproach, censure.

31 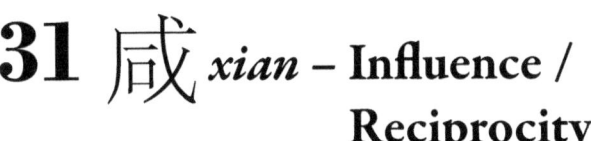 xian – Influence / Reciprocity

THE JUDGMENT

Influence. Success. The determination is favorable.
Taking a wife brings good fortune.

咸	xian2	2666	Influence, wooing; joined, together, to unite, completely; reciprocity (Lynn); feelings (Shaughnessy).
亨	heng1	2099	Success, prevalence, smooth progress, growth, consummate, triumph; pervade; offering, sacrifice.
利	li4	3867	Favorable, lucky, advantageous, profitable, beneficial, furthering, harvesting; sharp, sharp witted.
貞	zhen1	0346	Perseverance, persistence, determination, steadiness, firmness; straight, correct, verified, certain; pure, loyal. Its original meaning was "to determine an uncertain matter through divination".
取	qu3	1615	Take, take a wife, obtain, lay hold of, grasp.
女	nu3	4776	Maiden, woman, lady, girl, feminine.
吉	ji2	0476	Good fortune, auspicious, promising, fortunate, lucky, advantageous, happiness, good auspices. It is the only single character meaning good luck in the *YiJing*.

THE IMAGE

A Lake on the Mountain: The image of Influence.
Thus the noble is open-minded and welcoming for people.

山	shan1	5630	Mountain, hill, peak.
上	shang4	5669	Up, above, on, over, upwards, top, rise; higher, superior; first, best.
有	you3	7533	Have, possession, there be, there is.
澤	ze2	0277	Marsh, pool, pond, lake; flat body of water and the vapors rising from it; enrich, fertilize, benefit; moist, moisten; glossy, polished.

31   Matrix of Meanings of the Book of Changes

咸	xian2	2666	Influence, wooing; joined, together, to unite, completely; reciprocity (Lynn); feelings (Shaughnessy).
君	jun1	1715	Noble, prince, aristocrat, lord, chief, gentleman; honorable, a highly principled person, superior man. Most times, this character appears alongside another one, forming the word *JunZi*, whose original meaning was "son of a prince or ruler": 君子.
子	zi3	6939	Child, son or daughter, offspring; suffix; bride, wife; gentleman, officer, master, prince; young lady; the first of the *Earthly Branches*.
以	yi3	2932	Thus, in that way, by means of, with, for; instrument, medium, method, use (of), way (to).
虛	xu1	2821	Empty, vacant, hollow; hill, mound; abandoned city, ruins, waste; unsubstantial, unreal.
受	shou4	5840	Receive, accept, consent, agree; endure, suffer; compliant, tranquil.
人	ren2	3097	Man, person(s); people; others; human being, individual.

Six at the beginning

> Influence in the big toe of the foot.

咸	xian2	2666	Influence, wooing; joined, together, to unite, completely; reciprocity (Lynn); feelings (Shaughnessy).
其	qi2	0525	Their, his, its, the; this, that. A demonstrative and possessive pronoun.
拇	mu3	4584	Big toe or thumb; in the first line it means big toe, since the first line is related with the feet, but in the upper trigram it means big thumb.

Six in the second place

> Influence in the calves. Misfortune.
> Keeping still brings good fortune.

咸	xian2	2666	Influence, wooing; joined, together, to unite, completely; reciprocity (Lynn); feelings (Shaughnessy).
其	qi2	0525	Their, his, its, the; this, that. A demonstrative and possessive pronoun.
腓	fei2	1830	Calves of the legs.
凶	xiong1	2808	Misfortune, pitfall, ominous, bad, unlucky, disastrous, trouble, accident.
居	ju1	1535	Remain; rest (in); abides, dwell; to occupy a position or place; overbearing, arrogant.

INFLUENCE

吉	ji2	0476	Good fortune, auspicious, promising, fortunate, lucky, advantageous, happiness, good auspices. It is the only single character meaning good luck in the *YiJing*.

Nine in the third place

Influence on the thighs. He holds close to what he follows.
Going ahead causes humiliation.

咸	xian2	2666	Influence, wooing; joined, together, to unite, completely; reciprocity (Lynn); feelings (Shaughnessy).
其	qi2	0525	Their, his, its, the; this, that. A demonstrative and possessive pronoun.
股	gu3	3467	Thigh/s, haunches, rump, loins.
執	zhi2	0996	Catch, hold, size, capture; keep, retain; direct, control, manage.
其	qi2	0525	Their, his, its, the; this, that. A demonstrative and possessive pronoun.
隨	sui2	5523	Follow, pursue; conform to, respond, follow a way or religion; subsequently, in the course of time; listen to, submit; marrow, flesh.
往	wang3	7050	Go, to go to, go forward, go towards; depart, bygone, former.
吝	lin4	4040	Humiliation, regret, shame, distress, grief, sorrow; miserly, niggardly. It is a warning of trouble.

Nine in the fourth place

The determination brings good fortune. Regret vanishes.
Restless and indecisive comes and goes;
[only] his friends can follow his thoughts.

貞	zhen1	0346	Perseverance, persistence, determination, steadiness, firmness; straight, correct, verified, certain; pure, loyal. Its original meaning was "to determine an uncertain matter through divination".
吉	ji2	0476	Good fortune, auspicious, promising, fortunate, lucky, advantageous, happiness, good auspices. It is the only single character meaning good luck in the *YiJing*.
悔	hui3	2336	Repent, regret, contrition; trouble. This word indicates both an objective situation and a subjective reaction to such circumstance.
亡	wang2	7034	Go away, disappear, exile; fail; destroy, perish, not have, not exist.

31 — Matrix of Meanings of the Book of Changes

憧	chong1	1529	Agitated, unsettled, irresolute. It only appears here, but duplicated, which intensifies its meaning.
憧	chong1	1529	
往	wang3	7050	Go, to go to, go forward, go towards; depart, bygone, former. 攸往: have a place to go; have a goal.
來	lai2	3768	Come, arrive, return, bring.
朋	peng2	5054	Friend, companion, pair, equal, comrade; a string of cowries (small shiny shells used as coins in ancient China).
從	cong2	6919	Follow (somebody or a way or doctrine), adhere, obey, pursue; follower attendant; attend to business; from, by, since, whence, through.
爾	er3	1754	Your, you.
思	si1	5580	Think, consider, ponder; brood, reflect, plan.

Nine in the fifth place

Influence in the back of the neck. There is no repentance.

咸	xian2	2666	Influence, wooing; joined, together, to unite, completely; reciprocity (Lynn); feelings (Shaughnessy).
其	qi2	0525	Their, his, its, the; this, that. A demonstrative and possessive pronoun.
脢	mei2	8004	Back of the neck, neck, spinal flesh, meat on sides of the spine.
无	wu2	7173	No, not, negative; without, does not possess, not have.
悔	hui3	2336	Repent, regret, contrition; trouble. This word indicates both an objective situation and a subjective reaction to such circumstance.

Six at the top

Influence in the jaws, cheeks and tongue.

咸	xian2	2666	Influence, wooing; joined, together, to unite, completely; reciprocity (Lynn); feelings (Shaughnessy).
其	qi2	0525	Their, his, its, the; this, that. A demonstrative and possessive pronoun.
輔	fu3	1945	Jaws, cheeks, cheek bone; protect, help, support.
頰	jia2	0614	Cheeks; jowls.
舌	she2	5705	The tongue.

32 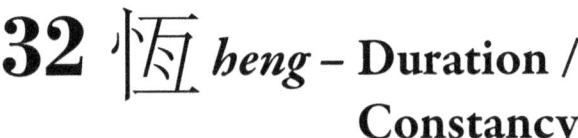 *heng* – Duration / Constancy

The Judgment

Duration. Success. No defect. The determination is favorable.
It is favorable to have a goal.

恆	heng2	2107	Duration, persistence, endurance, steadiness, continuity; for a long time.
亨	heng1	2099	Success, prevalence, smooth progress, growth, consummate, triumph; pervade; offering, sacrifice.
无	wu2	7173	No, not, negative; without, does not possess, not have.
咎	jiu4	1192	Fault, blame, mistake, wrong; inauspicious; misfortune, bad luck, calamity; reproach, censure.
利	li4	3867	Favorable, lucky, advantageous, profitable, beneficial, furthering, harvesting; sharp, sharp witted.
貞	zhen1	0346	Perseverance, persistence, determination, steadiness, firmness; straight, correct, verified, certain; pure, loyal. Its original meaning was "to determine an uncertain matter through divination".
利	li4	3867	Favorable, lucky, advantageous, profitable, beneficial, furthering, harvesting; sharp, sharp witted.
有	you3	7533	Have, possession, there be, there is.
攸	you1	7519	Goal, direction, destination, objective; distant, far away; a place; that which, whereby, thereby, for which; mark of the passive voice.
往	wang3	7050	Go, to go to, go forward, go towards; depart, bygone, former. 攸往: have a place to go; have a goal.

The Image

Thunder and Wind: The image of Duration.
Thus the noble stands up and does not change its course.

雷	lei2	4236	Thunder, shock, terrifying, arousing power surging from the earth.
風	feng1	1890	Wind, breath, air; manners, atmosphere.

恆	heng2	2107	Duration, persistence, endurance, steadiness, continuity; for a long time.
君	jun1	1715	Noble, prince, aristocrat, lord, chief, gentleman; honorable, a highly principled person, superior man. Most times, this character appears alongside another one, forming the word *JunZi*, whose original meaning was "son of a prince or ruler": 君子.
子	zi3	6939	Child, son or daughter, offspring; suffix; bride, wife; gentleman, officer, master, prince; young lady; the first of the *Earthly Branches*.
以	yi3	2932	Thus, in that way, by means of, with, for; instrument, medium, method, use (of), way (to).
立	li4	3921	Stand up or erect; set up, establish; raise, ascend; keep the position or the course, resist, endure.
不	bu4	5379	No, not, negative prefix; without, none, nothing, will not, need not, will not be.
易	yi4	2952	Change, versatility; ease, easy; name of a place (34.5, 56.6).
方	fang1	1802	Square, squarely, directly, straightforward, honest; a place, a region; on all sides; direction, trend, method; suddenly, quick, definite; take a place, occupy; sacrifice to the spirits of the four quarters.

Six at the beginning

He goes too far. The determination brings misfortune.
No goal is favorable.

浚	jun4	1729	Deep, deepen, dredge, dig out, dive (in deep water); profound, wise, recondite.
恆	heng2	2107	Duration, persistence, endurance, steadiness, continuity; for a long time.
貞	zhen1	0346	Perseverance, persistence, determination, steadiness, firmness; straight, correct, verified, certain; pure, loyal. Its original meaning was "to determine an uncertain matter through divination".
凶	xiong1	2808	Misfortune, pitfall, ominous, bad, unlucky, disastrous, trouble, accident.
无	wu2	7173	No, not, negative; without, does not possess, not have.
攸	you1	7519	Goal, direction, destination, objective; distant, far away; a place; that which, whereby, thereby, for which; mark of the passive voice.
利	li4	3867	Favorable, lucky, advantageous, profitable, beneficial, furthering, harvesting; sharp, sharp witted.

Nine in the second place
> Regret disappears.

悔	hui3	2336	Repent, regret, contrition; trouble. This word indicates both an objective situation and a subjective reaction to such circumstance.
亡	wang2	7034	Go away, disappear, exile; fail; destroy, perish, not have, not exist.

Nine in the third place
> His character is not constant. He may have to bear the shame. The determination is humiliating.

不	bu4	5379	No, not, negative prefix; without, none, nothing, will not, need not, will not be.
恆	heng2	2107	Duration, persistence, endurance, steadiness, continuity; for a long time.
其	qi2	0525	Their, his, its, the; this, that. A demonstrative and possessive pronoun.
德	de2	6162	Virtue, spiritual power, moral integrity; quality, nature, aptitude, ability, character.
或	huo4	2402	Perhaps, possibly, if, by chance; doubtful, uncertain; some, someone, something, sometime.
承	cheng2	0386	Support, assist, bear, serve; to present (54.6); receive, inherit (7.6).
之	zhi1	0935	Personal pronoun, he she, it; this, that, these, etc.; often used as a possessive.
羞	xiu1	2797	Shame, disgrace; inferior, unworthy; a prepared offering, prepared meat, sacrifice, offerings.
貞	zhen1	0346	Perseverance, persistence, determination, steadiness, firmness; straight, correct, verified, certain; pure, loyal. Its original meaning was "to determine an uncertain matter through divination".
吝	lin4	4040	Humiliation, regret, shame, distress, grief, sorrow; miserly, niggardly. It is a warning of trouble.

Nine in the fourth place
> No animals in the hunt.

田	tian2	6362	Field, cultivated land; hunt. The character is the picture of a cultivated field, divided in four sectors.
无	wu2	7173	No, not, negative; without, does not possess, not have.
禽	qin2	1100	Game, animals, birds, prey; quarry, captives, capture. It may be a deer, but it is not its specific meaning.

Six in the fifth place

> Perseverance in constancy is auspicious for a wife but wrong for a master.

恆	heng2	2107	Duration, persistence, endurance, steadiness, continuity; for a long time.
其	qi2	0525	Their, his, its, the; this, that. A demonstrative and possessive pronoun.
德	de2	6162	Virtue, spiritual power, moral integrity; quality, nature, aptitude, ability, character.
貞	zhen1	0346	Perseverance, persistence, determination, steadiness, firmness; straight, correct, verified, certain; pure, loyal. Its original meaning was "to determine an uncertain matter through divination".
婦	fu4	1963	Woman, lady, wife, married woman.
人	ren2	3097	Man, person(s); people; others; human being, individual.
吉	ji2	0476	Good fortune, auspicious, promising, fortunate, lucky, advantageous, happiness, good auspices. It is the only single character meaning good luck in the *YiJing*.
夫	fu1	1908	Man, male adult, husband; this, that, those.
子	zi3	6939	Child, son or daughter, offspring; suffix; bride, wife; gentleman, officer, master, prince; young lady; the first of the *Earthly Branches*.
凶	xiong1	2808	Misfortune, pitfall, ominous, bad, unlucky, disastrous, trouble, accident.

Six at the top

> Constantly agitated. Misfortune.

振	zhen4	0313	Excite, shake, quake (Kunst), arouse action; save help; arrange, to marshall troops; to restore order.
恆	heng2	2107	Duration, persistence, endurance, steadiness, continuity; for a long time.
凶	xiong1	2808	Misfortune, pitfall, ominous, bad, unlucky, disastrous, trouble, accident.

33 遯 *dun* – Retreat

The Judgment

Retreat. Success. Determination in small matters is favorable.

遯	dun4	6586	Retreat, escape, evade, withdraw; hide away, skulk; young pig, piglet.
亨	heng1	2099	Success, prevalence, smooth progress, growth, consummate, triumph; pervade; offering, sacrifice.
小	xiao3	2605	Small, insignificant, common, humble, mediocre; diminish, belittle.
利	li4	3867	Favorable, lucky, advantageous, profitable, beneficial, furthering, harvesting; sharp, sharp witted.
貞	zhen1	0346	Perseverance, persistence, determination, steadiness, firmness; straight, correct, verified, certain; pure, loyal. Its original meaning was "to determine an uncertain matter through divination".

The Image

Mountain under Heaven: The image of Retreat.
Thus the noble keeps at a distance the petty,
not with hatred but with reserve.

天	tian1	6361	Heaven, firmament, the sky, cosmos; celestial, divine, power above the human.
下	xia4	2520	Below, down, descend.
有	you3	7533	Have, possession, there be, there is.
山	shan1	5630	Mountain, hill, peak.
遯	dun4	6586	Retreat, escape, evade, withdraw; hide away, skulk; young pig, piglet.
君	jun1	1715	Noble, prince, aristocrat, lord, chief, gentleman; honorable, a highly principled person, superior man. Most times, this character appears alongside another one, forming the word *JunZi*, whose original meaning was "son of a prince or ruler": 君子.
子	zi3	6939	Child, son or daughter, offspring; suffix; bride, wife; gentleman, officer, master, prince; young lady; the first of the *Earthly Branches*.

以	yi3	2932	Thus, in that way, by means of, with, for; instrument, medium, method, use (of), way (to).
遠	yuan3	7734	Distance, far, remote; keep far from; leave.
小	xiao3	2605	Small, insignificant, common, humble, mediocre; diminish, belittle.
人	ren2	3097	Man, person(s); people; others; human being, individual.
不	bu4	5379	No, not, negative prefix; without, none, nothing, will not, need not, will not be.
惡	e4	4809	Evil, bad; ugly; wrong, fault, bad; hate.
而	er2	1756	And, then, but, nevertheless, also, only. Join and contrasts two words.
嚴	yan2	7347	Stern, strict, severe, rigorous; solemnity, dignity, gravity, majestic.

Six at the beginning

At the tail of the Retreat. Danger. Do not try to undertake anything.

遯	dun4	6586	Retreat, escape, evade, withdraw; hide away, skulk; young pig, piglet.
尾	wei3	7109	Tail, rear, back, behind, the end; last.
厲	li4	3906	Danger, threat; oppressive, cruel, wicked, brutal, harsh; sickness, malevolent devil; grind, polish, sharpen; discipline.
勿	wu4	7208	Do not, no. Negative imperative.
用	yong4	7567	Use, apply, put to use, apply the oracle to real world situations; hereby, thereby.
有	you3	7533	Have, possession, there be, there is.
攸	you1	7519	Goal, direction, destination, objective; distant, far away; a place; that which, whereby, thereby, for which; mark of the passive voice.
往	wang3	7050	Go, to go to, go forward, go towards; depart, bygone, former. 攸往: have a place to go; have a goal.

Six in the second place

Clutching a yellow ox leather no one can remove.

執	zhi2	0996	Catch, hold, size, capture; keep, retain; direct, control, manage.
之	zhi1	0935	Personal pronoun, he she, it; this, that, these, etc.; often used as a possessive.

Retreat (179) 33

用	yong4	7567	Use, apply, put to use, apply the oracle to real world situations; hereby, thereby.
黃	huang2	2297	Yellow, yellow-brown; color of the soil in central China. In the *YiJing* the yellow color is always favorable, it is the color of the middle and the moderation and it was the imperial color since the *Han* dynasty.
牛	niu2	4737	Cow, bull, ox.
之	zhi1	0935	Personal pronoun, he she, it; this, that, these, etc.; often used as a possessive.
革	ge2	3314	Change, change seasons, molt; revolution, overthrow; skin or hide, rawhide, hide without the hair, flay, peel off; ancient representations depict an animal hide spread out.
莫	mo4	4557	Nobody, nothing, none, no, not one, not at all, there is not, an absolute negative; evening, late.
之	zhi1	0935	Personal pronoun, he she, it; this, that, these, etc.; often used as a possessive.
勝	sheng4	5754	Defeat, subdue, vanquish, overcome; excel, surpass, be better than; victory, triumph, success.
說	tuo1	5939	Remove, take off, come off, let loose.

Nine in the third place

An entangled retreat is stressing and dangerous.
It is favorable to take charge of servants and maids.

係	xi4	2424	Cling to, attach to, bind to, (en)tangled, involved, relation.
遯	dun4	6586	Retreat, escape, evade, withdraw; hide away, skulk; young pig, piglet.
有	you3	7533	Have, possession, there be, there is.
疾	ji2	0492	Ill, harm, defect, stress; hurry; hate.
厲	li4	3906	Danger, threat; oppressive, cruel, wicked, brutal, harsh; sickness, malevolent devil; grind, polish, sharpen; discipline.
畜	chu4	1412	Accumulate, nurture, support, cultivate, domesticate.
臣	chen2	0327	Male slave, male bondservant or may be a slave couple, servant, retainer, vassal.
妾	qie4	0814	Concubine (secondary wife), handmaiden, servant girl, slave woman.
吉	ji2	0476	Good fortune, auspicious, promising, fortunate, lucky, advantageous, happiness, good auspices. It is the only single character meaning good luck in the *YiJing*.

Nine in the fourth place

> Retreat from what he is fond of.
> Good fortune for the noble, decline for the vulgar.

好	hao3	2062	Good, attractive, fine; to like, to be fond of.
遯	dun4	6586	Retreat, escape, evade, withdraw; hide away, skulk; young pig, piglet.
君	jun1	1715	Noble, prince, aristocrat, lord, chief, gentleman; honorable, a highly principled person, superior man. Most times, this character appears alongside another one, forming the word *JunZi*, whose original meaning was "son of a prince or ruler": 君子.
子	zi3	6939	Child, son or daughter, offspring; suffix; bride, wife; gentleman, officer, master, prince; young lady; the first of the *Earthly Branches*.
吉	ji2	0476	Good fortune, auspicious, promising, fortunate, lucky, advantageous, happiness, good auspices. It is the only single character meaning good luck in the *YiJing*.
小	xiao3	2605	Small, insignificant, common, humble, mediocre; diminish, belittle.
人	ren2	3097	Man, person(s); people; others; human being, individual.
否	pi3	1902	Standstill, stagnation, obstruction, stoppage, dead end; bad, wrong.

Nine in the fifth place

> Excellent retreat. The determination is favorable.

嘉	jia1	0592	Good, excellent, joyful; commendations, approbation; admirable, praiseworthy.
遯	dun4	6586	Retreat, escape, evade, withdraw; hide away, skulk; young pig, piglet.
貞	zhen1	0346	Perseverance, persistence, determination, steadiness, firmness; straight, correct, verified, certain; pure, loyal. Its original meaning was "to determine an uncertain matter through divination".
吉	ji2	0476	Good fortune, auspicious, promising, fortunate, lucky, advantageous, happiness, good auspices. It is the only single character meaning good luck in the *YiJing*.

Retreat

Nine at the top

> Fruitful retreat. Nothing that is not favorable.

肥	fei2	1839	Fat, rich, abundant (cheerful); fertile, fruitful.
遯	dun4	6586	Retreat, escape, evade, withdraw; hide away, skulk; young pig, piglet.
无	wu2	7173	No, not, negative; without, does not possess, not have.
不	bu4	5379	No, not, negative prefix; without, none, nothing, will not, need not, will not be.
利	li4	3867	Favorable, lucky, advantageous, profitable, beneficial, furthering, harvesting; sharp, sharp witted.

34 大壯 *da zhuang* – Great Power

THE JUDGMENT

Great Power. The determination is favorable.

大	da4	5943	Big, great, tall; excessive, arrogant; spread out and reach everywhere.
壯	zhuang4	1453	Power, strength, strong, robust, big, full grown male, in the prime of life; injure.
利	li4	3867	Favorable, lucky, advantageous, profitable, beneficial, furthering, harvesting; sharp, sharp witted.
貞	zhen1	0346	Perseverance, persistence, determination, steadiness, firmness; straight, correct, verified, certain; pure, loyal. Its original meaning was "to determine an uncertain matter through divination".

THE IMAGE

Thunder at the top of Heaven: The image of Great Power.
Thus the noble does not tread any path that deviates
from the established order.

雷	lei2	4236	Thunder, shock, terrifying, arousing power surging from the earth.
在	zai4	6657	Be at, at, in, on, within, be present; to lie in, depend upon, involved with; be living, dwell, located in.
天	tian1	6361	Heaven, firmament, the sky, cosmos; celestial, divine, power above the human.
上	shang4	5669	Up, above, on, over, upwards, top, rise; higher, superior; first, best.
大	da4	5943	Big, great, tall; excessive, arrogant; spread out and reach everywhere.
壯	zhuang4	1453	Power, strength, strong, robust, big, full grown male, in the prime of life; injure.
君	jun1	1715	Noble, prince, aristocrat, lord, chief, gentleman; honorable, a highly principled person, superior man. Most times, this character appears alongside another one, forming the word *JunZi*, whose original meaning was "son of a prince or ruler": 君子.

Great Power (183) 34

子	zi3	6939	Child, son or daughter, offspring; suffix; bride, wife; gentleman, officer, master, prince; young lady; the first of the *Earthly Branches*.
以	yi3	2932	Thus, in that way, by means of, with, for; instrument, medium, method, use (of), way (to).
非	fei1	1819	No, strong negative, oppose; wrong, bad; to blame or condemn.
禮	li3	3886	Social manners, politeness, propriety; ceremony, rituals.
弗	fu2	1981	Not (not able or not willing to), negative.
履	lu3	3893	Step on, treading, track, walk or follow a trail or way; footwear, shoes; conduct, behavior; ceremonies.

Nine at the beginning

Power in the toes. To push ahead brings misfortune. Have confidence.

壯	zhuang4	1453	Power, strength, strong, robust, big, full grown male, in the prime of life; injure.
于	yu2	7592	At, to, in, into, on, from, by, go, go to, move towards, proceed, be.
趾	zhi3	0944	Toes, feet, hoof, paw. Legs (of animals or furniture), footprints, tracks.
征	zheng1	0352	Punishing expedition ("to correct"), to reduce to submission, attack, punish; to levy taxes; comes, brings.
凶	xiong1	2808	Misfortune, pitfall, ominous, bad, unlucky, disastrous, trouble, accident.
有	you3	7533	Have, possession, there be, there is.
孚	fu2	1936	Truth; reliable, sincere; to inspire confidence in others; capture, prisoner, plunder.

Nine in the second place

The determination is favorable.

貞	zhen1	0346	Perseverance, persistence, determination, steadiness, firmness; straight, correct, verified, certain; pure, loyal. Its original meaning was "to determine an uncertain matter through divination".
吉	ji2	0476	Good fortune, auspicious, promising, fortunate, lucky, advantageous, happiness, good auspices. It is the only single character meaning good luck in the *YiJing*.

Nine in the third place

A common man uses the power.
The noble does not act like that. The determination is dangerous.
A ram butts the fence and his horns get stuck.

小	xiao3	2605	Small, insignificant, common, humble, mediocre; diminish, belittle.
人	ren2	3097	Man, person(s); people; others; human being, individual.
用	yong4	7567	Use, apply, put to use, apply the oracle to real world situations; hereby, thereby.
壯	zhuang4	1453	Power, strength, strong, robust, big, full grown male, in the prime of life; injure.
君	jun1	1715	Noble, prince, aristocrat, lord, chief, gentleman; honorable, a highly principled person, superior man. Most times, this character appears alongside another one, forming the word *JunZi*, whose original meaning was "son of a prince or ruler": 君子.
子	zi3	6939	Child, son or daughter, offspring; suffix; bride, wife; gentleman, officer, master, prince; young lady; the first of the *Earthly Branches*.
用	yong4	7567	Use, apply, put to use, apply the oracle to real world situations; hereby, thereby.
罔	wang3	7045	Not, no, negative, absence; a net (empty spaces between the threads), entangle, confusion.
貞	zhen1	0346	Perseverance, persistence, determination, steadiness, firmness; straight, correct, verified, certain; pure, loyal. Its original meaning was "to determine an uncertain matter through divination".
厲	li4	3906	Danger, threat; oppressive, cruel, wicked, brutal, harsh; sickness, malevolent devil; grind, polish, sharpen; discipline.
羝	di1	6195	Goat, ram, he-goat.
羊	yang2	7247	Sheep, ram, goat.
觸	chu4	1416	Butt, rush, charge, knock against; strike with the horns; offend or insult.
藩	fan1	1800	Hedge(row), fence, boundary, frontier; to protect.
羸	lei2	4240	Bound, entangled, tethered; break, damage; weak, lean, emaciated.

其	qi2	0525	Their, his, its, the; this, that. A demonstrative and possessive pronoun.
角	jiao3	1174	Horns, in the *YiJing*, is a symbol of violence and power, not always well employed.

Nine in the fourth place

> The determination is favorable. Regret vanishes.
> The fence is broken and there are no more entanglements.
> The power lies in the axle-brace of a great carriage.

貞	zhen1	0346	Perseverance, persistence, determination, steadiness, firmness; straight, correct, verified, certain; pure, loyal. Its original meaning was "to determine an uncertain matter through divination".
吉	ji2	0476	Good fortune, auspicious, promising, fortunate, lucky, advantageous, happiness, good auspices. It is the only single character meaning good luck in the *YiJing*.
悔	hui3	2336	Repent, regret, contrition; trouble. This word indicates both an objective situation and a subjective reaction to such circumstance.
亡	wang2	7034	Go away, disappear, exile; fail; destroy, perish, not have, not exist.
藩	fan1	1800	Hedge(row), fence, boundary, frontier; to protect.
決	jue2	1697	Burst open, break, rupture; open a passage for and lead forth a stream; break through an obstacle and scatter; determine, judge, decide.
不	bu4	5379	No, not, negative prefix; without, none, nothing, will not, need not, will not be.
羸	lei2	4240	Bound, entangled, tethered; break, damage; weak, lean, emaciated.
壯	zhuang4	1453	Power, strength, strong, robust, big, full grown male, in the prime of life; injure.
于	yu2	7592	At, to, in, into, on, from, by, go, go to, move towards, proceed, be.
大	da4	5943	Big, great, tall; excessive, arrogant; spread out and reach everywhere.
輿	yu2	7618	Wagon, cart, chariot, carriage; carrier, transport, transportation; carry on the shoulders; contain, hold.
之	zhi1	0935	Personal pronoun, he she, it; this, that, these, etc.; often used as a possessive.
輹	fu4	1997	Axletrees, axle-brace, two pieces of wood underneath a cart, which hold the axle firm on both sides.

Six in the fifth place

Loses the goat at *Yi*. There is no repentance.

喪	sang4	5429	Lose, let drop, disappear, destroy, perish, mourning, burial.
羊	yang2	7247	Sheep, ram, goat.
于	yu2	7592	At, to, in, into, on, from, by, go, go to, move towards, proceed, be.
易	yi4	2952	Name of a place; change, versatility; ease, easy.
无	wu2	7173	No, not, negative; without, does not possess, not have.
悔	hui3	2336	Repent, regret, contrition; trouble. This word indicates both an objective situation and a subjective reaction to such circumstance.

Six at the top

The ram butts the fence. Cannot retreat and cannot push through.
Nothing is favorable. Fortitude under trying conditions.
Good fortune.

羝	di1	6195	Goat, ram, he-goat.
羊	yang2	7247	Sheep, ram, goat.
觸	chu4	1416	Butt, rush, charge, knock against; strike with the horns; offend or insult.
藩	fan1	1800	Hedge(row), fence, boundary, frontier; to protect.
不	bu4	5379	No, not, negative prefix; without, none, nothing, will not, need not, will not be.
能	neng2	4648	Able, skill, power, talent, ability, expertise.
退	tui4	6568	Retreat, withdraw, back up, retire; decline, refuse.
不	bu4	5379	No, not, negative prefix; without, none, nothing, will not, need not, will not be.
能	neng2	4648	Able, skill, power, talent, ability, expertise.
遂	sui4	5530	Advance; push through, go forward; proceed, prolong; follow along, pursuit, comply with; consequently, then, next.
无	wu2	7173	No, not, negative; without, does not possess, not have.
攸	you1	7519	Goal, direction, destination, objective; distant, far away; a place; that which, whereby, thereby, for which; mark of the passive voice.
利	li4	3867	Favorable, lucky, advantageous, profitable, beneficial, furthering, harvesting; sharp, sharp witted.

艱	jian1	0834	Hardship, distressing, difficult, laborious.
則	ze2	6746	Then, thus, accordingly, consequently, and so, in that case; law, rule, pattern; follow a law.
吉	ji2	0476	Good fortune, auspicious, promising, fortunate, lucky, advantageous, happiness, good auspices. It is the only single character meaning good luck in the *YiJing*.

35 晉 *jin* – Progress / Advance

The Judgment

Progress. The Marquis of *Kang* is honored with numerous horses. On the same day he is received three times.

晉	jin4	1088	Progress, advance, promotion, flourishing.
康	kang1	3278	*Kang* was the title of nobility of one of the sons of the King *Wen*. It also means calm, peaceful, happy; prosperous; exalted; strong.
侯	hou2	2135	Feudal lord, (vassal) prince, marquis; officer, governor, chief; skilled archer.
用	yong4	7567	Use, apply, put to use, apply the oracle to real world situations; hereby, thereby.
錫	xi1	2505	Bestow (a reward), confer (honor, employment, rights or dignity), gift.
馬	ma3	4310	Horse.
蕃	fan2	1798	Numerous; prosper, propagate, breed, luxuriant growth of vegetation, multiply.
庶	shu4	5874	Numerous, many, multitude, the masses; ample, abundant; many chances for.
晝	zhou4	1302	Day, time of daylight.
日	ri4	3124	Sun, day, daylight, daytime; daily.
三	san1	5415	Three, thrice, third time or place.
接	jie1	0800	Receive, welcome, grant audience; to take with the hand; to accept; inherit; to succeed to.

The Image

The Brightness of the sun rises over the earth: The image of Progress. Thus the noble reveals his brilliant talents by himself.

明	ming2	4534	Light, brightness, clarity, clear; enlightenment, discernment; seeing, perception; agreement, contract.
出	chu1	1409	Go out, came out, appear, departure; arise, emerge; bring out, take out, expel, leave, get rid of; produce, beget.

地	di4	6198	Earth, soil, ground.
上	shang4	5669	Up, above, on, over, upwards, top, rise; higher, superior; first, best.
晉	jin4	1088	Progress, advance, promotion, flourishing.
君	jun1	1715	Noble, prince, aristocrat, lord, chief, gentleman; honorable, a highly principled person, superior man. Most times, this character appears alongside another one, forming the word *JunZi*, whose original meaning was "son of a prince or ruler": 君子.
子	zi3	6939	Child, son or daughter, offspring; suffix; bride, wife; gentleman, officer, master, prince; young lady; the first of the *Earthly Branches*.
以	yi3	2932	Thus, in that way, by means of, with, for; instrument, medium, method, use (of), way (to).
自	zi4	6960	From, origin, source, cause, reason; oneself, yourself.
昭	zhao1	0236	Bright, brilliant, brightness of the sun; enlighten, display, show, manifest; illustrious.
明	ming2	4534	Light, brightness, clarity, clear; enlightenment, discernment; seeing, perception; agreement, contract.
德	de2	6162	Virtue, spiritual power, moral integrity; quality, nature, aptitude, ability, character.

Six at the beginning

Progressing but repressed. The determination is favorable.
Be tolerant of the lack of confidence. No defect.

晉	jin4	1088	Progress, advance, promotion, flourishing.
如	ru2	3137	Thus, in this way, as, like, similar to, if (conditional).
摧	cui1	6866	Draw back; chop, destroy, break; repress, to cause to cease, to extinguish.
如	ru2	3137	Thus, in this way, as, like, similar to, if (conditional).
貞	zhen1	0346	Perseverance, persistence, determination, steadiness, firmness; straight, correct, verified, certain; pure, loyal. Its original meaning was "to determine an uncertain matter through divination".
吉	ji2	0476	Good fortune, auspicious, promising, fortunate, lucky, advantageous, happiness, good auspices. It is the only single character meaning good luck in the *YiJing*.
罔	wang3	7045	Not, no, negative, absence; a net (empty spaces between the threads), entangle, confusion.

孚	fu2	1936	Truth; reliable, sincere; to inspire confidence in others; capture, prisoner, plunder.
裕	yu4	7667	Tolerating, indulgent, forgiving, liberal; ample, abundant, opulent; neglect, postpone.
无	wu2	7173	No, not, negative; without, does not possess, not have.
咎	jiu4	1192	Fault, blame, mistake, wrong; inauspicious; misfortune, bad luck, calamity; reproach, censure.

Six in the second place

Progressing with grief. The determination is favorable.
Receives a great blessing from his ancestress.

晉	jin4	1088	Progress, advance, promotion, flourishing.
如	ru2	3137	Thus, in this way, as, like, similar to, if (conditional).
愁	chou2	1325	Anxious, in sorrow; fearful, melancholic, gloomy; mourning.
如	ru2	3137	Thus, in this way, as, like, similar to, if (conditional).
貞	zhen1	0346	Perseverance, persistence, determination, steadiness, firmness; straight, correct, verified, certain; pure, loyal. Its original meaning was "to determine an uncertain matter through divination".
吉	ji2	0476	Good fortune, auspicious, promising, fortunate, lucky, advantageous, happiness, good auspices. It is the only single character meaning good luck in the *YiJing*.
受	shou4	5840	Receive, accept, consent, agree; endure, suffer; compliant, tranquil.
茲	zi1	6935	This (loan); coarse straw mat.
介	jie4	0629	Great, important, solid; Limit, restriction, boundary; armour; protect, assist, depend on, support.
福	fu2	1978	Happiness, good fortune, blessings.
于	yu2	7592	At, to, in, into, on, from, by, go, go to, move towards, proceed, be.
其	qi2	0525	Their, his, its, the; this, that. A demonstrative and possessive pronoun.
王	wang2	7037	King, prince, sovereign, ruler.
母	mu3	4582	Mother; female elder; grandmother.

Six in the third place

All agree and trust. Regret disappears.

眾	zhong4	1517	Multitude, all, the whole of, majority.
允	yun3	7759	Trust, approval, consent, confidence; sincere, true, loyal; truly, indeed; earnestly.
悔	hui3	2336	Repent, regret, contrition; trouble. This word indicates both an objective situation and a subjective reaction to such circumstance.
亡	wang2	7034	Go away, disappear, exile; fail; destroy, perish, not have, not exist.

Nine in the fourth place

Progressing as a squirrel. The determination is dangerous.

晉	jin4	1088	Progress, advance, promotion, flourishing.
如	ru2	3137	Thus, in this way, as, like, similar to, if (conditional).
鼫	shi2	5816	Some kind of rodent with long tail: squirrel, long tailed marmot, field mouse.
鼠	shu3	5871	Rat, mouse, rodent.
貞	zhen1	0346	Perseverance, persistence, determination, steadiness, firmness; straight, correct, verified, certain; pure, loyal. Its original meaning was "to determine an uncertain matter through divination".
厲	li4	3906	Danger, threat; oppressive, cruel, wicked, brutal, harsh; sickness, malevolent devil; grind, polish, sharpen; discipline.

Six in the fifth place

Regret disappears. Do not worry about loss or gain.
Going forward brings happiness. Nothing that is not favorable.

悔	hui3	2336	Repent, regret, contrition; trouble. This word indicates both an objective situation and a subjective reaction to such circumstance.
亡	wang2	7034	Go away, disappear, exile; fail; destroy, perish, not have, not exist.
失	shi1	5806	Lose, let go, neglect, an omission; fail, err; lose control.
得	de2	6161	Get, obtain, gain; reach, achieve; can; attain the desired thing.
勿	wu4	7208	Do not, no. Negative imperative.

恤	xu4	2862	Worry, care about, fear, sorrow, pity.
往	wang3	7050	Go, to go to, go forward, go towards; depart, bygone, former.
吉	ji2	0476	Good fortune, auspicious, promising, fortunate, lucky, advantageous, happiness, good auspices. It is the only single character meaning good luck in the *YiJing*.
无	wu2	7173	No, not, negative; without, does not possess, not have.
不	bu4	5379	No, not, negative prefix; without, none, nothing, will not, need not, will not be.
利	li4	3867	Favorable, lucky, advantageous, profitable, beneficial, furthering, harvesting; sharp, sharp witted.

Nine at the top

Progressing with the horns. Use them only to punish your own city. Danger, but there will be good fortune. No defect. The determination is humiliating.

晉	jin4	1088	Progress, advance, promotion, flourishing.
其	qi2	0525	Their, his, its, the; this, that. A demonstrative and possessive pronoun.
角	jiao3	1174	Horns, in the *YiJing*, is a symbol of violence and power, not always well employed.
維	wei2	7067	Tie up, bound, bind together; guiding rope of a net; guiding principle, rule; but only.
用	yong4	7567	Use, apply, put to use, apply the oracle to real world situations; hereby, thereby.
伐	fa1	1765	Attack, punish (rebels), submit; beat, cut down, fell.
邑	yi4	3037	City, town; walled or fortified city, seat of the of government for a district.
厲	li4	3906	Danger, threat; oppressive, cruel, wicked, brutal, harsh; sickness, malevolent devil; grind, polish, sharpen; discipline.
吉	ji2	0476	Good fortune, auspicious, promising, fortunate, lucky, advantageous, happiness, good auspices. It is the only single character meaning good luck in the *YiJing*.
无	wu2	7173	No, not, negative; without, does not possess, not have.
咎	jiu4	1192	Fault, blame, mistake, wrong; inauspicious; misfortune, bad luck, calamity; reproach, censure.

貞	zhen1	0346	Perseverance, persistence, determination, steadiness, firmness; straight, correct, verified, certain; pure, loyal. Its original meaning was "to determine an uncertain matter through divination".
吝	lin4	4040	Humiliation, regret, shame, distress, grief, sorrow; miserly, niggardly. It is a warning of trouble.

36 明夷 *ming yi* – Suppressed Light

The Judgment

Suppressed Light. Fortitude under trying conditions brings good fortune.

明	ming2	4534	Light, brightness, clarity, clear; enlightenment, discernment; seeing, perception; agreement, contract.
夷	yi2	2982	Hide, wound, suppress, kill, darkening; pacified, at ease, common, ordinary; barbarian tribes in the East; crying pheasant.
利	li4	3867	Favorable, lucky, advantageous, profitable, beneficial, furthering, harvesting; sharp, sharp witted.
艱	jian1	0834	Hardship, distressing, difficult, laborious.
貞	zhen1	0346	Perseverance, persistence, determination, steadiness, firmness; straight, correct, verified, certain; pure, loyal. Its original meaning was "to determine an uncertain matter through divination".

The Image

Light has come into the Earth: The image of Suppressed Light. Thus the noble deals with the masses, concealing his talents, but still illuminating.

明	ming2	4534	Light, brightness, clarity, clear; enlightenment, discernment; seeing, perception; agreement, contract.
入	ru4	3152	Enter, go into (this is the meaning used in the *YiJing*); to make to enter; put into; bring in, present; encroach.
地	di4	6198	Earth, soil, ground.
中	zhong1	1504	Center, inner, in the inside, put in the center, hit (target); balanced, central, middle, correct.
明	ming2	4534	Light, brightness, clarity, clear; enlightenment, discernment; seeing, perception; agreement, contract.
夷	yi2	2982	Hide, wound, suppress, kill, darkening; pacified, at ease, common, ordinary; barbarian tribes in the East; crying pheasant.

Suppressed Light (195)   36

君	jun1	1715	Noble, prince, aristocrat, lord, chief, gentleman; honorable, a highly principled person, superior man. Most times, this character appears alongside another one, forming the word *JunZi*, whose original meaning was "son of a prince or ruler": 君子.
子	zi3	6939	Child, son or daughter, offspring; suffix; bride; wife; gentleman, officer, master, prince; young lady; the first of the *Earthly Branches*.
以	yi3	2932	Thus, in that way, by means of, with, for; instrument, medium, method, use (of), way (to).
涖	li4	3912	Treat; command, overlook, manage; come and inspect.
衆	zhong4	1517	Multitude, all, the whole of, majority.
用	yong4	7567	Use, apply, put to use, apply the oracle to real world situations; hereby, thereby.
晦	hui4	2337	Dark, to get dark, obscure, twilight, shading; the last day of the lunar month; reticent.
而	er2	1756	And, then, but, nevertheless, also, only. Join and contrasts two words.
明	ming2	4534	Light, brightness, clarity, clear; enlightenment, discernment; seeing, perception; agreement, contract.

Nine at the beginning

Suppressed Light during flight. He lowers his wings.
The noble goes along the road for three days without food,
but has somewhere to go. The host gossips about him.

明	ming2	4534	Light, brightness, clarity, clear; enlightenment, discernment; seeing, perception; agreement, contract.
夷	yi2	2982	Hide, wound, suppress, kill, darkening; pacified, at ease, common, ordinary; barbarian tribes in the East; crying pheasant.
于	yu2	7592	At, to, in, into, on, from, by, go, go to, move towards, proceed, be.
飛	fei1	1850	Fly, flying, soaring; go quickly.
垂	chui2	1478	Hang down, (let) drop, lower; bow.
其	qi2	0525	Their, his, its, the; this, that. A demonstrative and possessive pronoun.
翼	yi4	3051	Wings(s) of a bird, flanks of an army; to assist, to protect.

君	jun1	1715	Noble, prince, aristocrat, lord, chief, gentleman; honorable, a highly principled person, superior man. Most times, this character appears alongside another one, forming the word *JunZi*, whose original meaning was "son of a prince or ruler": 君子.
子	zi3	6939	Child, son or daughter, offspring; suffix; bride, wife; gentleman, officer, master, prince; young lady; the first of the *Earthly Branches*.
于	yu2	7592	At, to, in, into, on, from, by, go, go to, move towards, proceed, be.
行	xing2	2754	Move, go, advance, act, do.
三	san1	5415	Three, thrice, third time or place.
日	ri4	3124	Sun, day, daylight, daytime; daily.
不	bu4	5379	No, not, negative prefix; without, none, nothing, will not, need not, will not be.
食	shi2	5810	Eat, feed, ingest; food, give food to; nourishment; salary of an officer, livelihood; eclipse (eating of Sun or Moon).
有	you3	7533	Have, possession, there be, there is.
攸	you1	7519	Goal, direction, destination, objective; distant, far away; a place; that which, whereby, thereby, for which; mark of the passive voice.
往	wang3	7050	Go, to go to, go forward, go towards; depart, bygone, former. 攸往: have a place to go; have a goal.
主	zhu3	1336	Master, lord, chief; host, innkeeper.
人	ren2	3097	Man, person(s); people; others; human being, individual.
有	you3	7533	Have, possession, there be, there is.
言	yan2	7334	Talk, speech, words, sayings; big flute.

Six in the second place

Suppressed Light. Wounded in the left thigh.
Rescued by a powerful horse. Good fortune.

明	ming2	4534	Light, brightness, clarity, clear; enlightenment, discernment; seeing, perception; agreement, contract.
夷	yi2	2982	Hide, wound, suppress, kill, darkening; pacified, at ease, common, ordinary; barbarian tribes in the East; crying pheasant. Appearing duplicated intensifies its meaning.
夷	yi2	2982	

Suppressed Light (197)

于	yu2	7592	At, to, in, into, on, from, by, go, go to, move towards, proceed, be.
左	zuo3	6774	Left side, to the left; the left bank of a river, the East; help, assist, support.
股	gu3	3467	Thigh/s, haunches, rump, loins.
用	yong4	7567	Use, apply, put to use, apply the oracle to real world situations; hereby, thereby.
拯	zheng3	0360	Relief, rescue, to lift up, to raise; geld, remove (Kunst, Rutt).
馬	ma3	4310	Horse.
壯	zhuang4	1453	Power, strength, strong, robust, big, full grown male, in the prime of life; injure.
吉	ji2	0476	Good fortune, auspicious, promising, fortunate, lucky, advantageous, happiness, good auspices. It is the only single character meaning good luck in the *YiJing*.

Nine in the third place

Suppressed Light during the hunt in the south.
The great leader is caught. Cannot be hurriedly determined.

明	ming2	4534	Light, brightness, clarity, clear; enlightenment, discernment; seeing, perception; agreement, contract.
夷	yi2	2982	Hide, wound, suppress, kill, darkening (36); pacified, at ease, common, ordinary (59); barbarian tribes in the East; crying pheasant.
于	yu2	7592	At, to, in, into, on, from, by, go, go to, move towards, proceed, be.
南	nan2	4620	The South. The region associated with Summer, fire, work in community and vegetation.
狩	shou4	5845	Hunt, great winter hunt, inspection tour.
得	de2	6161	Get, obtain, gain; reach, achieve; can; attain the desired thing.
其	qi2	0525	Their, his, its, the; this, that. A demonstrative and possessive pronoun.
大	da4	5943	Big, great, tall; excessive, arrogant; spread out and reach everywhere.
首	shou3	5839	Head; foremost, first; leader, chief.
不	bu4	5379	No, not, negative prefix; without, none, nothing, will not, need not, will not be.

可	ke3	3381	Can, able, may; permit, allow; satisfactory, proper, suitable.
疾	ji2	0492	Ill, harm, defect, stress; hurry; hate.
貞	zhen1	0346	Perseverance, persistence, determination, steadiness, firmness; straight, correct, verified, certain; pure, loyal. Its original meaning was "to determine an uncertain matter through divination".

Six in the fourth place

Enters the left side of the belly. Grasps the heart of the Suppressed Light. Leaves the gate and courtyard.

入	ru4	3152	Enter, go into (this is the meaning used in the *YiJing*); to make to enter; put into; bring in, present; encroach.
于	yu2	7592	At, to, in, into, on, from, by, go, go to, move towards, proceed, be.
左	zuo3	6774	Left side, to the left; the left bank of a river, the East; help, assist, support.
腹	fu4	1994	Belly, stomach, gut: body cavity that contains the heart and the spleen, which were considered the source of the feelings.
獲	huo4	2412	Catch (in hunt), seize, get, obtain, hit the mark, find; succeed. What is caught, gotten or found may be a thing, a person, an opportunity, an idea or perception.
明	ming2	4534	Light, brightness, clarity, clear; enlightenment, discernment; seeing, perception; agreement, contract.
夷	yi2	2982	Hide, wound, suppress, kill, darkening; pacified, at ease, common, ordinary; barbarian tribes in the East; crying pheasant.
之	zhi1	0935	Personal pronoun, he she, it; this, that, these, etc.; often used as a possessive.
心	xin1	2735	Heart; conscience, moral nature; soul; core; mind; source of feelings, intentions, will.
于	yu2	7592	At, to, in, into, on, from, by, go, go to, move towards, proceed, be.
出	chu1	1409	Go out, came out, appear, departure; arise, emerge; bring out, take out, expel, leave, get rid of; produce, beget.
門	men2	4418	Gate, door. This is the external door, separating courtyard and street, meanwhile 戶 is the inner door, the entrance door.
庭	ting2	6405	Courtyard (of palace), court, audience chamber; hall, courtyard, chambers; family.

Suppressed Light (199) 36

Six in the fifth place

> Suppressed Light [as] Prince *Ji*.
> The determination is favorable.

箕	ji1	0402	Although this character means winnowing basket; a constellation; besides other meanings, in the *YiJing* it is a proper noun, the name of the Viscount *Ji*, who was a minister, and the uncle of the last *Shang* king; he was imprisoned for refusing to serve as minister and reproaching the king for his bad actions. It is told that he simulated madness to keep his life.
子	zi3	6939	Child, son or daughter, offspring; suffix; bride, wife; gentleman, officer, master, prince; young lady; the first of the *Earthly Branches*.
之	zhi1	0935	Personal pronoun, he she, it; this, that, these, etc.; often used as a possessive.
明	ming2	4534	Light, brightness, clarity, clear; enlightenment, discernment; seeing, perception; agreement, contract.
夷	yi2	2982	Hide, wound, suppress, kill, darkening (36); pacified, at ease, common, ordinary (59); barbarian tribes in the East; crying pheasant.
利	li4	3867	Favorable, lucky, advantageous, profitable, beneficial, furthering, harvesting; sharp, sharp witted.
貞	zhen1	0346	Perseverance, persistence, determination, steadiness, firmness; straight, correct, verified, certain; pure, loyal. Its original meaning was "to determine an uncertain matter through divination".

Six at the top

> No light, but darkness. First ascended to heaven.
> Later sank into the earth.

不	bu4	5379	No, not, negative prefix; without, none, nothing, will not, need not, will not be.
明	ming2	4534	Light, brightness, clarity, clear; enlightenment, discernment; seeing, perception; agreement, contract.
晦	hui4	2337	Dark, to get dark, obscure, twilight, shading; the last day of the lunar month; reticent.
初	chu1	1390	At first, beginning, initial, incipient, in the early stages.
登	deng1	6167	Rise, ascend, climb, mount, step up; ripen; raise.
于	yu2	7592	At, to, in, into, on, from, by, go, go to, move towards, proceed, be.

天	tian1	6361	Heaven, firmament, the sky, cosmos; celestial, divine, power above the human.
後	hou4	2143	Later, behind, rear, afterward, come after; follow; descendants, successor.
入	ru4	3152	Enter, go into (this is the meaning used in the *YiJing*); to make to enter; put into; bring in, present; encroach.
于	yu2	7592	At, to, in, into, on, from, by, go, go to, move towards, proceed, be.
地	di4	6198	Earth, soil, ground.

37 家人 *jia ren* – The Family / The Clan

THE JUDGMENT

The Family. The determination is favorable for a woman.

家	jia1	0594	Family, household, clan; home, to keep a home.
人	ren2	3097	Man, person(s); people; others; human being, individual.
利	li4	3867	Favorable, lucky, advantageous, profitable, beneficial, furthering, harvesting; sharp, sharp witted.
女	nu3	4776	Maiden, woman, lady, girl, feminine.
貞	zhen1	0346	Perseverance, persistence, determination, steadiness, firmness; straight, correct, verified, certain; pure, loyal. Its original meaning was "to determine an uncertain matter through divination".

THE IMAGE

The Wind comes from the Fire: The image of The Family.
So the noble words have substance and his actions duration.

風	feng1	1890	Wind, breath, air; manners, atmosphere.
自	zi4	6960	From, origin, source, cause, reason; oneself, yourself.
火	huo3	2395	Fire, flame.
出	chu1	1409	Go out, came out, appear, departure; arise, emerge; bring out, take out, expel, leave, get rid of; produce, beget.
家	jia1	0594	Family, household, clan; home, to keep a home.
人	ren2	3097	Man, person(s); people; others; human being, individual.
君	jun1	1715	Noble, prince, aristocrat, lord, chief, gentleman; honorable, a highly principled person, superior man. Most times, this character appears alongside another one, forming the word *JunZi*, whose original meaning was "son of a prince or ruler": 君子.
子	zi3	6939	Child, son or daughter, offspring; suffix; bride, wife; gentleman, officer, master, prince; young lady; the first of the *Earthly Branches*.

以	yi3	2932	Thus, in that way, by means of, with, for; instrument, medium, method, use (of), way (to).
言	yan2	7334	Talk, speech, words, sayings; big flute.
有	you3	7533	Have, possession, there be, there is.
物	wu4	7209	Thing/s, being/s, creature/s; substance, the physical world, all living things; others.
而	er2	1756	And, then, but, nevertheless, also, only. Join and contrasts two words.
行	xing2	2754	Move, go, advance, act, do.
有	you3	7533	Have, possession, there be, there is.
恆	heng2	2107	Duration, persistence, endurance, steadiness, continuity; for a long time.

Nine at the beginning

With firm boundaries in The Family regret vanishes.

閑	xian2	2679	Defend, guard, protect, barricade, enclose; enclosure, stables, corral; discipline, train, restrain, forbid.
有	you3	7533	Have, possession, there be, there is.
家	jia1	0594	Family, household, clan; home, to keep a home.
悔	hui3	2336	Repent, regret, contrition; trouble. This word indicates both an objective situation and a subjective reaction to such circumstance.
亡	wang2	7034	Go away, disappear, exile; fail; destroy, perish, not have, not exist.

Six in the second place

Unpretentious. Stays inside preparing food.
The determination is favorable.

无	wu2	7173	No, not, negative; without, does not possess, not have.
攸	you1	7519	Goal, direction, destination, objective; distant, far away; a place; that which, whereby, thereby, for which; mark of the passive voice.
遂	sui4	5530	Advance; push through, go forward; proceed, prolong; follow along, pursuit, comply with; consequently, then, next.
在	zai4	6657	Be at, at, in, on, within, be present; to lie in, depend upon, involved with; be living, dwell, located in.
中	zhong1	1504	Center, inner, in the inside, put in the center, hit (target); balanced, central, middle, correct.

饋	kui4	3669	Present food, offer food to a superior, to make a present; meal, food.
貞	zhen1	0346	Perseverance, persistence, determination, steadiness, firmness; straight, correct, verified, certain; pure, loyal. Its original meaning was "to determine an uncertain matter through divination".
吉	ji2	0476	Good fortune, auspicious, promising, fortunate, lucky, advantageous, happiness, good auspices. It is the only single character meaning good luck in the *YiJing*.

Nine in the third place

A family run with stern severity will cause regrets but there will be good fortune. If the woman and children are boisterously enjoying themselves, there will be humiliation in the end.

家	jia1	0594	Family, household, clan; home, to keep a home.
人	ren2	3097	Man, person(s); people; others; human being, individual.
嗃	he4	2134	To scold with severity; stern, severe. Appearing duplicated intensifies its meaning.
嗃	he4	2134	
悔	hui3	2336	Repent, regret, contrition; trouble. This word indicates both an objective situation and a subjective reaction to such circumstance.
厲	li4	3906	Danger, threat; oppressive, cruel, wicked, brutal, harsh; sickness, malevolent devil; grind, polish, sharpen; discipline.
吉	ji2	0476	Good fortune, auspicious, promising, fortunate, lucky, advantageous, happiness, good auspices. It is the only single character meaning good luck in the *YiJing*.
婦	fu4	1963	Woman, lady, wife, married woman.
子	zi3	6939	Child, son or daughter, offspring; suffix; bride, wife; gentleman, officer, master, prince; young lady; the first of the *Earthly Branches*.
嘻	xi1	2436	Laugh, giggle; merriment; an interjection of joy. Appearing duplicated intensifies its meaning.
嘻	xi1	2436	
終	zhong1	1500	End, finish, complete; for ever; end of a cycle; carried to conclusion, consummation, closure; death. The original meaning was: tied-off end of a thread.
吝	lin4	4040	Humiliation, regret, shame, distress, grief, sorrow; miserly, niggardly. It is a warning of trouble.

Six in the fourth place
A thriving family. Great good fortune.

富	fu4	1952	Rich, wealth, treasure, abundance, prosperity, to enrich.
家	jia1	0594	Family, household, clan; home, to keep a home.
大	da4	5943	Big, great, tall; excessive, arrogant; spread out and reach everywhere.
吉	ji2	0476	Good fortune, auspicious, promising, fortunate, lucky, advantageous, happiness, good auspices. It is the only single character meaning good luck in the *YiJing*.

Nine in the fifth place
The King approaches his family. Do not worry. Good fortune.

王	wang2	7037	King, prince, sovereign, ruler.
假	jia3	0599	Approaches, goes to, attains.
有	you3	7533	Have, possession, there be, there is.
家	jia1	0594	Family, household, clan; home, to keep a home.
勿	wu4	7208	Do not, no. Negative imperative.
恤	xu4	2862	Worry, care about, fear, sorrow, pity.
吉	ji2	0476	Good fortune, auspicious, promising, fortunate, lucky, advantageous, happiness, good auspices. It is the only single character meaning good luck in the *YiJing*.

Nine at the top
He inspires confidence and awe. At the end there will be good fortune.

有	you3	7533	Have, possession, there be, there is.
孚	fu2	1936	Truth; reliable, sincere; to inspire confidence in others; capture, prisoner, plunder.
威	wei1	7051	Dignity, respect; awesome, majestic; impress, terrify; the mother of one's husband.
如	ru2	3137	Thus, in this way, as, like, similar to, if (conditional).
終	zhong1	1500	End, finish, complete; for ever; end of a cycle; carried to conclusion, consummation, closure; death. The original meaning was: tied-off end of a thread.
吉	ji2	0476	Good fortune, auspicious, promising, fortunate, lucky, advantageous, happiness, good auspices. It is the only single character meaning good luck in the *YiJing*.

38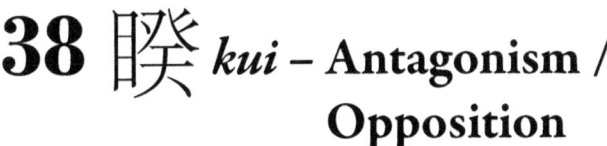

The Judgment

Antagonism. Good fortune in small matters.

睽	kui2	3660	Diverging, extraordinary; squint (eyes not aligned); opposition, polarization, estrangement.
小	xiao3	2605	Small, insignificant, common, humble, mediocre; diminish, belittle.
事	shi4	5787	Serve, service; affairs, business, matters.
吉	ji2	0476	Good fortune, auspicious, promising, fortunate, lucky, advantageous, happiness, good auspices. It is the only single character meaning good luck in the *YiJing*.

The Image

Fire is above, Lake below: The image of Antagonism.
Thus the noble is companionable, but maintains its uniqueness.

上	shang4	5669	Up, above, on, over, upwards, top, rise; higher, superior; first, best.
火	huo3	2395	Fire, flame.
下	xia4	2520	Below, down, descend.
澤	ze2	0277	Marsh, pool, pond, lake; flat body of water and the vapors rising from it; enrich, fertilize, benefit; moist, moisten; glossy, polished.
睽	kui2	3660	Diverging, extraordinary; squint (eyes not aligned); opposition, polarization, estrangement.
君	jun1	1715	Noble, prince, aristocrat, lord, chief, gentleman; honorable, a highly principled person, superior man. Most times, this character appears alongside another one, forming the word *JunZi*, whose original meaning was "son of a prince or ruler": 君子.
子	zi3	6939	Child, son or daughter, offspring; suffix; bride, wife; gentleman, officer, master, prince; young lady; the first of the *Earthly Branches*.

205

以	yi3	2932	Thus, in that way, by means of, with, for; instrument, medium, method, use (of), way (to).
同	tong2	6615	Gather people, assemble, join, partake in; identical, together, fellowship; in agreement, identical, identified.
而	er2	1756	And, then, but, nevertheless, also, only. Join and contrasts two words.
異	yi4	3009	Different, unique, separate, strange, extraordinary; a foreigner, a stranger.

Nine at the beginning

Repentance fades. Do not chase the horse that got away.
It will return on its own. You will find bad people,
but you will not make mistakes.

悔	hui3	2336	Repent, regret, contrition; trouble. This word indicates both an objective situation and a subjective reaction to such circumstance.
亡	wang2	7034	Go away, disappear, exile; fail; destroy, perish, not have, not exist.
喪	sang4	5429	Lose, let drop, disappear, destroy, perish, mourning, burial.
馬	ma3	4310	Horse.
勿	wu4	7208	Do not, no. Negative imperative.
逐	zhu2	1383	Chase, run after, hunt; expel, push out; in order, in succession; one by one.
自	zi4	6960	From, origin, source, cause, reason; oneself, yourself.
復	fu4	1992	Return, turn back; repeat, restore, revert, recommence.
見	jian4	0860	See, observe, look at, to be seen; cause to appear; be exposed to, display, reveal; interview, visit or call on, meet.
惡	e4	4809	Evil, bad; ugly; wrong, fault, bad; hate.
人	ren2	3097	Man, person(s); people; others; human being, individual.
无	wu2	7173	No, not, negative; without, does not possess, not have.
咎	jiu4	1192	Fault, blame, mistake, wrong; inauspicious; misfortune, bad luck, calamity; reproach, censure.

Nine in the second place

He meets his master in an alley. No defect.

| 遇 | yu4 | 7625 | Meet, encounter, come across, happen. |
| 主 | zhu3 | 1336 | Master, lord, chief; host, innkeeper. |

Antagonism (207) 38

于	yu2	7592	At, to, in, into, on, from, by, go, go to, move towards, proceed, be.
巷	xiang4	2553	Narrow street, lane, alley.
无	wu2	7173	No, not, negative; without, does not possess, not have.
咎	jiu4	1192	Fault, blame, mistake, wrong; inauspicious; misfortune, bad luck, calamity; reproach, censure.

Six in the third place

He sees his cart pulled back. His oxen and his men arrested, marked and mutilated. There is no [a good] beginning but [a good] end.

見	jian4	0860	See, observe, look at, to be seen; cause to appear; be exposed to; display, reveal; interview, visit or call on, meet.
輿	yu2	7618	Wagon, cart, chariot, carriage; carrier, transport, transportation; carry on the shoulders; contain, hold.
曳	yi4	3008	Drag, haul back; pull.
其	qi2	0525	Their, his, its, the; this, that. A demonstrative and possessive pronoun.
牛	niu2	4737	Cow, bull, ox.
掣	che4	0282	Drag, to trail, to hinder, obstruct.
其	qi2	0525	Their, his, its, the; this, that. A demonstrative and possessive pronoun.
人	ren2	3097	Man, person(s); people; others; human being, individual.
天	tian1	6361	In this place this character doesn't mean "heaven" (as usual), but "brand on forehead, head shaved", which is some kind of punishment designed to humiliate criminals.
且	qie3	0803	And; meanwhile; moreover; also; both; alternatively.
劓	yi4	3013	Cut off nose (as punishment for serious crime).
无	wu2	7173	No, not, negative; without, does not possess, not have.
初	chu1	1390	At first, beginning, initial, incipient, in the early stages.
有	you3	7533	Have, possession, there be, there is.
終	zhong1	1500	End, finish, complete; for ever; end of a cycle; carried to conclusion, consummation, closure; death. The original meaning was: tied-off end of a thread.

Nine in the fourth place

> Isolated by antagonism. One meets an outstanding man, [that can become] a truthful partner. Danger. No defect.

睽	kui2	3660	Diverging, extraordinary; squint (eyes not aligned); opposition, polarization, estrangement.
孤	gu1	3470	Isolated, solitary, alone; fatherless, orphan, without a protector.
遇	yu4	7625	Meet, encounter, come across, happen.
元	yuan2	7707	Outstanding, greatest, sublime, supreme, greatest, very great, grand; source, beginning, cause, first or paramount, fundamentality; head, chief; used as a superlative.
夫	fu1	1908	Man, male adult, husband; this, that, those.
交	jiao1	0702	Union, relation, meeting; exchange, do business; share; contact; have relations with; to hand in or over.
孚	fu2	1936	Truth; reliable, sincere; to inspire confidence in others; capture, prisoner, plunder.
厲	li4	3906	Danger, threat; oppressive, cruel, wicked, brutal, harsh; sickness, malevolent devil; grind, polish, sharpen; discipline.
无	wu2	7173	No, not, negative; without, does not possess, not have.
咎	jiu4	1192	Fault, blame, mistake, wrong; inauspicious; misfortune, bad luck, calamity; reproach, censure.

Six in the fifth place

> Repentance fades. In the temple of the clan they eat meat. How could it be a mistake to go there?

悔	hui3	2336	Repent, regret, contrition; trouble. This word indicates both an objective situation and a subjective reaction to such circumstance.
亡	wang2	7034	Go away, disappear, exile; fail; destroy, perish, not have, not exist.
厥	jue2	1680	Their, his, its.
宗	zong1	6896	Clan, kin, sect, faction, school; ancestor; ancestral temple; ancestral hall.
噬	shi4	5764	Bite, gnaw, snap at, chew.
膚	fu1	1958	Skin, flesh; cut meat, tender meat.
往	wang3	7050	Go, to go to, go forward, go towards; depart, bygone, former.

Antagonism (209)

何	he2	2109	What? how? why? what is? for that reason, therefore.
咎	jiu4	1192	Fault, blame, mistake, wrong; inauspicious; misfortune, bad luck, calamity; reproach, censure.

Nine at the top

Isolated by antagonism. He sees [the other as] a pig covered with mud, a carriage full of demons. First tenses his bow, but then puts it aside. It's not a robber but a marriage suitor. Going forward rain falls. Good fortune.

睽	kui2	3660	Diverging, extraordinary; squint (eyes not aligned); opposition, polarization, estrangement.
孤	gu1	3470	Isolated, solitary, alone; fatherless, orphan, without a protector.
見	jian4	0860	See, observe, look at, to be seen; cause to appear; be exposed to, display, reveal; interview, visit or call on, meet.
豕	shi3	5766	Pig, boar, swine. Symbol of wealth and luck.
負	fu4	1956	Bear, carry, carry in the back, to shoulder, to carry a burden; covered, caked with.
塗	tu2	6525	Dirt, mud; mire, plaster, smear.
載	zai4	6653	Transport, carry, load, bear; contain, sustain; load a vessel or cart, conveyance.
鬼	gui3	3634	*Gui* tribe (enemies of the *Zhou*), barbarians; ghosts, foreign devils, demons, disembodied spirits, goblins, ghouls.
一	yi1	3016	One, number one.
車	che1	0280	Chariot, wagon, cart, carriage.
先	xian1	2702	Before, first, foremost, in front, lead.
張	zhang1	0195	Draw taut (a bow), string the bow; stretch, extend. Has many other related meanings but only the previous ones are pertinent.
之	zhi1	0935	Personal pronoun, he she, it; this, that, these, etc.; often used as a possessive.
弧	hu2	2184	Bow (it is the only meaning used in the YiJing); bend, curved. It means the long wooden bow used for war and hunting.
後	hou4	2143	Later, behind, rear, afterward, come after; follow; descendants, successor.
說	tuo1	5939	Remove, take off, come off, let loose.

之	zhi1	0935	Personal pronoun, he she, it; this, that, these, etc.; often used as a possessive.
弧	hu2	2184	Bow (it is the only meaning used in the YiJing); bend, curved. It means the long wooden bow used for war and hunting.
匪	fei3	1820	No, strong negative.
寇	kou4	3444	Bandit, invader, enemy, robber, violent people, outcasts, plunderers.
婚	hun1	2360	Marriage, take a wife; bridegroom, ally.
媾	gou4	3426	Marriage, a second marriage, mating, match, families united by marriage; suitor, groom; allying, friendship, favor.
往	wang3	7050	Go, to go to, go forward, go towards; depart, bygone, former.
遇	yu4	7625	Meet, encounter, come across, happen.
雨	yu3	7662	Rain, shower, sudden downpour.
則	ze2	6746	Then, thus, accordingly, consequently, and so, in that case; law, rule, pattern; follow a law.
吉	ji2	0476	Good fortune, auspicious, promising, fortunate, lucky, advantageous, happiness, good auspices. It is the only single character meaning good luck in the *YiJing*.

39 蹇 *jian* – Hampered / Obstruction

THE JUDGMENT

Hampered. The South-West [withdrawal] is favorable, the North-East [going forward] is not advantageous. It is favorable to see the great man. Determination brings good fortune.

蹇	jian3	0843	Hobble, stumble, limp, proceed haltingly; impasse, obstruction, impediment, obstacle, troubles, difficulties.
利	li4	3867	Favorable, lucky, advantageous, profitable, beneficial, furthering, harvesting; sharp, sharp witted.
西	xi1	2460	The West, western. Related to the autumn.
南	nan2	4620	The South. The region associated with Summer, fire, work in community and vegetation. Here the South-West indicates withdrawal or return.
不	bu4	5379	No, not, negative prefix; without, none, nothing, will not, need not, will not be.
利	li4	3867	Favorable, lucky, advantageous, profitable, beneficial, furthering, harvesting; sharp, sharp witted.
東	dong1	6605	The East.
北	bei3	4974	The North. The character depicts two persons standing, back to back. In China, the north has traditionally been considered the "back side". Maps shown the south on top.
利	li4	3867	Favorable, lucky, advantageous, profitable, beneficial, furthering, harvesting; sharp, sharp witted.
見	jian4	0860	See, observe, look at, to be seen; cause to appear; be exposed to, display, reveal; interview, visit or call on, meet.
大	da4	5943	Big, great, tall; excessive, arrogant; spread out and reach everywhere.
人	ren2	3097	Man, person(s); people; others; human being, individual.
貞	zhen1	0346	Perseverance, persistence, determination, steadiness, firmness; straight, correct, verified, certain; pure, loyal. Its original meaning was "to determine an uncertain matter through divination".
吉	ji2	0476	Good fortune, auspicious, promising, fortunate, lucky, advantageous, happiness, good auspices. It is the only single character meaning good luck in the *YiJing*.

The Image

Above the Mountain there is Water: The image of Hampered.
Thus the noble goes back to himself to cultivate his nature.

山	shan1	5630	Mountain, hill, peak.
上	shang4	5669	Up, above, on, over, upwards, top, rise; higher, superior; first, best.
有	you3	7533	Have, possession, there be, there is.
水	shui3	5922	Water, river, stream, flood, liquid, fluid.
蹇	jian3	0843	Hobble, stumble, limp, proceed haltingly; impasse, obstruction, impediment, obstacle, troubles, difficulties.
君	jun1	1715	Noble, prince, aristocrat, lord, chief, gentleman; honorable, a highly principled person, superior man. Most times, this character appears alongside another one, forming the word *JunZi*, whose original meaning was "son of a prince or ruler": 君子.
子	zi3	6939	Child, son or daughter, offspring; suffix; bride, wife; gentleman, officer, master, prince; young lady; the first of the *Earthly Branches*.
以	yi3	2932	Thus, in that way, by means of, with, for; instrument, medium, method, use (of), way (to).
反	fan3	1781	Turn, reverse, come back, return.
身	shen1	5718	Body, trunk, torso, person, psyche, oneself, lifespan; pregnant woman.
脩	xiu1	2795	This character means "dried meat", but in the *YiJing* is used as a loan for 修 and hence takes its meaning: cultivate, put in order, arrange, repair, elaborate.
德	de2	6162	Virtue, spiritual power, moral integrity; quality, nature, aptitude, ability, character.

Six at the beginning

Going forward is Hampered, going back brings praise.

往	wang3	7050	Go, to go to, go forward, go towards; depart, bygone, former.
蹇	jian3	0843	Hobble, stumble, limp, proceed haltingly; impasse, obstruction, impediment, obstacle, troubles, difficulties.
來	lai2	3768	Come, arrive, return, bring.
譽	yu4	7617	Fame, renown, reputation, honor, honored, praised.

Hampered (213) 39

Six in the second place

> The King's servant [is struggling with] difficulties.
> Not because of himself.

王	wang2	7037	King, prince, sovereign, ruler.
臣	chen2	0327	Servant, retainer, vassal, statesman, officer; male slave, male bondservant or may be a slave couple.
蹇	jian3	0843	Hobble, stumble, limp, proceed haltingly; impasse, obstruction, impediment, obstacle, troubles, difficulties.
蹇	jian3	0843	Hobble, stumble, limp, proceed haltingly; impasse, obstruction, impediment, obstacle, troubles, difficulties.
匪	fei3	1820	No, strong negative.
躬	gong1	3704	Oneself, (own) body, person.
之	zhi1	0935	Personal pronoun, he she, it; this, that, these, etc.; often used as a possessive.
故	gu4	3455	Cause, reason; because of, come before as a cause; purpose.

Nine in the third place

> Going forward is Hampered. He comes back.

往	wang3	7050	Go, to go to, go forward, go towards; depart, bygone, former.
蹇	jian3	0843	Hobble, stumble, limp, proceed haltingly; impasse, obstruction, impediment, obstacle, troubles, difficulties.
來	lai2	3768	Come, arrive, return, bring.
反	fan3	1781	Turn, reverse, come back, return.

Six in the fourth place

> Going forward is Hampered. Coming back meets companions.

往	wang3	7050	Go, to go to, go forward, go towards; depart, bygone, former.
蹇	jian3	0843	Hobble, stumble, limp, proceed haltingly; impasse, obstruction, impediment, obstacle, troubles, difficulties.
來	lai2	3768	Come, arrive, return, bring.
連	lian2	4009	Union, alliance, connection; a kind of carriage, travel or carry on a carriage; toilsome, difficult, slow.

Nine in the fifth place
When the obstruction is greater, friends will come over.

大	da4	5943	Big, great, tall; excessive, arrogant; spread out and reach everywhere.
蹇	jian3	0843	Hobble, stumble, limp, proceed haltingly; impasse, obstruction, impediment, obstacle, troubles, difficulties.
朋	peng2	5054	Friend, companion, pair, equal, comrade; a string of cowries (small shiny shells used as coins in ancient China).
來	lai2	3768	Come, arrive, return, bring.

Six at the top
Going forward is Hampered, coming back brings great good fortune. It is favorable to see the great man.

往	wang3	7050	Go, to go to, go forward, go towards; depart, bygone, former.
蹇	jian3	0843	Hobble, stumble, limp, proceed haltingly; impasse, obstruction, impediment, obstacle, troubles, difficulties.
來	lai2	3768	Come, arrive, return, bring.
碩	shuo4	5815	Large, great, stately, eminent, ripe, full grown, maturity.
吉	ji2	0476	Good fortune, auspicious, promising, fortunate, lucky, advantageous, happiness, good auspices. It is the only single character meaning good luck in the *YiJing*.
利	li4	3867	Favorable, lucky, advantageous, profitable, beneficial, furthering, harvesting; sharp, sharp witted.
見	jian4	0860	See, observe, look at, to be seen; cause to appear; be exposed to, display, reveal; interview, visit or call on, meet.
大	da4	5943	Big, great, tall; excessive, arrogant; spread out and reach everywhere.
人	ren2	3097	Man, person(s); people; others; human being, individual.

40 解 *jie* – Liberation

THE JUDGMENT

Liberation. The South-West [going home] is favorable.
If there is no where to go [nothing to do] return brings good fortune.
If there is somewhere to go [to undertake something],
to be early brings good fortune.

解	jie3	0626	Deliver, deliverance; untie, loosen, divide; untangle; disjoin.
利	li4	3867	Favorable, lucky, advantageous, profitable, beneficial, furthering, harvesting; sharp, sharp witted.
西	xi1	2460	The West, western. Related to the autumn.
南	nan2	4620	The South. The region associated with Summer, fire, work in community and vegetation. Here South-West indicates returning home.
无	wu2	7173	No, not, negative; without, does not possess, not have.
所	suo3	5465	That which, place, location, residence, dwelling; reason, a cause, whereby; function, position, role; habitual focus or object.
往	wang3	7050	Go, to go to, go forward, go towards; depart, bygone, former.
其	qi2	0525	Their, his, its, the; this, that. A demonstrative and possessive pronoun.
來	lai2	3768	Come, arrive, return, bring.
復	fu4	1992	Return, turn back; repeat, restore, revert, recommence.
吉	ji2	0476	Good fortune, auspicious, promising, fortunate, lucky, advantageous, happiness, good auspices. It is the only single character meaning good luck in the *YiJing*.
有	you3	7533	Have, possession, there be, there is.
攸	you1	7519	Goal, direction, destination, objective; distant, far away; a place; that which, whereby, thereby, for which; mark of the passive voice.
往	wang3	7050	Go, to go to, go forward, go towards; depart, bygone, former. 攸往: have a place to go; have a goal.
夙	su4	5502	Early, soon, eager; early in the morning, after dawn.
吉	ji2	0476	Good fortune, auspicious, promising, fortunate, lucky, advantageous, happiness, good auspices. It is the only single character meaning good luck in the *YiJing*.

The Image

> Thunder and Rain in action: The image of Liberation.
> Thus the noble forgives excesses and excuses offenses.

雷	lei2	4236	Thunder, shock, terrifying, arousing power surging from the earth.
雨	yu3	7662	Rain, shower, sudden downpour.
作	zuo4	6780	Act, do, make, work, perform; rise, stand up, get to work; project, undertaking, ceremony, to sacrifice.
解	jie3	0626	Deliver, deliverance; untie, loosen, divide; untangle; disjoin.
君	jun1	1715	Noble, prince, aristocrat, lord, chief, gentleman; honorable, a highly principled person, superior man. Most times, this character appears alongside another one, forming the word *JunZi*, whose original meaning was "son of a prince or ruler": 君子.
子	zi3	6939	Child, son or daughter, offspring; suffix; bride, wife; gentleman, officer, master, prince; young lady; the first of the *Earthly Branches*.
以	yi3	2932	Thus, in that way, by means of, with, for; instrument, medium, method, use (of), way (to).
赦	she4	5702	Forgive, pardon, liberate, let go.
過	guo4	3730	Pass, pass through, go across, go beyond, excess, beyond the ordinary or proper limit; ; transgression, fault.
宥	you4	7536	Pardon, lenient, indulgent, to forgive; to be large minded.
罪	zui4	6860	Crime, offense, misdeed, wrongdoing, sin.

Six at the beginning

> No defect.

无	wu2	7173	No, not, negative; without, does not possess, not have.
咎	jiu4	1192	Fault, blame, mistake, wrong; inauspicious; misfortune, bad luck, calamity; reproach, censure.

Nine in the second place

> One catches three foxes in the hunt and receives a yellow arrow.
> Determination brings good fortune.

田	tian2	6362	Field, cultivated land; hunt. The character is the picture of a cultivated field, divided in four sectors.

LIBERATION (217) 40

獲	huo4	2412	Catch (in hunt), seize, get, obtain, hit the mark, find; succeed. What is caught, gotten or found may be a thing, a person, an opportunity, an idea or perception. 田獲: to catch a prey in hunting.
三	san1	5415	Three, thrice, third time or place.
狐	hu2	2185	Fox, foxes.
得	de2	6161	Get, obtain, gain; reach, achieve; can; attain the desired thing.
黃	huang2	2297	Yellow, yellow-brown; color of the soil in central China. In the *YiJing* the yellow color is always favorable, it is the color of the middle and the moderation and it was the imperial color since the *Han* dynasty.
矢	shi3	5784	Arrow.
貞	zhen1	0346	Perseverance, persistence, determination, steadiness, firmness; straight, correct, verified, certain; pure, loyal. Its original meaning was "to determine an uncertain matter through divination".
吉	ji2	0476	Good fortune, auspicious, promising, fortunate, lucky, advantageous, happiness, good auspices. It is the only single character meaning good luck in the *YiJing*.

Six in the third place

One who bears a burden on his back but rides on a carriage attracts bandits. The determination is humiliating.

負	fu4	1956	Bear, carry, carry in the back, to shoulder, to carry a burden; covered, caked with.
且	qie3	0803	And; meanwhile; moreover; also; both; alternatively.
乘	cheng2	0398	Ride, mount, ascend, climb up (13.4).
致	zhi4	0984	Bring about, cause; involve, induce; present, offer, hand over; send, transmit; extend, apply; carry on to the limit.
寇	kou4	3444	Bandit, invader, enemy, robber, violent people, outcasts, plunderers.
至	zhi4	0982	Arrive, culminate, reach the highest point, utmost, superlative.
貞	zhen1	0346	Perseverance, persistence, determination, steadiness, firmness; straight, correct, verified, certain; pure, loyal. Its original meaning was "to determine an uncertain matter through divination".
吝	lin4	4040	Humiliation, regret, shame, distress, grief, sorrow; miserly, niggardly. It is a warning of trouble.

Nine in the fourth place

Free yourself from your big toe. Then a trusty companion will come.

解	jie3	0626	Deliver, deliverance; untie, loosen, divide; untangle; disjoin.
而	er2	1756	And, then, but, nevertheless, also, only. Join and contrasts two words.
拇	mu3	4584	Big toe or thumb; in the first line it means big toe, since the first line is related with the feet, but in the upper trigram it means big thumb.
朋	peng2	5054	Friend, companion, pair, equal, comrade; a string of cowries (small shiny shells used as coins in ancient China).
至	zhi4	0982	Arrive, culminate, reach the highest point, utmost, superlative.
斯	si1	5574	Then, this, thereupon, so, thus; cleave, tear apart.
孚	fu2	1936	Truth; reliable, sincere; to inspire confidence in others; capture, prisoner, plunder.

Six in the fifth place

Only the noble can have Liberation. Good fortune.
Inferior people trust him.

君	jun1	1715	Noble, prince, aristocrat, lord, chief, gentleman; honorable, a highly principled person, superior man. Most times, this character appears alongside another one, forming the word *JunZi*, whose original meaning was "son of a prince or ruler": 君子.
子	zi3	6939	Child, son or daughter, offspring; suffix; bride, wife; gentleman, officer, master, prince; young lady; the first of the *Earthly Branches*.
維	wei2	7067	Tie up, bound, bind together; guiding rope of a net; guiding principle, rule; but only.
有	you3	7533	Have, possession, there be, there is.
解	jie3	0626	Deliver, deliverance; untie, loosen, divide; untangle; disjoin.
吉	ji2	0476	Good fortune, auspicious, promising, fortunate, lucky, advantageous, happiness, good auspices. It is the only single character meaning good luck in the *YiJing*.
有	you3	7533	Have, possession, there be, there is.
孚	fu2	1936	Truth; reliable, sincere; to inspire confidence in others; capture, prisoner, plunder.

Liberation (219) 40

于	yu2	7592	At, to, in, into, on, from, by, go, go to, move towards, proceed, be.
小	xiao3	2605	Small, insignificant, common, humble, mediocre; diminish, belittle.
人	ren2	3097	Man, person(s); people; others; human being, individual.

Six at the top

The prince shoots at a hawk on a high wall and hits the target. Nothing that is not favorable.

公	gong1	3701	Prince, feudal lord, duke, noble of rank; public, impartial, with justice, fair.
用	yong4	7567	Use, apply, put to use, apply the oracle to real world situations; hereby, thereby.
射	she4	5703	Shoot with a bow; aim and hit the target.
隼	sun3	1487	Hawk, bird of prey.
于	yu2	7592	At, to, in, into, on, from, by, go, go to, move towards, proceed, be.
高	gao1	3290	High, elevated, exalted, eminent, lofty, illustrious, higher.
墉	yong1	7578	Wall, a fortified wall, defensive wall.
之	zhi1	0935	Personal pronoun, he she, it; this, that, these, etc.; often used as a possessive.
上	shang4	5669	Up, above, on, over, upwards, top, rise; higher, superior; first, best.
獲	huo4	2412	Catch (in hunt), seize, get, obtain, hit the mark, find; succeed. What is caught, gotten or found may be a thing, a person, an opportunity, an idea or perception.
之	zhi1	0935	Personal pronoun, he she, it; this, that, these, etc.; often used as a possessive.
无	wu2	7173	No, not, negative; without, does not possess, not have.
不	bu4	5379	No, not, negative prefix; without, none, nothing, will not, need not, will not be.
利	li4	3867	Favorable, lucky, advantageous, profitable, beneficial, furthering, harvesting; sharp, sharp witted.

41 損 *sun* – Decrease

THE JUDGMENT

Decrease with sincerity brings outstanding good fortune. No defect. Satisfactory determination. It is favorable to have a goal. What should be done? Two bowls can be used for the offering.

損	sun3	5548	Decrease, diminish, lessen; damage, injure.
有	you3	7533	Have, possession, there be, there is.
孚	fu2	1936	Truth; reliable, sincere; to inspire confidence in others; capture, prisoner, plunder.
元	yuan2	7707	Outstanding, greatest, sublime, supreme, greatest, very great, grand; source, beginning, cause, first or paramount, fundamentality; head, chief; used as a superlative.
吉	ji2	0476	Good fortune, auspicious, promising, fortunate, lucky, advantageous, happiness, good auspices. It is the only single character meaning good luck in the *YiJing*.
无	wu2	7173	No, not, negative; without, does not possess, not have.
咎	jiu4	1192	Fault, blame, mistake, wrong; inauspicious; misfortune, bad luck, calamity; reproach, censure.
可	ke3	3381	Can, able, may; permit, allow; satisfactory, proper, suitable.
貞	zhen1	0346	Perseverance, persistence, determination, steadiness, firmness; straight, correct, verified, certain; pure, loyal. Its original meaning was "to determine an uncertain matter through divination".
利	li4	3867	Favorable, lucky, advantageous, profitable, beneficial, furthering, harvesting; sharp, sharp witted.
有	you3	7533	Have, possession, there be, there is.
攸	you1	7519	Goal, direction, destination, objective; distant, far away; a place; that which, whereby, thereby, for which; mark of the passive voice.
往	wang3	7050	Go, to go to, go forward, go towards; depart, bygone, former. 攸往: have a place to go; have a goal.
曷	he2	2122	How? what? where? when? why? why not?

Decrease (221) 41

之	zhi1	0935	Personal pronoun, he she, it; this, that, these, etc.; often used as a possessive.
用	yong4	7567	Use, apply, put to use, apply the oracle to real world situations; hereby, thereby.
二	er4	1751	Two, twice, the second, to divide en two, dual.
簋	gui3	3633	Bowl, square basket of bamboo, tureen of rice, small or plain rice basket; a kind of vessel or basked used at sacrifices.
可	ke3	3381	Can, able, may; permit, allow; satisfactory, proper, suitable.
用	yong4	7567	Use, apply, put to use, apply the oracle to real world situations; hereby, thereby.
享	xiang3	2552	Sacrifice, offering to a god or a superior; consecrate; treat.

The Image

Down the Mountain is the Lake: The image of Decrease.
Thus the noble controls his anger and restrains his passions.

山	shan1	5630	Mountain, hill, peak.
下	xia4	2520	Below, down, descend.
有	you3	7533	Have, possession, there be, there is.
澤	ze2	0277	Marsh, pool, pond, lake; flat body of water and the vapors rising from it; enrich, fertilize, benefit; moist, moisten; glossy, polished.
損	sun3	5548	Decrease, diminish, lessen; damage, injure.
君	jun1	1715	Noble, prince, aristocrat, lord, chief, gentleman; honorable, a highly principled person, superior man. Most times, this character appears alongside another one, forming the word *JunZi*, whose original meaning was "son of a prince or ruler": 君子.
子	zi3	6939	Child, son or daughter, offspring; suffix; bride, wife; gentleman, officer, master, prince; young lady; the first of the *Earthly Branches*.
以	yi3	2932	Thus, in that way, by means of, with, for; instrument, medium, method, use (of), way (to).
懲	cheng2	0384	Restrain, curb; correct, chastise, reprimand, corrective punishment; a warning.
忿	fen4	1854	Anger, fury, resentment, exasperation.
窒	zhi4	0994	Obstruct, block, restrain; block-headed; frightened.
欲	yu4	7671	Desire, wish, expectation, longing; lust, passion.

Nine at the beginning

> There is no defect if after finishing your work you go quickly,
> but think about how much you can decrease [sacrifice] yourself.

巳	si4	5590	6th earthly branch. The period from 9.00 a.m. to 11.00 a.m. Usually it is replaced with other characters:
事	shi4	5787	Serve, service; affairs, business, matters.
遄	chuan2	1444	Quickly, hurry, rapid, rushed, with dispatch.
往	wang3	7050	Go, to go to, go forward, go towards; depart, bygone, former.
无	wu2	7173	No, not, negative; without, does not possess, not have.
咎	jiu4	1192	Fault, blame, mistake, wrong; inauspicious; misfortune, bad luck, calamity; reproach, censure.
酌	zhuo2	1257	Consider, think about, deliberate, consult; pour out wine in a cup.
損	sun3	5548	Decrease, diminish, lessen; damage, injure.
之	zhi1	0935	Personal pronoun, he she, it; this, that, these, etc.; often used as a possessive.

Nine in the second place

> The determination is favorable.
> Going forward with violence brings misfortune.
> Without loss one may increase [the other].

利	li4	3867	Favorable, lucky, advantageous, profitable, beneficial, furthering, harvesting; sharp, sharp witted.
貞	zhen1	0346	Perseverance, persistence, determination, steadiness, firmness; straight, correct, verified, certain; pure, loyal. Its original meaning was "to determine an uncertain matter through divination".
征	zheng1	0352	Punishing expedition ("to correct"), to reduce to submission, attack, punish; to levy taxes; comes, brings.
凶	xiong1	2808	Misfortune, pitfall, ominous, bad, unlucky, disastrous, trouble, accident.
弗	fu2	1981	Not (not able or not willing to), negative.
損	sun3	5548	Decrease, diminish, lessen; damage, injure.
益	yi4	3052	Increase, augment; more; benefit, profit, advantage.
之	zhi1	0935	Personal pronoun, he she, it; this, that, these, etc.; often used as a possessive.

Decrease

Six in the third place

> Three man walking along the road together are decreased,
> but one man walking [alone] gains a companion.

三	san1	5415	Three, thrice, third time or place.
人	ren2	3097	Man, person(s); people; others; human being, individual.
行	xing2	2754	Move, go, advance, act, do.
則	ze2	6746	Then, thus, accordingly, consequently, and so, in that case; law, rule, pattern; follow a law.
損	sun3	5548	Decrease, diminish, lessen; damage, injure.
一	yi1	3016	One, number one.
人	ren2	3097	Man, person(s); people; others; human being, individual.
一	yi1	3016	One, number one.
人	ren2	3097	Man, person(s); people; others; human being, individual.
行	xing2	2754	Move, go, advance, act, do.
則	ze2	6746	Then, thus, accordingly, consequently, and so, in that case; law, rule, pattern; follow a law.
得	de2	6161	Get, obtain, gain; reach, achieve; can; attain the desired thing.
其	qi2	0525	Their, his, its, the; this, that. A demonstrative and possessive pronoun.
友	you3	7540	Companion, friend, associate, partner, couple, boy/girl friend.

Six in the fourth place

> As a result of reducing his anxiety, he will have joy quickly.
> No defect.

損	sun3	5548	Decrease, diminish, lessen; damage, injure.
其	qi2	0525	Their, his, its, the; this, that. A demonstrative and possessive pronoun.
疾	ji2	0492	Ill, harm, defect, stress; hurry; hate.
使	shi3	5770	Send on a mission, order, cause, envoy, messenger, ambassador, agent.
遄	chuan2	1444	Quickly, hurry, rapid, rushed, with dispatch.
有	you3	7533	Have, possession, there be, there is.

喜	xi3	2434	Pleasure, joy, happiness, gratification, delight.
无	wu2	7173	No, not, negative; without, does not possess, not have.
咎	jiu4	1192	Fault, blame, mistake, wrong; inauspicious; misfortune, bad luck, calamity; reproach, censure.

Six in the fifth place

> Someone increases him by ten pairs of tortoise shells.
> Nobody can resist. Outstanding happiness.

或	huo4	2402	Perhaps, possibly, if, by chance; doubtful, uncertain; some, someone, something, sometime.
益	yi4	3052	Increase, augment; more; benefit, profit, advantage.
之	zhi1	0935	Personal pronoun, he she, it; this, that, these, etc.; often used as a possessive.
十	shi2	5807	Ten; complete, perfect, whole.
朋	peng2	5054	Friend, companion, pair, equal, comrade; a string of cowries (small shiny shells used as coins in ancient China).
之	zhi1	0935	Personal pronoun, he she, it; this, that, these, etc.; often used as a possessive.
龜	gui1	3621	Turtle, symbol of longevity.
弗	fu2	1981	Not (not able or not willing to), negative.
克	ke4	3320	Can, able, carry, sustain; conquest, dominate, prevail.
違	wei2	7093	Oppose, go against; disobey, disregard, refuse; go away, leave; deviate from; error; perverse.
元	yuan2	7707	Outstanding, greatest, sublime, supreme, greatest, very great, grand; source, beginning, cause, first or paramount, fundamentality; head, chief; used as a superlative.
吉	ji2	0476	Good fortune, auspicious, promising, fortunate, lucky, advantageous, happiness, good auspices. It is the only single character meaning good luck in the YiJing.

Nine at the top

> There is no decrease but increase. No defect.
> The determination brings good fortune. It is favorable to have a goal.
> One gets servants but not a household.

弗	fu2	1981	Not (not able or not willing to), negative.
損	sun3	5548	Decrease, diminish, lessen; damage, injure.
益	yi4	3052	Increase, augment; more; benefit, profit, advantage.

Decrease 41

之	zhi1	0935	Personal pronoun, he she, it; this, that, these, etc.; often used as a possessive.
无	wu2	7173	No, not, negative; without, does not possess, not have.
咎	jiu4	1192	Fault, blame, mistake, wrong; inauspicious; misfortune, bad luck, calamity; reproach, censure.
貞	zhen1	0346	Perseverance, persistence, determination, steadiness, firmness; straight, correct, verified, certain; pure, loyal. Its original meaning was "to determine an uncertain matter through divination".
吉	ji2	0476	Good fortune, auspicious, promising, fortunate, lucky, advantageous, happiness, good auspices. It is the only single character meaning good luck in the *YiJing*.
利	li4	3867	Favorable, lucky, advantageous, profitable, beneficial, furthering, harvesting; sharp, sharp witted.
有	you3	7533	Have, possession, there be, there is.
攸	you1	7519	Goal, direction, destination, objective; distant, far away; a place; that which, whereby, thereby, for which; mark of the passive voice.
往	wang3	7050	Go, to go to, go forward, go towards; depart, bygone, former. 攸往: have a place to go; have a goal.
得	de2	6161	Get, obtain, gain; reach, achieve; can; attain the desired thing.
臣	chen2	0327	Servant, retainer, vassal, statesman, officer; male slave, male bondservant or may be a slave couple.
无	wu2	7173	No, not, negative; without, does not possess, not have.
家	jia1	0594	Family, household, clan; home, to keep a home.

42 益 yi – Increase

The Judgment

> Increase. It is favorable to have a goal.
> It is favorable to cross the great river.

益	yi4	3052	Increase, augment; more; benefit, profit, advantage.
利	li4	3867	Favorable, lucky, advantageous, profitable, beneficial, furthering, harvesting; sharp, sharp witted.
有	you3	7533	Have, possession, there be, there is.
攸	you1	7519	Goal, direction, destination, objective; distant, far away; a place; that which, whereby, thereby, for which; mark of the passive voice.
往	wang3	7050	Go, to go to, go forward, go towards; depart, bygone, former. 攸往: have a place to go; have a goal.
利	li4	3867	Favorable, lucky, advantageous, profitable, beneficial, furthering, harvesting; sharp, sharp witted.
涉	she4	5707	Cross, wade across (a river, stream), ford, pass through or over.
大	da4	5943	Big, great, tall; excessive, arrogant; spread out and reach everywhere.
川	chuan1	1439	River, flowing water; flood.

The Image

> Wind and Thunder: The image of Increase.
> Thus when the noble sees the good changes [imitates it];
> and if he has defects he corrects them.

風	feng1	1890	Wind, breath, air; manners, atmosphere.
雷	lei2	4236	Thunder, shock, terrifying, arousing power surging from the earth.
益	yi4	3052	Increase, augment; more; benefit, profit, advantage.

Increase (227) 42

君	jun1	1715	Noble, prince, aristocrat, lord, chief, gentleman; honorable, a highly principled person, superior man. Most times, this character appears alongside another one, forming the word *JunZi*, whose original meaning was "son of a prince or ruler": 君子.
子	zi3	6939	Child, son or daughter, offspring; suffix; bride, wife; gentleman, officer, master, prince; young lady; the first of the *Earthly Branches*.
以	yi3	2932	Thus, in that way, by means of, with, for; instrument, medium, method, use (of), way (to).
見	jian4	0860	See, observe, look at, to be seen; cause to appear; be exposed to, display, reveal; interview, visit or call on, meet.
善	shan4	5657	Good, virtuous; perfect, improve.
則	ze2	6746	Then, thus, accordingly, consequently, and so, in that case; law, rule, pattern; follow a law.
遷	qian1	0911	Move, remove, shift, change, transfer; promotion or change of position or job.
有	you3	7533	Have, possession, there be, there is.
過	guo4	3730	Pass, pass through, go across, go beyond, excess, beyond the ordinary or proper limit; ; transgression, fault.
則	ze2	6746	Then, thus, accordingly, consequently, and so, in that case; law, rule, pattern; follow a law.
改	gai3	3196	Change, reform, correct, amend.

Nine at the beginning

It is favorable to begin great endeavors.
Outstanding good fortune. No defect.

利	li4	3867	Favorable, lucky, advantageous, profitable, beneficial, furthering, harvesting; sharp, sharp witted.
用	yong4	7567	Use, apply, put to use, apply the oracle to real world situations; hereby, thereby.
爲	wei2	7059	Act, do, accomplish, make, to be; act for, stand for, support, help; become.
大	da4	5943	Big, great, tall; excessive, arrogant; spread out and reach everywhere.
作	zuo4	6780	Act, do, make, work, perform; rise, stand up, get to work; project, undertaking, ceremony, to sacrifice.
元	yuan2	7707	Outstanding, greatest, sublime, supreme, greatest, very great, grand; source, beginning, cause, first or paramount, fundamentality; head, chief; used as a superlative.

吉	ji2	0476	Good fortune, auspicious, promising, fortunate, lucky, advantageous, happiness, good auspices. It is the only single character meaning good luck in the *YiJing*.
无	wu2	7173	No, not, negative; without, does not possess, not have.
咎	jiu4	1192	Fault, blame, mistake, wrong; inauspicious; misfortune, bad luck, calamity; reproach, censure.

Six in the second place

Someone increases him by ten pairs of tortoise shells. Nobody can resist. Long-term determination brings good fortune. Used by the King in an offering to the Divine Ruler. Good fortune.

或	huo4	2402	Perhaps, possibly, if, by chance; doubtful, uncertain; some, someone, something, sometime.
益	yi4	3052	Increase, augment; more; benefit, profit, advantage.
之	zhi1	0935	Personal pronoun, he she, it; this, that, these, etc.; often used as a possessive.
十	shi2	5807	Ten; complete, perfect, whole.
朋	peng2	5054	Friend, companion, pair, equal, comrade; a string of cowries (small shiny shells used as coins in ancient China).
之	zhi1	0935	Personal pronoun, he she, it; this, that, these, etc.; often used as a possessive.
龜	gui1	3621	Turtle, symbol of longevity.
弗	fu2	1981	Not (not able or not willing to), negative.
克	ke4	3320	Can, able, carry, sustain; conquest, dominate, prevail.
違	wei2	7093	Oppose, go against; disobey, disregard, refuse; go away, leave; deviate from; error; perverse.
永	yong3	7589	For a long time, constant, permanent, everlasting; prolong; distant, far reaching.
貞	zhen1	0346	Perseverance, persistence, determination, steadiness, firmness; straight, correct, verified, certain; pure, loyal. Its original meaning was "to determine an uncertain matter through divination".
吉	ji2	0476	Good fortune, auspicious, promising, fortunate, lucky, advantageous, happiness, good auspices. It is the only single character meaning good luck in the *YiJing*.
王	wang2	7037	King, prince, sovereign, ruler.

Increase

用	yong4	7567	Use, apply, put to use, apply the oracle to real world situations; hereby, thereby.
享	xiang3	2552	Sacrifice, offering to a god or a superior; consecrate; treat.
于	yu2	7592	At, to, in, into, on, from, by, go, go to, move towards, proceed, be.
帝	di4	6204	Sovereign, emperor, god.
吉	ji2	0476	Good fortune, auspicious, promising, fortunate, lucky, advantageous, happiness, good auspices. It is the only single character meaning good luck in the *YiJing*.

Six in the third place

Increased by unfortunate events. If your service is sincere there is no defect. Walk in the middle and report to the Prince with a credential.

益	yi4	3052	Increase, augment; more; benefit, profit, advantage.
之	zhi1	0935	Personal pronoun, he she, it; this, that, these, etc.; often used as a possessive.
用	yong4	7567	Use, apply, put to use, apply the oracle to real world situations; hereby, thereby.
凶	xiong1	2808	Misfortune, pitfall, ominous, bad, unlucky, disastrous, trouble, accident.
事	shi4	5787	Serve, service; affairs, business, matters.
无	wu2	7173	No, not, negative; without, does not possess, not have.
咎	jiu4	1192	Fault, blame, mistake, wrong; inauspicious; misfortune, bad luck, calamity; reproach, censure.
有	you3	7533	Have, possession, there be, there is.
孚	fu2	1936	Truth; reliable, sincere; to inspire confidence in others; capture, prisoner, plunder.
中	zhong1	1504	Center, inner, in the inside, put in the center, hit (target); balanced, central, middle, correct.
行	xing2	2754	Move, go, advance, act, do.
告	gao4	3287	Inform, announce, report, proclaim.
公	gong1	3701	Prince, feudal lord, duke, noble of rank (the nobiliary titles, from high to low, were: duke, marquis, count, viscount, baron); public, impartial, with justice, fair.
用	yong4	7567	Use, apply, put to use, apply the oracle to real world situations; hereby, thereby.
圭	gui1	3609	Jade tablet or baton as token of rank; official seal, seal of office. It was conferrer by the king in official ceremonies and its size and shape varied with the rank.

Six in the fourth place

> If you walk i the middle and report to the Prince,
> he will follow [your advice].
> It is favorable to be assigned to relocate the capital.

中	zhong1	1504	Center, inner, in the inside, put in the center, hit (target); balanced, central, middle, correct.
行	xing2	2754	Move, go, advance, act, do.
告	gao4	3287	Inform, announce, report, proclaim.
公	gong1	3701	Prince, feudal lord, duke, noble of rank (the nobiliary titles, from high to low, were: duke, marquis, count, viscount, baron); public, impartial, with justice, fair.
從	cong2	6919	Follow (somebody or a way or doctrine), adhere, obey, pursue; follower attendant; attend to business; from, by, since, whence, through.
利	li4	3867	Favorable, lucky, advantageous, profitable, beneficial, furthering, harvesting; sharp, sharp witted.
用	yong4	7567	Use, apply, put to use, apply the oracle to real world situations; hereby, thereby.
爲	wei2	7059	Act, do, accomplish, make, to be; act for, stand for, support, help; become.
依	yi1	2990	Depend on, lean upon; accord with, obey; trust.
遷	qian1	0911	Move, remove, shift, change, transfer; promotion or change of position or job.
國	guo2	3738	State, country, nation, kingdom, a dynasty; capital city.

Nine in the fifth place

> If you have a sincere and kind heart you do not need to ask.
> Outstanding good fortune.
> Your sincerity will be favored with spiritual power.

有	you3	7533	Have, possession, there be, there is.
孚	fu2	1936	Truth; reliable, sincere; to inspire confidence in others; capture, prisoner, plunder.
惠	hui4	2339	Kindness, benevolence; favor, benefit; affectionate; gracious.
心	xin1	2735	Heart; conscience, moral nature; soul; core; mind; source of feelings, intentions, will.
勿	wu4	7208	Do not, no. Negative imperative.
問	wen4	7141	Ask, make inquiries, interrogate, question.

INCREASE (231) 42

元	yuan2	7707	Outstanding, greatest, sublime, supreme, greatest, very great, grand; source, beginning, cause, first or paramount, fundamentality; head, chief; used as a superlative.
吉	ji2	0476	Good fortune, auspicious, promising, fortunate, lucky, advantageous, happiness, good auspices. It is the only single character meaning good luck in the *YiJing*.
有	you3	7533	Have, possession, there be, there is.
孚	fu2	1936	Truth; reliable, sincere; to inspire confidence in others; capture, prisoner, plunder.
惠	hui4	2339	Kindness, benevolence; favor, benefit; affectionate; gracious.
我	wo3	4778	We, us, I, my, mine, our.
德	de2	6162	Virtue, spiritual power, moral integrity; quality, nature, aptitude, ability, character.

Nine at the top

He increases no one. Perhaps somebody will attack him.
Does not keep his heart constant. Misfortune.

莫	mo4	4557	Nobody, nothing, none, no, not one, not at all, there is not, an absolute negative; evening, late.
益	yi4	3052	Increase, augment; more; benefit, profit, advantage.
之	zhi1	0935	Personal pronoun, he she, it; this, that, these, etc.; often used as a possessive.
或	huo4	2402	Perhaps, possibly, if, by chance; doubtful, uncertain; some, someone, something, sometime.
擊	ji1	0481	Strike, repel, beat, attack.
之	zhi1	0935	Personal pronoun, he she, it; this, that, these, etc.; often used as a possessive.
立	li4	3921	Stand up or erect; set up, establish; raise, ascend; keep the position or the course, resist, endure.
心	xin1	2735	Heart; conscience, moral nature; soul; core; mind; source of feelings, intentions, will.
勿	wu4	7208	Do not, no. Negative imperative.
恆	heng2	2107	Duration, persistence, endurance, steadiness, continuity; for a long time.
凶	xiong1	2808	Misfortune, pitfall, ominous, bad, unlucky, disastrous, trouble, accident.

43 夬 *guai* – Breakthrough / Resoluteness / Parting

THE JUDGMENT

Breakthrough. Proclaim the matter truthfully in the King's court. Danger. Report to your own city.
It is not favorable to resort to weapons. It is favorable to have a goal.

夬	guai4	3535	Breakthrough, make a breach, split, cut off, pull off; resolute, decisive.
揚	yang2	7259	Display, make known, announce, extol; scatter, spread; lift, raise; stir.
于	yu2	7592	At, to, in, into, on, from, by, go, go to, move towards, proceed, be.
王	wang2	7037	King, prince, sovereign, ruler.
庭	ting2	6405	Courtyard (of palace), court, audience chamber; hall, courtyard, chambers; family.
孚	fu2	1936	Truth; reliable, sincere; to inspire confidence in others; capture, prisoner, plunder.
號	hao4	2064	Weep; cry out, call out, scream, cry for help; signal, command.
有	you3	7533	Have, possession, there be, there is.
厲	li4	3906	Danger, threat; oppressive, cruel, wicked, brutal, harsh; sickness, malevolent devil; grind, polish, sharpen; discipline.
告	gao4	3287	Inform, announce, report, proclaim.
自	zi4	6960	From, origin, source, cause, reason; oneself, yourself.
邑	yi4	3037	City, town; walled or fortified city, seat of the of government for a district.
不	bu4	5379	No, not, negative prefix; without, none, nothing, will not, need not, will not be.
利	li4	3867	Favorable, lucky, advantageous, profitable, beneficial, furthering, harvesting; sharp, sharp witted.
即	ji2	0495	Approach, come to; promptly.
戎	rong2	3181	Weapons, arms; war chariot; violence, attack.

利	li4	3867	Favorable, lucky, advantageous, profitable, beneficial, furthering, harvesting; sharp, sharp witted.
有	you3	7533	Have, possession, there be, there is.
攸	you1	7519	Goal, direction, destination, objective; distant, far away; a place; that which, whereby, thereby, for which; mark of the passive voice.
往	wang3	7050	Go, to go to, go forward, go towards; depart, bygone, former. 攸往: have a place to go; have a goal.

THE IMAGE

The Lake rises above Heaven: The image of Breakthrough.
Thus the noble distributes benefits downward,
while avoiding presumption of virtue.

澤	ze2	0277	Marsh, pool, pond, lake; flat body of water and the vapors rising from it; enrich, fertilize, benefit; moist, moisten; glossy, polished.
上	shang4	5669	Up, above, on, over, upwards, top, rise; higher, superior; first, best.
於	yu2	7643	On, in, at, by, from; with reference to; interjection.
天	tian1	6361	Heaven, firmament, the sky, cosmos; celestial, divine, power above the human.
夬	guai4	3535	Breakthrough, make a breach, split, cut off, pull off; resolute, decisive.
君	jun1	1715	Noble, prince, aristocrat, lord, chief, gentleman; honorable, a highly principled person, superior man. Most times, this character appears alongside another one, forming the word *JunZi*, whose original meaning was "son of a prince or ruler": 君子.
子	zi3	6939	Child, son or daughter, offspring; suffix; bride, wife; gentleman, officer, master, prince; young lady; the first of the *Earthly Branches*.
以	yi3	2932	Thus, in that way, by means of, with, for; instrument, medium, method, use (of), way (to).
施	shi1	5768	Expand, spread out, dispense, distribute, give, bestow.
祿	lu4	4196	Prosperity, revenue, salary, favors, official recognition, blessings.
及	ji2	0468	Reach, come to, draw out, approach to.
下	xia4	2520	Below, down, descend.

居	ju1	1535	Remain; rest (in); abides, dwell; to occupy a position or place; overbearing, arrogant.
德	de2	6162	Virtue, spiritual power, moral integrity; quality, nature, aptitude, ability, character.
則	ze2	6746	Then, thus, accordingly, consequently, and so, in that case; law, rule, pattern; follow a law.
忌	ji4	0432	Avoid, kept distant, shun, hate; prevent, abstain from, taboo; superstitious fear.

Nine at the beginning

> Powerful in the toes. He goes forward but cannot triumph,
> and makes a mistake.

壯	zhuang4	1453	Power, strength, strong, robust, big, full grown male, in the prime of life; injure.
于	yu2	7592	At, to, in, into, on, from, by, go, go to, move towards, proceed, be.
前	qian2	0919	Forward, ahead, front, foremost; formerly, before, come before in time, anterior, ancient.
趾	zhi3	0944	Toes, feet, hoof, paw. Legs (of animals or furniture), footprints, tracks.
往	wang3	7050	Go, to go to, go forward, go towards; depart, bygone, former.
不	bu4	5379	No, not, negative prefix; without, none, nothing, will not, need not, will not be.
勝	sheng4	5754	Defeat, subdue, vanquish, overcome; excel, surpass, be better than; victory, triumph, success.
爲	wei2	7059	Act, do, accomplish, make, to be; act for, stand for, support, help; become.
咎	jiu4	1192	Fault, blame, mistake, wrong; inauspicious; misfortune, bad luck, calamity; reproach, censure.

Nine in the second place

> Cries of alarm at evening and night.
> If you are armed there is nothing to fear.

惕	ti4	6263	Wary, cautious, alert, alarmed; fear, respect, to stand in awe of.
號	hao4	2064	Weep; cry out, call out, scream, cry for help; signal, command.
莫	mo4	4557	Nobody, nothing, none, no, not one, not at all, there is not, an absolute negative; evening, late.

夜	ye4	7315	Night, darkness.
有	you3	7533	Have, possession, there be, there is.
戎	rong2	3181	Weapons, arms; war chariot; violence, attack.
勿	wu4	7208	Do not, no. Negative imperative.
恤	xu4	2862	Worry, care about, fear, sorrow, pity.

Nine in the third place

To be powerful in the cheeks brings misfortune.
The noble is utterly resolved. Walks alone in the rain,
wet and grieved. No defect.

壯	zhuang4	1453	Power, strength, strong, robust, big, full grown male, in the prime of life; injure.
于	yu2	7592	At, to, in, into, on, from, by, go, go to, move towards, proceed, be.
頄	qiu2	8007	Cheekbones, bones of the face, face. High cheekbones indicates cruelty or a pushy character. 壯于頄: "mighty in his cheekbones", or "cruel or overbearing".
有	you3	7533	Have, possession, there be, there is.
凶	xiong1	2808	Misfortune, pitfall, ominous, bad, unlucky, disastrous, trouble, accident.
君	jun1	1715	Noble, prince, aristocrat, lord, chief, gentleman; honorable, a highly principled person, superior man. Most times, this character appears alongside another one, forming the word *JunZi*, whose original meaning was "son of a prince or ruler": 君子.
子	zi3	6939	Child, son or daughter, offspring; suffix; bride, wife; gentleman, officer, master, prince; young lady; the first of the *Earthly Branches*.
夬	guai4	3535	Breakthrough, make a breach, split, cut off, pull off; resolute, decisive. Appearing duplicated intensifies its meaning.
夬	guai4	3535	
獨	du2	6512	Alone, single, solitary, only; isolated; meditative.
行	xing2	2754	Move, go, advance, act, do.
遇	yu4	7625	Meet, encounter, come across, happen.
雨	yu3	7662	Rain, shower, sudden downpour.
若	ruo4	3126	Like, just as, to be like; agree, conform to; approve; concordant; compliant.

濡	ru2	3149	Moist, soak, immerse, wet.
有	you3	7533	Have, possession, there be, there is.
愠	yun4	7766	Angry, indignant, vexed, irritated, grieved, displeasure, hate.
无	wu2	7173	No, not, negative; without, does not possess, not have.
咎	jiu4	1192	Fault, blame, mistake, wrong; inauspicious; misfortune, bad luck, calamity; reproach, censure.

Nine in the fourth place

There is no skin on his buttocks. Walks haltingly leading a sheep. Regret disappears. Hearing complaints, not to be believed.

臀	tun2	6602	Buttocks, rump.
无	wu2	7173	No, not, negative; without, does not possess, not have.
膚	fu1	1958	Skin, flesh; cut meat, tender meat.
其	qi2	0525	Their, his, its, the; this, that. A demonstrative and possessive pronoun.
行	xing2	2754	Move, go, advance, act, do.
次	ci4	6980	Camp, take a position, to stop at a place, halt; lodge, hostel, lodging place, hut; hard-going; put in order, sequel, next in order, second, second rate.
且	qie3	0803	And; meanwhile; moreover; also; both; alternatively.
牽	qian1	0881	Lead by hand, lead; haul, drag; to drag into an affair, to connect.
羊	yang2	7247	Sheep, ram, goat.
悔	hui3	2336	Repent, regret, contrition; trouble. This word indicates both an objective situation and a subjective reaction to such circumstance.
亡	wang2	7034	Go away, disappear, exile; fail; destroy, perish, not have, not exist.
聞	wen2	7142	Hear; to be heard; make known, fame; smell.
言	yan2	7334	Talk, speech, words, sayings; big flute.
不	bu4	5379	No, not, negative prefix; without, none, nothing, will not, need not, will not be.
信	xin4	2748	Trust, belief, confidence, good faith; truthful, sincere, reliable.

Breakthrough (237) 43

Nine in the fifth place

A mountain goat breaks through and goes along the middle of the road. No defect.

莧	xian4	2686	Weeds, edible greens of various sorts, spinach. Many scholars think that it is a variant character or an error for other character similar, 莧, which means some kind of goat antelope, genus *Nemorhaedus*.
陸	lu4	4191	Highland, plateau, heights, dry land.
夬	guai4	3535	Breakthrough, make a breach, split, cut off, pull off; resolute, decisive. Appearing duplicated intensifies its meaning.
夬	guai4	3535	
中	zhong1	1504	Center, inner, in the inside, put in the center, hit (target); balanced, central, middle, correct.
行	xing2	2754	Move, go, advance, act, do.
无	wu2	7173	No, not, negative; without, does not possess, not have.
咎	jiu4	1192	Fault, blame, mistake, wrong; inauspicious; misfortune, bad luck, calamity; reproach, censure.

Six at the top

There is no cry. At the end there will be misfortune.

无	wu2	7173	No, not, negative; without, does not possess, not have.
號	hao4	2064	Weep; cry out, call out, scream, cry for help; signal, command.
終	zhong1	1500	End, finish, complete; for ever; end of a cycle; carried to conclusion, consummation, closure; death. The original meaning was: tied-off end of a thread.
有	you3	7533	Have, possession, there be, there is.
凶	xiong1	2808	Misfortune, pitfall, ominous, bad, unlucky, disastrous, trouble, accident.

44 姤 *gou* – Close Encounter / Meeting

THE JUDGMENT

Close Encounter. The woman is powerful.
Do not take her as wife.

姤	gou4	3422	Couple, mate, meet, interlock, locking; coming to meet; good.
女	nu3	4776	Maiden, woman, lady, girl, feminine.
壯	zhuang4	1453	Power, strength, strong, robust, big, full grown male, in the prime of life; injure.
勿	wu4	7208	Do not, no. Negative imperative.
用	yong4	7567	Use, apply, put to use, apply the oracle to real world situations; hereby, thereby.
取	qu3	1615	Take, take a wife, obtain, lay hold of, grasp.
女	nu3	4776	Maiden, woman, lady, girl, feminine.

THE IMAGE

Under Heaven is the Wind: The image of Close Encounter.
Thus the sovereign dispenses his orders
to the four corners of the world.

天	tian1	6361	Heaven, firmament, the sky, cosmos; celestial, divine, power above the human.
下	xia4	2520	Below, down, descend.
有	you3	7533	Have, possession, there be, there is.
風	feng1	1890	Wind, breath, air; manners, atmosphere.
姤	gou4	3422	Couple, mate, meet, interlock, locking; coming to meet; good.
后	hou4	2144	Sovereign, lord, prince; empress; descendants, heirs.
以	yi3	2932	Thus, in that way, by means of, with, for; instrument, medium, method, use (of), way (to).
施	shi1	5768	Expand, spread out, dispense, distribute, give, bestow.

Close Encounter (239) 44

命	ming4	4537	Heaven's will; command(s), fate, destiny; will; investiture; birth and death as limits of life.
誥	gao4	3288	Command, order, decree, imperial mandate, notification, proclamation.
四	si4	5598	Four, four times, quadruple.
方	fang1	1802	Square, squarely, directly, straightforward, honest; a place, a region; on all sides; direction, trend, method; suddenly, quick, definite; take a place, occupy; sacrifice to the spirits of the four quarters.

Six at the beginning

Tied it to a metal brake. The determination brings good fortune.
Has where to go but sees pitfalls.
The skinny pig will waver back and forth.

繫	xi4	2458	Tie, attach, bind, connect, tether, restrain; suspend, hang from a cord; keep in mind.
于	yu2	7592	At, to, in, into, on, from, by, go, go to, move towards, proceed, be.
金	jin1	1057	Metal, bronze, gold, golden; money, riches.
柅	ni3	4659	Brake, chock for stopping a car; spindle.
貞	zhen1	0346	Perseverance, persistence, determination, steadiness, firmness; straight, correct, verified, certain; pure, loyal. Its original meaning was "to determine an uncertain matter through divination".
吉	ji2	0476	Good fortune, auspicious, promising, fortunate, lucky, advantageous, happiness, good auspices. It is the only single character meaning good luck in the *YiJing*.
有	you3	7533	Have, possession, there be, there is.
攸	you1	7519	Goal, direction, destination, objective; distant, far away; a place; that which, whereby, thereby, for which; mark of the passive voice.
往	wang3	7050	Go, to go to, go forward, go towards; depart, bygone, former. 攸往: have a place to go; have a goal.
見	jian4	0860	See, observe, look at, to be seen; cause to appear; be exposed to, display, reveal; interview, visit or call on, meet.
凶	xiong1	2808	Misfortune, pitfall, ominous, bad, unlucky, disastrous, trouble, accident.
羸	lei2	4240	Bound, entangled, tethered; break, damage; weak, lean, emaciated.

豕	shi3	5766	Pig, boar, swine. Symbol of wealth and luck.
孚	fu2	1936	Truth; reliable, sincere; to inspire confidence in others; capture, prisoner, plunder.
蹢	zhi2	8000	Plant feet, dig in, balk, stop walking; animal's foot, hoof. 蹢躅: faltering, hesitant.
躅	zhu2	1388	Stop walking; falter, limping, halter, hesitate; stamp the foot, fight, struggle.

Nine in the second place

There is a fish in the wrapping. No defect. Not fitting for guests.

包	bao1	4937	Bundle, wrap, reed mat for wrapping; kitchen, butchering room; contain, support, take responsibility over.
有	you3	7533	Have, possession, there be, there is.
魚	yu2	7668	Fish, symbol of abundance.
无	wu2	7173	No, not, negative; without, does not possess, not have.
咎	jiu4	1192	Fault, blame, mistake, wrong; inauspicious; misfortune, bad luck, calamity; reproach, censure.
不	bu4	5379	No, not, negative prefix; without, none, nothing, will not, need not, will not be.
利	li4	3867	Favorable, lucky, advantageous, profitable, beneficial, furthering, harvesting; sharp, sharp witted.
賓	bin1	5259	Guest, visitor.

Nine in the third place

There is no skin on his buttocks and his walk is hard-going. Danger. There will be no great defect.

臀	tun2	6602	Buttocks, rump.
无	wu2	7173	No, not, negative; without, does not possess, not have.
膚	fu1	1958	Skin, flesh; cut meat, tender meat.
其	qi2	0525	Their, his, its, the; this, that. A demonstrative and possessive pronoun.
行	xing2	2754	Move, go, advance, act, do.
次	ci4	6980	Camp, take a position, to stop at a place, halt; lodge, hostel, lodging place, hut; hard-going; put in order, sequel, next in order, second, second rate.
且	qie3	0803	And; meanwhile; moreover; also; both; alternatively.

Close Encounter (241) 44

厲	li4	3906	Danger, threat; oppressive, cruel, wicked, brutal, harsh; sickness, malevolent devil; grind, polish, sharpen; discipline.
无	wu2	7173	No, not, negative; without, does not possess, not have.
大	da4	5943	Big, great, tall; excessive, arrogant; spread out and reach everywhere.
咎	jiu4	1192	Fault, blame, mistake, wrong; inauspicious; misfortune, bad luck, calamity; reproach, censure.

Nine in the fourth place

There are no fish in the wrapping. This causes misfortune.

包	bao1	4937	Bundle, wrap, reed mat for wrapping; kitchen, butchering room; contain, support, take responsibility over.
无	wu2	7173	No, not, negative; without, does not possess, not have.
魚	yu2	7668	Fish, symbol of abundance.
起	qi3	0548	Originate, begin; rise, go up.
凶	xiong1	2808	Misfortune, pitfall, ominous, bad, unlucky, disastrous, trouble, accident.

Nine in the fifth place

A melon wrapped in willow leaves. Hidden brilliance.
It falls from Heaven.

以	yi3	2932	Thus, in that way, by means of, with, for; instrument, medium, method, use (of), way (to).
杞	qi3	0547	Willow leaves; willow (*Lycium chinense*).
包	bao1	4937	Bundle, wrap, reed mat for wrapping; kitchen, butchering room; contain, support, take responsibility over.
瓜	gua1	3504	Melon, gourd, cucumber.
含	han2	2017	Hidden, hold in the mouth; contain, restrain, tolerate.
章	zhang1	0182	Brilliance, splendor, refinement, distinction; ornament, emblem of distinction, jade tablet; amulet. Its short form, with the jade radical means "jade baton".
有	you3	7533	Have, possession, there be, there is.
隕	yun3	7756	Fall, drop or throw down; fall from the sky; tumbled, tumble.
自	zi4	6960	From, origin, source, cause, reason; oneself, yourself.
天	tian1	6361	Heaven, firmament, the sky, cosmos; celestial, divine, power above the human.

Nine at the top

> Close encounter with his horns.
> Humiliation. No defect.

姤	gou4	3422	Couple, mate, meet, interlock, locking; coming to meet; good.
其	qi2	0525	Their, his, its, the; this, that. A demonstrative and possessive pronoun.
角	jiao3	1174	Horns, in the *YiJing*, is a symbol of violence and power, not always well employed.
吝	lin4	4040	Humiliation, regret, shame, distress, grief, sorrow; miserly, niggardly. It is a warning of trouble.
无	wu2	7173	No, not, negative; without, does not possess, not have.
咎	jiu4	1192	Fault, blame, mistake, wrong; inauspicious; misfortune, bad luck, calamity; reproach, censure.

45 萃 cui – Gathering Together

The Judgment

Gathering Together. Success. The King approaches his temple.
It is favorable to see the great man.
Success. The determination is favorable. Offering great sacrifices brings good fortune. It is favorable to have a goal.

萃	cui4	6880	Collect, assemble, gather together, massing; bunched, thick, dense; crowd, collection, group.
亨	heng1	2099	Success, prevalence, smooth progress, growth, consummate, triumph; pervade; offering, sacrifice.
王	wang2	7037	King, prince, sovereign, ruler.
假	jia3	0599	Approaches, goes to.
有	you3	7533	Have, possession, there be, there is.
廟	miao4	4473	(Ancestral) temple, a shrine, used to honor gods and ancestors.
利	li4	3867	Favorable, lucky, advantageous, profitable, beneficial, furthering, harvesting; sharp, sharp witted.
見	jian4	0860	See, observe, look at, to be seen; cause to appear; be exposed to, display, reveal; interview, visit or call on, meet.
大	da4	5943	Big, great, tall; excessive, arrogant; spread out and reach everywhere.
人	ren2	3097	Man, person(s); people; others; human being, individual.
亨	heng1	2099	Success, prevalence, smooth progress, growth, consummate, triumph; pervade; offering, sacrifice.
利	li4	3867	Favorable, lucky, advantageous, profitable, beneficial, furthering, harvesting; sharp, sharp witted.
貞	zhen1	0346	Perseverance, persistence, determination, steadiness, firmness; straight, correct, verified, certain; pure, loyal. Its original meaning was "to determine an uncertain matter through divination".
用	yong4	7567	Use in sacrifice; hereby, thereby, herewith (Shaugnessy), like "hereby offer sacrifice". Use, apply, put to use, apply the oracle to real world situations, act.

大	da4	5943	Big, great, tall; excessive, arrogant; spread out and reach everywhere.
牲	sheng1	5739	Offering, sacrificial victim.
吉	ji2	0476	Good fortune, auspicious, promising, fortunate, lucky, advantageous, happiness, good auspices. It is the only single character meaning good luck in the *YiJing*.
利	li4	3867	Favorable, lucky, advantageous, profitable, beneficial, furthering, harvesting; sharp, sharp witted.
有	you3	7533	Have, possession, there be, there is.
攸	you1	7519	Goal, direction, destination, objective; distant, far away; a place; that which, whereby, thereby, for which; mark of the passive voice.
往	wang3	7050	Go, to go to, go forward, go towards; depart, bygone, former. 攸往: have a place to go; have a goal.

The Image

> The Lake rises above Earth: The image of Gathering Together.
> Thus the noble gets his weapons in order, to be on guard against the unexpected.

澤	ze2	0277	Marsh, pool, pond, lake; flat body of water and the vapors rising from it; enrich, fertilize, benefit; moist, moisten; glossy, polished.
上	shang4	5669	Up, above, on, over, upwards, top, rise; higher, superior; first, best.
於	yu2	7643	On, in, at, by, from; with reference to; interjection.
地	di4	6198	Earth, soil, ground.
萃	cui4	6880	Collect, assemble, gather together, massing; bunched, thick, dense; crowd, collection, group.
君	jun1	1715	Noble, prince, aristocrat, lord, chief, gentleman; honorable, a highly principled person, superior man. Most times, this character appears alongside another one, forming the word *JunZi*, whose original meaning was "son of a prince or ruler": 君子.
子	zi3	6939	Child, son or daughter, offspring; suffix; bride, wife; gentleman, officer, master, prince; young lady; the first of the *Earthly Branches*.
以	yi3	2932	Thus, in that way, by means of, with, for; instrument, medium, method, use (of), way (to).

Gathering Together (245)   45

除	chu2	1391	Store up, save for future use, put aside, hide in a safe place; eliminate, remove, deduct, divide.
戎	rong2	3181	Weapons, arms; war chariot; violence, attack.
器	qi4	0549	Tools, artifact, weapon; ability, talent.
戒	jie4	0627	Warn, caution, limit, on guard, wary.
不	bu4	5379	No, not, negative prefix; without, none, nothing, will not, need not, will not be.
虞	yu2	7648	Eventuality; contingency; take precautions, to provide against; foresee; anxious, not at ease; forester, game-keeper.

Six at the beginning

If you are sincere, but not to the end,
sometimes there will be confusion, sometimes Gathering Together.
If you call, a handshake can bring smiles. Do not worry.
Going has no defect.

有	you3	7533	Have, possession, there be, there is.
孚	fu2	1936	Truth; reliable, sincere; to inspire confidence in others; capture, prisoner, plunder.
不	bu4	5379	No, not, negative prefix; without, none, nothing, will not, need not, will not be.
終	zhong1	1500	End, finish, complete; for ever; end of a cycle; carried to conclusion, consummation, closure; death. The original meaning was: tied-off end of a thread.
乃	nai3	4612	Then, and, also, thereupon, as it turned out, namely, after all, only then; really, indeed.
亂	luan4	4220	Disorder, confusion, rebellion, anarchy, chaos, a mess, confused and tangled situation.
乃	nai3	4612	Then, and, also, thereupon, as it turned out, namely, after all, only then; really, indeed.
萃	cui4	6880	Collect, assemble, gather together, massing; bunched, thick, dense; crowd, collection, group.
若	ruo4	3126	Like, just as, to be like; agree, conform to; approve; concordant; compliant.
號	hao4	2064	Weep; cry out, call out, scream, cry for help; signal, command.
一	yi1	3016	One, number one.
握	wo4	7161	Grasp, squeeze; restrain; handful.

爲	wei2	7059	Act, do, accomplish, make, to be; act for, stand for, support, help; become.
笑	xiao4	2615	Laugh, smile, merriment, good humor.
勿	wu4	7208	Do not, no. Negative imperative.
恤	xu4	2862	Worry, care about, fear, sorrow, pity.
往	wang3	7050	Go, to go to, go forward, go towards; depart, bygone, former.
无	wu2	7173	No, not, negative; without, does not possess, not have.
咎	jiu4	1192	Fault, blame, mistake, wrong; inauspicious; misfortune, bad luck, calamity; reproach, censure.

Six in the second place

Following the lead brings good fortune. No defect.
If one is sincere is favorable to make a small offering.

引	yin3	7429	Guide, lead, pull, attract, stretch, draw the bow.
吉	ji2	0476	Good fortune, auspicious, promising, fortunate, lucky, advantageous, happiness, good auspices. It is the only single character meaning good luck in the *YiJing*.
无	wu2	7173	No, not, negative; without, does not possess, not have.
咎	jiu4	1192	Fault, blame, mistake, wrong; inauspicious; misfortune, bad luck, calamity; reproach, censure.
孚	fu2	1936	Truth; reliable, sincere; to inspire confidence in others; capture, prisoner, plunder.
乃	nai3	4612	Then, and, also, thereupon, as it turned out, namely, after all, only then; really, indeed.
利	li4	3867	Favorable, lucky, advantageous, profitable, beneficial, furthering, harvesting; sharp, sharp witted.
用	yong4	7567	Use, apply, put to use, apply the oracle to real world situations; hereby, thereby.
禴	yue4	7498	*Yue* summer sacrifice to all the ancestors entitled to special sacrifices, when food is sparse; small offering, a sacrifice offered with few resources.

Six in the third place

Gathering Together between moans. Nothing is favorable.
Going is without defect. Small humiliation.

| 萃 | cui4 | 6880 | Collect, assemble, gather together, massing; bunched, thick, dense; crowd, collection, group. |

Gathering Together (247) 45

如	ru2	3137	Thus, in this way, as, like, similar to, if (conditional).
嗟	jie1	0763	Lament, sigh, interjection of regret or sorrow, alas, groan.
如	ru2	3137	Thus, in this way, as, like, similar to, if (conditional).
无	wu2	7173	No, not, negative; without, does not possess, not have.
攸	you1	7519	Goal, direction, destination, objective; distant, far away; a place; that which, whereby, thereby, for which; mark of the passive voice.
利	li4	3867	Favorable, lucky, advantageous, profitable, beneficial, furthering, harvesting; sharp, sharp witted.
往	wang3	7050	Go, to go to, go forward, go towards; depart, bygone, former.
无	wu2	7173	No, not, negative; without, does not possess, not have.
咎	jiu4	1192	Fault, blame, mistake, wrong; inauspicious; misfortune, bad luck, calamity; reproach, censure.
小	xiao3	2605	Small, insignificant, common, humble, mediocre; diminish, belittle.
吝	lin4	4040	Humiliation, regret, shame, distress, grief, sorrow; miserly, niggardly. It is a warning of trouble.

Nine in the fourth place
Great good fortune. No defect.

大	da4	5943	Big, great, tall; excessive, arrogant; spread out and reach everywhere.
吉	ji2	0476	Good fortune, auspicious, promising, fortunate, lucky, advantageous, happiness, good auspices. It is the only single character meaning good luck in the *YiJing*.
无	wu2	7173	No, not, negative; without, does not possess, not have.
咎	jiu4	1192	Fault, blame, mistake, wrong; inauspicious; misfortune, bad luck, calamity; reproach, censure.

Nine in the fifth place
One has a good position in the Gathering. No defect.
There is no trust. If one has outstanding long term determination regret disappears.

萃	cui4	6880	Collect, assemble, gather together, massing; bunched, thick, dense; crowd, collection, group.
有	you3	7533	Have, possession, there be, there is.

Matrix of Meanings of the Book of Changes

位	wei4	7116	Position, location; category, rank, status; situation.
无	wu2	7173	No, not, negative; without, does not possess, not have.
咎	jiu4	1192	Fault, blame, mistake, wrong; inauspicious; misfortune, bad luck, calamity; reproach, censure.
匪	fei3	1820	No, strong negative.
孚	fu2	1936	Truth; reliable, sincere; to inspire confidence in others; capture, prisoner, plunder.
元	yuan2	7707	Outstanding, greatest, sublime, supreme, greatest, very great, grand; source, beginning, cause, first or paramount, fundamentality; head, chief; used as a superlative.
永	yong3	7589	For a long time, constant, permanent, everlasting; prolong; distant, far reaching.
貞	zhen1	0346	Perseverance, persistence, determination, steadiness, firmness; straight, correct, verified, certain; pure, loyal. Its original meaning was "to determine an uncertain matter through divination".
悔	hui3	2336	Repent, regret, contrition; trouble. This word indicates both an objective situation and a subjective reaction to such circumstance.
亡	wang2	7034	Go away, disappear, exile; fail; destroy, perish, not have, not exist.

Six at the top

Sighing and moaning, Copious tears. No defect.

齎	ji1	0464	Sigh; bring, give a present.
咨	zi1	6923	Sigh, lament, sob.
涕	ti4	6250	Tears, weep, snivel, mucus.
洟	yi2	2986	Mucus from nose, to have a runny nose, snivel.
无	wu2	7173	No, not, negative; without, does not possess, not have.
咎	jiu4	1192	Fault, blame, mistake, wrong; inauspicious; misfortune, bad luck, calamity; reproach, censure.

46  *sheng* – Ascending

THE JUDGMENT

    Ascending has outstanding success.
It is useful seeing the great man. Do not worry.
Marching forth toward the South brings good fortune.

升	sheng1	5745	Climb, push upwards, rise, go up, arise.
元	yuan2	7707	Outstanding, greatest, sublime, supreme, greatest, very great, grand; source, beginning, cause, first or paramount, fundamentality; head, chief; used as a superlative.
亨	heng1	2099	Success, prevalence, smooth progress, growth, consummate, triumph; pervade; offering, sacrifice.
用	yong4	7567	Use, apply, put to use, apply the oracle to real world situations; hereby, thereby.
見	jian4	0860	See, observe, look at, to be seen; cause to appear; be exposed to, display, reveal; interview, visit or call on, meet.
大	da4	5943	Big, great, tall; excessive, arrogant; spread out and reach everywhere.
人	ren2	3097	Man, person(s); people; others; human being, individual.
勿	wu4	7208	Do not, no. Negative imperative.
恤	xu4	2862	Worry, care about, fear, sorrow, pity.
南	nan2	4620	The South. The region associated with Summer, fire, work in community and vegetation.
征	zheng1	0352	Punishing expedition ("to correct"), to reduce to submission, attack, punish; to levy taxes; comes, brings.
吉	ji2	0476	Good fortune, auspicious, promising, fortunate, lucky, advantageous, happiness, good auspices. It is the only single character meaning good luck in the *YiJing*.

THE IMAGE

In the middle of the Earth grows Wood: The image of Ascending.
Thus the noble lets virtue be his guide,
he accumulates the small in order to achieve the high and the great.

地	di4	6198	Earth, soil, ground.
中	zhong1	1504	Center, inner, in the inside, put in the center, hit (target); balanced, central, middle, correct.
生	sheng1	5738	Live, give birth to, to be born living being; produce; sacrificial animal, victim.
木	mu4	4593	Tree, wood, timber, wooden.
升	sheng1	5745	Climb, push upwards, rise, go up, arise.
君	jun1	1715	Noble, prince, aristocrat, lord, chief, gentleman; honorable, a highly principled person, superior man. Most times, this character appears alongside another one, forming the word *JunZi*, whose original meaning was "son of a prince or ruler": 君子.
子	zi3	6939	Child, son or daughter, offspring; suffix; bride, wife; gentleman, officer, master, prince; young lady; the first of the *Earthly Branches*.
以	yi3	2932	Thus, in that way, by means of, with, for; instrument, medium, method, use (of), way (to).
順	shun4	5935	Follow, obey, yield, agree, submissive, docile.
德	de2	6162	Virtue, spiritual power, moral integrity; quality, nature, aptitude, ability, character.
積	ji1	0500	Accumulate, store up, hoard provisions.
小	xiao3	2605	Small, insignificant, common, humble, mediocre; diminish, belittle.
以	yi3	2932	Thus, in that way, by means of, with, for; instrument, medium, method, use (of), way (to).
高	gao1	3290	High, elevated, exalted, eminent, lofty, illustrious, higher.
大	da4	5943	Big, great, tall; excessive, arrogant; spread out and reach everywhere.

Six at the beginning

Trusted and ascending. Great good fortune.

允	yun3	7759	Trust, approval, consent, confidence; sincere, true, loyal; truly, indeed; earnestly.
升	sheng1	5745	Climb, push upwards, rise, go up, arise.

大	da4	5943	Big, great, tall; excessive, arrogant; spread out and reach everywhere.
吉	ji2	0476	Good fortune, auspicious, promising, fortunate, lucky, advantageous, happiness, good auspices. It is the only single character meaning good luck in the *YiJing*.

Nine in the second place

If one is sincere is favorable to present a small offering.
No defect.

孚	fu2	1936	Truth; reliable, sincere; to inspire confidence in others; capture, prisoner, plunder.
乃	nai3	4612	Then, and, also, thereupon, as it turned out, namely, after all, only then; really, indeed.
利	li4	3867	Favorable, lucky, advantageous, profitable, beneficial, furthering, harvesting; sharp, sharp witted.
用	yong4	7567	Use, apply, put to use, apply the oracle to real world situations; hereby, thereby.
禴	yue4	7498	*Yue* summer sacrifice to all the ancestors entitled to special sacrifices, when food is sparse; small offering, a sacrifice offered with few resources.
无	wu2	7173	No, not, negative; without, does not possess, not have.
咎	jiu4	1192	Fault, blame, mistake, wrong; inauspicious; misfortune, bad luck, calamity; reproach, censure.

Nine in the third place

Ascends into an empty city.

升	sheng1	5745	Climb, push upwards, rise, go up, arise.
虛	xu1	2821	Empty, vacant, hollow; hill, mound; abandoned city, ruins, waste; unsubstantial, unreal.
邑	yi4	3037	City, town; walled or fortified city, seat of the of government for a district.

Six in the fourth place

The King presents an offering on Mount *Qi*.
Good fortune. No defect.

王	wang2	7037	King, prince, sovereign, ruler.
用	yong4	7567	Use, apply, put to use, apply the oracle to real world situations; hereby, thereby.
亨	heng1	2099	Success, prevalence, smooth progress, growth, consummate, triumph; pervade; offering, sacrifice.

于	yu2	7592	At, to, in, into, on, from, by, go, go to, move towards, proceed, be.
岐	qi2	0522	Name of a mountain, the home of the ancestors of the *Zhou* dynasty. Also means split, fork in the road.
山	shan1	5630	Mountain, hill, peak.
吉	ji2	0476	Good fortune, auspicious, promising, fortunate, lucky, advantageous, happiness, good auspices. It is the only single character meaning good luck in the *YiJing*.
无	wu2	7173	No, not, negative; without, does not possess, not have.
咎	jiu4	1192	Fault, blame, mistake, wrong; inauspicious; misfortune, bad luck, calamity; reproach, censure.

Six in the fifth place

The determination brings good fortune. Ascends on stairs.

貞	zhen1	0346	Perseverance, persistence, determination, steadiness, firmness; straight, correct, verified, certain; pure, loyal. Its original meaning was "to determine an uncertain matter through divination".
吉	ji2	0476	Good fortune, auspicious, promising, fortunate, lucky, advantageous, happiness, good auspices. It is the only single character meaning good luck in the *YiJing*.
升	sheng1	5745	Climb, push upwards, rise, go up, arise.
階	jie1	0625	Steps, stairs; stages; degree; rank.

Six at the top

Ascending in the dark. It is favorable an untiring determination.

冥	ming2	4528	Dark, darkness, obscured; benighted, confused, ignorant, blind; deep, the underworld.
升	sheng1	5745	Climb, push upwards, rise, go up, arise.
利	li4	3867	Favorable, lucky, advantageous, profitable, beneficial, furthering, harvesting; sharp, sharp witted.
于	yu2	7592	At, to, in, into, on, from, by, go, go to, move towards, proceed, be.
不	bu4	5379	No, not, negative prefix; without, none, nothing, will not, need not, will not be.
息	xi1	2495	Rest, pause; breathe, breathing-spell, take breath, enjoy the rest, well-being, prosper.

之	zhi1	0935	Personal pronoun, he she, it; this, that, these, etc.; often used as a possessive.
貞	zhen1	0346	Perseverance, persistence, determination, steadiness, firmness; straight, correct, verified, certain; pure, loyal. Its original meaning was "to determine an uncertain matter through divination".

47 困 *kun* – Oppression / Besieged / Impasse

THE JUDGMENT

Oppression. Success.
The determination brings good fortune
to the great man. No defect.
Talk is not to be trusted.

困	kun4	3688	Oppression, obstruction; besieged, surrounded; entangled; distress, exhaustion, anxiety.
亨	heng1	2099	Success, prevalence, smooth progress, growth, consummate, triumph; pervade; offering, sacrifice.
貞	zhen1	0346	Perseverance, persistence, determination, steadiness, firmness; straight, correct, verified, certain; pure, loyal. Its original meaning was "to determine an uncertain matter through divination".
大	da4	5943	Big, great, tall; excessive, arrogant; spread out and reach everywhere.
人	ren2	3097	Man, person(s); people; others; human being, individual.
吉	ji2	0476	Good fortune, auspicious, promising, fortunate, lucky, advantageous, happiness, good auspices. It is the only single character meaning good luck in the *YiJing*.
无	wu2	7173	No, not, negative; without, does not possess, not have.
咎	jiu4	1192	Fault, blame, mistake, wrong; inauspicious; misfortune, bad luck, calamity; reproach, censure.
有	you3	7533	Have, possession, there be, there is.
言	yan2	7334	Talk, speech, words, sayings; big flute.
不	bu4	5379	No, not, negative prefix; without, none, nothing, will not, need not, will not be.
信	xin4	2748	Trust, belief, confidence, good faith; truthful, sincere, reliable.

Oppression

The Image

The Lake has no Water: The image of Oppression.
Thus the noble will sacrifice his own life to achieve his objective.

澤	ze2	0277	Marsh, pool, pond, lake; flat body of water and the vapors rising from it; enrich, fertilize, benefit; moist, moisten; glossy, polished.
无	wu2	7173	No, not, negative; without, does not possess, not have.
水	shui3	5922	Water, river, stream, flood, liquid, fluid.
困	kun4	3688	Oppression, obstruction; besieged, surrounded; entangled; distress, exhaustion, anxiety.
君	jun1	1715	Noble, prince, aristocrat, lord, chief, gentleman; honorable, a highly principled person, superior man. Most times, this character appears alongside another one, forming the word *JunZi*, whose original meaning was "son of a prince or ruler": 君子.
子	zi3	6939	Child, son or daughter, offspring; suffix; bride, wife; gentleman, officer, master, prince; young lady; the first of the *Earthly Branches*.
以	yi3	2932	Thus, in that way, by means of, with, for; instrument, medium, method, use (of), way (to).
致	zhi4	0984	Bring about, cause; involve, induce; present, offer, hand over; send, transmit; extend, apply; carry on to the limit.
命	ming4	4537	Heaven's will; command(s), fate, destiny; will; investiture; birth and death as limits of life.
遂	sui4	5530	Advance; push through, go forward; proceed, prolong; follow along, pursuit, comply with; consequently, then, next.
志	zhi4	0971	Purpose, will, determination, goal; keep the mind on target; treaty; annals.

Six at the beginning

Buttocks oppressed by a tree stump.
Enters a dark valley and is not seen for three years.

臀	tun2	6602	Buttocks, rump.
困	kun4	3688	Oppression, obstruction; besieged, surrounded; entangled; distress, exhaustion, anxiety.
于	yu2	7592	At, to, in, into, on, from, by, go, go to, move towards, proceed, be.
株	zhu1	1348	Stump, trunk or root of a tree; cane.

Matrix of Meanings of the Book of Changes

木	mu4	4593	Tree, wood, timber, wooden.
入	ru4	3152	Enter, go into (this is the meaning used in the *YiJing*); to make to enter; put into; bring in, present; encroach.
于	yu2	7592	At, to, in, into, on, from, by, go, go to, move towards, proceed, be.
幽	you1	7505	Dark, obscure; solitary, secluded, hidden from view; secret, difficult to understand.
谷	gu3	3483	Valley, hollow, ditch, gully, river bed, a river separating hills.
三	san1	5415	Three, thrice, third time or place.
歲	sui4	5538	Years, seasons, harvests.
不	bu4	5379	No, not, negative prefix; without, none, nothing, will not, need not, will not be.
覿	di2	6230	See face to face; to be admitted to an audience; encounter; to be visible.

Nine in the second place

Oppressed between wine and food.
Scarlet knee bands arrive from all sides. Offering a sacrifice is favorable.
Marching forth will bring misfortune. No defect.

困	kun4	3688	Oppression, obstruction; besieged, surrounded; entangled; distress, exhaustion, anxiety.
于	yu2	7592	At, to, in, into, on, from, by, go, go to, move towards, proceed, be.
酒	jiu3	1208	Drink, wine, liquor, spirits.
食	shi2	5810	Eat, feed, ingest; food, give food to; nourishment; salary of an officer, livelihood; eclipse (eating of Sun or Moon).
朱	zhu1	1346	Scarlet, red, vermilion; symbol of loyalty and sincerity, honor.
紱	fu2	1971	Knee bands, knee shields; a silk band in which the seal of office was tied to the waist; a band or ribbon worn about the waist, as for ornament, or over the shoulder as a symbol of rank; ceremonial leather apron. Indicates rank and authority.
方	fang1	1802	Square, squarely, directly, straightforward, honest; a place, a region; on all sides; direction, trend, method; suddenly, quick, definite; take a place, occupy; sacrifice to the spirits of the four quarters.

來	lai2	3768	Come, arrive, return, bring.
利	li4	3867	Favorable, lucky, advantageous, profitable, beneficial, furthering, harvesting; sharp, sharp witted.
用	yong4	7567	Use, apply, put to use, apply the oracle to real world situations; hereby, thereby.
享	xiang3	2552	Sacrifice, offering to a god or a superior; consecrate; treat.
祀	si4	5592	Sacrifice, autumnal sacrifice after harvest, libation, offering to the gods or the dead ancestors.
征	zheng1	0352	Punishing expedition ("to correct"), to reduce to submission, attack, punish; to levy taxes; comes, brings.
凶	xiong1	2808	Misfortune, pitfall, ominous, bad, unlucky, disastrous, trouble, accident.
无	wu2	7173	No, not, negative; without, does not possess, not have.
咎	jiu4	1192	Fault, blame, mistake, wrong; inauspicious; misfortune, bad luck, calamity; reproach, censure.

Six in the third place

Oppressed by stones. Leans on thorny bushes and thistles. Enters his house but does not see his wife. Misfortune.

困	kun4	3688	Oppression, obstruction; besieged, surrounded; entangled; distress, exhaustion, anxiety.
于	yu2	7592	At, to, in, into, on, from, by, go, go to, move towards, proceed, be.
石	shi2	5813	Rock, stone.
據	ju4	1563	Grasp, seize; lean on, depend on.
于	yu2	7592	At, to, in, into, on, from, by, go, go to, move towards, proceed, be.
蒺	ji2	0494	Thorns, spiny shrubs, *Tribulus terrestris*.
藜	li2	3877	*Tribulus terrestris*, it is a flowering plant in the family *Zygophyllaceae*, its thorns are sharp enough to puncture bicycle tires and to cause painful injury to bare feet; thistles, brambles.
入	ru4	3152	Enter, go into (this is the meaning used in the *YiJing*); to make to enter; put into; bring in, present; encroach.
于	yu2	7592	At, to, in, into, on, from, by, go, go to, move towards, proceed, be.
其	qi2	0525	Their, his, its, the; this, that. A demonstrative and possessive pronoun.

宮	gong1	3705	House, palace, dwelling place, chambers, mansion, temple.
不	bu4	5379	No, not, negative prefix; without, none, nothing, will not, need not, will not be.
見	jian4	0860	See, observe, look at, to be seen; cause to appear; be exposed to, display, reveal; interview, visit or call on, meet.
其	qi2	0525	Their, his, its, the; this, that. A demonstrative and possessive pronoun.
妻	qi1	0555	Wife, consort. A legal wife (first wife).
凶	xiong1	2808	Misfortune, pitfall, ominous, bad, unlucky, disastrous, trouble, accident.

Nine in the fourth place

He comes very slowly, oppressed in a metal carriage.
Humiliation, but it will be carried to conclusion.

來	lai2	3768	Come, arrive, return, bring.
徐	xu2	2841	Walk slowly, grave, slow, dignified; gently, quietly, leisurely; tardy, hesitant. Appearing duplicated intensifies its meaning.
徐	xu2	2841	
困	kun4	3688	Oppression, obstruction; besieged, surrounded; entangled; distress, exhaustion, anxiety.
于	yu2	7592	At, to, in, into, on, from, by, go, go to, move towards, proceed, be.
金	jin1	1057	Metal, bronze, gold, golden; money, riches.
車	che1	0280	Chariot, wagon, cart, carriage.
吝	lin4	4040	Humiliation, regret, shame, distress, grief, sorrow; miserly, niggardly. It is a warning of trouble.
有	you3	7533	Have, possession, there be, there is.
終	zhong1	1500	End, finish, complete; for ever; end of a cycle; carried to conclusion, consummation, closure; death. The original meaning was: tied-off end of a thread.

Nine in the fifth place

His nose and feet are severed. Oppressed by scarlet knee bands.
The joy comes slowly. It is favorable to present offerings and libations.

劓	yi4	3013	Cut off nose (as punishment for serious crime).
刖	yue4	7697	Cut off the feet as a punishment (for serious crimes).

OPPRESSION (259) 47

困	kun4	3688	Oppression, obstruction; besieged, surrounded; entangled; distress, exhaustion, anxiety.
于	yu2	7592	At, to, in, into, on, from, by, go, go to, move towards, proceed, be.
赤	chi4	1048	Purple, red; the color of the fire, associated with the South; sign of official rank.
紱	fu2	1971	Knee bands, knee shields; a silk band in which the seal of office was tied to the waist; a band or ribbon worn about the waist, as for ornament, or over the shoulder as a symbol of rank; ceremonial leather apron. Indicates rank and authority.
乃	nai3	4612	Then, and, also, thereupon, as it turned out, namely, after all, only then; really, indeed.
徐	xu2	2841	Walk slowly, grave, slow, dignified; gently, quietly, leisurely; tardy, hesitant.
有	you3	7533	Have, possession, there be, there is.
說	shuo1	5939	Pleasure, joy, satisfaction; talk, persuade, stimulate, say, explain, exhort.
利	li4	3867	Favorable, lucky, advantageous, profitable, beneficial, furthering, harvesting; sharp, sharp witted.
用	yong4	7567	Use, apply, put to use, apply the oracle to real world situations; hereby, thereby.
祭	ji4	0465	Sacrifice, offering to gods or spirits, worship.
祀	si4	5592	Sacrifice, autumnal sacrifice after harvest, libation, offering to the gods or the dead ancestors.

Six at the top

> Oppressed by climbing plants. He is anxious and insecure, telling himself that movement will bring regret. There will be trouble. Marching forth brings good fortune.

困	kun4	3688	Oppression, obstruction; besieged, surrounded; entangled; distress, exhaustion, anxiety.
于	yu2	7592	At, to, in, into, on, from, by, go, go to, move towards, proceed, be.
葛	ge2	3377	Climbing plant, creeping edible bean. Its common name is *kudzu*, it is a vine that grows everywhere.
藟	lei3	4235	Vines, climbing plant, creeper.
于	yu2	7592	At, to, in, into, on, from, by, go, go to, move towards, proceed, be.

臲	nie4	4700	Unstable, unsteady, jittery, on edge, worried.
卼	wu4	7211	Unsafe, unsteady, uncertain, uncomfortable, to limp; stump, stake.
曰	yue1	7694	To say, says, said, tell, calling, called, appointed, speaking, say. It is a verbal prefix.
動	dong4	6611	Move, stir, take action, excite, arouse.
悔	hui3	2336	Repent, regret, contrition; trouble. This word indicates both an objective situation and a subjective reaction to such circumstance.
有	you3	7533	Have, possession, there be, there is.
悔	hui3	2336	Repent, regret, contrition; trouble. This word indicates both an objective situation and a subjective reaction to such circumstance.
征	zheng1	0352	Punishing expedition ("to correct"), to reduce to submission, attack, punish; to levy taxes; comes, brings.
吉	ji2	0476	Good fortune, auspicious, promising, fortunate, lucky, advantageous, happiness, good auspices. It is the only single character meaning good luck in the *YiJing*.

48 井 *jing* – The Well

THE JUDGMENT

The Well. Changing the town, not changing the Well.
No loss, no gain. Going to take water from the Well nearly dry.
The rope does not reach the water or the jar breaks. Misfortune.

井	jing3	1143	Water well; source. The ideogram indicates eight fields with a well at the center.
改	gai3	3196	Change, reform, correct, amend.
邑	yi4	3037	City, town; walled or fortified city, seat of the of government for a district.
不	bu4	5379	No, not, negative prefix; without, none, nothing, will not, need not, will not be.
改	gai3	3196	Change, reform, correct, amend.
井	jing3	1143	Water well; source. The ideogram indicates eight fields with a well at the center.
无	wu2	7173	No, not, negative; without, does not possess, not have.
喪	sang4	5429	Lose, let drop, disappear, destroy, perish, mourning, burial.
无	wu2	7173	No, not, negative; without, does not possess, not have.
得	de2	6161	Get, obtain, gain; reach, achieve; can; attain the desired thing.
往	wang3	7050	Go, to go to, go forward, go towards; depart, bygone, former.
來	lai2	3768	Come, arrive, return, bring.
井	jing3	1143	Water well; source. The ideogram indicates eight fields with a well at the center. Appearing duplicated emphasizes its meaning.
井	jing3	1143	
汔	qi4	8006	Almost, nearly; water drying up, dried up.
至	zhi4	0982	Arrive, culminate, reach the highest point, utmost, superlative.
亦	yi4	3021	And, also, too, likewise, however.

未	wei4	7114	Not yet, before. The eight of the twelve *Earthly Branches*. 13-15 hs.
繘	yu4	8009	Rope used to draw water from a well.
井	jing3	1143	Water well; source. The ideogram indicates eight fields with a well at the center.
羸	lei2	4240	Bound, entangled, tethered; break, damage; weak, lean, emaciated.
其	qi2	0525	Their, his, its, the; this, that. A demonstrative and possessive pronoun.
瓶	ping2	5301	Earthen jar, jug, base, bottle.
凶	xiong1	2808	Misfortune, pitfall, ominous, bad, unlucky, disastrous, trouble, accident.

THE IMAGE

Wood above the Water: The image of the Well. Thus the noble encourages people at their work to cooperate among themselves.

木	mu4	4593	Tree, wood, timber, wooden.
上	shang4	5669	Up, above, on, over, upwards, top, rise; higher, superior; first, best.
有	you3	7533	Have, possession, there be, there is.
水	shui3	5922	Water, river, stream, flood, liquid, fluid.
井	jing3	1143	Water well; source. The ideogram indicates eight fields with a well at the center.
君	jun1	1715	Noble, prince, aristocrat, lord, chief, gentleman; honorable, a highly principled person, superior man. Most times, this character appears alongside another one, forming the word *JunZi*, whose original meaning was "son of a prince or ruler": 君子.
子	zi3	6939	Child, son or daughter, offspring; suffix; bride, wife; gentleman, officer, master, prince; young lady; the first of the *Earthly Branches*.
以	yi3	2932	Thus, in that way, by means of, with, for; instrument, medium, method, use (of), way (to).
勞	lao2	3826	Toil, diligent work; deeds, achievements, merits.
民	min2	4508	People, the masses, citizenry, the common people, crowd.
勸	quan4	1662	Encourage, exhort, stimulate, urge, advice, persuade.
相	xiang1	2562	Each other, mutual, reciprocal, cooperative; look to, look at, assist, aid.

The Well (263) 48

Six at the beginning

One does not drink from a muddy Well
There are no animals in an old Well.

井	jing3	1143	Water well; source. The ideogram indicates eight fields with a well at the center.
泥	ni2	4660	Mud, sludge; mire, an area of wet, soggy ground, to be mired; to paste, to plaster; impeded, obstructed.
不	bu4	5379	No, not, negative prefix; without, none, nothing, will not, need not, will not be.
食	shi2	5810	Eat, feed, ingest; food, give food to; nourishment; salary of an officer, livelihood; eclipse (eating of Sun or Moon).
舊	jiu4	1205	Ancient, old; past, long ago, for a long time; obsolete. It is used for people, places and things.
井	jing3	1143	Water well; source. The ideogram indicates eight fields with a well at the center.
无	wu2	7173	No, not, negative; without, does not possess, not have.
禽	qin2	1100	Game, animals, birds, prey; quarry, captives, capture. It may be a deer, but it is not its specific meaning.

Nine in the second place

Shooting fishes in the Well. The jar is broken and leaks.

井	jing3	1143	Water well; source. The ideogram indicates eight fields with a well at the center.
谷	gu3	3483	Valley, hollow, ditch, gully, river bed, a river separating hills.
射	she4	5703	Shoot with a bow; aim and hit the target.
鮒	fu4	1927	Fish, silver carp, perch, freshwater fish.
甕	weng4	7151	Earthen vessel, jug.
敝	bi4	5101	Broken, worn out, shabby, tattered, ruined; damage; unworthy, poor, vile.
漏	lou4	4152	Leak, drip.

Nine in the third place

The Well is cleaned but its water is not drank.
Our hearts grieve, because the water might be drawn out and used.
If the King were clear-minded all would receive the blessings.

井	jing3	1143	Water well; source. The ideogram indicates eight fields with a well at the center.

漊	xie4	6318	Clear, filter, purify (these are the preferred meaning for 48.3, the only place where this character appears); ooze, seep, leak; turbid, muddy, unsettled.
不	bu4	5379	No, not, negative prefix; without, none, nothing, will not, need not, will not be.
食	shi2	5810	Eat, feed, ingest; food, give food to; nourishment; salary of an officer, livelihood; eclipse (eating of Sun or Moon).
爲	wei2	7059	Act, do, accomplish, make, to be; act for, stand for, support, help; become.
我	wo3	4778	We, us, I, my, mine, our.
心	xin1	2735	Heart; conscience, moral nature; soul; core; mind; source of feelings, intentions, will.
惻	ce4	6758	Sorrow, grief, sadness, deeply pained; to pity, sympathize.
可	ke3	3381	Can, able, may; permit, allow; satisfactory, proper, suitable.
用	yong4	7567	Use, apply, put to use, apply the oracle to real world situations; hereby, thereby.
汲	ji2	0472	Draw water (from a well or an underground water body); pull towards oneself.
王	wang2	7037	King, prince, sovereign, ruler.
明	ming2	4534	Light, brightness, clarity, clear; enlightenment, discernment; seeing, perception; agreement, contract.
並	bing4	5292	In common, together, both, side by side; all, many.
受	shou4	5840	Receive, accept, consent, agree; endure, suffer; compliant, tranquil.
其	qi2	0525	Their, his, its, the; this, that. A demonstrative and possessive pronoun.
福	fu2	1978	Happiness, good fortune, blessings.

Six in the fourth place

> The Well is lined. No defect.

井	jing3	1143	Water well; source. The ideogram indicates eight fields with a well at the center.
甃	zhou4	1305	To repair a well, brickwork of a well, to line a well.
无	wu2	7173	No, not, negative; without, does not possess, not have.
咎	jiu4	1192	Fault, blame, mistake, wrong; inauspicious; misfortune, bad luck, calamity; reproach, censure.

The Well (265) 48

Nine in the fifth place

The Well has a clear, cold spring-water for drinking.

井	jing3	1143	Water well; source. The ideogram indicates eight fields with a well at the center.
洌	lie4	3987	Clear, limpid, pure.
寒	han2	2048	Cold, icy, chilly, wintry; poor needy.
泉	quan2	1674	Spring, fountain.
食	shi2	5810	Eat, feed, ingest; food, give food to; nourishment; salary of an officer, livelihood; eclipse (eating of Sun or Moon).

Six at the top

Taking water from the Well. It should not be covered.
It inspires confidence. Outstanding good fortune.

井	jing3	1143	Water well; source. The ideogram indicates eight fields with a well at the center.
收	shou1	5837	Take, gather together, collect, catch, receive, take and remove; harvest.
勿	wu4	7208	Do not, no. Negative imperative.
幕	mu4	4559	Cover, covering, curtain, screen, tent, canopy, baldachin.
有	you3	7533	Have, possession, there be, there is.
孚	fu2	1936	Truth; reliable, sincere; to inspire confidence in others; capture, prisoner, plunder.
元	yuan2	7707	Outstanding, greatest, sublime, supreme, greatest, very great, grand; source, beginning, cause, first or paramount, fundamentality; head, chief; used as a superlative.
吉	ji2	0476	Good fortune, auspicious, promising, fortunate, lucky, advantageous, happiness, good auspices. It is the only single character meaning good luck in the *YiJing*.

49 革 *ge* – Revolution / Getting rid of

The Judgment

The Revolution is trusted after it has been accomplished. Outstanding good fortune. The determination is favorable. Repentance fades.

革	ge2	3314	Change, change seasons, molt; revolution, overthrow; skin or hide, rawhide, hide without the hair, flay, peel off; ancient representations depict an animal hide spread out.
巳	si4	5590	6th earthly branch. The period from 9.00 a.m. to 11.00 a.m. Usually it is replaced with other characters:
日	ri4	3124	Sun, day, daylight, daytime; daily.
乃	nai3	4612	Then, and, also, thereupon, as it turned out, namely, after all, only then; really, indeed.
孚	fu2	1936	Truth; reliable, sincere; to inspire confidence in others; capture, prisoner, plunder.
元	yuan2	7707	Outstanding, greatest, sublime, supreme, greatest, very great, grand; source, beginning, cause, first or paramount, fundamentality; head, chief; used as a superlative.
亨	heng1	2099	Success, prevalence, smooth progress, growth, consummate, triumph; pervade; offering, sacrifice.
利	li4	3867	Favorable, lucky, advantageous, profitable, beneficial, furthering, harvesting; sharp, sharp witted.
貞	zhen1	0346	Perseverance, persistence, determination, steadiness, firmness; straight, correct, verified, certain; pure, loyal. Its original meaning was "to determine an uncertain matter through divination".
悔	hui3	2336	Repent, regret, contrition; trouble. This word indicates both an objective situation and a subjective reaction to such circumstance.
亡	wang2	7034	Go away, disappear, exile; fail; destroy, perish, not have, not exist.

Revolution (267)

The Image

>Within the Lake is Fire: The image of Revolution.
>Thus the noble regulates the calendar and makes clear the seasons.

澤	ze2	0277	Marsh, pool, pond, lake; flat body of water and the vapors rising from it; enrich, fertilize, benefit; moist, moisten; glossy, polished.
中	zhong1	1504	Center, inner, in the inside, put in the center, hit (target); balanced, central, middle, correct.
有	you3	7533	Have, possession, there be, there is.
火	huo3	2395	Fire, flame.
革	ge2	3314	Change, change seasons, molt; revolution, overthrow; skin or hide, rawhide, hide without the hair, flay, peel off; ancient representations depict an animal hide spread out.
君	jun1	1715	Noble, prince, aristocrat, lord, chief, gentleman; honorable, a highly principled person, superior man. Most times, this character appears alongside another one, forming the word *JunZi*, whose original meaning was "son of a prince or ruler": 君子.
子	zi3	6939	Child, son or daughter, offspring; suffix; bride, wife; gentleman, officer, master, prince; young lady; the first of the *Earthly Branches*.
以	yi3	2932	Thus, in that way, by means of, with, for; instrument, medium, method, use (of), way (to).
治	zhi4	1021	Regulate, govern, direct, rule, put in order.
歷	li4	3931	Calendar, calculate; number; successively, a sequence; classification; history, era, age, past; experience.
明	ming2	4534	Light, brightness, clarity, clear; enlightenment, discernment; seeing, perception; agreement, contract.
時	shi2	5780	Time, season, epoch, period, opportune moment.

Nine at the beginning

>The Revolution is tied with a yellow cow hide.

鞏	gong3	3718	Bind, bind with thongs; strengthen, secure, guard.
用	yong4	7567	Use, apply, put to use, apply the oracle to real world situations; hereby, thereby.
黃	huang2	2297	Yellow, yellow-brown; color of the soil in central China. In the *YiJing* the yellow color is always favorable, it is the color of the middle and the moderation and it was the imperial color since the *Han* dynasty.

牛	niu2	4737	Cow, bull, ox.
之	zhi1	0935	Personal pronoun, he she, it; this, that, these, etc.; often used as a possessive.
革	ge2	3314	Change, change seasons, molt; revolution, overthrow; skin or hide, rawhide, hide without the hair, flay, peel off; ancient representations depict an animal hide spread out.

Six in the second place

Revolution after the end of the day.
It is favorable to attack. No defect.

巳	si4	5590	6th earthly branch. The period from 9.00 a.m. to 11.00 a.m. Usually it is replaced with other characters:
日	ri4	3124	Sun, day, daylight, daytime; daily.
乃	nai3	4612	Then, and, also, thereupon, as it turned out, namely, after all, only then; really, indeed.
革	ge2	3314	Change, change seasons, molt; revolution, overthrow; skin or hide, rawhide, hide without the hair, flay, peel off; ancient representations depict an animal hide spread out.
之	zhi1	0935	Personal pronoun, he she, it; this, that, these, etc.; often used as a possessive.
征	zheng1	0352	Punishing expedition ("to correct"), to reduce to submission, attack, punish; to levy taxes; comes, brings.
吉	ji2	0476	Good fortune, auspicious, promising, fortunate, lucky, advantageous, happiness, good auspices. It is the only single character meaning good luck in the *YiJing*.
无	wu2	7173	No, not, negative; without, does not possess, not have.
咎	jiu4	1192	Fault, blame, mistake, wrong; inauspicious; misfortune, bad luck, calamity; reproach, censure.

Nine in the third place

Attacking brings misfortune. The determination is dangerous.
Only after Revolution has been talked about three times
there will be trust.

| 征 | zheng1 | 0352 | Punishing expedition ("to correct"), to reduce to submission, attack, punish; to levy taxes; comes, brings. |
| 凶 | xiong1 | 2808 | Misfortune, pitfall, ominous, bad, unlucky, disastrous, trouble, accident. |

Revolution (269) 49

貞	zhen1	0346	Perseverance, persistence, determination, steadiness, firmness; straight, correct, verified, certain; pure, loyal. Its original meaning was "to determine an uncertain matter through divination".
厲	li4	3906	Danger, threat; oppressive, cruel, wicked, brutal, harsh; sickness, malevolent devil; grind, polish, sharpen; discipline.
革	ge2	3314	Change, change seasons, molt; revolution, overthrow; skin or hide, rawhide, hide without the hair, flay, peel off; ancient representations depict an animal hide spread out.
言	yan2	7334	Talk, speech, words, sayings; big flute.
三	san1	5415	Three, thrice, third time or place.
就	jiu4	1210	Approach, come to, go to, go-around; proceed; follow; accomplish, finish.
有	you3	7533	Have, possession, there be, there is.
孚	fu2	1936	Truth; reliable, sincere; to inspire confidence in others; capture, prisoner, plunder.

Nine in the fourth place

> Repentance fades. There is confidence.
> Reforming the form of government brings good fortune.

悔	hui3	2336	Repent, regret, contrition; trouble. This word indicates both an objective situation and a subjective reaction to such circumstance.
亡	wang2	7034	Go away, disappear, exile; fail; destroy, perish, not have, not exist.
有	you3	7533	Have, possession, there be, there is.
孚	fu2	1936	Truth; reliable, sincere; to inspire confidence in others; capture, prisoner, plunder.
改	gai3	3196	Change, reform, correct, amend.
命	ming4	4537	Heaven's will; command(s), fate, destiny; will; investiture; birth and death as limits of life.
吉	ji2	0476	Good fortune, auspicious, promising, fortunate, lucky, advantageous, happiness, good auspices. It is the only single character meaning good luck in the *YiJing*.

Nine in the fifth place

> The great man changes like a tiger.
> Even before asking the oracle has confidence.

大	da4	5943	Big, great, tall; excessive, arrogant; spread out and reach everywhere.
人	ren2	3097	Man, person(s); people; others; human being, individual.
虎	hu3	2161	Tiger. Emblem of bravery and cruelty: strong, wild, extreme.
變	bian4	5245	Change, transform, metamorphose, alter.
未	wei4	7114	Not yet, before. The eight of the twelve *Earthly Branches*. 13-15 hs.
占	zhan1	0125	Divine by casting lots, prognosticating; observe signs; foretell by looking at an augury or using yarrow wands (*Achillea sibirica* or *mongolica*).
有	you3	7533	Have, possession, there be, there is.
孚	fu2	1936	Truth; reliable, sincere; to inspire confidence in others; capture, prisoner, plunder.

Six at the top

> The noble changes as a panther. The petty man changes its face.
> Attacking brings misfortune. The determination brings good fortune.

君	jun1	1715	Noble, prince, aristocrat, lord, chief, gentleman; honorable, a highly principled person, superior man. Most times, this character appears alongside another one, forming the word *JunZi*, whose original meaning was "son of a prince or ruler": 君子.
子	zi3	6939	Child, son or daughter, offspring; suffix; bride, wife; gentleman, officer, master, prince; young lady; the first of the *Earthly Branches*.
豹	bao4	4954	Panther, leopard. 豹變: the leopard's versatility, from rags to riches.
變	bian4	5245	Change, transform, metamorphose, alter.
小	xiao3	2605	Small, insignificant, common, humble, mediocre; diminish, belittle.
人	ren2	3097	Man, person(s); people; others; human being, individual.
革	ge2	3314	Change, change seasons, molt; revolution, overthrow; skin or hide, rawhide, hide without the hair, flay, peel off; ancient representations depict an animal hide spread out.

面	mian4	4497	Face, countenance; reputation, facade.
征	zheng1	0352	Punishing expedition ("to correct"), to reduce to submission, attack, punish; to levy taxes; comes, brings.
凶	xiong1	2808	Misfortune, pitfall, ominous, bad, unlucky, disastrous, trouble, accident.
居	ju1	1535	Remain; rest (in); abides, dwell; to occupy a position or place; overbearing, arrogant.
貞	zhen1	0346	Perseverance, persistence, determination, steadiness, firmness; straight, correct, verified, certain; pure, loyal. Its original meaning was "to determine an uncertain matter through divination".
吉	ji2	0476	Good fortune, auspicious, promising, fortunate, lucky, advantageous, happiness, good auspices. It is the only single character meaning good luck in the *YiJing*.

50 鼎 *ding* – The Caldron

THE JUDGMENT

The Caldron. Outstanding good fortune. Success.

鼎	ding3	6392	Caldron; three-legged bronze cauldron with two ears.
元	yuan2	7707	Outstanding, greatest, sublime, supreme, greatest, very great, grand; source, beginning, cause, first or paramount, fundamentality; head, chief; used as a superlative.
吉	ji2	0476	Good fortune, auspicious, promising, fortunate, lucky, advantageous, happiness, good auspices. It is the only single character meaning good luck in the *YiJing*.
亨	heng1	2099	Success, prevalence, smooth progress, growth, consummate, triumph; pervade; offering, sacrifice.

THE IMAGE

Fire over Wood: The image of the Caldron.
Thus the noble corrects his position to consolidate his fate.

木	mu4	4593	Tree, wood, timber, wooden.
上	shang4	5669	Up, above, on, over, upwards, top, rise; higher, superior; first, best.
有	you3	7533	Have, possession, there be, there is.
火	huo3	2395	Fire, flame.
鼎	ding3	6392	Caldron; three-legged bronze cauldron with two ears.
君	jun1	1715	Noble, prince, aristocrat, lord, chief, gentleman; honorable, a highly principled person, superior man. Most times, this character appears alongside another one, forming the word *JunZi*, whose original meaning was "son of a prince or ruler": 君子.
子	zi3	6939	Child, son or daughter, offspring; suffix; bride, wife; gentleman, officer, master, prince; young lady; the first of the *Earthly Branches*.

The Caldron (273) 50

以	yi3	2932	Thus, in that way, by means of, with, for; instrument, medium, method, use (of), way (to).
正	zheng4	0351	Correct, proper, upright, straight; regulate; chief, ruler; just, exactly.
位	wei4	7116	Position, location; category, rank, status; situation.
凝	ning2	4732	Consolidate, secure, fix; concentrate, achieve; congeal, coagulate, harden, solidify.
命	ming4	4537	Heaven's will; command(s), fate, destiny; will; investiture; birth and death as limits of life.

Six at the beginning

The Caldron is lying upside down. It is favorable to remove debris. One takes a concubine to bear a child. No defect.

鼎	ding3	6392	Caldron; three-legged bronze cauldron with two ears.
顛	dian1	6337	Summit, peak, top, top of head; invert, upturn, topple, fall on the head; overthrow.
趾	zhi3	0944	Toes, feet, hoof, paw. Legs (of animals or furniture), footprints, tracks.
利	li4	3867	Favorable, lucky, advantageous, profitable, beneficial, furthering, harvesting; sharp, sharp witted.
出	chu1	1409	Go out, came out, appear, departure; arise, emerge; bring out, take out, expel, leave, get rid of; produce, beget.
否	pi3	1902	Standstill, stagnation, obstruction, stoppage, dead end; bad, wrong.
得	de2	6161	Get, obtain, gain; reach, achieve; can; attain the desired thing.
妾	qie4	0814	Concubine (secondary wife), handmaiden, servant girl, slave woman.
以	yi3	2932	Thus, in that way, by means of, with, for; instrument, medium, method, use (of), way (to).
其	qi2	0525	Their, his, its, the; this, that. A demonstrative and possessive pronoun.
子	zi3	6939	Child, son or daughter, offspring; suffix; bride, wife; gentleman, officer, master, prince; young lady; the first of the *Earthly Branches*.
无	wu2	7173	No, not, negative; without, does not possess, not have.
咎	jiu4	1192	Fault, blame, mistake, wrong; inauspicious; misfortune, bad luck, calamity; reproach, censure.

Nine in the second place

The Caldron is full. My enemy is anxious, but cannot get at me.
Good fortune.

鼎	ding3	6392	Caldron; three-legged bronze cauldron with two ears.
有	you3	7533	Have, possession, there be, there is.
實	shi2	5821	Contents, substance; actual, real; full, fill; solid, truthful, honest; fruit.
我	wo3	4778	We, us, I, my, mine, our.
仇	chou2	1332	Enemy, antagonist; feud, hate; comrade, mate; counterpart. The *Mawangdui* manuscript has an unknown character composed of the 'dagger-ax' signific. Hence, using 'enemy' may be the best option.
有	you3	7533	Have, possession, there be, there is.
疾	ji2	0492	Ill, harm, defect, stress; hurry; hate.
不	bu4	5379	No, not, negative prefix; without, none, nothing, will not, need not, will not be.
我	wo3	4778	We, us, I, my, mine, our.
能	neng2	4648	Able, skill, power, talent, ability, expertise.
即	ji2	0495	Approach, come to; promptly.
吉	ji2	0476	Good fortune, auspicious, promising, fortunate, lucky, advantageous, happiness, good auspices. It is the only single character meaning good luck in the *YiJing*.

Nine in the third place

The handles of the Caldron are removed. Progress is impeded.
The fat pheasant meat is not eaten. Rain falls all around
and regrets disappear. Finally there will be good fortune.

鼎	ding3	6392	Caldron; three-legged bronze cauldron with two ears.
耳	er3	1744	Ear/s, handle/s; that which is at the side (as handles).
革	ge2	3314	Change, change seasons, molt; revolution, overthrow; skin or hide, rawhide, hide without the hair, flay, peel off; ancient representations depict an animal hide spread out.
其	qi2	0525	Their, his, its, the; this, that. A demonstrative and possessive pronoun.
行	xing2	2754	Move, go, advance, act, do.

The Caldron (275) 50

塞	se4	5446	To stop up, block, hinder, impede, seal, close; a (frontier) pass, strait.
雉	zhi4	0968	Pheasant. Bird associated with the trigram *Li*, The Adherent, the Fire.
膏	gao1	3296	Fat, grease, far meat; richness, favors, dispensing favors.
不	bu4	5379	No, not, negative prefix; without, none, nothing, will not, need not, will not be.
食	shi2	5810	Eat, feed, ingest; food, give food to; nourishment; salary of an officer, livelihood; eclipse (eating of Sun or Moon).
方	fang1	1802	Square, squarely, directly, straightforward, honest; a place, a region; on all sides; direction, trend, method; suddenly, quick, definite; take a place, occupy; sacrifice to the spirits of the four quarters.
雨	yu3	7662	Rain, shower, sudden downpour.
虧	kui1	3650	Wane, diminish, lessen; failure, loss, deficiency; danger.
悔	hui3	2336	Repent, regret, contrition; trouble. This word indicates both an objective situation and a subjective reaction to such circumstance.
終	zhong1	1500	End, finish, complete; for ever; end of a cycle; carried to conclusion, consummation, closure; death. The original meaning was: tied-off end of a thread.
吉	ji2	0476	Good fortune, auspicious, promising, fortunate, lucky, advantageous, happiness, good auspices. It is the only single character meaning good luck in the *YiJing*.

Nine in the fourth place

> The Caldron legs are broken. The stew is spilled
> and stains the Prince's figure. Misfortune.

鼎	ding3	6392	Caldron; three-legged bronze cauldron with two ears.
折	zhe2	0267	Sever, break; bend, destroy, execute; decide a cause, discriminate, judge.
足	zu2	6824	Leg, foot, base, support.
覆	fu4	1993	Overturn, tip over, spill.
公	gong1	3701	Prince, feudal lord, duke, noble of rank (the nobiliary titles, from high to low, were: duke, marquis, count, viscount, baron); public, impartial, with justice, fair.
餗	su4	5506	Stew of meat and vegetables, meal, rice stew.

其	qi2	0525	Their, his, its, the; this, that. A demonstrative and possessive pronoun.
形	xing2	2759	Figure, shape, appearance.
渥	wo4	7162	Soak, smear, moisten, stain.
凶	xiong1	2808	Misfortune, pitfall, ominous, bad, unlucky, disastrous, trouble, accident.

Six in the fifth place

> The Caldron has yellow handles and metal rings.
> The determination is favorable.

鼎	ding3	6392	Caldron; three-legged bronze cauldron with two ears.
黃	huang2	2297	Yellow, yellow-brown; color of the soil in central China. In the *YiJing* the yellow color is always favorable, it is the color of the middle and the moderation and it was the imperial color since the *Han* dynasty.
耳	er3	1744	Ear/s, handle/s; that which is at the side (as handles).
金	jin1	1057	Metal, bronze, gold, golden; money, riches.
鉉	xuan4	2886	Rings, carrying rings, ears or bar for carrying a three-legged bronze caldron.
利	li4	3867	Favorable, lucky, advantageous, profitable, beneficial, furthering, harvesting; sharp, sharp witted.
貞	zhen1	0346	Perseverance, persistence, determination, steadiness, firmness; straight, correct, verified, certain; pure, loyal. Its original meaning was "to determine an uncertain matter through divination".

Nine at the top

> The Caldron has rings of jade. Great good fortune.
> Nothing that is not favorable.

鼎	ding3	6392	Caldron; three-legged bronze cauldron with two ears.
玉	yu4	7666	Jade, a precious stone, a gem; precious.
鉉	xuan4	2886	Rings, carrying rings, ears or bar for carrying a three-legged bronze caldron.
大	da4	5943	Big, great, tall; excessive, arrogant; spread out and reach everywhere.
吉	ji2	0476	Good fortune, auspicious, promising, fortunate, lucky, advantageous, happiness, good auspices. It is the only single character meaning good luck in the *YiJing*.

无	wu2	7173	No, not, negative; without, does not possess, not have.
不	bu4	5379	No, not, negative prefix; without, none, nothing, will not, need not, will not be.
利	li4	3867	Favorable, lucky, advantageous, profitable, beneficial, furthering, harvesting; sharp, sharp witted.

51 震 zhen – The Arousing / Shock / Thunder

The Judgment

Shock. Success. The arrival of Shock causes great fear. But afterwards there are laughing words. Shock terrifies for a hundred *li*, but he doesn't drop the libation in the sacrificial ladle.

震	zhen4	0315	Shock; clap of thunder; fear; awe inspiring; stimulation, movement, excitation; to excite, to terrify; to quicken; endow, succor.
亨	heng1	2099	Success, prevalence, smooth progress, growth, consummate, triumph; pervade; offering, sacrifice.
震	zhen4	0315	Shock; clap of thunder; fear; awe inspiring; stimulation, movement, excitation; to excite, to terrify; to quicken; endow, succor.
來	lai2	3768	Come, arrive, return, bring.
虩	xi4	2480	Fear, fright, terror; sound of thunder (Kunst).
虩	xi4	2480	震來虩虩: scared of the thunder.
笑	xiao4	2615	Laugh, smile, merriment, good humor.
言	yan2	7334	Talk, speech, words, sayings; big flute.
啞	e4	7226	Laugh, sound of laughter. When duplicated it also means: the raucous sounds of crows; the sound of a baby learning to speak; babble, confused noise.
啞	e4	7226	Laugh, sound of laughter. When duplicated it also means: the raucous sounds of crows; the sound of a baby learning to speak; babble, confused noise.
震	zhen4	0315	Shock; clap of thunder; fear; awe inspiring; stimulation, movement, excitation; to excite, to terrify; to quicken; endow, succor.
驚	jing1	1140	Frighten, to be afraid, alarmed, startled; stampede.
百	bai3	4976	Hundred, hundredth, a hundred times, numerous, many.

The Arousing (279) 51

里	li3	3857	Unit of distance, about 500 m or 1800 feet; a village with 25-50 families; place of residence.
不	bu4	5379	No, not, negative prefix; without, none, nothing, will not, need not, will not be.
喪	sang4	5429	Lose, let drop, disappear, destroy, perish, mourning, burial.
匕	bi3	5076	Sacrificial spoon, used to pour libations in the sacrifices, ladle.
鬯	chang4	0232	Aromatic spirits, libation, sacrificial spirits made up by fermenting millet (*Panicum miliaceum*) and fragrant herbs.

The Image

Thunder repeated: The image of Shock.
Thus the noble puts his life in order with apprehension and fear, and evaluates himself.

洊	jian4	0880	Continuous flow, repeated, for a second time; flowing water.
雷	lei2	4236	Thunder, shock, terrifying, arousing power surging from the earth.
震	zhen4	0315	Shock; clap of thunder; fear; awe inspiring; stimulation, movement, excitation; to excite, to terrify; to quicken; endow, succor.
君	jun1	1715	Noble, prince, aristocrat, lord, chief, gentleman; honorable, a highly principled person, superior man. Most times, this character appears alongside another one, forming the word *JunZi*, whose original meaning was "son of a prince or ruler": 君子.
子	zi3	6939	Child, son or daughter, offspring; suffix; bride, wife; gentleman, officer, master, prince; young lady; the first of the *Earthly Branches*.
以	yi3	2932	Thus, in that way, by means of, with, for; instrument, medium, method, use (of), way (to).
恐	kong3	3721	Fear, apprehensive, anxious, worried.
懼	ju4	1560	Fear, dread, alarm, apprehension.
脩	xiu1	2795	This character means "dried meat", but in the *YiJing* is used as a loan for 修 and hence takes its meaning: cultivate, put in order, arrange, repair, elaborate.
省	xing3	5744	Visit, inspect, study, go and visit, inspection visit; examine oneself; frugal, to save, to reduce.

51

Nine at the beginning

The arrival of Shock causes great fear.
But afterwards there are laughing words. Good fortune.

震	zhen4	0315	Shock; clap of thunder; fear; awe inspiring; stimulation, movement, excitation; to excite, to terrify; to quicken; endow, succor.
來	lai2	3768	Come, arrive, return, bring.
虩	xi4	2480	Fear, fright, terror; sound of thunder (Kunst).
虩	xi4	2480	震來虩虩: scared of the thunder.
後	hou4	2143	Later, behind, rear, afterward, come after; follow; descendants, successor.
笑	xiao4	2615	Laugh, smile, merriment, good humor.
言	yan2	7334	Talk, speech, words, sayings; big flute.
啞	e4	7226	Laugh, sound of laughter. When duplicated it also means:
啞	e4	7226	the raucous sounds of crows; the sound of a baby learning to speak; babble, confused noise.
吉	ji2	0476	Good fortune, auspicious, promising, fortunate, lucky, advantageous, happiness, good auspices. It is the only single character meaning good luck in the *YiJing*.

Six in the second place

Shock comes with risk. You lose one hundred thousand cowries
and climb the nine hills. Do not go in pursuit.
In seven days you will get them.

震	zhen4	0315	Shock; clap of thunder; fear; awe inspiring; stimulation, movement, excitation; to excite, to terrify; to quicken; endow, succor.
來	lai2	3768	Come, arrive, return, bring.
厲	li4	3906	Danger, threat; oppressive, cruel, wicked, brutal, harsh; sickness, malevolent devil; grind, polish, sharpen; discipline.
億	yi4	3042	Hundred-thousand; many, great number; exclamation: alas, oh!; quiet, satisfied.
喪	sang4	5429	Lose, let drop, disappear, destroy, perish, mourning, burial.
貝	bei4	5005	Coins, cowry shells, formerly used in China for currency.
躋	ji1	0461	Climb, ascend, scale, go up, rise; steep.

The Arousing (281)

于	yu2	7592	At, to, in, into, on, from, by, go, go to, move towards, proceed, be.
九	jiu3	1198	The number nine, nine times, ninth.
陵	ling2	4067	Hill, mound (the meanings it seems to have in the *YiJing*); tumulus, barrow; ascend a hill, ascend; transgress, overstep the limits, invade, encroach upon, usurp.
勿	wu4	7208	Do not, no. Negative imperative.
逐	zhu2	1383	Chase, run after, hunt; expel, push out; in order, in succession; one by one.
七	qi1	0579	Seven, seventh; seventh day when the moon reaches a major phase after the new moon.
日	ri4	3124	Sun, day, daylight, daytime; daily.
得	de2	6161	Get, obtain, gain; reach, achieve; can; attain the desired thing.

Six in the third place

Shock stimulates and terrifies one.
If shock excites one to [the right] action, there will be no defect.

震	zhen4	0315	Shock; clap of thunder; fear; awe inspiring; stimulation, movement, excitation; to excite, to terrify; to quicken; endow, succor.
蘇	su1	5488	Distraught; tremble, fear, sound of thunder, rumbling sound; revive, awakens, enlivens, stimulate, excitate. Being duplicated intensifies its quality.
蘇	su1	5488	Distraught; tremble, fear, sound of thunder, rumbling sound; revive, awakens, enlivens, stimulate, excitate. Being duplicated intensifies its quality.
震	zhen4	0315	Shock; clap of thunder; fear; awe inspiring; stimulation, movement, excitation; to excite, to terrify; to quicken; endow, succor.
行	xing2	2754	Move, go, advance, act, do.
无	wu2	7173	No, not, negative; without, does not possess, not have.
眚	sheng3	5741	Disaster, calamity, serious mistake; offense by mishap or fault; cloudy eyes, disease of the eye, new moon, eclipse, meanings that indicate blindness or lack of light, a mistake due to ignorance or an error of judgment.

Nine in the fourth place

After Shock mud.

震	zhen4	0315	Shock; clap of thunder; fear; awe inspiring; stimulation, movement, excitation; to excite, to terrify; to quicken; endow, succor.
遂	sui4	5530	Advance; push through, go forward; proceed, prolong; follow along, pursuit, comply with; consequently, then, next.
泥	ni2	4660	Mud, sludge; mire, an area of wet, soggy ground, to be mired; to paste, to plaster; impeded, obstructed.

Six in the fifth place

Shock comes and goes. Danger. But nothing is lost.
There are things to do.

震	zhen4	0315	Shock; clap of thunder; fear; awe inspiring; stimulation, movement, excitation; to excite, to terrify; to quicken; endow, succor.
往	wang3	7050	Go, to go to, go forward, go towards; depart, bygone, former.
來	lai2	3768	Come, arrive, return, bring.
厲	li4	3906	Danger, threat; oppressive, cruel, wicked, brutal, harsh; sickness, malevolent devil; grind, polish, sharpen; discipline.
意	yi4	2960	Think, thought, intention, will.
无	wu2	7173	No, not, negative; without, does not possess, not have.
喪	sang4	5429	Lose, let drop, disappear, destroy, perish, mourning, burial.
有	you3	7533	Have, possession, there be, there is.
事	shi4	5787	Serve, service; affairs, business, matters.

Six at the top

Shock causes fear and agitation. One looks around in terror.
Marching forth brings misfortune. Shock does not reach you
but your neighbor. No defect. There is talk of marriage.

震	zhen4	0315	Shock; clap of thunder; fear; awe inspiring; stimulation, movement, excitation; to excite, to terrify; to quicken; endow, succor.

The Arousing

索	suo3	5459	Disquieted, apprehensive, tremble, fear. 震索索: startled and agitated, fear suscitated by the sound of thunder, which is intensified because the character is repeated.
索	suo3	5459	
視	shi4	5789	See, look, inspect, observe, regard.
矍	jue2	1704	Terrified, look around in fright or alarm, wild-eyed. Appearing duplicated intensifies its meaning.
矍	jue2	1704	
征	zheng1	0352	Punishing expedition ("to correct"), to reduce to submission, attack, punish; to levy taxes; comes, brings.
凶	xiong1	2808	Misfortune, pitfall, ominous, bad, unlucky, disastrous, trouble, accident.
震	zhen4	0315	Shock; clap of thunder; fear; awe inspiring; stimulation, movement, excitation; to excite, to terrify; to quicken; endow, succor.
不	bu4	5379	No, not, negative prefix; without, none, nothing, will not, need not, will not be.
于	yu2	7592	At, to, in, into, on, from, by, go, go to, move towards, proceed, be.
其	qi2	0525	Their, his, its, the; this, that. A demonstrative and possessive pronoun.
躬	gong1	3704	Oneself, (own) body, person.
于	yu2	7592	At, to, in, into, on, from, by, go, go to, move towards, proceed, be.
其	qi2	0525	Their, his, its, the; this, that. A demonstrative and possessive pronoun.
鄰	lin2	4033	Neighbor, neighborhood, extended family, associate, assistant.
无	wu2	7173	No, not, negative; without, does not possess, not have.
咎	jiu4	1192	Fault, blame, mistake, wrong; inauspicious; misfortune, bad luck, calamity; reproach, censure.
婚	hun1	2360	Marriage, take a wife; bridegroom, ally.
媾	gou4	3426	Marriage, a second marriage, mating, match, families united by marriage; suitor, groom; allying, friendship, favor.
有	you3	7533	Have, possession, there be, there is.
言	yan2	7334	Talk, speech, words, sayings; big flute.

52  gen – Restraint / Mountain

THE JUDGMENT

> Restraining his back. Doesn't feel his body.
> Goes to his courtyard and doesn't see his people. No defect.

艮	gen4	3327	Keeping still, limit, check, restrain, stop, enclose; obstinate, opposed; obstacle.
其	qi2	0525	Their, his, its, the; this, that. A demonstrative and possessive pronoun.
背	bei4	4989	Back, spine, back side, behind.
不	bu4	5379	No, not, negative prefix; without, none, nothing, will not, need not, will not be.
獲	huo4	2412	Catch (in hunt), seize, get, obtain, hit the mark, find; succeed. What is caught, gotten or found may be a thing, a person, an opportunity, an idea or perception.
其	qi2	0525	Their, his, its, the; this, that. A demonstrative and possessive pronoun.
身	shen1	5718	Body, trunk, torso, person, psyche, oneself, lifespan; pregnant woman, womb (Kunst).
行	xing2	2754	Move, go, advance, act, do.
其	qi2	0525	Their, his, its, the; this, that. A demonstrative and possessive pronoun.
庭	ting2	6405	Courtyard (of palace), court, audience chamber; hall, courtyard, chambers; family.
不	bu4	5379	No, not, negative prefix; without, none, nothing, will not, need not, will not be.
見	jian4	0860	See, observe, look at, to be seen; cause to appear; be exposed to, display, reveal; interview, visit or call on, meet.
其	qi2	0525	Their, his, its, the; this, that. A demonstrative and possessive pronoun.
人	ren2	3097	Man, person(s); people; others; human being, individual.
无	wu2	7173	No, not, negative; without, does not possess, not have.
咎	jiu4	1192	Fault, blame, mistake, wrong; inauspicious; misfortune, bad luck, calamity; reproach, censure.

Restraint (285) 52

The Image

> Joined Mountains: The image of Restraint.
> Thus the noble doesn't let his thoughts wander beyond his position.

兼	jian1	0830	Adjacent, joined, connected, combined; together both, equally, double; at the same time.
山	shan1	5630	Mountain, hill, peak.
艮	gen4	3327	Keeping still, limit, check, restrain, stop, enclose; obstinate, opposed; obstacle.
君	jun1	1715	Noble, prince, aristocrat, lord, chief, gentleman; honorable, a highly principled person, superior man. Most times, this character appears alongside another one, forming the word *JunZi*, whose original meaning was "son of a prince or ruler": 君子.
子	zi3	6939	Child, son or daughter, offspring; suffix; bride, wife; gentleman, officer, master, prince; young lady; the first of the *Earthly Branches*.
以	yi3	2932	Thus, in that way, by means of, with, for; instrument, medium, method, use (of), way (to).
思	si1	5580	Think, consider, ponder; brood, reflect, plan.
不	bu4	5379	No, not, negative prefix; without, none, nothing, will not, need not, will not be.
出	chu1	1409	Go out, came out, appear, departure; arise, emerge; bring out, take out, expel, leave, get rid of; produce, beget.
其	qi2	0525	Their, his, its, the; this, that. A demonstrative and possessive pronoun.
位	wei4	7116	Position, location; category, rank, status; situation.

Six at the beginning

> Restraining his toes. No defect. Long term determination is favorable.

艮	gen4	3327	Keeping still, limit, check, restrain, stop, enclose; obstinate, opposed; obstacle.
其	qi2	0525	Their, his, its, the; this, that. A demonstrative and possessive pronoun.
趾	zhi3	0944	Toes, feet, hoof, paw. Legs (of animals or furniture), footprints, tracks.
无	wu2	7173	No, not, negative; without, does not possess, not have.
咎	jiu4	1192	Fault, blame, mistake, wrong; inauspicious; misfortune, bad luck, calamity; reproach, censure.

利	li4	3867	Favorable, lucky, advantageous, profitable, beneficial, furthering, harvesting; sharp, sharp witted.
永	yong3	7589	For a long time, constant, permanent, everlasting; prolong; distant, far reaching.
貞	zhen1	0346	Perseverance, persistence, determination, steadiness, firmness; straight, correct, verified, certain; pure, loyal. Its original meaning was "to determine an uncertain matter through divination".

Six in the second place

Restraining his calves doesn't help out his followers.
His heart is not happy.

艮	gen4	3327	Keeping still, limit, check, restrain, stop, enclose; obstinate, opposed; obstacle.
其	qi2	0525	Their, his, its, the; this, that. A demonstrative and possessive pronoun.
腓	fei2	1830	Calves of the legs.
不	bu4	5379	No, not, negative prefix; without, none, nothing, will not, need not, will not be.
拯	zheng3	0360	Relief, rescue, to lift up, to raise; geld, remove (Kunst, Rutt).
其	qi2	0525	Their, his, its, the; this, that. A demonstrative and possessive pronoun.
隨	sui2	5523	Follow, pursue; conform to, respond, follow a way or religion; subsequently, in the course of time; listen to, submit; marrow, flesh.
其	qi2	0525	Their, his, its, the; this, that. A demonstrative and possessive pronoun.
心	xin1	2735	Heart; conscience, moral nature; soul; core; mind; source of feelings, intentions, will.
不	bu4	5379	No, not, negative prefix; without, none, nothing, will not, need not, will not be.
快	kuai4	3547	Glad, pleased, cheerful, satisfied.

Nine in the third place

Restraining his hips. Tears the region of the reins.
Danger. The heart is suffocated.

艮	gen4	3327	Keeping still, limit, check, restrain, stop, enclose; obstinate, opposed; obstacle.

Restraint (287) 52

其	qi2	0525	Their, his, its, the; this, that. A demonstrative and possessive pronoun.
限	xian4	2696	Hips, waist, loins, midsection; boundary (the waist is the boundary between the upper and the lower body parts); limit, frontier, divisory line.
列	lie4	3984	Rend, tear, divide; sort, distribute, arrange in order, classify, organize.
其	qi2	0525	Their, his, its, the; this, that. A demonstrative and possessive pronoun.
夤	yin2	7427	Sacrum, lumbar area, small of the back, lower back, loins; spinal meat.
厲	li4	3906	Danger, threat; oppressive, cruel, wicked, brutal, harsh; sickness, malevolent devil; grind, polish, sharpen; discipline.
熏	xun1	2906	To smoke (meat), choke, suffocate; smoke out; fog, vapor, mist.
心	xin1	2735	Heart; conscience, moral nature; soul; core; mind; source of feelings, intentions, will.

Six in the fourth place

Restrains his torso. No defect.

艮	gen4	3327	Keeping still, limit, check, restrain, stop, enclose; obstinate, opposed; obstacle.
其	qi2	0525	Their, his, its, the; this, that. A demonstrative and possessive pronoun.
身	shen1	5718	Body, trunk, torso, person, psyche, oneself, lifespan; pregnant woman, womb (Kunst, 52.4).
无	wu2	7173	No, not, negative; without, does not possess, not have.
咎	jiu4	1192	Fault, blame, mistake, wrong; inauspicious; misfortune, bad luck, calamity; reproach, censure.

Six in the fifth place

Restrains his jaws. What he says is orderly. Repentance fades.

艮	gen4	3327	Keeping still, limit, check, restrain, stop, enclose; obstinate, opposed; obstacle.
其	qi2	0525	Their, his, its, the; this, that. A demonstrative and possessive pronoun.
輔	fu3	1945	Jaws, cheeks, cheek bone; protect, help, support.
言	yan2	7334	Talk, speech, words, sayings; big flute.

有	you3	7533	Have, possession, there be, there is.
序	xu4	2851	Order, sequence, sequential, put in order.
悔	hui3	2336	Repent, regret, contrition; trouble. This word indicates both an objective situation and a subjective reaction to such circumstance.
亡	wang2	7034	Go away, disappear, exile; fail; destroy, perish, not have, not exist.

Nine at the top

Sincere restrain. Good fortune.

敦	dun1	6571	Earnest, generous, authentic, honest, sincere; staunch, strong, thick, solid.
艮	gen4	3327	Keeping still, limit, check, restrain, stop, enclose; obstinate, opposed; obstacle.
吉	ji2	0476	Good fortune, auspicious, promising, fortunate, lucky, advantageous, happiness, good auspices. It is the only single character meaning good luck in the *YiJing*.

53 漸 *jian* – Gradual Development

The Judgment

Gradual Development. The maiden's marriage brings good fortune. The determination is favorable.

漸	jian4	0878	Gradual development, gradually, increasingly; advance by degrees; moisten, dip down into, imbue, influence. Advance like the water, infiltrating gradually.
女	nu3	4776	Maiden, woman, lady, girl, feminine.
歸	gui1	3617	Send in marriage, marriage of a woman, go as a bride to the new home; return to, revert to, to send back.
吉	ji2	0476	Good fortune, auspicious, promising, fortunate, lucky, advantageous, happiness, good auspices. It is the only single character meaning good luck in the *YiJing*.
利	li4	3867	Favorable, lucky, advantageous, profitable, beneficial, furthering, harvesting; sharp, sharp witted.
貞	zhen1	0346	Perseverance, persistence, determination, steadiness, firmness; straight, correct, verified, certain; pure, loyal. Its original meaning was "to determine an uncertain matter through divination".

The Image

On the Mountain is a Tree: The image of Gradual Development.
Thus the noble dwells in virtue
and so improves the mores of the people.

山	shan1	5630	Mountain, hill, peak.
上	shang4	5669	Up, above, on, over, upwards, top, rise; higher, superior; first, best.
有	you3	7533	Have, possession, there be, there is.
木	mu4	4593	Tree, wood, timber, wooden.
漸	jian4	0878	Gradual development, gradually, increasingly; advance by degrees; moisten, dip down into, imbue, influence. Advance like the water, infiltrating gradually.

君	jun1	1715	Noble, prince, aristocrat, lord, chief, gentleman; honorable, a highly principled person, superior man. Most times, this character appears alongside another one, forming the word *JunZi*, whose original meaning was "son of a prince or ruler": 君子.
子	zi3	6939	Child, son or daughter, offspring; suffix; bride, wife; gentleman, officer, master, prince; young lady; the first of the *Earthly Branches*.
以	yi3	2932	Thus, in that way, by means of, with, for; instrument, medium, method, use (of), way (to).
居	ju1	1535	Remain; rest (in); abides, dwell; to occupy a position or place; overbearing, arrogant.
賢	xian2	2671	Virtuous and able, worthy, superior, wise, morally good. 賢德: virtue and kindheartedness.
德	de2	6162	Virtue, spiritual power, moral integrity; quality, nature, aptitude, ability, character.
善	shan4	5657	Good, virtuous; perfect, improve.
俗	su2	5497	Mores, popular usage; common, vulgar, unrefined, current.

Six at the beginning

The goose gradually moves toward the riverbank.
The child is in danger and will be spoken against him. No defect.

鴻	hong2	2386	Wild goose or swan.
漸	jian4	0878	Gradual development, gradually, increasingly; advance by degrees; moisten, dip down into, imbue, influence. Advance like the water, infiltrating gradually.
于	yu2	7592	At, to, in, into, on, from, by, go, go to, move towards, proceed, be.
干	gan1	3211	Shore, riverbank (this is the meaning used in the *YiJing*); invade, violate, oppose, offend against.
小	xiao3	2605	Small, insignificant, common, humble, mediocre; diminish, belittle.
子	zi3	6939	Child, son or daughter, offspring; suffix; bride, wife; gentleman, officer, master, prince; young lady; the first of the *Earthly Branches*.
厲	li4	3906	Danger, threat; oppressive, cruel, wicked, brutal, harsh; sickness, malevolent devil; grind, polish, sharpen; discipline.
有	you3	7533	Have, possession, there be, there is.

Gradual Development (291)

言	yan2	7334	Talk, speech, words, sayings; big flute.
無	wu2	7173	No, not, negative; without, does not possess, not have.
咎	jiu4	1192	Fault, blame, mistake, wrong; inauspicious; misfortune, bad luck, calamity; reproach, censure.

Six in the second place

The goose gradually moves toward the rock;
eats and drinks joyfully. Good fortune.

鴻	hong2	2386	Wild goose or swan.
漸	jian4	0878	Gradual development, gradually, increasingly; advance by degrees; moisten, dip down into, imbue, influence. Advance like the water, infiltrating gradually.
于	yu2	7592	At, to, in, into, on, from, by, go, go to, move towards, proceed, be.
磐	pan2	4904	Boulder, large rock; stable, immovable.
飲	yin3	7454	Drink; swallow; give to drink. 飲食: drink and eat; eating together.
食	shi2	5810	Eat, feed, ingest; food, give food to; nourishment; salary of an officer, livelihood; eclipse (eating of Sun or Moon).
衎	kan4	3252	Rejoice, to be pleased, to give pleasure; geese honking sounds, calls.
衎	kan4	3252	Rejoice, to be pleased, to give pleasure; geese honking sounds, calls.
吉	ji2	0476	Good fortune, auspicious, promising, fortunate, lucky, advantageous, happiness, good auspices. It is the only single character meaning good luck in the *YiJing*.

Nine in the third place

The goose gradually moves to the highlands.
The man goes on an expedition but does not return,
the woman is pregnant but does not give birth. Misfortune.
It is favorable to fend off bandits.

鴻	hong2	2386	Wild goose or swan.
漸	jian4	0878	Gradual development, gradually, increasingly; advance by degrees; moisten, dip down into, imbue, influence. Advance like the water, infiltrating gradually.
于	yu2	7592	At, to, in, into, on, from, by, go, go to, move towards, proceed, be.

陸	lu4	4191	Highland, plateau, heights, dry land.
夫	fu1	1908	Man, male adult, husband; this, that, those.
征	zheng1	0352	Punishing expedition ("to correct"), to reduce to submission, attack, punish; to levy taxes; comes, brings.
不	bu4	5379	No, not, negative prefix; without, none, nothing, will not, need not, will not be.
復	fu4	1992	Return, turn back; repeat, restore, revert, recommence.
婦	fu4	1963	Woman, lady, wife, married woman.
孕	yun4	7765	Pregnancy, to conceive.
不	bu4	5379	No, not, negative prefix; without, none, nothing, will not, need not, will not be.
育	yu4	7687	Give birth; rear, breed, raise, nurture, nourish, bring up, educate.
凶	xiong1	2808	Misfortune, pitfall, ominous, bad, unlucky, disastrous, trouble, accident.
利	li4	3867	Favorable, lucky, advantageous, profitable, beneficial, furthering, harvesting; sharp, sharp witted.
禦	yu4	7665	Defend against, fight off, resist, withstand, hold out against, hinder.
寇	kou4	3444	Bandit, invader, enemy, robber, violent people, outcasts, plunderers.

Six in the fourth place

The goose gradually moves toward the woods.
It may find a flat branch. No defect.

鴻	hong2	2386	Wild goose or swan.
漸	jian4	0878	Gradual development, gradually, increasingly; advance by degrees; moisten, dip down into, imbue, influence. Advance like the water, infiltrating gradually.
于	yu2	7592	At, to, in, into, on, from, by, go, go to, move towards, proceed, be.
木	mu4	4593	Tree, wood, timber, wooden.
或	huo4	2402	Perhaps, possibly, if, by chance; doubtful, uncertain; some, someone, something, sometime.
得	de2	6161	Get, obtain, gain; reach, achieve; can; attain the desired thing.
其	qi2	0525	Their, his, its, the; this, that. A demonstrative and possessive pronoun.

Gradual Development (293)

桷	jue2	1175	Flat or horizontal branch; rafter, roof beams.
无	wu2	7173	No, not, negative; without, does not possess, not have.
咎	jiu4	1192	Fault, blame, mistake, wrong; inauspicious; misfortune, bad luck, calamity; reproach, censure.

Nine in the fifth place

> The goose gradually moves toward the top of the hill.
> The woman can not conceive for three years.
> Finally, nothing can stop it. Good fortune.

鴻	hong2	2386	Wild goose or swan.
漸	jian4	0878	Gradual development, gradually, increasingly; advance by degrees; moisten, dip down into, imbue, influence. Advance like the water, infiltrating gradually.
于	yu2	7592	At, to, in, into, on, from, by, go, go to, move towards, proceed, be.
陵	ling2	4067	Hill, mound (the meanings it seems to have in the *YiJing*); tumulus, barrow; ascend a hill, ascend; transgress, overstep the limits, invade, encroach upon, usurp.
婦	fu4	1963	Woman, lady, wife, married woman.
三	san1	5415	Three, thrice, third time or place.
歲	sui4	5538	Years, seasons, harvests.
不	bu4	5379	No, not, negative prefix; without, none, nothing, will not, need not, will not be.
孕	yun4	7765	Pregnancy, to conceive.
終	zhong1	1500	End, finish, complete; for ever; end of a cycle; carried to conclusion, consummation, closure; death. The original meaning was: tied-off end of a thread.
莫	mo4	4557	Nobody, nothing, none, no, not one, not at all, there is not, an absolute negative; evening, late.
之	zhi1	0935	Personal pronoun, he she, it; this, that, these, etc.; often used as a possessive.
勝	sheng4	5754	Defeat, subdue, vanquish, overcome; excel, surpass, be better than; victory, triumph, success.
吉	ji2	0476	Good fortune, auspicious, promising, fortunate, lucky, advantageous, happiness, good auspices. It is the only single character meaning good luck in the *YiJing*.

Nine at the top

> The goose gradually moves toward the highlands.
> Its feathers can be used to practice the rites. Good fortune.

鴻	hong2	2386	Wild goose or swan.
漸	jian4	0878	Gradual development, gradually, increasingly; advance by degrees; moisten, dip down into, imbue, influence. Advance like the water, infiltrating gradually.
于	yu2	7592	At, to, in, into, on, from, by, go, go to, move towards, proceed, be.
陸	lu4	4191	Highland, plateau, heights, dry land.
其	qi2	0525	Their, his, its, the; this, that. A demonstrative and possessive pronoun.
羽	yu3	7658	Feathers, wings, plums.
可	ke3	3381	Can, able, may; permit, allow; satisfactory, proper, suitable.
用	yong4	7567	Use, apply, put to use, apply the oracle to real world situations; hereby, thereby.
爲	wei2	7059	Act, do, accomplish, make, to be; act for, stand for, support, help; become.
儀	yi2	3003	Ceremony, ritual, sacred dances; protocol, decorum, courtesy, proper behavior.
吉	ji2	0476	Good fortune, auspicious, promising, fortunate, lucky, advantageous, happiness, good auspices. It is the only single character meaning good luck in the *YiJing*.

54 歸妹 *gui mei*
The Marrying Maiden

THE JUDGMENT

The Marrying Maiden. Marching forth brings misfortune.
Nothing that is favorable.

歸	gui1	3617	Send in marriage, marriage of a woman, go as a bride to the new home; return to, revert to, to send back.
妹	mei4	4410	Younger sister, maiden, daughter, daughter of a secondary wife; virgin.
征	zheng1	0352	Punishing expedition ("to correct"), to reduce to submission, attack, punish; to levy taxes; comes, brings.
凶	xiong1	2808	Misfortune, pitfall, ominous, bad, unlucky, disastrous, trouble, accident.
无	wu2	7173	No, not, negative; without, does not possess, not have.
攸	you1	7519	Goal, direction, destination, objective; distant, far away; a place; that which, whereby, thereby, for which; mark of the passive voice.
利	li4	3867	Favorable, lucky, advantageous, profitable, beneficial, furthering, harvesting; sharp, sharp witted.

THE IMAGE

On the Lake is the Thunder: The image of the Marrying Maiden.
Thus the noble persists to the end and knows the cause of the damage.

澤	ze2	0277	Marsh, pool, pond, lake; flat body of water and the vapors rising from it; enrich, fertilize, benefit; moist, moisten; glossy, polished.
上	shang4	5669	Up, above, on, over, upwards, top, rise; higher, superior; first, best.
有	you3	7533	Have, possession, there be, there is.
雷	lei2	4236	Thunder, shock, terrifying, arousing power surging from the earth.
歸	gui1	3617	Send in marriage, marriage of a woman, go as a bride to the new home; return to, revert to, to send back.

妹	mei4	4410	Younger sister, maiden, daughter, daughter of a secondary wife; virgin.
君	jun1	1715	Noble, prince, aristocrat, lord, chief, gentleman; honorable, a highly principled person, superior man. Most times, this character appears alongside another one, forming the word *JunZi*, whose original meaning was "son of a prince or ruler": 君子.
子	zi3	6939	Child, son or daughter, offspring; suffix; bride, wife; gentleman, officer, master, prince; young lady; the first of the *Earthly Branches*.
以	yi3	2932	Thus, in that way, by means of, with, for; instrument, medium, method, use (of), way (to).
永	yong3	7589	For a long time, constant, permanent, everlasting; prolong; distant, far reaching.
終	zhong1	1500	End, finish, complete; for ever; end of a cycle; carried to conclusion, consummation, closure; death. The original meaning was: tied-off end of a thread.
知	zhi1	0932	Knows, understands; informed, wise.
敝	bi4	5101	Broken, worn out, shabby, tattered, ruined; damage; unworthy, poor, vile.

Nine at the beginning

She marries as a concubine. A lame man can walk.
Marching forth brings good fortune.

歸	gui1	3617	Send in marriage, marriage of a woman, go as a bride to the new home; return to, revert to, to send back.
妹	mei4	4410	Younger sister, maiden, daughter, daughter of a secondary wife; virgin.
以	yi3	2932	Thus, in that way, by means of, with, for; instrument, medium, method, use (of), way (to).
娣	di4	6202	Younger secondary wife, under the authority of the first wife; concubine.
跛	bo3	5317	Lame, limping, crippled.
能	neng2	4648	Able, skill, power, talent, ability, expertise.
履	lu3	3893	Step on, treading, track, walk or follow a trail or way; footwear, shoes; conduct, behavior; ceremonies.
征	zheng1	0352	Punishing expedition ("to correct"), to reduce to submission, attack, punish; to levy taxes; comes, brings.
吉	ji2	0476	Good fortune, auspicious, promising, fortunate, lucky, advantageous, happiness, good auspices. It is the only single character meaning good luck in the *YiJing*.

The Marrying Maiden (297) 54

Nine in the second place

A one-eyed man can see.
The determination of a secluded man is favorable.

眇	miao3	4476	Weak-sighted, one-eyed, having one eye smaller than the other.
能	neng2	4648	Able, skill, power, talent, ability, expertise.
視	shi4	5789	See, look, inspect, observe, regard.
利	li4	3867	Favorable, lucky, advantageous, profitable, beneficial, furthering, harvesting; sharp, sharp witted.
幽	you1	7505	Dark, obscure; solitary, secluded, hidden from view; secret, difficult to understand.
人	ren2	3097	Man, person(s); people; others; human being, individual.
之	zhi1	0935	Personal pronoun, he she, it; this, that, these, etc.; often used as a possessive.
貞	zhen1	0346	Perseverance, persistence, determination, steadiness, firmness; straight, correct, verified, certain; pure, loyal. Its original meaning was "to determine an uncertain matter through divination".

Six in the third place

The Marrying Maiden in servitude.
She returns and marries as a secondary wife.

歸	gui1	3617	Send in marriage, marriage of a woman, go as a bride to the new home; return to, revert to, to send back.
妹	mei4	4410	Younger sister, maiden, daughter, daughter of a secondary wife; virgin.
以	yi3	2932	Thus, in that way, by means of, with, for; instrument, medium, method, use (of), way (to).
嬬	xu1	8011	Concubine, mistress, slave.
反	fan3	1781	Turn, reverse, come back, return.
歸	gui1	3617	Send in marriage, marriage of a woman, go as a bride to the new home; return to, revert to, to send back.
以	yi3	2932	Thus, in that way, by means of, with, for; instrument, medium, method, use (of), way (to).
娣	di4	6202	Younger secondary wife, under the authority of the first wife; concubine.

Nine in the fourth place

The Marrying Maiden delays marriage, waiting for the right time. There will be a late marriage.

歸	gui1	3617	Send in marriage, marriage of a woman, go as a bride to the new home; return to, revert to, to send back.
妹	mei4	4410	Younger sister, maiden, daughter, daughter of a secondary wife; virgin.
愆	qian1	0889	Exceed, pass the limit; error, transgression.
期	qi2	0526	Period, time limit, a full fixed time, a year, seasons.
遲	chi2	1024	Hesitation, delay, slow, dilatory, late, procrastinate.
歸	gui1	3617	Send in marriage, marriage of a woman, go as a bride to the new home; return to, revert to, to send back.
有	you3	7533	Have, possession, there be, there is.
時	shi2	5780	Time, season, epoch, period, opportune moment.

Six in the fifth place

The Emperor *Yi* gives her daughter in marriage. The sleeves of her dress were less gorgeous than those of the secondary wife. The moon is almost full. Good fortune.

帝	di4	6204	Sovereign, emperor, god.
乙	yi3	3017	*Yi*, name of the penultimate *Shang* Emperor; cyclic character: second stem.
歸	gui1	3617	Send in marriage, marriage of a woman, go as a bride to the new home; return to, revert to, to send back.
妹	mei4	4410	Younger sister, maiden, daughter, daughter of a secondary wife; virgin.
其	qi2	0525	Their, his, its, the; this, that. A demonstrative and possessive pronoun.
君	jun1	1715	Noble, prince, aristocrat, lord, chief, gentleman; honorable, a highly principled person, superior man. Most times, this character appears alongside another one, forming the word *JunZi*, whose original meaning was "son of a prince or ruler": 君子.
之	zhi1	0935	Personal pronoun, he she, it; this, that, these, etc.; often used as a possessive.
袂	mei4	4456	Sleeves, sleeve of a robe, embroidered garments, gown.

The Marrying Maiden (299) 54

不	bu4	5379	No, not, negative prefix; without, none, nothing, will not, need not, will not be.
如	ru2	3137	Thus, in this way, as, like, similar to, if (conditional).
其	qi2	0525	Their, his, its, the; this, that. A demonstrative and possessive pronoun.
娣	di4	6202	Younger secondary wife, under the authority of the first wife; concubine.
之	zhi1	0935	Personal pronoun, he she, it; this, that, these, etc.; often used as a possessive.
袂	mei4	4456	Sleeves, sleeve of a robe, embroidered garments, gown.
良	liang2	3941	Good, fine, gorgeous, excellent; virtuous; natural.
月	yue4	7696	The Moon, lunar month.
幾	ji1	0409	Almost; imminent, nearly; occasion; minutiae, first subtle signs; approaches.
望	wang4	7043	Full Moon; the 15th day of the lunar calendar; hope; expect; look forward to.
吉	ji2	0476	Good fortune, auspicious, promising, fortunate, lucky, advantageous, happiness, good auspices. It is the only single character meaning good luck in the *YiJing*.

Six at the top

The woman presents a basket, but it contains no fruit.
The man stabs a sheep but this does not bleed. Nothing is favorable.

女	nu3	4776	Maiden, woman, lady, girl, feminine.
承	cheng2	0386	To present; support, assist, bear, serve; receive, inherit.
筐	kuang1	3598	Open, square basket woven with strips of bamboo.
无	wu2	7173	No, not, negative; without, does not possess, not have.
實	shi2	5821	Contents, substance; actual, real; full, fill; solid, truthful, honest; fruit.
士	shi4	5776	Young man, bachelor, man, gentleman, warrior, soldier, officer.
刲	kui1	3642	Stab, cut, to cut open and clean (as fish), prepare for sacrifice (disembowel).
羊	yang2	7247	Sheep, ram, goat.
无	wu2	7173	No, not, negative; without, does not possess, not have.
血	xue4	2901	Blood, bleeding. Its ancient form shows a sacrificial vessel with its content.

无	wu2	7173	No, not, negative; without, does not possess, not have.
攸	you1	7519	Goal, direction, destination, objective; distant, far away; a place; that which, whereby, thereby, for which; mark of the passive voice.
利	li4	3867	Favorable, lucky, advantageous, profitable, beneficial, furthering, harvesting; sharp, sharp witted.

55 豐 *feng* – Abundance / Wholeness

THE JUDGMENT

Abundance has success. The King approaches.
Do not be sad. Suitable at midday.

豐	feng1	1897	Abundance, fullness; abundant, luxurious, bountiful, fruitful.
亨	heng1	2099	Success, prevalence, smooth progress, growth, consummate, triumph; pervade; offering, sacrifice.
王	wang2	7037	King, prince, sovereign, ruler.
假	jia3	0599	Approaches, goes to, attains.
之	zhi1	0935	Personal pronoun, he she, it; this, that, these, etc.; often used as a possessive.
勿	wu4	7208	Do not, no. Negative imperative.
憂	you1	7508	Grieved, sad, mournful; grief, melancholy.
宜	yi2	2993	Right, proper, sacrifice to the deity of the soil.
日	ri4	3124	Sun, day, daylight, daytime; daily.
中	zhong1	1504	Center, inner, in the inside, put in the center, hit (target); balanced, central, middle, correct.

THE IMAGE

Thunder and Lightning culminate altogether:
The image of Abundance. Thus the noble decides legal cases
and applies punishments.

雷	lei2	4236	Thunder, shock, terrifying, arousing power surging from the earth.
電	dian4	6358	Lightning, sudden illumination, complete clarity.
皆	jie1	0620	Altogether; everybody; in accord; together; complete.
至	zhi4	0982	Arrive, culminate, reach the highest point, utmost, superlative.

55 — MATRIX OF MEANINGS OF THE BOOK OF CHANGES

豐	feng1	1897	Abundance, fullness; abundant, luxurious, bountiful, fruitful.
君	jun1	1715	Noble, prince, aristocrat, lord, chief, gentleman; honorable, a highly principled person, superior man. Most times, this character appears alongside another one, forming the word *JunZi*, whose original meaning was "son of a prince or ruler": 君子.
子	zi3	6939	Child, son or daughter, offspring; suffix; bride, wife; gentleman, officer, master, prince; young lady; the first of the *Earthly Branches*.
以	yi3	2932	Thus, in that way, by means of, with, for; instrument, medium, method, use (of), way (to).
折	zhe2	0267	Sever, break; bend, destroy, execute; decide a cause, discriminate, judge.
獄	yu4	7685	Justice, litigation, lawsuit, criminal cases; prison, jail.
致	zhi4	0984	Bring about, cause; involve, induce; present, offer, hand over; send, transmit; extend, apply; carry on to the limit.
刑	xing2	2755	Punishment, discipline, sanction.

Nine at the beginning

Meets the master that is his match.
Even if they are together for ten days there will be no mistake.
Going forward attains rewards.

遇	yu4	7625	Meet, encounter, come across, happen.
其	qi2	0525	Their, his, its, the; this, that. A demonstrative and possessive pronoun.
配	pei4	5019	Match, equal, pair, colleague, consort; worthy, to be qualified.
主	zhu3	1336	Master, lord, chief; host, innkeeper.
雖	sui1	5519	Although, even if, still, though it be, supposing.
旬	xun2	2915	Ten-day week; period of time.
无	wu2	7173	No, not, negative; without, does not possess, not have.
咎	jiu4	1192	Fault, blame, mistake, wrong; inauspicious; misfortune, bad luck, calamity; reproach, censure.
往	wang3	7050	Go, to go to, go forward, go towards; depart, bygone, former.

Abundance (303) 55

有	you3	7533	Have, possession, there be, there is.
尚	shang4	5670	High, ascend, admirable, superior, surpass, respected, esteemed, reward; still, yet an besides, in addition to.

Six in the second place

> The curtain has such fullness that the Big Dipper could be seen at noon. Going forwards attains distrust and hatred. Manifest sincerity will have good fortune.

豐	feng1	1897	Abundance, fullness; abundant, luxurious, bountiful, fruitful.
其	qi2	0525	Their, his, its, the; this, that. A demonstrative and possessive pronoun.
蔀	bu4	8001	Screen, curtain, awning, hanging mat; old unit of time (cycle of 76 years).
日	ri4	3124	Sun, day, daylight, daytime; daily.
中	zhong1	1504	Center, inner, in the inside, put in the center, hit (target); balanced, central, middle, correct.
見	jian4	0860	See, observe, look at, to be seen; cause to appear; be exposed to, display, reveal; interview, visit or call on, meet.
斗	dou3	6472	Big Dipper (a cluster of seven stars in the constellation *Ursa Major*, four forming the bowl and three the handle of a dipper-shaped configuration, also called Plow or Plough); dipper; a unit of measure for grain.
往	wang3	7050	Go, to go to, go forward, go towards; depart, bygone, former.
得	de2	6161	Get, obtain, gain; reach, achieve; can; attain the desired thing.
疑	yi2	2940	Doubt, mistrust, suspect, hesitate.
疾	ji2	0492	Ill, harm, defect, stress; hurry; hate.
有	you3	7533	Have, possession, there be, there is.
孚	fu2	1936	Truth; reliable, sincere; to inspire confidence in others; capture, prisoner, plunder.
發	fa1	1768	Develop, expand, open, manifest, send out, emit, arouse.
若	ruo4	3126	Like, just as, to be like; agree, conform to; approve; concordant; compliant.
吉	ji2	0476	Good fortune, auspicious, promising, fortunate, lucky, advantageous, happiness, good auspices. It is the only single character meaning good luck in the *YiJing*.

Nine in the third place

> The veil has such fullness that the star *Mei* could be seen at noon. Breaks his right arm. No defect.

豐	feng1	1897	Abundance, fullness; abundant, luxurious, bountiful, fruitful.
其	qi2	0525	Their, his, its, the; this, that. A demonstrative and possessive pronoun.
沛	pei4	5020	Covering, veil, darkened, abundant, copious or/and sudden rain.
日	ri4	3124	Sun, day, daylight, daytime; daily.
中	zhong1	1504	Center, inner, in the inside, put in the center, hit (target); balanced, central, middle, correct.
見	jian4	0860	See, observe, look at, to be seen; cause to appear; be exposed to, display, reveal; interview, visit or call on, meet.
沬	mei4	4412	*Mei* star; small stars, a faint light. It is not clear if it is the name of a star or to which star is related.
折	zhe2	0267	Sever, break; bend, destroy, execute; decide a cause, discriminate, judge.
其	qi2	0525	Their, his, its, the; this, that. A demonstrative and possessive pronoun.
右	you4	7541	Right, the right hand, on the right, make things right.
肱	gong1	3706	Arm (esp. the upper arm, from elbow to shoulder).
无	wu2	7173	No, not, negative; without, does not possess, not have.
咎	jiu4	1192	Fault, blame, mistake, wrong; inauspicious; misfortune, bad luck, calamity; reproach, censure.

Nine in the fourth place

> The curtain has such fullness that the Big Dipper could be seen at noon. He meets his master in secret. Good fortune.

豐	feng1	1897	Abundance, fullness; abundant, luxurious, bountiful, fruitful.
其	qi2	0525	Their, his, its, the; this, that. A demonstrative and possessive pronoun.
蔀	bu4	8001	Screen, curtain, awning, hanging mat; old unit of time (cycle of 76 years).
日	ri4	3124	Sun, day, daylight, daytime; daily.
中	zhong1	1504	Center, inner, in the inside, put in the center, hit (target); balanced, central, middle, correct.

Abundance (305) 55

見	jian4	0860	See, observe, look at, to be seen; cause to appear; be exposed to, display, reveal; interview, visit or call on, meet.
斗	dou3	6472	Big Dipper (a cluster of seven stars in the constellation *Ursa Major*, four forming the bowl and three the handle of a dipper-shaped configuration, also called Plow or Plough); dipper; a unit of measure for grain.
遇	yu4	7625	Meet, encounter, come across, happen.
其	qi2	0525	Their, his, its, the; this, that. A demonstrative and possessive pronoun.
夷	yi2	2982	Hidden, obscure, dark; hide, wound, suppress, kill, darkening (36); pacified, at ease, common, ordinary (59); barbarian tribes in the East; crying pheasant.
主	zhu3	1336	Master, lord, chief; host, innkeeper.
吉	ji2	0476	Good fortune, auspicious, promising, fortunate, lucky, advantageous, happiness, good auspices. It is the only single character meaning good luck in the *YiJing*.

Six in the fifth place

Brilliance is coming, with blessings and fame. Good fortune.

來	lai2	3768	Come, arrive, return, bring.
章	zhang1	0182	Brilliance, splendor, refinement, distinction; ornament, emblem of distinction, jade tablet; amulet. Its short form, with the jade radical means "jade baton".
有	you3	7533	Have, possession, there be, there is.
慶	qing4	1167	Blessings, good luck; rejoice, happiness; congratulate with gifts, reward.
譽	yu4	7617	Fame, renown, reputation, honor, honored, praised.
吉	ji2	0476	Good fortune, auspicious, promising, fortunate, lucky, advantageous, happiness, good auspices. It is the only single character meaning good luck in the *YiJing*.

Six at the top

A large canopy hides his house. He peeks from his door, silent and with no one at his side. For three years he sees nothing. Misfortune.

豐	feng1	1897	Abundance, fullness; abundant, luxurious, bountiful, fruitful.
其	qi2	0525	Their, his, its, the; this, that. A demonstrative and possessive pronoun.

屋	wu1	7212	Roof, canopy, shelter, room, house.
蔀	bu4	8001	Screen, curtain, awning, hanging mat; old unit of time (cycle of 76 years).
其	qi2	0525	Their, his, its, the; this, that. A demonstrative and possessive pronoun.
家	jia1	0594	Family, household, clan; home, to keep a home.
闚	kui1	3649	Peek, observe furtively; to pry, spy.
其	qi2	0525	Their, his, its, the; this, that. A demonstrative and possessive pronoun.
戶	hu4	2180	Door, inner door, the house entrance door; household, family.
闃	qu4	1627	Quiet, alone, silent, lonely; deserted, abandoned.
其	qi2	0525	Their, his, its, the; this, that. A demonstrative and possessive pronoun.
无	wu2	7173	No, not, negative; without, does not possess, not have.
人	ren2	3097	Man, person(s); people; others; human being, individual.
三	san1	5415	Three, thrice, third time or place.
歲	sui4	5538	Years, seasons, harvests.
不	bu4	5379	No, not, negative prefix; without, none, nothing, will not, need not, will not be.
覿	di2	6230	See face to face; to be admitted to an audience; encounter; to be visible.
凶	xiong1	2808	Misfortune, pitfall, ominous, bad, unlucky, disastrous, trouble, accident.

56 旅 *lu* – The Wanderer

The Judgment

The Wanderer. Success in small things.
The determination of the Wanderer brings good fortune.

旅	lu3	4286	Wanderer, traveler; stranger; stay away from home; guest, to lodge; multitude, troops.
小	xiao3	2605	Small, insignificant, common, humble, mediocre; diminish, belittle.
亨	heng1	2099	Success, prevalence, smooth progress, growth, consummate, triumph; pervade; offering, sacrifice.
旅	lu3	4286	Wanderer, traveler; stranger; stay away from home; guest, to lodge; multitude, troops.
貞	zhen1	0346	Perseverance, persistence, determination, steadiness, firmness; straight, correct, verified, certain; pure, loyal. Its original meaning was "to determine an uncertain matter through divination".
吉	ji2	0476	Good fortune, auspicious, promising, fortunate, lucky, advantageous, happiness, good auspices. It is the only single character meaning good luck in the *YiJing*.

The Image

Above the Mountain is Fire: The image of the Wanderer.
Thus the noble applies punishments with clarity
and doesn't prolong litigation.

山	shan1	5630	Mountain, hill, peak.
上	shang4	5669	Up, above, on, over, upwards, top, rise; higher, superior; first, best.
有	you3	7533	Have, possession, there be, there is.
火	huo3	2395	Fire, flame.
旅	lu3	4286	Wanderer, traveler; stranger; stay away from home; guest, to lodge; multitude, troops.

君	jun1	1715	Noble, prince, aristocrat, lord, chief, gentleman; honorable, a highly principled person, superior man. Most times, this character appears alongside another one, forming the word *JunZi*, whose original meaning was "son of a prince or ruler": 君子.
子	zi3	6939	Child, son or daughter, offspring; suffix; bride, wife; gentleman, officer, master, prince; young lady; the first of the *Earthly Branches*.
以	yi3	2932	Thus, in that way, by means of, with, for; instrument, medium, method, use (of), way (to).
明	ming2	4534	Light, brightness, clarity, clear; enlightenment, discernment; seeing, perception; agreement, contract.
慎	shen4	5734	Careful, cautious, circumspect.
用	yong4	7567	Use, apply, put to use, apply the oracle to real world situations; hereby, thereby.
刑	xing2	2755	Punishment, discipline, sanction.
而	er2	1756	And, then, but, nevertheless, also, only. Join and contrasts two words.
不	bu4	5379	No, not, negative prefix; without, none, nothing, will not, need not, will not be.
留	liu2	4083	Detain, protract, delay, tarry, a long time.
獄	yu4	7685	Justice, litigation, lawsuit, criminal cases; prison, jail.

Six at the beginning

The Wanderer is too fussy. He will bring calamity upon himself.

旅	lu3	4286	Wanderer, traveler; stranger; stay away from home; guest, to lodge; multitude, troops.
瑣	suo3	5466	Trivial, small, petty, annoying, touchy, fussy, contemptible; in tiny pieces. Being duplicated intensifies its meaning.
瑣	suo3	5466	
斯	si1	5574	Then, this, thereupon, so, thus; cleave, tear apart.
其	qi2	0525	Their, his, its, the; this, that. A demonstrative and possessive pronoun.
所	suo3	5465	That which, place, location, residence, dwelling; reason, a cause, whereby; function, position, role; habitual focus or object.
取	qu3	1615	Take, take a wife, obtain, lay hold of, grasp.
災	zai1	6652	Calamity, disaster, injury; misfortune from without (undeserved); calamities from Heaven, as floods, famines, pestilence, etc.

Six in the second place

> The Wanderer comes to a resting place. Keeps his belongings safely and gets a young and loyal servant.

旅	lu3	4286	Wanderer, traveler; stranger; stay away from home; guest, to lodge; multitude, troops.
即	ji2	0495	Approach, come to; promptly.
次	ci4	6980	Camp, take a position, to stop at a place, halt; lodge, hostel, lodging place, hut; hard-going; put in order, sequel, next in order, second, second rate.
懷	huai2	2233	Carry, hold; keep in the bosom; carry in the heart or breast; to cherish in the mind, be anxious about; to love, yearn, cling to.
其	qi2	0525	Their, his, its, the; this, that. A demonstrative and possessive pronoun.
資	zi1	6927	Property, wealth, goods, provisions, materials; means of living, rely on, depend on.
得	de2	6161	Get, obtain, gain; reach, achieve; can; attain the desired thing.
童	tong2	6626	Youth, boy, young person (boy or girl); page, pupil; servant; a virgin, pure, undefiled; young animal without horns (esp. calf or lamb).
僕	pu2	5401	Servant, slave, follower, retainer, vassal; a charioteer.
貞	zhen1	0346	Perseverance, persistence, determination, steadiness, firmness; straight, correct, verified, certain; pure, loyal. Its original meaning was "to determine an uncertain matter through divination".

Nine in the third place

> The Wanderer burns his resting place. He loses his young servant. The determination is dangerous.

旅	lu3	4286	Wanderer, traveler; stranger; stay away from home; guest, to lodge; multitude, troops.
焚	fen2	1866	Burn, set fire; destroy, overthrow.
其	qi2	0525	Their, his, its, the; this, that. A demonstrative and possessive pronoun.
次	ci4	6980	Camp, take a position, to stop at a place, halt; lodge, hostel, lodging place, hut; hard-going; put in order, sequel, next in order, second, second rate.

喪	sang4	5429	Lose, let drop, disappear, destroy, perish, mourning, burial.
其	qi2	0525	Their, his, its, the; this, that. A demonstrative and possessive pronoun.
童	tong2	6626	Youth, boy, young person (boy or girl); page, pupil; servant; a virgin, pure, undefiled; young animal without horns (esp. calf or lamb).
僕	pu2	5401	Servant, slave, follower, retainer, vassal; a charioteer.
貞	zhen1	0346	Perseverance, persistence, determination, steadiness, firmness; straight, correct, verified, certain; pure, loyal. Its original meaning was "to determine an uncertain matter through divination".
厲	li4	3906	Danger, threat; oppressive, cruel, wicked, brutal, harsh; sickness, malevolent devil; grind, polish, sharpen; discipline.

Nine in the fourth place

The Wanderer stays at one place and obtains property and an ax.
My heart is not happy.

旅	lu3	4286	Wanderer, traveler; stranger; stay away from home; guest, to lodge; multitude, troops.
于	yu2	7592	At, to, in, into, on, from, by, go, go to, move towards, proceed, be.
處	chu3	1407	Rest, stop, stay; dwell in a place for a while.
得	de2	6161	Get, obtain, gain; reach, achieve; can; attain the desired thing.
其	qi2	0525	Their, his, its, the; this, that. A demonstrative and possessive pronoun.
資	zi1	6927	Property, wealth, goods, provisions, materials; means of living, rely on, depend on.
斧	fu3	1934	An axe; a hatchet.
我	wo3	4778	We, us, I, my, mine, our.
心	xin1	2735	Heart; conscience, moral nature; soul; core; mind; source of feelings, intentions, will.
不	bu4	5379	No, not, negative prefix; without, none, nothing, will not, need not, will not be.
快	kuai4	3547	Glad, pleased, cheerful, satisfied.

The Wanderer (311) 56

Six in the fifth place

> He shoots a pheasant. Although the first arrow fails,
> finally is praised and given employment.

射	she4	5703	Shoot with a bow; aim and hit the target.
雉	zhi4	0968	Pheasant. Bird associated with the trigram *Li*, The Adherent, the Fire.
一	yi1	3016	One, number one.
矢	shi3	5784	Arrow.
亡	wang2	7034	Go away, disappear, exile; fail; destroy, perish, not have, not exist.
終	zhong1	1500	End, finish, complete; for ever; end of a cycle; carried to conclusion, consummation, closure; death. The original meaning was: tied-off end of a thread.
以	yi3	2932	Thus, in that way, by means of, with, for; instrument, medium, method, use (of), way (to).
譽	yu4	7617	Fame, renown, reputation, honor, honored, praised.
命	ming4	4537	Heaven's will; command(s), fate, destiny; will; investiture; birth and death as limits of life.

Nine at the top

> The bird burns its nest. The Wanderer laughs at first but afterward
> cries out and weeps. He loses his cow in *Yi*. Misfortune.

鳥	niao3	4688	Bird.
焚	fen2	1866	Burn, set fire; destroy, overthrow.
其	qi2	0525	Their, his, its, the; this, that. A demonstrative and possessive pronoun.
巢	chao2	0253	Nest, a nest in a tree; haunt, retreat, den.
旅	lu3	4286	Wanderer, traveler; stranger; stay away from home; guest, to lodge; multitude, troops.
人	ren2	3097	Man, person(s); people; others; human being, individual.
先	xian1	2702	Before, first, foremost, in front, lead.
笑	xiao4	2615	Laugh, smile, merriment, good humor.
後	hou4	2143	Later, behind, rear, afterward, come after; follow; descendants, successor.
號	hao4	2064	Weep; cry out, call out, scream, cry for help; signal, command.

咷	tao2	6152	Wail, weep, cry loudly, lament, moaning.
喪	sang4	5429	Lose, let drop, disappear, destroy, perish, mourning, burial.
牛	niu2	4737	Cow, bull, ox.
于	yu2	7592	At, to, in, into, on, from, by, go, go to, move towards, proceed, be.
易	yi4	2952	Name of a place; change, versatility; ease, easy.
凶	xiong1	2808	Misfortune, pitfall, ominous, bad, unlucky, disastrous, trouble, accident.

57 巽 Xun – Gentle Influence / Compliance / Penetration / Wind

THE JUDGMENT

Gentle Influence. Success in small things.
It is favorable to have a goal.
It is favorable to see the great man.

巽	xun4	5550	Humble, yield, compliant, obedient, mild, bland, insinuating, subtly penetrating. Kunst and Rutt say it means "food offering".
小	xiao3	2605	Small, insignificant, common, humble, mediocre; diminish, belittle.
亨	heng1	2099	Success, prevalence, smooth progress, growth, consummate, triumph; pervade; offering, sacrifice.
利	li4	3867	Favorable, lucky, advantageous, profitable, beneficial, furthering, harvesting; sharp, sharp witted.
有	you3	7533	Have, possession, there be, there is.
攸	you1	7519	Goal, direction, destination, objective; distant, far away; a place; that which, whereby, thereby, for which; mark of the passive voice.
往	wang3	7050	Go, to go to, go forward, go towards; depart, bygone, former. 攸往: have a place to go; have a goal.
利	li4	3867	Favorable, lucky, advantageous, profitable, beneficial, furthering, harvesting; sharp, sharp witted.
見	jian4	0860	See, observe, look at, to be seen; cause to appear; be exposed to, display, reveal; interview, visit or call on, meet.
大	da4	5943	Big, great, tall; excessive, arrogant; spread out and reach everywhere.
人	ren2	3097	Man, person(s); people; others; human being, individual.

The Image

Winds that follow each other: The image of Gentle Influence.
Thus the noble proclaims his commands and acts to carry out his tasks.

隨	sui2	5523	Follow, pursue; conform to, respond, follow a way or religion; subsequently, in the course of time; listen to, submit; marrow, flesh.
風	feng1	1890	Wind, breath, air; manners, atmosphere.
巽	xun4	5550	Humble, yield, compliant, obedient, mild, bland, insinuating, subtly penetrating. Kunst and Rutt say it means "food offering".
君	jun1	1715	Noble, prince, aristocrat, lord, chief, gentleman; honorable, a highly principled person, superior man. Most times, this character appears alongside another one, forming the word *JunZi*, whose original meaning was "son of a prince or ruler": 君子.
子	zi3	6939	Child, son or daughter, offspring; suffix; bride, wife; gentleman, officer, master, prince; young lady; the first of the *Earthly Branches*.
以	yi3	2932	Thus, in that way, by means of, with, for; instrument, medium, method, use (of), way (to).
申	shen1	5712	Spread, extend, prolong, stretch; repeat, again, further; exhibit; explain, express; the 9th of the Twelve Earthly Branches. 3-5 pm.
命	ming4	4537	Heaven's will; command(s), fate, destiny; will; investiture; birth and death as limits of life.
行	xing2	2754	Move, go, advance, act, do.
事	shi4	5787	Serve, service; affairs, business, matters.

Six at the beginning

Advancing and retreating.
The determination is favorable for a warrior.

進	jin4	1091	Advance, to urge forward, progress; present, introduce, recommend, propose.
退	tui4	6568	Retreat, withdraw, back up, retire; decline, refuse.
利	li4	3867	Favorable, lucky, advantageous, profitable, beneficial, furthering, harvesting; sharp, sharp witted.
武	wu3	7195	Martial, military; warlike, warrior.
人	ren2	3097	Man, person(s); people; others; human being, individual.
之	zhi1	0935	Personal pronoun, he she, it; this, that, these, etc.; often used as a possessive.

Gentle Influence (315)

貞	zhen1	0346	Perseverance, persistence, determination, steadiness, firmness; straight, correct, verified, certain; pure, loyal. Its original meaning was "to determine an uncertain matter through divination".

Nine in the second place

Penetration under the bed. Using diviners and sorcerers in large number brings good fortune. No defect.

巽	xun4	5550	Humble, yield, compliant, obedient, mild, bland, insinuating, subtly penetrating. Kunst and Rutt say it means "food offering".
在	zai4	6657	Be at, at, in, on, within, be present; to lie in, depend upon, involved with; be living, dwell, located in.
牀	chuang2	1459	Bed, couch; platform, place to sleep. Rutt says "bed, means a platform on which other things rest, such as offerings before a spirit table".
下	xia4	2520	Below, down, descend.
用	yong4	7567	Use, apply, put to use, apply the oracle to real world situations; hereby, thereby.
史	shi3	5769	Scribe, historian, chronicles, annals; diviner; invoker (of spirits) (Kunst).
巫	wu1	7164	Magician, sorcerer, shaman, wizard, witch.
紛	fen1	1859	Numerous, many; mixed, assorted; confused, scattered, tangled, confusion, disorder.
若	ruo4	3126	Like, just as, to be like; agree, conform to; approve; concordant; compliant.
吉	ji2	0476	Good fortune, auspicious, promising, fortunate, lucky, advantageous, happiness, good auspices. It is the only single character meaning good luck in the *YiJing*.
无	wu2	7173	No, not, negative; without, does not possess, not have.
咎	jiu4	1192	Fault, blame, mistake, wrong; inauspicious; misfortune, bad luck, calamity; reproach, censure.

Nine in the third place

Repeated penetration. Humiliation.

頻	pin2	5275	Repeated, incessant, urgent, pressing; on the brink of.
巽	xun4	5550	Humble, yield, compliant, obedient, mild, bland, insinuating, subtly penetrating. Kunst and Rutt say it means "food offering".
吝	lin4	4040	Humiliation, regret, shame, distress, grief, sorrow; miserly, niggardly. It is a warning of trouble.

Six in the fourth place

> Repentance fades. Captures three types of prey in hunting.

悔	hui3	2336	Repent, regret, contrition; trouble. This word indicates both an objective situation and a subjective reaction to such circumstance.
亡	wang2	7034	Go away, disappear, exile; fail; destroy, perish, not have, not exist.
田	tian2	6362	Field, cultivated land; hunt. The character is the picture of a cultivated field, divided in four sectors.
獲	huo4	2412	Catch (in hunt), seize, get, obtain, hit the mark, find; succeed. What is caught, gotten or found may be a thing, a person, an opportunity, an idea or perception. 田獲: to catch a prey in hunting.
三	san1	5415	Three, thrice, third time or place.
品	pin3	5281	Kind, variety, classes, categories.

Nine in the fifth place

> The determination is fortunate. Repentance fades.
> Nothing that is not favorable. There is no beginning, but an end.
> Before the seventh day three days, after the seventh day, three days.
> Good fortune.

貞	zhen1	0346	Perseverance, persistence, determination, steadiness, firmness; straight, correct, verified, certain; pure, loyal. Its original meaning was "to determine an uncertain matter through divination".
吉	ji2	0476	Good fortune, auspicious, promising, fortunate, lucky, advantageous, happiness, good auspices. It is the only single character meaning good luck in the *YiJing*.
悔	hui3	2336	Repent, regret, contrition; trouble. This word indicates both an objective situation and a subjective reaction to such circumstance.
亡	wang2	7034	Go away, disappear, exile; fail; destroy, perish, not have, not exist.
无	wu2	7173	No, not, negative; without, does not possess, not have.
不	bu4	5379	No, not, negative prefix; without, none, nothing, will not, need not, will not be.
利	li4	3867	Favorable, lucky, advantageous, profitable, beneficial, furthering, harvesting; sharp, sharp witted.
无	wu2	7173	No, not, negative; without, does not possess, not have.

Gentle Influence (317) 57

初	chu1	1390	At first, beginning, initial, incipient, in the early stages.
有	you3	7533	Have, possession, there be, there is.
終	zhong1	1500	End, finish, complete; for ever; end of a cycle; carried to conclusion, consummation, closure; death. The original meaning was: tied-off end of a thread.
先	xian1	2702	Before, first, foremost, in front, lead.
庚	geng1	3339	A date in the Chinese calendar; 7th heavenly stem, cyclical character.
三	san1	5415	Three, thrice, third time or place.
日	ri4	3124	Sun, day, daylight, daytime; daily.
後	hou4	2143	Later, behind, rear, afterward, come after; follow; descendants, successor.
庚	geng1	3339	A date in the Chinese calendar; 7th heavenly stem, cyclical character.
三	san1	5415	Three, thrice, third time or place.
日	ri4	3124	Sun, day, daylight, daytime; daily.
吉	ji2	0476	Good fortune, auspicious, promising, fortunate, lucky, advantageous, happiness, good auspices. It is the only single character meaning good luck in the *YiJing*.

Nine at the top

Penetration under the bed. He loses his belongings and an ax.
The determination is ominous.

巽	xun4	5550	Humble, yield, compliant, obedient, mild, bland, insinuating, subtly penetrating. Kunst and Rutt say it means "food offering".
在	zai4	6657	Be at, at, in, on, within, be present; to lie in, depend upon, involved with; be living, dwell, located in.
牀	chuang2	1459	Bed, couch; platform, place to sleep. Rutt says "bed, means a platform on which other things rest, such as offerings before a spirit table".
下	xia4	2520	Below, down, descend.
喪	sang4	5429	Lose, let drop, disappear, destroy, perish, mourning, burial.
其	qi2	0525	Their, his, its, the; this, that. A demonstrative and possessive pronoun.
資	zi1	6927	Property, wealth, goods, provisions, materials; means of living, rely on, depend on.

斧	fu3	1934	An axe; a hatchet.
貞	zhen1	0346	Perseverance, persistence, determination, steadiness, firmness; straight, correct, verified, certain; pure, loyal. Its original meaning was "to determine an uncertain matter through divination".
凶	xiong1	2808	Misfortune, pitfall, ominous, bad, unlucky, disastrous, trouble, accident.

58 兑 *dui* – Joyousness / Lake

The Judgment

Joyousness. Success. The determination is favorable.

兌	dui4	6560	Joyousness, happiness; cheerful talk, openness, interaction, exchange, mouth; barter.
亨	heng1	2099	Success, prevalence, smooth progress, growth, consummate, triumph; pervade; offering, sacrifice.
利	li4	3867	Favorable, lucky, advantageous, profitable, beneficial, furthering, harvesting; sharp, sharp witted.
貞	zhen1	0346	Perseverance, persistence, determination, steadiness, firmness; straight, correct, verified, certain; pure, loyal. Its original meaning was "to determine an uncertain matter through divination".

The Image

Two Lakes together: The image of Joyousness.
Thus the noble joins his friends for discussion and training.

麗	li4	3914	Attached, interconnected, tied, interdependent, depend on; congregate; couple, pair.
澤	ze2	0277	Marsh, pool, pond, lake; flat body of water and the vapors rising from it; enrich, fertilize, benefit; moist, moisten; glossy, polished.
兌	dui4	6560	Joyousness, happiness; cheerful talk, openness, interaction, exchange, mouth; barter.
君	jun1	1715	Noble, prince, aristocrat, lord, chief, gentleman; honorable, a highly principled person, superior man. Most times, this character appears alongside another one, forming the word *JunZi*, whose original meaning was "son of a prince or ruler": 君子.
子	zi3	6939	Child, son or daughter, offspring; suffix; bride, wife; gentleman, officer, master, prince; young lady; the first of the *Earthly Branches*.
以	yi3	2932	Thus, in that way, by means of, with, for; instrument, medium, method, use (of), way (to).

朋	peng2	5054	Friend, companion, pair, equal, comrade; a string of cowries (small shiny shells used as coins in ancient China).
友	you3	7540	Companion, friend, associate, partner, couple, boy/girlfriend.
講	jiang3	0645	Conversation, explication, study; to discuss, to speak, to preach.
習	xi2	2499	Double, duplicate; repeated, repeatedly; practice, exercise, rehearsal, learning; to practice flying (young birds learning to fly flapping its wings).

Nine at the beginning

Harmonious Joyousness. Good fortune.

和	he2	2115	Harmony, concord, conciliation, peace, contented; respond; balance, rhythm.
兌	dui4	6560	Joyousness, happiness; cheerful talk, openness, interaction, exchange, mouth; barter.
吉	ji2	0476	Good fortune, auspicious, promising, fortunate, lucky, advantageous, happiness, good auspices. It is the only single character meaning good luck in the *YiJing*.

Nine in the second place

Sincere Joyousness. Good fortune. Regrets go away.

孚	fu2	1936	Truth; reliable, sincere; to inspire confidence in others; capture, prisoner, plunder.
兌	dui4	6560	Joyousness, happiness; cheerful talk, openness, interaction, exchange, mouth; barter.
吉	ji2	0476	Good fortune, auspicious, promising, fortunate, lucky, advantageous, happiness, good auspices. It is the only single character meaning good luck in the *YiJing*.
悔	hui3	2336	Repent, regret, contrition; trouble. This word indicates both an objective situation and a subjective reaction to such circumstance.
亡	wang2	7034	Go away, disappear, exile; fail; destroy, perish, not have, not exist.

Six in the third place

He goes after Joyousness. Misfortune.

來	lai2	3768	Come, arrive, return, bring.
兌	dui4	6560	Joyousness, happiness; cheerful talk, openness, interaction, exchange, mouth; barter.
凶	xiong1	2808	Misfortune, pitfall, ominous, bad, unlucky, disastrous, trouble, accident.

Nine in the fourth place

Haggling Joyousness. Still not at peace.
After limiting your anxiety there will be happiness.

商	shang1	5673	Bargain, discuss, deliberate, negotiate, calculate; merchant, trader.
兌	dui4	6560	Joyousness, happiness; cheerful talk, openness, interaction, exchange, mouth; barter.
未	wei4	7114	Not yet, before. The eight of the twelve *Earthly Branches*. 13-15 hs.
寧	ning2	4725	Peace, peaceful, rest, serenity, at ease, body and mind at ease.
介	jie4	0629	Curb, limit, restriction, boundary; armour; protect, assist, depend on, support; great, important, solid, firm.
疾	ji2	0492	Ill, harm, defect, stress; hurry; hate.
有	you3	7533	Have, possession, there be, there is.
喜	xi3	2434	Pleasure, joy, happiness, gratification, delight.

Nine in the fifth place

Trusting degrading influences is dangerous.

孚	fu2	1936	Truth; reliable, sincere; to inspire confidence in others; capture, prisoner, plunder.
于	yu2	7592	At, to, in, into, on, from, by, go, go to, move towards, proceed, be.
剝	bo1	5337	Flay, strip, peel; pluck, lay bare, strip (as clothes or badges of office); split, slice, crack.
有	you3	7533	Have, possession, there be, there is.
厲	li4	3906	Danger, threat; oppressive, cruel, wicked, brutal, harsh; sickness, malevolent devil; grind, polish, sharpen; discipline.

Six at the top

Alluring Joyousness.

引	yin3	7429	Guide, lead, pull, attract, stretch, draw the bow.
兌	dui4	6560	Joyousness, happiness; cheerful talk, openness, interaction, exchange, mouth; barter.

59 渙 *huan* – Dispersion / Dissolution / The Flood

THE JUDGMENT

Dispersion. Success. The King approaches his temple.
It is favorable to cross the great river.
The determination is favorable.

渙	huan4	2252	Dispersion, dissolution, scattering; dispel misunderstandings, fantasies and fears; gush, splash; slack, relaxed.
亨	heng1	2099	Success, prevalence, smooth progress, growth, consummate, triumph; pervade; offering, sacrifice.
王	wang2	7037	King, prince, sovereign, ruler.
假	jia3	0599	Approaches, goes to, attains.
有	you3	7533	Have, possession, there be, there is.
廟	miao4	4473	(Ancestral) temple, a shrine, used to honor gods and ancestors.
利	li4	3867	Favorable, lucky, advantageous, profitable, beneficial, furthering, harvesting; sharp, sharp witted.
涉	she4	5707	Cross, wade across (a river, stream), ford, pass through or over.
大	da4	5943	Big, great, tall; excessive, arrogant; spread out and reach everywhere.
川	chuan1	1439	River, flowing water; flood.
利	li4	3867	Favorable, lucky, advantageous, profitable, beneficial, furthering, harvesting; sharp, sharp witted.
貞	zhen1	0346	Perseverance, persistence, determination, steadiness, firmness; straight, correct, verified, certain; pure, loyal. Its original meaning was "to determine an uncertain matter through divination".

Dispersion (323) 59

The Image

Wind moving over Water: The image of Dispersion.
Thus the Ancient Kings made offerings to the Supreme Lord
and erected temples.

風	feng1	1890	Wind, breath, air; manners, atmosphere.
行	xing2	2754	Move, go, advance, act, do.
水	shui3	5922	Water, river, stream, flood, liquid, fluid.
上	shang4	5669	Up, above, on, over, upwards, top, rise; higher, superior; first, best.
渙	huan4	2252	Dispersion, dissolution, scattering; dispel misunderstandings, fantasies and fears; gush, splash; slack, relaxed.
先	xian1	2702	Before, first, foremost, in front, lead.
王	wang2	7037	King, prince, sovereign, ruler.
以	yi3	2932	Thus, in that way, by means of, with, for; instrument, medium, method, use (of), way (to).
享	xiang3	2552	Sacrifice, offering to a god or a superior; consecrate; treat.
于	yu2	7592	At, to, in, into, on, from, by, go, go to, move towards, proceed, be.
帝	di4	6204	Sovereign, emperor, god.
立	li4	3921	Stand up or erect; set up, establish; raise, ascend; keep the position or the course, resist, endure.
廟	miao4	4473	(Ancestral) temple, a shrine, used to honor gods and ancestors.

Six at the beginning

Uses the strength of a horse for rescue. Good fortune.

用	yong4	7567	Use, apply, put to use, apply the oracle to real world situations; hereby, thereby.
拯	zheng3	0360	Relief, rescue, to lift up, to raise; geld, remove (Kunst, Rutt).
馬	ma3	4310	Horse.
壯	zhuang4	1453	Power, strength, strong, robust, big, full grown male, in the prime of life; injure.
吉	ji2	0476	Good fortune, auspicious, promising, fortunate, lucky, advantageous, happiness, good auspices. It is the only single character meaning good luck in the *YiJing*.

Nine in the second place

> Dispersion. Run to your support.
> Repentance fades.

渙	huan4	2252	Dispersion, dissolution, scattering; dispel misunderstandings, fantasies and fears; gush, splash; slack, relaxed.
奔	ben1	5028	Hurry, hasten, rush toward, run away.
其	qi2	0525	Their, his, its, the; this, that. A demonstrative and possessive pronoun.
机	ji1	0411	Support, stool, low or small table.
悔	hui3	2336	Repent, regret, contrition; trouble. This word indicates both an objective situation and a subjective reaction to such circumstance.
亡	wang2	7034	Go away, disappear, exile; fail; destroy, perish, not have, not exist.

Six in the third place

> Disperses himself. No repentance.

渙	huan4	2252	Dispersion, dissolution, scattering; dispel misunderstandings, fantasies and fears; gush, splash; slack, relaxed.
其	qi2	0525	Their, his, its, the; this, that. A demonstrative and possessive pronoun.
躬	gong1	3704	Oneself, (own) body, person.
无	wu2	7173	No, not, negative; without, does not possess, not have.
悔	hui3	2336	Repent, regret, contrition; trouble. This word indicates both an objective situation and a subjective reaction to such circumstance.

Six in the fourth place

> Disperses his group. Outstanding good fortune. Dispersion is great.
> Common people do not consider that point.

渙	huan4	2252	Dispersion, dissolution, scattering; dispel misunderstandings, fantasies and fears; gush, splash; slack, relaxed.
其	qi2	0525	Their, his, its, the; this, that. A demonstrative and possessive pronoun.
羣	qun2	1737	Group, herd, flock, crowd, host, multitude, congregation.
元	yuan2	7707	Outstanding, greatest, sublime, supreme, greatest, very great, grand; source, beginning, cause, first or paramount, fundamentality; head, chief; used as a superlative.

Dispersion (325) 59

吉	ji2	0476	Good fortune, auspicious, promising, fortunate, lucky, advantageous, happiness, good auspices. It is the only single character meaning good luck in the *YiJing*.
渙	huan4	2252	Dispersion, dissolution, scattering; dispel misunderstandings, fantasies and fears; gush, splash; slack, relaxed.
有	you3	7533	Have, possession, there be, there is.
丘	qiu1	1213	Hill, mound, small hill; great; waste, ruins.
匪	fei3	1820	No, strong negative.
夷	yi2	2982	Pacified, at ease, common, ordinary (59); hide, wound, suppress, kill, darkening (36); barbarian tribes in the East; crying pheasant.
所	suo3	5465	That which, place, location, residence, dwelling; reason, a cause, whereby; function, position, role; habitual focus or object.
思	si1	5580	Think, consider, ponder; brood, reflect, plan.

Nine in the fifth place

Dispersing sweat, aloud proclamations.
Disperses the King dwelling. No defect.

渙	huan4	2252	Dispersion, dissolution, scattering; dispel misunderstandings, fantasies and fears; gush, splash; slack, relaxed.
汗	han4	2028	Sweat, perspiration. 渙汗: imperial edict.
其	qi2	0525	Their, his, its, the; this, that. A demonstrative and possessive pronoun.
大	da4	5943	Big, great, tall; excessive, arrogant; spread out and reach everywhere.
號	hao4	2064	Weep; cry out, call out, scream, cry for help; signal, command.
渙	huan4	2252	Dispersion, dissolution, scattering; dispel misunderstandings, fantasies and fears; gush, splash; slack, relaxed.
王	wang2	7037	King, prince, sovereign, ruler.
居	ju1	1535	Remain; rest (in); abides, dwell; to occupy a position or place; overbearing, arrogant.
无	wu2	7173	No, not, negative; without, does not possess, not have.
咎	jiu4	1192	Fault, blame, mistake, wrong; inauspicious; misfortune, bad luck, calamity; reproach, censure.

Nine at the top

Disperses his blood. Going away, keeping at a distance, departing. No defect.

渙	huan4	2252	Dispersion, dissolution, scattering; dispel misunderstandings, fantasies and fears; gush, splash; slack, relaxed.
其	qi2	0525	Their, his, its, the; this, that. A demonstrative and possessive pronoun.
血	xue4	2901	Blood, bleeding. Its ancient form shows a sacrificial vessel with its content.
去	qu4	1594	Go away, leave, depart; remove, put away, eliminate, reject.
逖	ti4	6265	Far, distant; removed, remove, send away, keep at distance.
出	chu1	1409	Go out, came out, appear, departure; arise, emerge; bring out, take out, expel, leave, get rid of; produce, beget.
无	wu2	7173	No, not, negative; without, does not possess, not have.
咎	jiu4	1192	Fault, blame, mistake, wrong; inauspicious; misfortune, bad luck, calamity; reproach, censure.

60 節 *jie* – Limitation

The Judgment

Limitation. Success.
A severe limitation can not be applied with persistence.

節	jie2	0795	Regulate, moderate, articulate, rule; moral integrity; degree, rank; regular division; juncture, circumstance; baton, token of authority. Knot, node, joint, in bamboo of other plants.
亨	heng1	2099	Success, prevalence, smooth progress, growth, consummate, triumph; pervade; offering, sacrifice.
苦	ku3	3493	Bitter, galling, suffering; *Sonchus* (a wild herb), *Lactuca* (lettuce).
節	jie2	0795	Regulate, moderate, articulate, rule; moral integrity; degree, rank; regular division; juncture, circumstance; baton, token of authority. Knot, node, joint, in bamboo of other plants.
不	bu4	5379	No, not, negative prefix; without, none, nothing, will not, need not, will not be.
可	ke3	3381	Can, able, may; permit, allow; satisfactory, proper, suitable.
貞	zhen1	0346	Perseverance, persistence, determination, steadiness, firmness; straight, correct, verified, certain; pure, loyal. Its original meaning was "to determine an uncertain matter through divination".

The Image

Above the Lake is Water: The image of Limitation.
Thus the noble establishes the number and measure
and deliberates about morality and conduct.

澤	ze2	0277	Marsh, pool, pond, lake; flat body of water and the vapors rising from it; enrich, fertilize, benefit; moist, moisten; glossy, polished.
上	shang4	5669	Up, above, on, over, upwards, top, rise; higher, superior; first, best.

有	you3	7533	Have, possession, there be, there is.
水	shui3	5922	Water, river, stream, flood, liquid, fluid.
節	jie2	0795	Regulate, moderate, articulate, rule; moral integrity; degree, rank; regular division; juncture, circumstance; baton, token of authority. Knot, node, joint, in bamboo of other plants.
君	jun1	1715	Noble, prince, aristocrat, lord, chief, gentleman; honorable, a highly principled person, superior man. Most times, this character appears alongside another one, forming the word *JunZi*, whose original meaning was "son of a prince or ruler": 君子.
子	zi3	6939	Child, son or daughter, offspring; suffix; bride, wife; gentleman, officer, master, prince; young lady; the first of the *Earthly Branches*.
以	yi3	2932	Thus, in that way, by means of, with, for; instrument, medium, method, use (of), way (to).
制	zhi4	0986	Make, create, establish; institute, law, regulation; limit, restrain; tailor, trim.
數	shu3	5865	Number, count, calculate; method, norm, rule; degree.
度	du4	6504	Measure (of length); law, rule; limits, regulate; calculate; consider; interval in music.
議	yi4	3006	Discuss, deliberate, negotiate, weigh the options, plan for.
德	de2	6162	Virtue, spiritual power, moral integrity; quality, nature, aptitude, ability, character.
行	xing2	2754	Move, go, advance, act, do.

Nine at the beginning

Not going out of the door to the courtyard. No defect.

不	bu4	5379	No, not, negative prefix; without, none, nothing, will not, need not, will not be.
出	chu1	1409	Go out, came out, appear, departure; arise, emerge; bring out, take out, expel, leave, get rid of; produce, beget.
戶	hu4	2180	Door, inner door, the house entrance door; household, family.
庭	ting2	6405	Courtyard (of palace), court, audience chamber; hall, courtyard, chambers; family.
无	wu2	7173	No, not, negative; without, does not possess, not have.
咎	jiu4	1192	Fault, blame, mistake, wrong; inauspicious; misfortune, bad luck, calamity; reproach, censure.

Limitation (329) 60

Nine in the second place
Not going out of the gate of the courtyard. Misfortune.

不	bu4	5379	No, not, negative prefix; without, none, nothing, will not, need not, will not be.
出	chu1	1409	Go out, came out, appear, departure; arise, emerge; bring out, take out, expel, leave, get rid of; produce, beget.
門	men2	4418	Gate, door. This is the external door, separating courtyard and street, meanwhile 戶 is the inner door, the entrance door.
庭	ting2	6405	Courtyard (of palace), court, audience chamber; hall, courtyard, chambers; family.
凶	xiong1	2808	Misfortune, pitfall, ominous, bad, unlucky, disastrous, trouble, accident.

Six in the third place
Disregarding the limits leads to sorrow. No defect.

不	bu4	5379	No, not, negative prefix; without, none, nothing, will not, need not, will not be.
節	jie2	0795	Regulate, moderate, articulate, rule; moral integrity; degree, rank; regular division; juncture, circumstance; baton, token of authority. Knot, node, joint, in bamboo of other plants.
若	ruo4	3126	Like, just as, to be like; agree, conform to; approve; concordant; compliant.
則	ze2	6746	Then, thus, accordingly, consequently, and so, in that case; law, rule, pattern; follow a law.
嗟	jie1	0763	Lament, sigh, interjection of regret or sorrow, alas, groan.
若	ruo4	3126	Like, just as, to be like; agree, conform to; approve; concordant; compliant.
无	wu2	7173	No, not, negative; without, does not possess, not have.
咎	jiu4	1192	Fault, blame, mistake, wrong; inauspicious; misfortune, bad luck, calamity; reproach, censure.

Six in the fourth place
Contented Limitation. Success.

安	an1	0026	Quiet, at peace, calm; tranquility, safety, security; settled, comfort, contentment.
節	jie2	0795	Regulate, moderate, articulate, rule; moral integrity; degree, rank; regular division; juncture, circumstance; baton, token of authority. Knot, node, joint, in bamboo of other plants.
亨	heng1	2099	Success, prevalence, smooth progress, growth, consummate, triumph; pervade; offering, sacrifice.

Nine in the fifth place

Pleasant Limitation. Good fortune. Going forward has praise.

甘	gan1	3223	Sweet, pleasant, happy, enjoy.
節	jie2	0795	Regulate, moderate, articulate, rule; moral integrity; degree, rank; regular division; juncture, circumstance; baton, token of authority. Knot, node, joint, in bamboo of other plants.
吉	ji2	0476	Good fortune, auspicious, promising, fortunate, lucky, advantageous, happiness, good auspices. It is the only single character meaning good luck in the *YiJing*.
往	wang3	7050	Go, to go to, go forward, go towards; depart, bygone, former.
有	you3	7533	Have, possession, there be, there is.
尚	shang4	5670	High, ascend, admirable, superior, surpass, respected, esteemed, reward; still, yet an besides, in addition to.

Six at the top

Bitter Limitation. The determination is ominous. Repentance fades.

苦	ku3	3493	Bitter, galling, suffering; *Sonchus* (a wild herb), *Lactuca* (lettuce).
節	jie2	0795	Regulate, moderate, articulate, rule; moral integrity; degree, rank; regular division; juncture, circumstance; baton, token of authority. Knot, node, joint, in bamboo of other plants.
貞	zhen1	0346	Perseverance, persistence, determination, steadiness, firmness; straight, correct, verified, certain; pure, loyal. Its original meaning was "to determine an uncertain matter through divination".
凶	xiong1	2808	Misfortune, pitfall, ominous, bad, unlucky, disastrous, trouble, accident.
悔	hui3	2336	Repent, regret, contrition; trouble. This word indicates both an objective situation and a subjective reaction to such circumstance.
亡	wang2	7034	Go away, disappear, exile; fail; destroy, perish, not have, not exist.

61 中孚 *zhong fu* – Inner Truth

THE JUDGMENT

Inner truth. Pigs and fishes. Good fortune.
It is favorable to cross the great river. The determination is favorable.

中	zhong1	1504	Center, inner, in the inside, put in the center, hit (target); balanced, central, middle, correct.
孚	fu2	1936	Truth; reliable, sincere; to inspire confidence in others; capture, prisoner, plunder.
豚	tun2	6600	A small, suckling pig. *Shuowen* says "pig meat".
魚	yu2	7668	Fish, symbol of abundance.
吉	ji2	0476	Good fortune, auspicious, promising, fortunate, lucky, advantageous, happiness, good auspices. It is the only single character meaning good luck in the *YiJing*.
利	li4	3867	Favorable, lucky, advantageous, profitable, beneficial, furthering, harvesting; sharp, sharp witted.
涉	she4	5707	Cross, wade across (a river, stream), ford, pass through or over.
大	da4	5943	Big, great, tall; excessive, arrogant; spread out and reach everywhere.
川	chuan1	1439	River, flowing water; flood.
利	li4	3867	Favorable, lucky, advantageous, profitable, beneficial, furthering, harvesting; sharp, sharp witted.
貞	zhen1	0346	Perseverance, persistence, determination, steadiness, firmness; straight, correct, verified, certain; pure, loyal. Its original meaning was "to determine an uncertain matter through divination".

THE IMAGE

Above the Lake is the Wind: The image of Inner Truth.
Thus the noble discusses criminal cases and delays executions.

澤	ze2	0277	Marsh, pool, pond, lake; flat body of water and the vapors rising from it; enrich, fertilize, benefit; moist, moisten; glossy, polished.

上	shang4	5669	Up, above, on, over, upwards, top, rise; higher, superior; first, best.
有	you3	7533	Have, possession, there be, there is.
風	feng1	1890	Wind, breath, air; manners, atmosphere.
中	zhong1	1504	Center, inner, in the inside, put in the center, hit (target); balanced, central, middle, correct.
孚	fu2	1936	Truth; reliable, sincere; to inspire confidence in others; capture, prisoner, plunder.
君	jun1	1715	Noble, prince, aristocrat, lord, chief, gentleman; honorable, a highly principled person, superior man. Most times, this character appears alongside another one, forming the word *JunZi*, whose original meaning was "son of a prince or ruler": 君子.
子	zi3	6939	Child, son or daughter, offspring; suffix; bride, wife; gentleman, officer, master, prince; young lady; the first of the *Earthly Branches*.
以	yi3	2932	Thus, in that way, by means of, with, for; instrument, medium, method, use (of), way (to).
議	yi4	3006	Discuss, deliberate, negotiate, weigh the options, plan for.
獄	yu4	7685	Justice, litigation, lawsuit, criminal cases; prison, jail.
緩	huan3	2242	Slow, delay; indulgent, lax; remiss, negligent; let things take their course.
死	si3	5589	Die, death, doomed.

Nine at the beginning

It is auspicious to be prepared.
There are others who are not at peace.

虞	yu2	7648	Take precautions, to provide against; foresee; anxious, not at ease; eventuality; contingency; forester, gamekeeper.
吉	ji2	0476	Good fortune, auspicious, promising, fortunate, lucky, advantageous, happiness, good auspices. It is the only single character meaning good luck in the *YiJing*.
有	you3	7533	Have, possession, there be, there is.
他	ta1	5961	Harm, obstacle, calamity; other.
不	bu4	5379	No, not, negative prefix; without, none, nothing, will not, need not, will not be.
燕	yan4	7399	At peace, calm, soothed, rest; swallow.

Inner Truth (333)

Nine in the second place

A crane calling from the shadows.
His young replies. I have a good cup.
I will share it with you.

鳴	ming2	4535	Cry of a bird or animal, a sound, to make sounds, distinctive sound, voice, express, proclaim.
鶴	he4	2131	Crane. This bird is the most favored of all Chinese bird symbols. It is an emblem of longevity, wisdom and nobility.
在	zai4	6657	Be at, at, in, on, within, be present; to lie in, depend upon, involved with; be living, dwell, located in.
陰	yin1	7444	Shade, darkness, mysterious; northern slope of a height; cloudy. In the *YiJing*, with his philosophy of change and transformation of opposites, there is the germ of the ideas that lead to the doctrine of *Yin-Yang*, several centuries later.
其	qi2	0525	Their, his, its, the; this, that. A demonstrative and possessive pronoun.
子	zi3	6939	Child, son or daughter, offspring; suffix; bride, wife; gentleman, officer, master, prince; young lady; the first of the *Earthly Branches*.
和	he2	2115	Harmony, concord, conciliation, peace, contented; respond; balance, rhythm.
之	zhi1	0935	Personal pronoun, he she, it; this, that, these, etc.; often used as a possessive.
我	wo3	4778	We, us, I, my, mine, our.
有	you3	7533	Have, possession, there be, there is.
好	hao3	2062	Good, attractive, fine; to like, to be fond of.
爵	jue2	1179	Goblet, libation cup, wine cup for ritual libations with bird shaped lid. A cup with tree legs and two handles; sparrow; rank of nobility.
吾	wu2	7188	I, my, we, our. First person pronoun.
與	yu3	7615	With, and; associate with, together with, participate in, be present at; help; give.
爾	er3	1754	Your, you.
靡	mi2	4455	Share, empty, consume, scatter, to waste.
之	zhi1	0935	Personal pronoun, he she, it; this, that, these, etc.; often used as a possessive.

Six in the third place

> Gets a mate. Sometimes beats the drum, sometimes stops.
> Sometimes weeps, sometimes sings.

得	de2	6161	Get, obtain, gain; reach, achieve; can; attain the desired thing.
敵	di2	6221	Enemy, opponent that is an equal; an equal, comrade, a match, mate.
或	huo4	2402	Perhaps, possibly, if, by chance; doubtful, uncertain; some, someone, something, sometime.
鼓	gu3	3479	Drum, drumbeating.
或	huo4	2402	Perhaps, possibly, if, by chance; doubtful, uncertain; some, someone, something, sometime.
罷	ba4	4841	Stop, cease, leave off, give up; finish; weary, exhausted.
或	huo4	2402	Perhaps, possibly, if, by chance; doubtful, uncertain; some, someone, something, sometime.
泣	qi4	0563	Weep, tears, sob, to weep silent tears, broken heart.
或	huo4	2402	Perhaps, possibly, if, by chance; doubtful, uncertain; some, someone, something, sometime.
歌	ge1	3364	Sing, song, sad or mournful songs.

Six in the fourth place

> The moon is almost full.
> One of the team's horses goes away.
> No defect.

月	yue4	7696	The Moon, lunar month.
幾	ji1	0409	Almost; imminent, nearly; occasion; minutiae, first subtle signs; approaches.
望	wang4	7043	Full Moon; the 15th day of the lunar calendary; hope; expect; look forward to.
馬	ma3	4310	Horse.
匹	pi3	5170	Companion, one of a team or yoke, peer, mate, match.
亡	wang2	7034	Go away, disappear, exile; fail; destroy, perish, not have, not exist.
无	wu2	7173	No, not, negative; without, does not possess, not have.
咎	jiu4	1192	Fault, blame, mistake, wrong; inauspicious; misfortune, bad luck, calamity; reproach, censure.

Inner Truth (335)

Nine in the fifth place
Has confidence that links them together. No defect.

有	you3	7533	Have, possession, there be, there is.
孚	fu2	1936	Truth; reliable, sincere; to inspire confidence in others; capture, prisoner, plunder.
攣	luan2	4300	Attach, link, bind, tie together; connect, continue.
如	ru2	3137	Thus, in this way, as, like, similar to, if (conditional).
无	wu2	7173	No, not, negative; without, does not possess, not have.
咎	jiu4	1192	Fault, blame, mistake, wrong; inauspicious; misfortune, bad luck, calamity; reproach, censure.

Nine at the top
The cry of the pheasant rises up into heaven.
The determination is ominous.

翰	han4	2042	Pheasant feather; wing, winged, in flight, soaring.
音	yin1	7418	Sound, tone, pronunciation of words, message, noise.
登	deng1	6167	Rise, ascend, climb, mount, step up; ripen; raise.
于	yu2	7592	At, to, in, into, on, from, by, go, go to, move towards, proceed, be.
天	tian1	6361	Heaven, firmament, the sky, cosmos; celestial, divine, power above the human.
貞	zhen1	0346	Perseverance, persistence, determination, steadiness, firmness; straight, correct, verified, certain; pure, loyal. Its original meaning was "to determine an uncertain matter through divination".
凶	xiong1	2808	Misfortune, pitfall, ominous, bad, unlucky, disastrous, trouble, accident.

62 小過 *xiao guo* – Excess of the Small

THE JUDGMENT

Excess of the Small. Success. The determination is favorable.
Proper for small matters, not suitable for great matters.
The flying bird leaves the message: It is not right to ascend,
it is fit to go below. Great good fortune.

小	xiao3	2605	Small, insignificant, common, humble, mediocre; diminish, belittle.
過	guo4	3730	Pass, pass through, go across, go beyond, excess, beyond the ordinary or proper limit; ; transgression, fault.
亨	heng1	2099	Success, prevalence, smooth progress, growth, consummate, triumph; pervade; offering, sacrifice.
利	li4	3867	Favorable, lucky, advantageous, profitable, beneficial, furthering, harvesting; sharp, sharp witted.
貞	zhen1	0346	Perseverance, persistence, determination, steadiness, firmness; straight, correct, verified, certain; pure, loyal. Its original meaning was "to determine an uncertain matter through divination".
可	ke3	3381	Can, able, may; permit, allow; satisfactory, proper, suitable.
小	xiao3	2605	Small, insignificant, common, humble, mediocre; diminish, belittle.
事	shi4	5787	Serve, service; affairs, business, matters.
不	bu4	5379	No, not, negative prefix; without, none, nothing, will not, need not, will not be.
可	ke3	3381	Can, able, may; permit, allow; satisfactory, proper, suitable.
大	da4	5943	Big, great, tall; excessive, arrogant; spread out and reach everywhere.
事	shi4	5787	Serve, service; affairs, business, matters.
飛	fei1	1850	Fly, flying, soaring; go quickly.
鳥	niao3	4688	Bird.

Excess of the Small (337)

遺	yi2	2995	Leave behind, reject, abandon, neglect, lose through carelessness.
之	zhi1	0935	Personal pronoun, he she, it; this, that, these, etc.; often used as a possessive.
音	yin1	7418	Sound, tone, pronunciation of words, message, noise.
不	bu4	5379	No, not, negative prefix; without, none, nothing, will not, need not, will not be.
宜	yi2	2993	Right, proper, sacrifice to the deity of the soil.
上	shang4	5669	Up, above, on, over, upwards, top, rise; higher, superior; first, best.
宜	yi2	2993	Right, proper, sacrifice to the deity of the soil.
下	xia4	2520	Below, down, descend.
大	da4	5943	Big, great, tall; excessive, arrogant; spread out and reach everywhere.
吉	ji2	0476	Good fortune, auspicious, promising, fortunate, lucky, advantageous, happiness, good auspices. It is the only single character meaning good luck in the *YiJing*.

THE IMAGE

On Top of the Mountain is the Thunder:
The image of Excess of the Small.
Thus the noble in his behavior is exceedingly reverent,
in mourning is exceedingly sorrow,
and in his expenditures is exceedingly frugal.

山	shan1	5630	Mountain, hill, peak.
上	shang4	5669	Up, above, on, over, upwards, top, rise; higher, superior; first, best.
有	you3	7533	Have, possession, there be, there is.
雷	lei2	4236	Thunder, shock, terrifying, arousing power surging from the earth.
小	xiao3	2605	Small, insignificant, common, humble, mediocre; diminish, belittle.
過	guo4	3730	Pass, pass through, go across, go beyond, excess, beyond the ordinary or proper limit; ; transgression, fault.
君	jun1	1715	Noble, prince, aristocrat, lord, chief, gentleman; honorable, a highly principled person, superior man. Most times, this character appears alongside another one, forming the word *JunZi*, whose original meaning was "son of a prince or ruler": 君子.

子	zi3	6939	Child, son or daughter, offspring; suffix; bride, wife; gentleman, officer, master, prince; young lady; the first of the *Earthly Branches*.
以	yi3	2932	Thus, in that way, by means of, with, for; instrument, medium, method, use (of), way (to).
行	xing2	2754	Move, go, advance, act, do.
過	guo4	3730	Pass, pass through, go across, go beyond, excess, beyond the ordinary or proper limit; ; transgression, fault.
乎	hu1	2154	Exclamatory or interrogatory particle; preposition: in, at, on, over, beside.
恭	gong1	3711	Respect, reverence, courtesy.
喪	sang4	5429	Lose, let drop, disappear, destroy, perish, mourning, burial.
過	guo4	3730	Pass, pass through, go across, go beyond, excess, beyond the ordinary or proper limit; ; transgression, fault.
乎	hu1	2154	Exclamatory or interrogatory particle; preposition: in, at, on, over, beside.
哀	ai1	0003	Grief, sorrow, regret; mourn, lament; to wail, to pity or have compassion for other person or oneself; alas!
用	yong4	7567	Use, apply, put to use, apply the oracle to real world situations; hereby, thereby.
過	guo4	3730	Pass, pass through, go across, go beyond, excess, beyond the ordinary or proper limit; ; transgression, fault.
乎	hu1	2154	Exclamatory or interrogatory particle; preposition: in, at, on, over, beside.
儉	jian3	0848	Thrift, temperate, restricted, frugal, meager; poor harvest.

Six at the beginning

    The flying bird will have misfortune.

飛	fei1	1850	Fly, flying, soaring; go quickly.
鳥	niao3	4688	Bird.
以	yi3	2932	Thus, in that way, by means of, with, for; instrument, medium, method, use (of), way (to).
凶	xiong1	2808	Misfortune, pitfall, ominous, bad, unlucky, disastrous, trouble, accident.

Excess of the Small (339)

Six in the second place

> Passing by his ancestor, meeting his ancestress.
> Not reaching his ruler, meeting his minister. No defect.

過	guo4	3730	Pass, pass through, go across, go beyond, excess, beyond the ordinary or proper limit; ; transgression, fault.
其	qi2	0525	Their, his, its, the; this, that. A demonstrative and possessive pronoun.
祖	zu3	6815	Ancestor, grandfather.
遇	yu4	7625	Meet, encounter, come across, happen.
其	qi2	0525	Their, his, its, the; this, that. A demonstrative and possessive pronoun.
妣	bi3	5082	Ancestress, foremother, deceased mother or grandmother.
不	bu4	5379	No, not, negative prefix; without, none, nothing, will not, need not, will not be.
及	ji2	0468	Reach, come to, draw out, approach to.
其	qi2	0525	Their, his, its, the; this, that. A demonstrative and possessive pronoun.
君	jun1	1715	Noble, prince, aristocrat, lord, chief, gentleman; honorable, a highly principled person, superior man. Most times, this character appears alongside another one, forming the word *JunZi*, whose original meaning was "son of a prince or ruler": 君子.
遇	yu4	7625	Meet, encounter, come across, happen.
其	qi2	0525	Their, his, its, the; this, that. A demonstrative and possessive pronoun.
臣	chen2	0327	Servant, retainer, vassal, statesman, minister, officer; male slave, male bondservant or may be a slave couple.
无	wu2	7173	No, not, negative; without, does not possess, not have.
咎	jiu4	1192	Fault, blame, mistake, wrong; inauspicious; misfortune, bad luck, calamity; reproach, censure.

Nine in the third place

> If he is not exceedingly careful, somebody may follow
> and strike him. Misfortune.

弗	fu2	1981	Not (not able or not willing to), negative.
過	guo4	3730	Pass, pass through, go across, go beyond, excess, beyond the ordinary or proper limit; ; transgression, fault.

防	fang2	1817	Prevent, careful, protect against; embankment, erect a protective barrier; withstand, be a match for.
之	zhi1	0935	Personal pronoun, he she, it; this, that, these, etc.; often used as a possessive.
從	cong2	6919	Follow (somebody or a way or doctrine), adhere, obey, pursue; follower attendant; attend to business; from, by, since, whence, through.
或	huo4	2402	Perhaps, possibly, if, by chance; doubtful, uncertain; some, someone, something, sometime.
戕	qiang1	0673	Strike, kill, injure, violent assault, maltreat.
之	zhi1	0935	Personal pronoun, he she, it; this, that, these, etc.; often used as a possessive.
凶	xiong1	2808	Misfortune, pitfall, ominous, bad, unlucky, disastrous, trouble, accident.

Nine in the fourth place

No defect. Not passing, meeting. Moving on is dangerous.
One must be alert. Do not be unyielding.

无	wu2	7173	No, not, negative; without, does not possess, not have.
咎	jiu4	1192	Fault, blame, mistake, wrong; inauspicious; misfortune, bad luck, calamity; reproach, censure.
弗	fu2	1981	Not (not able or not willing to), negative.
過	guo4	3730	Pass, pass through, go across, go beyond, excess, beyond the ordinary or proper limit; ; transgression, fault.
遇	yu4	7625	Meet, encounter, come across, happen.
之	zhi1	0935	Personal pronoun, he she, it; this, that, these, etc.; often used as a possessive.
往	wang3	7050	Go, to go to, go forward, go towards; depart, bygone, former.
厲	li4	3906	Danger, threat; oppressive, cruel, wicked, brutal, harsh; sickness, malevolent devil; grind, polish, sharpen; discipline.
必	bi4	5109	Must, necessarily, certainly, unavoidably.
戒	jie4	0627	Warn, caution, limit, on guard, wary.
勿	wu4	7208	Do not, no. Negative imperative.
用	yong4	7567	Use, apply, put to use, apply the oracle to real world situations; hereby, thereby.

Excess of the Small (341)

永	yong3	7589	For a long time, constant, permanent, everlasting; prolong; distant, far reaching.
貞	zhen1	0346	Perseverance, persistence, determination, steadiness, firmness; straight, correct, verified, certain; pure, loyal. Its original meaning was "to determine an uncertain matter through divination".

Six in the fifth place

> Heavy clouds but no rain from our western frontier.
> The prince shoots and captures the one in the cave.

密	mi4	4464	Dense, thick, intimate, confidential; hidden, secret; silent.
雲	yun2	7750	Clouds.
不	bu4	5379	No, not, negative prefix; without, none, nothing, will not, need not, will not be.
雨	yu3	7662	Rain, shower, sudden downpour.
自	zi4	6960	From, origin, source, cause, reason; oneself, yourself.
我	wo3	4778	We, us, I, my, mine, our.
西	xi1	2460	The West, western. Related to the autumn.
郊	jiao1	0714	Countryside, suburbs, outskirts, frontier; suburban altar and sacrifice.
公	gong1	3701	Prince, feudal lord, duke, noble of rank (the nobiliary titles, from high to low, were: duke, marquis, count, viscount, baron); public, impartial, with justice, fair.
弋	yi4	3018	Shoot with arrow and string attached. It was used to hunt birds and fishes to prevent the prey from bolting.
取	qu3	1615	Take, take a wife, obtain, lay hold of, grasp.
彼	bi3	5093	That one, that, there, those, other, another.
在	zai4	6657	Be at, at, in, on, within, be present; to lie in, depend upon, involved with; be living, dwell, located in.
穴	xue2	2899	Pit, cave, den, hole, underground dwellings.

Six at the top

> Passes without finding him. The flying bird is netted. Misfortune.
> This means disaster.

弗	fu2	1981	Not (not able or not willing to), negative.
遇	yu4	7625	Meet, encounter, come across, happen.

過	guo4	3730	Pass, pass through, go across, go beyond, excess, beyond the ordinary or proper limit; ; transgression, fault.
之	zhi1	0935	Personal pronoun, he she, it; this, that, these, etc.; often used as a possessive.
飛	fei1	1850	Fly, flying, soaring; go quickly.
鳥	niao3	4688	Bird.
離	li2	3902	Brightness, radiance, attach, cling; name of a bird. The modern meaning is leave, separate.
之	zhi1	0935	Personal pronoun, he she, it; this, that, these, etc.; often used as a possessive.
凶	xiong1	2808	Misfortune, pitfall, ominous, bad, unlucky, disastrous, trouble, accident.
是	shi4	5794	This, that; this is, is; to be right; indeed, correctly; preceding statement.
謂	wei4	7079	Say, tell; call; mean; name. 是謂: this is what is called...
災	zai1	6652	Calamity, disaster, injury; misfortune from without (undeserved); calamities from Heaven, as floods, famines, pestilence, etc.
眚	sheng3	5741	Disaster, calamity, serious mistake; offense by mishap or fault; cloudy eyes, disease of the eye, new moon, eclipse, meanings that indicate blindness or lack of light, a mistake due to ignorance or an error of judgment.

63 既濟 *jiji* – Already Across

The Judgment

Already Across. Success.
The determination is favorable
for small things.
At first good fortune, at the end chaos.

既	ji4	0453	Already, consummated, completed, finished; to be done with, get done.
濟	ji4	0459	Ford, cross a stream at a shallow place; complete a task, fulfill, consummate; increase; help.
亨	heng1	2099	Success, prevalence, smooth progress, growth, consummate, triumph; pervade; offering, sacrifice.
小	xiao3	2605	Small, insignificant, common, humble, mediocre; diminish, belittle.
利	li4	3867	Favorable, lucky, advantageous, profitable, beneficial, furthering, harvesting; sharp, sharp witted.
貞	zhen1	0346	Perseverance, persistence, determination, steadiness, firmness; straight, correct, verified, certain; pure, loyal. Its original meaning was "to determine an uncertain matter through divination".
初	chu1	1390	At first, beginning, initial, incipient, in the early stages.
吉	ji2	0476	Good fortune, auspicious, promising, fortunate, lucky, advantageous, happiness, good auspices. It is the only single character meaning good luck in the *YiJing*.
終	zhong1	1500	End, finish, complete; for ever; end of a cycle; carried to conclusion, consummation, closure; death. The original meaning was: tied-off end of a thread.
亂	luan4	4220	Disorder, confusion, rebellion, anarchy, chaos, a mess, confused and tangled situation.

63 — MATRIX OF MEANINGS OF THE BOOK OF CHANGES

THE IMAGE

Water over Fire: The image of Already Across.
Thus the noble meditates on misfortune in advance to prevent it.

水	shui3	5922	Water, river, stream, flood, liquid, fluid.
在	zai4	6657	Be at, at, in, on, within, be present; to lie in, depend upon, involved with; be living, dwell, located in.
火	huo3	2395	Fire, flame.
上	shang4	5669	Up, above, on, over, upwards, top, rise; higher, superior; first, best.
既	ji4	0453	Already, consummated, completed, finished; to be done with, get done.
濟	ji4	0459	Ford, cross a stream at a shallow place; complete a task, fulfill, consummate; increase; help.
君	jun1	1715	Noble, prince, aristocrat, lord, chief, gentleman; honorable, a highly principled person, superior man. Most times, this character appears alongside another one, forming the word *JunZi*, whose original meaning was "son of a prince or ruler": 君子.
子	zi3	6939	Child, son or daughter, offspring; suffix; bride, wife; gentleman, officer, master, prince; young lady; the first of the *Earthly Branches*.
以	yi3	2932	Thus, in that way, by means of, with, for; instrument, medium, method, use (of), way (to).
思	si1	5580	Think, consider, ponder; brood, reflect, plan.
患	huan4	2240	Misfortune, calamity, disaster, tribulation; distress, grief, suffering.
而	er2	1756	And, then, but, nevertheless, also, only. Join and contrasts two words.
豫	yu4	7603	Think beforehand, take precautions, anticipate, hesitate; joy, happy, amusement, recreation, enthusiasm, contentment, at ease.
防	fang2	1817	Prevent, careful, protect against; embankment, erect a protective barrier; withstand, be a match for.
之	zhi1	0935	Personal pronoun, he she, it; this, that, these, etc.; often used as a possessive.

Nine at the beginning

Drags his wheels and wets his tail. No defect.

曳	yi4	3008	Drag, haul back; pull.

Already Across (345)

其	qi2	0525	Their, his, its, the; this, that. A demonstrative and possessive pronoun.
輪	lun2	4254	Wheel/s.
濡	ru2	3149	Moist, soak, immerse, wet.
其	qi2	0525	Their, his, its, the; this, that. A demonstrative and possessive pronoun.
尾	wei3	7109	Tail, rear, back, behind, the end; last.
无	wu2	7173	No, not, negative; without, does not possess, not have.
咎	jiu4	1192	Fault, blame, mistake, wrong; inauspicious; misfortune, bad luck, calamity; reproach, censure.

Six in the second place

The woman loses the curtain of her carriage.
Do not chase it, you will get it in seven days.

婦	fu4	1963	Woman, lady, wife, married woman.
喪	sang4	5429	Lose, let drop, disappear, destroy, perish, mourning, burial.
其	qi2	0525	Their, his, its, the; this, that. A demonstrative and possessive pronoun.
茀	fu2	1989	Carriage curtain, carriage blind (to kept women protected from prying eyes), veil; head ornament, ornamental hairpin, hairpiece, wig.
勿	wu4	7208	Do not, no. Negative imperative.
逐	zhu2	1383	Chase, run after, hunt; expel, push out; in order, in succession; one by one.
七	qi1	0579	Seven, seventh; seventh day when the moon reaches a major phase after the new moon.
日	ri4	3124	Sun, day, daylight, daytime; daily.
得	de2	6161	Get, obtain, gain; reach, achieve; can; attain the desired thing.

Nine in the third place

The eminent ancestor attacks the Land of the Devil,
after three years conquest it. Petty man must not be used.

高	gao1	3290	High, elevated, exalted, eminent, lofty, illustrious, higher.
宗	zong1	6896	Clan, kin, sect, faction, school; ancestor; ancestral temple; ancestral hall.

伐	fa1	1765	Attack, punish (rebels), submit; beat, cut down, fell.
鬼	gui3	3634	*Gui* tribe (enemies of the *Zhou*), barbarians; ghosts, foreign devils, demons, disembodied spirits, goblins, ghouls.
方	fang1	1802	Square, squarely, directly, straightforward, honest; a place, a region; on all sides; direction, trend, method; suddenly, quick, definite; take a place, occupy; sacrifice to the spirits of the four quarters.
三	san1	5415	Three, thrice, third time or place.
年	nian2	4711	Year(s), season(s), harvest(s).
克	ke4	3320	Can, able, carry, sustain; conquest, dominate, prevail.
之	zhi1	0935	Personal pronoun, he she, it; this, that, these, etc.; often used as a possessive.
小	xiao3	2605	Small, insignificant, common, humble, mediocre; diminish, belittle.
人	ren2	3097	Man, person(s); people; others; human being, individual.
勿	wu4	7208	Do not, no. Negative imperative.
用	yong4	7567	Use, apply, put to use, apply the oracle to real world situations; hereby, thereby.

Six in the fourth place

He has torn silk and caulking rags.
Be cautious until the end of the day.

繻	xu1	2845	Torn piece of silk; silk torn in two pieces, one of which was given as a token and the other retained, to identify the bearers when joined; fine silk clothing, jacket.
有	you3	7533	Have, possession, there be, there is.
衣	yi1	2989	Clothes, garment, to wear.
袽	ru2	3140	Rags, tatters, caulking rags; silk thread.
終	zhong1	1500	End, finish, complete; for ever; end of a cycle; carried to conclusion, consummation, closure; death. The original meaning was: tied-off end of a thread.
日	ri4	3124	Sun, day, daylight, daytime; daily.
戒	jie4	0627	Warn, caution, limit, on guard, wary.

Nine in the fifth place

The eastern neighbor sacrifices an ox,
but this falls short of the neighbor in the west with his small offering,
whose sincerity receives the blessing.

Already Across (347) 63

東	dong1	6605	The East.
鄰	lin2	4033	Neighbor, neighborhood, extended family, associate, assistant.
殺	sha1	5615	Kill, slaughter, slay; diminish, reduce.
牛	niu2	4737	Cow, bull, ox.
不	bu4	5379	No, not, negative prefix; without, none, nothing, will not, need not, will not be.
如	ru2	3137	Thus, in this way, as, like, similar to, if (conditional).
西	xi1	2460	The West, western. Related to the autumn.
鄰	lin2	4033	Neighbor, neighborhood, extended family, associate, assistant.
之	zhi1	0935	Personal pronoun, he she, it; this, that, these, etc.; often used as a possessive.
禴	yue4	7498	*Yue* summer sacrifice to all the ancestors entitled to special sacrifices, when food is sparse; small offering, a sacrifice offered with few resources.
祭	ji4	0465	Sacrifice, offering to gods or spirits, worship.
實	shi2	5821	Contents, substance; actual, real; full, fill; solid, truthful, honest; fruit.
受	shou4	5840	Receive, accept, consent, agree; endure, suffer; compliant, tranquil.
其	qi2	0525	Their, his, its, the; this, that. A demonstrative and possessive pronoun.
福	fu2	1978	Happiness, good fortune, blessings.

Six at the top

He soaks his head. Danger.

濡	ru2	3149	Moist, soak, immerse, wet.
其	qi2	0525	Their, his, its, the; this, that. A demonstrative and possessive pronoun.
首	shou3	5839	Head; foremost, first; leader, chief.
厲	li4	3906	Danger, threat; oppressive, cruel, wicked, brutal, harsh; sickness, malevolent devil; grind, polish, sharpen; discipline.

64 未濟 *wei ji* – Before Crossing

THE JUDGMENT

Before Crossing. Success.
[If] the little fox tail gets wet when finishes fording the river, nothing is favorable.

未	wei4	7114	Not yet, before. The eight of the twelve *Earthly Branches*. 13-15 hs.
濟	ji4	0459	Ford, cross a stream at a shallow place; complete a task, fulfill, consummate; increase; help.
亨	heng1	2099	Success, prevalence, smooth progress, growth, consummate, triumph; pervade; offering, sacrifice.
小	xiao3	2605	Small, insignificant, common, humble, mediocre; diminish, belittle.
狐	hu2	2185	Fox, foxes.
汔	qi4	8006	Almost, nearly; water drying up, dried up.
濟	ji4	0459	Ford, cross a stream at a shallow place; complete a task, fulfill, consummate; increase; help.
濡	ru2	3149	Moist, soak, immerse, wet.
其	qi2	0525	Their, his, its, the; this, that. A demonstrative and possessive pronoun.
尾	wei3	7109	Tail, rear, back, behind, the end; last.
无	wu2	7173	No, not, negative; without, does not possess, not have.
攸	you1	7519	Goal, direction, destination, objective; distant, far away; a place; that which, whereby, thereby, for which; mark of the passive voice.
利	li4	3867	Favorable, lucky, advantageous, profitable, beneficial, furthering, harvesting; sharp, sharp witted.

Before Crossing (349) 64

The Image

> Fire over Water: The image of Before Crossing.
> So the noble is careful discriminating things,
> so that each one is left in place.

火	huo3	2395	Fire, flame.
在	zai4	6657	Be at, at, in, on, within, be present; to lie in, depend upon, involved with; be living, dwell, located in.
水	shui3	5922	Water, river, stream, flood, liquid, fluid.
上	shang4	5669	Up, above, on, over, upwards, top, rise; higher, superior; first, best.
未	wei4	7114	Not yet, before. The eight of the twelve *Earthly Branches*. 13-15 hs.
濟	ji4	0459	Ford, cross a stream at a shallow place; complete a task, fulfill, consummate; increase; help.
君	jun1	1715	Noble, prince, aristocrat, lord, chief, gentleman; honorable, a highly principled person, superior man. Most times, this character appears alongside another one, forming the word *JunZi*, whose original meaning was "son of a prince or ruler": 君子.
子	zi3	6939	Child, son or daughter, offspring; suffix; bride, wife; gentleman, officer, master, prince; young lady; the first of the *Earthly Branches*.
以	yi3	2932	Thus, in that way, by means of, with, for; instrument, medium, method, use (of), way (to).
慎	shen4	5734	Careful, cautious, circumspect.
辨	bian4	5240	Discriminate, distinguish, discern, identify; divide, distribute; frame that divides a bed from its stand.
物	wu4	7209	Thing/s, being/s, creature/s; substance, the physical world, all living things; others.
居	ju1	1535	Remain; rest (in); abides, dwell; to occupy a position or place; overbearing, arrogant.
方	fang1	1802	Square, squarely, directly, straightforward, honest; a place, a region; on all sides; direction, trend, method; suddenly, quick, definite; take a place, occupy; sacrifice to the spirits of the four quarters.

Six at the beginning

> He dips his tail. Humiliation.

濡	ru2	3149	Moist, soak, immerse, wet.

其	qi2	0525	Their, his, its, the; this, that. A demonstrative and possessive pronoun.
尾	wei3	7109	Tail, rear, back, behind, the end; last.
吝	lin4	4040	Humiliation, regret, shame, distress, grief, sorrow; miserly, niggardly. It is a warning of trouble.

Nine in the second place

Dragging his wheels. The determination is fortunate.

曳	yi4	3008	Drag, haul back; pull.
其	qi2	0525	Their, his, its, the; this, that. A demonstrative and possessive pronoun.
輪	lun2	4254	Wheel/s.
貞	zhen1	0346	Perseverance, persistence, determination, steadiness, firmness; straight, correct, verified, certain; pure, loyal. Its original meaning was "to determine an uncertain matter through divination".
吉	ji2	0476	Good fortune, auspicious, promising, fortunate, lucky, advantageous, happiness, good auspices. It is the only single character meaning good luck in the *YiJing*.

Six in the third place

Before Crossing. Attack brings misfortune.
It is favorable to ford the great river.

未	wei4	7114	Not yet, before. The eight of the twelve *Earthly Branches*. 13-15 hs.
濟	ji4	0459	Ford, cross a stream at a shallow place; complete a task, fulfill, consummate; increase; help.
征	zheng1	0352	Punishing expedition ("to correct"), to reduce to submission, attack, punish; to levy taxes; comes, brings.
凶	xiong1	2808	Misfortune, pitfall, ominous, bad, unlucky, disastrous, trouble, accident.
利	li4	3867	Favorable, lucky, advantageous, profitable, beneficial, furthering, harvesting; sharp, sharp witted.
涉	she4	5707	Cross, wade across (a river, stream), ford, pass through or over.
大	da4	5943	Big, great, tall; excessive, arrogant; spread out and reach everywhere.
川	chuan1	1439	River, flowing water; flood.

Before Crossing (351) 64

Nine in the fourth place

The determination is fortunate. Repentance fades.
Shock to conquer the Land of the Devil.
Three years of rewards from the great kingdom.

貞	zhen1	0346	Perseverance, persistence, determination, steadiness, firmness; straight, correct, verified, certain; pure, loyal. Its original meaning was "to determine an uncertain matter through divination".
吉	ji2	0476	Good fortune, auspicious, promising, fortunate, lucky, advantageous, happiness, good auspices. It is the only single character meaning good luck in the *YiJing*.
悔	hui3	2336	Repent, regret, contrition; trouble. This word indicates both an objective situation and a subjective reaction to such circumstance.
亡	wang2	7034	Go away, disappear, exile; fail; destroy, perish, not have, not exist.
震	zhen4	0315	Shock; clap of thunder; fear; awe inspiring; stimulation, movement, excitation; to excite, to terrify; to quicken; endow, succor.
用	yong4	7567	Use, apply, put to use, apply the oracle to real world situations; hereby, thereby.
伐	fa1	1765	Attack, punish (rebels), submit; beat, cut down, fell.
鬼	gui3	3634	*Gui* tribe (enemies of the *Zhou*), barbarians; ghosts, foreign devils, demons, disembodied spirits, goblins, ghouls.
方	fang1	1802	Square, squarely, directly, straightforward, honest; a place, a region; on all sides; direction, trend, method; suddenly, quick, definite; take a place, occupy; sacrifice to the spirits of the four quarters.
三	san1	5415	Three, thrice, third time or place.
年	nian2	4711	Year(s), season(s), harvest(s).
有	you3	7533	Have, possession, there be, there is.
賞	shang3	5672	Reward, award, gifts, tributes.
于	yu2	7592	At, to, in, into, on, from, by, go, go to, move towards, proceed, be.
大	da4	5943	Big, great, tall; excessive, arrogant; spread out and reach everywhere.
國	guo2	3738	State, country, nation, kingdom, a dynasty; capital city.

Six in the fifth place

>The determination is fortunate. There is no repentance.
>The glory of the noble is true. Good fortune.

貞	zhen1	0346	Perseverance, persistence, determination, steadiness, firmness; straight, correct, verified, certain; pure, loyal. Its original meaning was "to determine an uncertain matter through divination".
吉	ji2	0476	Good fortune, auspicious, promising, fortunate, lucky, advantageous, happiness, good auspices. It is the only single character meaning good luck in the *YiJing*.
无	wu2	7173	No, not, negative; without, does not possess, not have.
悔	hui3	2336	Repent, regret, contrition; trouble. This word indicates both an objective situation and a subjective reaction to such circumstance.
君	jun1	1715	Noble, prince, aristocrat, lord, chief, gentleman; honorable, a highly principled person, superior man. Most times, this character appears alongside another one, forming the word *JunZi*, whose original meaning was "son of a prince or ruler": 君子.
子	zi3	6939	Child, son or daughter, offspring; suffix; bride, wife; gentleman, officer, master, prince; young lady; the first of the *Earthly Branches*.
之	zhi1	0935	Personal pronoun, he she, it; this, that, these, etc.; often used as a possessive.
光	guang1	3583	Light, illumination, brilliance, glory, honor.
有	you3	7533	Have, possession, there be, there is.
孚	fu2	1936	Truth; reliable, sincere; to inspire confidence in others; capture, prisoner, plunder.
吉	ji2	0476	Good fortune, auspicious, promising, fortunate, lucky, advantageous, happiness, good auspices. It is the only single character meaning good luck in the *YiJing*.

Nine at the top

>They drink wine in confidence. No defect.
>But confidence will be lost if your head gets wet.

有	you3	7533	Have, possession, there be, there is.
孚	fu2	1936	Truth; reliable, sincere; to inspire confidence in others; capture, prisoner, plunder.
于	yu2	7592	At, to, in, into, on, from, by, go, go to, move towards, proceed, be.

Before Crossing

飲	yin3	7454	Drink; swallow; give to drink.
酒	jiu3	1208	Drink, wine, liquor, spirits.
无	wu2	7173	No, not, negative; without, does not possess, not have.
咎	jiu4	1192	Fault, blame, mistake, wrong; inauspicious; misfortune, bad luck, calamity; reproach, censure.
濡	ru2	3149	Moist, soak, immerse, wet.
其	qi2	0525	Their, his, its, the; this, that. A demonstrative and possessive pronoun.
首	shou3	5839	Head; foremost, first; leader, chief.
有	you3	7533	Have, possession, there be, there is.
孚	fu2	1936	Truth; reliable, sincere; to inspire confidence in others; capture, prisoner, plunder.
失	shi1	5806	Lose, let go, neglect, an omission; fail, err; lose control.
是	shi4	5794	This, that; this is, is; to be right; indeed, correctly; preceding statement.

Concordance

The location of the characters is indicated by adding a point and a letter or number after the number of the hexagram.
0   indicates The Judgment;
1 to 6 indicate a Line number;
7   indicates the comment when all lines change, in hexagrams 1 and 2;
X   indicates The Image.

哀
0003: appears 1 time in: 62.X.

安
0026: appears 4 times in: 2.0, 6.4, 23.X and 60.4.

占
0125: appears 1 time in: 49.5.

戰
0147: appears 1 time in: 2.6.

章
0182: appears 3 times in: 2.3, 44.5 and 5.5.

張
0195: appears 1 time in: 38.6.

丈
0200: appears 3 times in: 7.0, 17.2 and 17.3.

長
0213: appears 1 time in: 7.5.

常
0221: appears 1 time in: 29.X.

邕
0232: appears 1 time in: 51.0.

朝
0233: appears 1 time in: 6.6.

昭
0236: appears 1 time in: 35.X.

照
0238: appears 1 time in: 30.X.

巢
0253: appears 1 time in: 56.6.

折
0267: appears 5 times in: 22.X, 30.6, 50.4, 55.3 and 55.X.

宅
0275: appears 1 time in: 23.X.

澤
0277: appears 15 times in: 10.X, 17.X, 19.X, 28.X, 31.X, 38.X, 41.X, 43.X, 45.X, 47.X, 49.X, 54.X, 58.X, 60.X and 61.X.

車
0280: appears 4 times in: 14.2, 22.1, 38.6 and 47.4.

掣
0282: appears 1 time in: 38.3.

枕
0308: appears 1 time in: 29.3.

振
0313: appears 2 times in: 18.X and 32.6.

震
0315: appears 9 times in: 51.0, 51.1, 51.2, 51.3, 51.4, 51.5, 51.6, 51.X and 64.4.

臣
0327: appears 4 times in: 33.3, 39.2, 41.6 and 62.2.

貞
0346: appears 109 times in: 1.0, 2.0, 2.3, 2.7, 3.0, 3.1, 3.2, 3.5, 4.0, 5.0, 5.5, 6.3, 6.4, 7.0, 7.5, 8.0, 8.2, 8.4, 9.6, 10.2, 10.5, 11.3, 11.6, 12.0, 12.1, 13.0, 15.2, 16.2, 16.5, 17.0, 17.1, 17.3, 17.4, 18.2, 19.0, 19.1, 20.2, 21.4, 21.5, 22.3, 23.1, 23.2, 25.0, 25.4, 26.0, 26.3, 27.0, 27.3, 27.5, 30.0, 31.0, 31.4, 32.0, 32.1, 32.3, 32.5, 33.0, 33.5, 34.0, 34.2, 34.3, 34.4, 35.1, 35.2, 35.4, 35.6, 36.0, 36.3, 36.5, 37.0, 37.2, 39.0, 40.2, 40.3, 41.0, 41.2, 41.6, 42.2, 44.1, 45.0, 45.5, 46.5, 46.6, 47.0, 49.0, 49.3, 49.6, 50.5, 52.1, 53.0, 54.2, 56.0, 56.2, 56.3, 57.1, 57.5, 57.6, 58.0, 59.0, 60.0, 60.6, 61.0, 61.6, 62.0, 62.4, 63.0, 64.2, 64.4 and 64.5.

正
0351: appears 2 times in: 25.0 and 50.X.

征
0352: appears 19 times in: 9.6, 11.1, 15.6, 24.6, 27.2, 30.6, 34.1, 41.2, 46.0, 47.2, 47.6, 49.2, 49.3, 49.6, 51.6, 53.3, 54.0, 54.1 and 64.3.

政
0355: appears 1 time in: 22.X.

拯
0360: appears 3 times in: 36.2, 52.2 and 59.1.

成
0379: appears 4 times in: 2.3, 6.3, 11.X and 16.6.

城
0380: appears 1 time in: 11.6.

稱
0383: appears 1 time in: 15.X.

懲
0384: appears 1 time in: 41.X.

承
0386: appears 4 times in: 7.6, 12.2, 32.3 and 54.6.

乘
0398: appears 5 times in: 3.2, 3.4, 3.6, 13.4 and 40.3.

箕
0402: appears 1 time in: 36.5.

幾
0409: appears 4 times in: 3.3, 9.6, 54.5 and 61.4.

机
0411: appears 1 time in: 59.2.

忌
0432: appears 1 time in: 43.X.

繼
0452: appears 1 time in: 30.X.

Concordance

既
0453: appears 5 times in: 9.6, 19.3, 29.5, 63.0 and 63.X.

濟
0459: appears 5 times in: 63.0, 63.X, 64.0, 64.3 and 64.X.

躋
0461: appears 1 time in: 51.2.

齋
0464: appears 1 time in: 45.6.

祭
0465: appears 2 times in: 47.5 and 63.5.

及
0468: appears 2 times in: 43.X and 62.2.

汲
0472: appears 1 time in: 48.3.

吉
0476: appears 142 times in: 1.7, 2.0, 2.5, 3.4, 3.5, 4.2, 4.5, 5.0, 5.2, 5.5, 5.6, 6.0, 6.1, 6.3, 6.4, 6.5, 7.0, 7.2, 8.0, 8.1, 8.2, 8.4, 8.5, 9.1, 9.2, 10.2, 10.4, 10.6, 11.0, 11.1, 11.5, 12.1, 12.2, 12.5, 13.4, 14.5, 14.6, 15.1, 15.2, 15.3, 16.2, 17.1, 17.5, 18.1, 19.1, 19.2, 19.5, 19.6, 21.4, 22.3, 22.5, 24.1, 24.2, 25.1, 26.0, 26.4, 26.5, 27.0, 27.4, 27.5, 27.6, 28.4, 30.0, 30.2, 30.5, 31.0, 31.2, 31.4, 32.5, 33.3, 33.4, 33.5, 34.2, 34.4, 34.6, 35.1, 35.2, 35.5, 35.6, 36.2, 37.2, 37.3, 37.4, 37.5, 37.6, 38.0, 38.6, 39.0, 39.6, 40.0, 40.2, 40.5, 41.0, 41.5, 41.6, 42.1, 42.2, 42.5, 44.1, 45.0, 45.2, 45.4, 46.0, 46.1, 46.4, 46.5, 47.0, 47.6, 48.6, 49.2, 49.4, 49.6, 50.0, 50.2, 50.3, 50.6, 51.1, 52.6, 53.0, 53.2, 53.5, 53.6, 54.1, 54.5, 55.2, 55.4, 55.5, 56.0, 57.2, 57.5, 58.1, 58.2, 59.1, 59.4, 60.5, 61.0, 61.1, 62.0, 63.0, 64.2, 64.4 and 64.5.

擊
0481: appears 2 times in: 4.6 and 42.6.

棘
0486: appears 1 time in: 29.6.

疾
0492: appears 9 times in: 16.5, 24.0, 25.5, 33.3, 36.3, 41.4, 50.2, 55.2 and 58.4.

蒺
0494: appears 1 time in: 47.3.

卽
0495: appears 5 times in: 3.3, 6.4, 43.0, 50.2 and 56.2.

積
0500: appears 1 time in: 46.X.

岐
0522: appears 1 time in: 46.4.

其
0525: appears 90 times in: 2.6, 3.5, 6.2, 9.1, 9.5, 10.6, 11.1, 11.3, 11.4, 12.1, 12.5, 13.3, 13.4, 14.4, 15.5, 18.6, 20.6, 22.1, 22.2, 24.0, 24.6, 25.0, 26.X, 27.4, 28.2, 28.5, 30.4, 30.6, 31.1, 31.2, 31.3, 31.5, 31.6, 32.3, 32.5, 34.3, 35.2, 35.6, 36.1, 36.3, 38.3, 40.0, 41.3, 41.4, 43.4, 44.3, 44.6, 47.3, 48.0, 48.3, 50.1, 50.3, 50.4, 51.6, 52.0, 52.1, 52.2, 52.3, 52.4, 52.5, 52.X, 53.4, 53.6, 54.5, 55.1, 55.2, 55.3, 55.4, 55.6, 56.1, 56.2, 56.3, 56.4, 56.6, 57.6, 59.2, 59.3, 59.4, 59.5, 59.6, 61.2, 62.2, 63.1, 63.2, 63.5, 63.6, 64.0, 64.1, 64.2 and 64.6.

期
0526: appears 1 time in: 54.4.

杞
0547: appears 1 time in: 44.5.

起
0548: appears 1 time in: 44.4.

器
0549: appears 1 time in: 45.X.

棄
0550: appears 1 time in: 30.4.

妻
0555: appears 3 times in: 9.3, 28.2 and 47.3.

泣
0563: appears 2 times in: 3.6 and 61.3.

戚
0575: appears 1 time in: 30.5.

七
0579: appears 3 times in: 24.0, 51.2 and 63.2.

嘉
0592: appears 3 times in: 17.5, 30.6 and 33.5.

家
0594: appears 11 times in: 4.2, 7.6, 26.0, 37.0, 37.1, 37.3, 37.4, 37.5, 37.X, 41.6 and 55.6.

假
0599: appears 4 times in: 37.5, 45.0, 55.0 and 59.0.

甲
0610: appears 1 time in: 18.0.

頰
0614: appears 1 time in: 31.6.

皆
0620: appears 1 time in: 55.X.

階
0625: appears 1 time in: 46.5.

解
0626: appears 4 times in: 40.0, 40.4, 40.5 and 40.X.

戒
0627: appears 4 times in: 11.4, 45.X, 62.4 and 63.4.

誡
0628: appears 1 time in: 8.5.

介
0629: appears 3 times in: 16.2, 35.2 and 58.4.

疆
0643: appears 1 time in: 19.X.

講
0645: appears 1 time in: 58.X.

疅
0668: appears 1 time in: 1.X.

戕
0673: appears 1 time in: 62.3.

交
0702: appears 6 times in: 11.X, 12.X, 14.1, 14.5, 17.1 and 38.4.

校
0706: appears 2 times in: 21.1 and 21.6.

郊
0714: appears 4 times in: 5.1, 9.0, 13.6 and 62.5.

教
0719: appears 3 times in: 19.X, 20.X and 29.X.

嗟
0763: appears 4 times in: 30.3, 30.5, 45.3 and 60.3.

藉
0767: appears 1 time in: 28.1.

節
0795: appears 7 times in: 27.X, 60.0, 60.3, 60.4, 60.5, 60.6 and 60.X.

Concordance

接
0800: appears 1 time in: 35.0.

且
0803: appears 5 times in: 29.3, 38.3, 40.3, 43.4 and 44.3.

妾
0814: appears 2 times in: 33.3 and 50.1.

堅
0825: appears 1 time in: 2.1.

兼
0830: appears 1 time in: 52.X.

艱
0834: appears 6 times in: 11.3, 14.1, 21.4, 26.3, 34.6 and 36.0.

蹇
0843: appears 8 times in: 39.0, 39.1, 39.2, 39.3, 39.4, 39.5, 39.6 and 39.X.

儉
0848: appears 2 times in: 12.X and 62.X.

建
0853: appears 4 times in: 3.0, 3.1, 8.X and 16.0.

健
0854: appears 1 time in: 1.X.

見
0860: appears 21 times in: 1.2, 1.5, 1.7, 4.3, 6.0, 18.4, 38.1, 38.3, 38.6, 39.0, 39.6, 42.X, 44.1, 45.0, 46.0, 47.3, 52.0, 55.2, 55.3, 55.4 and 57.0.

戔
0866: appears 1 time in: 22.5.

薦
0872: appears 2 times in: 16.X and 20.0.

漸
0878: appears 8 times in: 53.0, 53.1, 53.2, 53.3, 53.4, 53.5, 53.6 and 53.X.

洊
0880: appears 2 times in: 29.X and 51.X.

牽
0881: appears 2 times in: 9.2 and 43.4.

謙
0885: appears 7 times in: 15.0, 15.1, 15.2, 15.3, 15.4, 15.6 and 15.X.

愆
0889: appears 1 time in: 54.4.

遷
0911: appears 2 times in: 42.4 and 42.X.

潛
0918: appears 1 time in: 1.1.

前
0919: appears 3 times in: 8.5, 26.X and 43.1.

知
0932: appears 2 times in: 19.5 and 54.X.

之
0935: appears 63 times in: 2.0, 5.6, 6.6, 8.1, 8.2, 8.3, 8.4, 8.6, 11.X, 12.0, 14.6, 16.X, 17.6, 18.1, 18.2, 18.3, 18.4, 18.5, 19.3, 19.5, 20.4, 23.3, 25.3, 25.5, 26.4, 26.5, 26.6, 29.3, 30.1, 30.3, 32.3, 33.2, 34.4, 36.4, 36.5, 38.6, 39.2, 40.6, 41.0, 41.1, 41.2, 41.5, 41.6, 42.2, 42.3, 42.6, 46.6, 49.1, 49.2, 53.5, 54.2, 54.5, 55.0, 57.1, 61.2, 62.0, 62.3, 62.4, 62.6, 63.3, 63.5, 63.X and 64.5.

祉
0942: appears 2 times in: 11.5 and 12.4.

趾
0944: appears 6 times in: 21.1, 22.1, 34.1, 43.1, 50.1 and 52.1.

祇
0952: appears 2 times in: 24.1 and 29.5.

雉
0968: appears 2 times in: 50.3 and 56.5.

志
0971: appears 2 times in: 10.X and 47.X.

實
0976: appears 1 time in: 29.6.

至
0982: appears 11 times in: 2.1, 5.3, 19.0, 19.4, 24.6, 24.X, 29.X, 40.3, 40.4, 48.0 and 55.X.

致
0984: appears 4 times in: 5.3, 40.3, 47.X and 55.X.

制
0986: appears 1 time in: 60.X.

桎
0993: appears 1 time in: 4.1.

窒
0994: appears 2 times in: 6.0 and 41.X.

執
0996: appears 3 times in: 7.5, 31.3 and 33.2.

直
1006: appears 1 time in: 2.2.

治
1021: appears 1 time in: 49.X.

遲
1024: appears 2 times in: 16.3 and 54.4.

褫
1028: appears 1 time in: 6.6.

赤
1048: appears 1 time in: 47.5.

敕
1050: appears 1 time in: 21.X.

金
1057: appears 6 times in: 4.3, 21.4, 21.5, 44.1, 47.4 and 50.5.

晉
1088: appears 6 times in: 35.0, 35.1, 35.2, 35.4, 35.6 and 35.X.

進
1091: appears 2 times in: 20.3 and 57.1.

禽
1100: appears 4 times in: 7.5, 8.5, 32.4 and 48.1.

親
1107: appears 1 time in: 8.X.

侵
1108: appears 1 time in: 15.5.

經
1123: appears 3 times in: 3.X, 27.2 and 27.5.

敬
1138: appears 2 times in: 5.6 and 30.1.

驚
1140: appears 1 time in: 51.0.

井
1143: appears 8 times in: 48.0, 48.1, 48.2, 48.3, 48.4, 48.5, 48.6 and 48.X.

傾
1161: appears 1 time in: 12.6.

慶
1167: appears 1 time in: 55.5.

角
1174: appears 3 times in: 34.3, 35.6 and 44.6.

CONCORDANCE

桷
1175: appears 1 time in: 53.4.

爵
1179: appears 1 time in: 61.2.

咎
1192: appears 99 times in: 1.3, 1.4, 2.4, 5.1, 7.0, 7.2, 7.4, 7.5, 8.0, 8.1, 9.1, 9.4, 10.1, 11.3, 12.4, 13.1, 14.1, 14.2, 14.4, 16.6, 17.0, 17.4, 18.1, 18.3, 19.3, 19.4, 19.6, 20.1, 20.5, 20.6, 21.1, 21.2, 21.3, 21.5, 22.6, 23.3, 24.0, 24.3, 25.4, 27.4, 28.1, 28.5, 28.6, 29.4, 29.5, 30.1, 30.6, 32.0, 35.1, 35.6, 38.1, 38.2, 38.4, 38.5, 40.1, 41.0, 41.1, 41.4, 41.6, 42.1, 42.3, 43.1, 43.3, 43.5, 44.2, 44.3, 44.6, 45.1, 45.2, 45.3, 45.4, 45.5, 45.6, 46.2, 46.4, 47.0, 47.2, 48.4, 49.2, 50.1, 51.6, 52.0, 52.1, 52.4, 53.1, 53.4, 55.1, 55.3, 57.2, 59.5, 59.6, 60.1, 60.3, 61.4, 61.5, 62.2, 62.4, 63.1 and 64.6.

九
1198: appears 1 time in: 51.2.

舊
1205: appears 2 times in: 6.3 and 48.1.

酒
1208: appears 4 times in: 5.5, 29.4, 47.2 and 64.6.

就
1210: appears 1 time in: 49.3.

丘
1213: appears 3 times in: 22.5, 27.2 and 59.4.

求
1217: appears 5 times in: 3.4, 4.0, 17.3, 27.0 and 29.2.

窮
1247: appears 1 time in: 19.X.

酌
1257: appears 1 time in: 41.1.

晝
1302: appears 1 time in: 35.0.

甃
1305: appears 1 time in: 48.4.

疇
1322: appears 1 time in: 12.4.

愁
1325: appears 1 time in: 35.2.

醜
1327: appears 1 time in: 30.6.

仇
1332: appears 1 time in: 50.2.

主
1336: appears 5 times in: 2.0, 36.1, 38.2, 55.1 and 55.4.

朱
1346: appears 1 time in: 47.2.

株
1348: appears 1 time in: 47.1.

諸
1362: appears 1 time in: 8.X.

逐
1383: appears 5 times in: 26.3, 27.4, 38.1, 51.2 and 63.2.

躅
1388: appears 1 time in: 44.1.

初
1390: appears 5 times in: 4.0, 36.6, 38.3, 57.5 and 63.0.

除
1391: appears 1 time in: 45.X.

處
1407: appears 2 times in: 9.6 and 56.4.

出
1409: appears 17 times in: 4.X, 5.4, 7.1, 9.4, 16.X, 17.1, 24.0, 30.5, 30.6, 35.X, 36.4, 37.X, 50.1, 52.X, 59.6, 60.1 and 60.2.

畜
1412: appears 7 times in: 7.X, 9.0, 9.X, 26.0, 26.X, 30.0 and 33.3.

觸
1416: appears 2 times in: 34.3 and 34.6.

川
1439: appears 12 times in: 5.0, 6.0, 13.0, 15.1, 18.0, 26.0, 27.5, 27.6, 42.0, 59.0, 61.0 and 64.3.

遄
1444: appears 2 times in: 41.1 and 41.4.

壯
1453: appears 10 times in: 34.0, 34.1, 34.3, 34.4, 34.X, 36.2, 43.1, 43.3, 44.0 and 59.1.

牀
1459: appears 5 times in: 23.1, 23.2, 23.4, 57.2 and 57.6.

垂
1478: appears 1 time in: 36.1.

隼
1487: appears 1 time in: 40.6.

終
1500: appears 30 times in: 1.3, 2.3, 5.2, 5.6, 6.0, 6.1, 6.3, 6.6, 8.1, 10.4, 15.0, 15.3, 16.2, 18.1, 22.5, 24.6, 29.4, 37.3, 37.6, 38.3, 43.6, 45.1, 47.4, 50.3, 53.5, 54.X, 56.5, 57.5, 63.0 and 63.4.

中
1504: appears 23 times in: 3.3, 6.0, 7.2, 7.X, 11.2, 15.X, 17.X, 24.4, 24.X, 26.X, 36.X, 37.2, 42.3, 42.4, 43.5, 46.X, 49.2, 55.0, 55.2, 55.3, 55.4, 61.0 and 61.X.

眾
1517: appears 3 times in: 7.X, 35.3 and 36.X.

崇
1528: appears 1 time in: 16.X.

憧
1529: appears 1 time in: 31.4.

寵
1534: appears 1 time in: 23.5.

居
1535: appears 9 times in: 3.1, 17.3, 27.5, 31.2, 43.X, 49.6, 53.X, 59.5 and 64.X.

拘
1542: appears 1 time in: 17.6.

懼
1560: appears 2 times in: 28.X and 51.X.

據
1563: appears 1 time in: 47.3.

履
1572: appears 1 time in: 21.1.

去
1594: appears 2 times in: 9.4 and 59.6.

驅
1602: appears 1 time in: 8.5.

衢
1611: appears 1 time in: 26.6.

取
1615: appears 5 times in: 4.3, 31.0, 44.0, 56.1 and 62.5.

闃
1627: appears 1 time in: 55.6.

勸
1662: appears 1 time in: 48.X.

Concordance

泉
1674: appears 2 times in: 4.X and 48.5.

厥
1680: appears 2 times in: 14.5 and 38.5.

決
1697: appears 1 time in: 34.4.

矍
1704: appears 1 time in: 51.6.

君
1715: appears 79 times in: 1.3, 1.X, 2.0, 2.X, 3.3, 3.X, 4.X, 5.X, 6.X, 7.X, 7.X, 9.6, 9.X, 10.3, 10.X, 12.0, 12.X, 13.0, 13.X, 14.X, 15.0, 15.1, 15.3, 15.X, 17.X, 18.X, 19.5, 19.X, 20.1, 20.5, 20.6, 22.X, 23.6, 24.6, 26.X, 27.X, 28.X, 29.X, 31.X, 32.X, 33.4, 33.X, 34.3, 34.X, 35.X, 36.1, 36.X, 37.X, 38.X, 39.X, 40.5, 40.X, 41.X, 42.X, 43.3, 43.X, 45.X, 46.X, 47.X, 48.X, 49.6, 49.X, 50.X, 51.X, 52.X, 53.X, 54.5, 54.X, 55.X, 56.X, 57.X, 58.X, 60.X, 61.X, 62.2, 62.X, 63.X, 64.5 and 64.X.

浚
1729: appears 1 time in: 32.1.

羣
1737: appears 2 times in: 1.7 and 59.4.

耳
1744: appears 3 times in: 21.6, 50.3 and 50.5.

二
1751: appears 1 time in: 41.0.

貳
1752: appears 1 time in: 29.4.

爾
1754: appears 3 times in: 27.1, 31.4 and 61.2.

而
1756: appears 12 times in: 6.2, 13.5, 20.0, 22.1, 30.3, 33.X, 36.X, 37.X, 38.X, 40.4, 56.X and 63.X.

法
1762: appears 1 time in: 21.X.

伐
1765: appears 4 times in: 15.5, 35.6, 63.3 and 64.4.

發
1768: appears 2 times in: 4.1 and 55.2.

罰
1769: appears 1 time in: 21.X.

反
1781: appears 5 times in: 9.3, 24.0, 39.3, 39.X and 54.3.

蕃
1798: appears 1 time in: 35.0.

藩
1800: appears 3 times in: 34.3, 34.4 and 34.6.

方
1802: appears 12 times in: 2.2, 8.0, 20.X, 24.X, 30.X, 32.X, 44.X, 47.2, 50.3, 63.3, 64.4 and 64.X.

防
1817: appears 2 times in: 62.3 and 63.X.

非
1819: appears 1 time in: 34.X.

匪
1820: appears 13 times in: 3.2, 4.0, 8.3, 12.0, 14.1, 14.4, 22.4, 25.0, 30.6, 38.6, 39.2, 45.5 and 59.4.

腓
1830: appears 2 times in: 31.2 and 52.2.

肥
1839: appears 1 time in: 33.6.

飛
1850: appears 5 times in: 1.5, 36.1, 62.0, 62.1 and 62.6.

忿
1854: appears 1 time in: 41.X.

紛
1859: appears 1 time in: 57.2.

焚
1866: appears 3 times in: 30.4, 56.3 and 56.6.

豶
1873: appears 1 time in: 26.5.

奮
1874: appears 1 time in: 16.X.

風
1890: appears 10 times in: 9.X, 18.X, 20.X, 32.X, 37.X, 42.X, 44.X, 57.X, 59.X and 61.X.

馮
1895: appears 1 time in: 11.2.

豐
1897: appears 6 times in: 55.0, 55.2, 55.3, 55.4, 55.6 and 55.X.

否
1902: appears 8 times in: 7.1, 12.0, 12.2, 12.5, 12.6, 12.X, 33.4 and 50.1.

缶
1905: appears 3 times in: 8.1, 29.4 and 30.3.

夫
1908: appears 10 times in: 4.3, 8.0, 9.3, 17.2, 17.3, 28.2, 28.5, 32.5, 38.4 and 53.3.

鮒
1927: appears 1 time in: 48.2.

父
1933: appears 4 times in: 18.1, 18.3, 18.4 and 18.5.

斧
1934: appears 2 times in: 56.4 and 57.6.

孚
1936: appears 40 times in: 5.0, 6.0, 8.1, 9.4, 9.5, 11.3, 11.4, 14.5, 17.4, 17.5, 20.0, 29.0, 34.1, 35.1, 37.6, 38.4, 40.4, 40.5, 41.0, 42.3, 42.5, 43.0, 44.1, 45.1, 45.2, 45.5, 46.2, 48.6, 49.0, 49.3, 49.4, 49.5, 55.2, 58.2, 58.5, 61.0, 61.5, 61.X, 64.5 and 64.6.

輔
1945: appears 3 times in: 11.X, 31.6 and 52.5.

富
1952: appears 4 times in: 9.5, 11.4, 15.5 and 37.4.

負
1956: appears 2 times in: 38.6 and 40.3.

膚
1958: appears 5 times in: 21.2, 23.4, 38.5, 43.4 and 44.3.

婦
1963: appears 8 times in: 4.2, 9.6, 28.5, 32.5, 37.3, 53.3, 53.5 and 63.2.

伏
1964: appears 1 time in: 13.3.

紱
1971: appears 2 times in: 47.2 and 47.5.

福
1978: appears 4 times in: 11.3, 35.2, 48.3 and 63.5.

輻
1980: appears 1 time in: 9.3.

弗
1981: appears 10 times in: 13.4, 14.3, 34.X, 41.2, 41.5, 41.6, 42.2, 62.3, 62.4 and 62.6.

茀
1989: appears 1 time in: 63.2.

復
1992: appears 16 times in: 6.4, 9.1, 9.2, 11.3, 11.6, 24.0, 24.1, 24.2, 24.3, 24.4, 24.5, 24.6, 24.X, 38.1, 40.0 and 53.3.

覆
1993: appears 1 time in: 50.4.

腹
1994: appears 1 time in: 36.4.

輹
1997: appears 2 times in: 26.2 and 34.4.

害
2015: appears 1 time in: 14.1.

含
2017: appears 2 times in: 2.3 and 44.5.

汗
2028: appears 1 time in: 59.5.

翰
2042: appears 2 times in: 22.4 and 61.6.

寒
2048: appears 1 time in: 48.5.

好
2062: appears 2 times in: 33.4 and 61.2.

號
2064: appears 7 times in: 13.5, 43.0, 43.2, 43.6, 45.1, 56.6 and 59.5.

亨
2099: appears 46 times in: 1.0, 2.0, 3.0, 4.0, 5.0, 9.0, 10.0, 11.0, 12.1, 12.2, 13.0, 14.0, 14.3, 15.0, 17.0, 17.6, 18.0, 19.0, 21.0, 22.0, 24.0, 25.0, 26.6, 28.0, 29.0, 30.0, 31.0, 32.0, 33.0, 45.0, 46.0, 46.4, 47.0, 49.0, 50.0, 51.0, 55.0, 56.0, 57.0, 58.0, 59.0, 60.0, 60.4, 62.0, 63.0 and 64.0.

恆
2107: appears 10 times in: 5.1, 16.5, 32.0, 32.1, 32.3, 32.5, 32.6, 32.X, 37.X and 42.6.

何
2109: appears 5 times in: 9.1, 17.4, 21.6, 26.6 and 38.5.

河
2111: appears 1 time in: 11.2.

和
2115: appears 2 times in: 58.1 and 61.2.

盍
2119: appears 1 time in: 16.4.

嗑
2120: appears 2 times in: 21.0 and 21.X.

曷
2122: appears 1 time in: 41.0.

鶴
2131: appears 1 time in: 61.2.

嗃
2134: appears 1 time in: 37.3.

侯
2135: appears 6 times in: 3.0, 3.1, 8.X, 16.0, 18.6 and 35.0.

後
2143: appears 10 times in: 2.0, 8.0, 12.6, 13.5, 18.0, 36.6, 38.6, 51.1, 56.6 and 57.5.

后
2144: appears 3 times in: 11.X, 24.X and 44.X.

厚
2147: appears 2 times in: 2.X and 23.X.

乎
2154: appears 1 time in: 62.X.

虎
2161: appears 5 times in: 10.0, 10.3, 10.4, 27.4 and 49.5.

戶
2180: appears 3 times in: 6.2, 55.6 and 60.1.

弧
2184: appears 1 time in: 38.6.

狐
2185: appears 2 times in: 40.2 and 64.0.

穫
2207: appears 1 time in: 25.2.

華
2217: appears 1 time in: 28.5.

懷
2233: appears 1 time in: 56.2.

桓
2236: appears 1 time in: 3.1.

患
2240: appears 1 time in: 63.X.

緩
2242: appears 1 time in: 61.X.

渙
2252: appears 7 times in: 59.0, 59.2, 59.3, 59.4, 59.5, 59.6 and 59.X.

荒
2271: appears 1 time in: 11.2.

隍
2295: appears 1 time in: 11.6.

黃
2297: appears 8 times in: 2.5, 2.6, 21.5, 30.2, 33.2, 40.2, 49.1 and 50.5.

悔
2336: appears 32 times in: 1.6, 13.6, 16.3, 18.3, 24.1, 24.5, 31.4, 31.5, 32.2, 34.4, 34.5, 35.3, 35.5, 37.1, 37.3, 38.1, 38.5, 43.4, 45.5, 47.6, 49.0, 49.4, 50.3, 52.5, 57.4, 57.5, 58.2, 59.2, 59.3, 60.6, 64.4 and 64.5.

晦
2337: appears 3 times in: 17.X, 36.6 and 36.X.

惠
2339: appears 1 time in: 42.5.

彙
2349: appears 2 times in: 11.1 and 12.1.

徽
2354: appears 1 time in: 29.6.

撝
2356: appears 1 time in: 15.4.

婚
2360: appears 5 times in: 3.2, 3.4, 22.4, 38.6 and 51.6.

鴻
2386: appears 6 times in: 53.1, 53.2, 53.3, 53.4, 53.5 and 53.6.

火
2395: appears 10 times in: 13.X, 14.X, 22.X, 37.X, 38.X, 49.X, 50.X, 56.X, 63.X and 64.X.

或
2402: appears 13 times in: 1.4, 2.3, 6.3, 6.6, 7.3, 25.3, 32.3, 41.5, 42.2, 42.6, 53.4, 61.3 and 62.3.

獲
2412: appears 7 times in: 17.4, 30.6, 36.4, 40.2, 40.6, 52.0 and 57.4.

係
2424: appears 5 times in: 17.2, 17.3, 17.6, 29.6 and 33.3.

Concordance

喜
2434: appears 4 times in: 12.6, 25.5, 41.4 and 58.4.

嘻
2436: appears 1 time in: 37.3.

哑
2456: appears 2 times in: 10.0 and 10.3.

繫
2458: appears 3 times in: 12.5, 25.3 and 44.1.

西
2460: appears 7 times in: 2.0, 9.0, 17.6, 39.0, 40.0, 62.5 and 63.5.

虩
2480: appears 2 times in: 51.0 and 51.1.

夕
2485: appears 1 time in: 1.3.

息
2495: appears 3 times in: 1.X, 17.X and 46.6.

習
2499: appears 5 times in: 2.2, 29.0, 29.1, 29.X and 58.X.

錫
2505: appears 3 times in: 6.6, 7.2 and 35.0.

退
2517: appears 1 time in: 11.2.

下
2520: appears 15 times in: 4.X, 10.X, 18.X, 22.X, 23.X, 25.X, 27.X, 33.X, 38.X, 41.X, 43.X, 44.X, 57.2, 57.6 and 62.0.

享
2552: appears 4 times in: 41.0, 42.2, 47.2 and 59.X.

巷
2553: appears 1 time in: 38.2.

嚮
2561: appears 1 time in: 17.X.

相
2562: appears 3 times in: 11.X, 13.5 and 48.X.

祥
2577: appears 1 time in: 10.6.

小
2605: appears 35 times in: 3.5, 5.2, 6.1, 7.6, 9.0, 9.X, 11.0, 12.0, 12.2, 14.3, 17.2, 17.3, 18.3, 20.1, 21.3, 22.0, 23.6, 29.2, 33.0, 33.4, 33.X, 34.3, 38.0, 40.5, 45.3, 46.X, 49.6, 53.1, 56.0, 57.0, 62.0, 62.X, 63.0, 63.3 and 64.0.

笑
2615: appears 5 times in: 13.5, 45.1, 51.0, 51.1 and 56.6.

咸
2666: appears 9 times in: 19.1, 19.2, 31.0, 31.1, 31.2, 31.3, 31.5, 31.6 and 31.X.

賢
2671: appears 1 time in: 53.X.

閑
2679: appears 2 times in: 26.3 and 37.1.

莧
2686: appears 1 time in: 43.5.

險
2689: appears 2 times in: 29.2 and 29.3.

顯
2692: appears 1 time in: 8.5.

限
2696: appears 1 time in: 52.3.

先
2702: appears 14 times in: 2.0, 8.X, 12.6, 13.5, 16.X, 18.0, 20.X, 21.X, 24.X, 25.X, 38.6, 56.6, 57.5 and 59.X.

心
2735: appears 8 times in: 29.0, 36.4, 42.5, 42.6, 48.3, 52.2, 52.3 and 56.4.

信
2748: appears 2 times in: 43.4 and 47.0.

興
2753: appears 1 time in: 13.3.

行
2754: appears 33 times in: 1.X, 4.X, 6.X, 9.X, 11.2, 15.6, 16.0, 20.X, 24.4, 24.6, 24.X, 25.3, 25.6, 25.X, 26.X, 29.0, 29.X, 36.1, 37.X, 41.3, 42.3, 42.4, 43.3, 43.4, 43.5, 44.3, 50.3, 51.3, 52.0, 57.X, 59.X, 60.X and 62.X.

刑
2755: appears 3 times in: 4.1, 55.X and 56.X.

形
2759: appears 1 time in: 50.4.

休
2786: appears 3 times in: 12.5, 14.X and 24.2.

脩
2795: appears 2 times in: 39.X and 51.X.

羞
2797: appears 2 times in: 12.3 and 32.3.

凶
2808: appears 57 times in: 3.5, 6.0, 7.1, 7.3, 7.5, 8.0, 8.6, 9.6, 10.3, 16.1, 17.4, 19.0, 21.6, 23.1, 23.2, 23.4, 24.6, 27.1, 27.2, 27.3, 28.3, 28.6, 29.1, 29.6, 30.3, 31.2, 32.1, 32.5, 32.6, 34.1, 41.2, 42.3, 42.6, 43.3, 43.6, 44.1, 44.4, 47.2, 47.3, 48.0, 49.3, 49.6, 50.4, 51.6, 53.3, 54.0, 55.6, 56.6, 57.6, 58.3, 60.2, 60.6, 61.6, 62.1, 62.3, 62.6 and 64.3.

旰
2819: appears 1 time in: 16.3.

虛
2821: appears 2 times in: 31.X and 46.3.

徐
2841: appears 2 times in: 47.4 and 47.5.

需
2844: appears 7 times in: 5.0, 5.1, 5.2, 5.3, 5.4, 5.5 and 5.X.

繻
2845: appears 1 time in: 63.4.

須
2847: appears 1 time in: 22.2.

序
2851: appears 1 time in: 52.5.

恤
2862: appears 6 times in: 11.3, 35.5, 37.5, 43.2, 45.1 and 46.0.

玄
2881: appears 1 time in: 2.6.

鉉
2886: appears 2 times in: 50.5 and 50.6.

旋
2894: appears 1 time in: 10.6.

穴
2899: appears 3 times in: 5.4, 5.6 and 62.5.

血
2901: appears 6 times in: 2.6, 3.6, 5.4, 9.4, 54.6 and 59.6.

Concordance

熏
2906: appears 1 time in: 52.3.

旬
2915: appears 1 time in: 55.1.

已
2930: appears 1 time in: 26.1.

以
2932: appears 85 times in: 1.X, 2.X, 3.X, 4.1, 4.X, 5.X, 6.X, 7.1, 7.X, 8.X, 9.5, 9.X, 10.X, 11.1, 11.4, 11.5, 11.X, 12.1, 12.X, 13.X, 14.2, 14.X, 15.5, 15.X, 16.X, 17.4, 17.X, 18.X, 19.X, 20.X, 21.X, 22.X, 23.1, 23.2, 23.4, 23.5, 23.X, 24.6, 24.X, 25.X, 26.X, 27.X, 28.X, 29.X, 30.X, 31.X, 32.X, 33.X, 34.X, 35.X, 36.X, 37.X, 38.X, 39.X, 40.X, 41.X, 42.X, 43.X, 44.5, 44.X, 45.X, 46.X, 47.X, 48.X, 49.X, 50.1, 50.X, 51.X, 52.X, 53.X, 54.1, 54.3, 54.X, 55.X, 56.5, 56.X, 57.X, 58.X, 59.X, 60.X, 61.X, 62.1, 62.X, 63.X and 64.X.

疑
2940: appears 2 times in: 16.4 and 55.2.

易
2952: appears 3 times in: 32.X, 34.5 and 56.6.

意
2960: appears 1 time in: 51.5.

頤
2969: appears 7 times in: 27.0, 27.1, 27.2, 27.3, 27.4, 27.6 and 27.X.

夷
2982: appears 9 times in: 36.0, 36.1, 36.2, 36.3, 36.4, 36.5, 36.X, 55.4 and 59.4.

洟
2986: appears 1 time in: 45.6.

衣
2989: appears 1 time in: 63.4.

依
2990: appears 1 time in: 42.4.

宜
2993: appears 4 times in: 11.X, 19.5, 55.0 and 62.0.

遺
2995: appears 2 times in: 11.2 and 62.0.

懿
2999: appears 1 time in: 9.X.

儀
3003: appears 1 time in: 53.6.

議
3006: appears 2 times in: 60.X and 61.X.

曳
3008: appears 3 times in: 38.3, 63.1 and 64.2.

異
3009: appears 1 time in: 38.X.

劓
3013: appears 2 times in: 38.3 and 47.5.

一
3016: appears 4 times in: 38.6, 41.3, 45.1 and 56.5.

乙
3017: appears 2 times in: 11.5 and 54.5.

弋
3018: appears 1 time in: 62.5.

亦
3021: appears 1 time in: 48.0.

邑
3037: appears 9 times in: 6.2, 8.5, 11.6, 15.6, 25.3, 35.6, 43.0, 46.3 and 48.0.

億
3042: appears 1 time in: 51.2.

翼
3051: appears 1 time in: 36.1.

益
3052: appears 9 times in: 15.X, 41.2, 41.5, 41.6, 42.0, 42.2, 42.3, 42.6 and 42.X.

然
3072: appears 1 time in: 30.1.

橈
3087: appears 2 times in: 28.0 and 28.3.

人
3097: appears 55 times in: 1.2, 1.5, 4.1, 5.6, 6.0, 6.2, 7.0, 7.6, 8.3, 8.5, 10.0, 10.2, 10.3, 12.0, 12.2, 12.5, 13.0, 13.1, 13.2, 13.5, 13.6, 13.X, 14.3, 20.1, 23.5, 23.6, 25.3, 30.X, 31.X, 32.5, 33.4, 33.X, 34.3, 36.1, 37.0, 37.3, 37.X, 38.1, 38.3, 39.0, 39.6, 40.5, 41.3, 45.0, 46.0, 47.0, 49.5, 49.6, 52.0, 54.2, 55.6, 56.6, 57.0, 57.1 and 63.3.

日
3124: appears 18 times in: 1.3, 16.2, 18.0, 24.0, 24.X, 30.3, 35.0, 36.1, 49.0, 49.2, 51.2, 55.0, 55.2, 55.3, 55.4, 57.5, 63.2 and 63.4.

若
3126: appears 8 times in: 1.3, 20.0, 30.5, 43.3, 45.1, 55.2, 57.2 and 60.3.

如
3137: appears 17 times in: 3.2, 3.3, 3.4, 3.6, 9.5, 14.5, 22.3, 22.4, 30.4, 35.1, 35.2, 35.4, 37.6, 45.3, 54.5, 61.5 and 63.5.

茹
3139: appears 2 times in: 11.1 and 12.1.

衵
3140: appears 1 time in: 63.4.

濡
3149: appears 7 times in: 22.3, 43.3, 63.1, 63.6, 64.0, 64.1 and 64.6.

入
3152: appears 11 times in: 3.3, 5.6, 17.X, 24.0, 29.1, 29.3, 36.4, 36.6, 36.X, 47.1 and 47.3.

肉
3153: appears 2 times in: 21.3 and 21.5.

戎
3181: appears 4 times in: 13.3, 43.0, 43.2 and 45.X.

改
3196: appears 3 times in: 42.X, 48.0 and 49.4.

開
3204: appears 1 time in: 7.6.

干
3211: appears 1 time in: 53.1.

甘
3223: appears 2 times in: 19.3 and 60.5.

敢
3229: appears 1 time in: 22.X.

乾
3233: appears 4 times in: 1.0, 1.3, 21.4 and 21.5.

幹
3235: appears 4 times in: 18.1, 18.2, 18.3 and 18.5.

坎
3245: appears 6 times in: 29.0, 29.1, 29.2, 29.3, 29.5 and 29.X.

衎
3252: appears 1 time in: 53.2.

Concordance

亢
3273: appears 1 time in: 1.6.

康
3278: appears 1 time in: 35.0.

告
3287: appears 5 times in: 4.0, 11.6, 42.3, 42.4 and 43.0.

誥
3288: appears 1 time in: 44.X.

高
3290: appears 5 times in: 13.3, 18.6, 40.6, 46.X and 63.3.

膏
3296: appears 2 times in: 3.5 and 50.3.

考
3299: appears 3 times in: 10.6, 16.X and 18.1.

革
3314: appears 8 times in: 33.2, 49.0, 49.1, 49.2, 49.3, 49.6, 49.X and 50.3.

克
3320: appears 10 times in: 4.2, 6.2, 6.4, 13.4, 13.5, 14.3, 24.6, 41.5, 42.2 and 63.3.

客
3324: appears 1 time in: 5.6.

艮
3327: appears 8 times in: 52.0, 52.1, 52.2, 52.3, 52.4, 52.5, 52.6 and 52.X.

庚
3339: appears 1 time in: 57.5.

耕
3343: appears 1 time in: 25.2.

歌
3364: appears 2 times in: 30.3 and 61.3.

葛
3377: appears 1 time in: 47.6.

可
3381: appears 11 times in: 2.3, 12.X, 18.2, 25.4, 27.5, 36.3, 41.0, 48.3, 53.6, 60.0 and 62.0.

姤
3422: appears 3 times in: 44.0, 44.6 and 44.X.

媾
3426: appears 5 times in: 3.2, 3.4, 22.4, 38.6 and 51.6.

口
3434: appears 1 time in: 27.0.

寇
3444: appears 7 times in: 3.2, 4.6, 5.3, 22.4, 38.6, 40.3 and 53.3.

故
3455: appears 1 time in: 39.2.

股
3467: appears 2 times in: 31.3 and 36.2.

孤
3470: appears 2 times in: 38.4 and 38.6.

蠱
3475: appears 7 times in: 18.0, 18.1, 18.2, 18.3, 18.4, 18.5 and 18.X.

鼓
3479: appears 2 times in: 30.3 and 61.3.

谷
3483: appears 2 times in: 47.1 and 48.2.

梏
3484: appears 1 time in: 4.1.

枯
3492: appears 2 times in: 28.2 and 28.5.

苦
3493: appears 2 times in: 60.0 and 60.6.

瓜
3504: appears 1 time in: 44.5.

寡
3517: appears 1 time in: 15.X.

括
3519: appears 1 time in: 2.4.

夬
3535: appears 5 times in: 10.5, 43.0, 43.3, 43.5 and 43.X.

快
3547: appears 2 times in: 52.2 and 56.4.

官
3552: appears 1 time in: 17.1.

貫
3566: appears 1 time in: 23.5.

盥
3569: appears 1 time in: 20.0.

關
3571: appears 1 time in: 24.X.

觀
3575: appears 10 times in: 20.0, 20.1, 20.2, 20.3, 20.4, 20.5, 20.6, 20.X, 27.0 and 27.1.

光
3583: appears 3 times in: 5.0, 20.4 and 64.5.

筐
3598: appears 1 time in: 54.6.

圭
3609: appears 1 time in: 42.3.

歸
3617: appears 9 times in: 6.2, 11.5, 53.0, 54.0, 54.1, 54.3, 54.4, 54.5 and 54.X.

龜
3621: appears 3 times in: 27.1, 41.5 and 42.2.

簋
3633: appears 2 times in: 29.4 and 41.0.

鬼
3634: appears 3 times in: 38.6, 63.3 and 64.4.

刲
3642: appears 1 time in: 54.6.

闚
3649: appears 2 times in: 20.2 and 55.6.

虧
3650: appears 1 time in: 50.3.

睽
3660: appears 4 times in: 38.0, 38.4, 38.6 and 38.X.

饋
3669: appears 1 time in: 37.2.

坤
3684: appears 2 times in: 2.0 and 2.X.

困
3688: appears 9 times in: 4.4, 47.0, 47.1, 47.2, 47.3, 47.4, 47.5, 47.6 and 47.X.

功
3698: appears 1 time in: 17.1.

攻
3699: appears 1 time in: 13.4.

公
3701: appears 6 times in: 14.3, 40.6, 42.3, 42.4, 50.4 and 62.5.

躬
3704: appears 4 times in: 4.3, 39.2, 51.6 and 59.3.

宮
3705: appears 2 times in: 23.5 and 47.3.

肱
3706: appears 1 time in: 55.3.

Concordance

恭
3711: appears 1 time in: 62.X.

鞏
3718: appears 1 time in: 49.1.

恐
3721: appears 1 time in: 51.X.

過
3730: appears 11 times in: 28.0, 28.6, 28.X, 40.X, 42.X, 62.0, 62.2, 62.3, 62.4, 62.6 and 62.X.

果
3732: appears 2 times in: 4.X and 23.6.

國
3738: appears 7 times in: 7.6, 8.X, 15.6, 20.4, 24.6, 42.4 and 64.4.

臘
3763: appears 1 time in: 21.3.

來
3768: appears 24 times in: 5.6, 8.0, 8.1, 11.0, 12.0, 24.0, 29.3, 30.4, 31.4, 39.1, 39.3, 39.4, 39.5, 39.6, 40.0, 47.2, 47.4, 48.0, 51.0, 51.1, 51.2, 51.5, 55.5 and 58.3.

勞
3826: appears 2 times in: 15.3 and 48.X.

老
3833: appears 2 times in: 28.2 and 28.5.

里
3857: appears 1 time in: 51.0.

利
3867: appears 99 times in: 1.0, 1.2, 1.5, 2.0, 2.2, 2.7, 3.0, 3.1, 3.4, 4.0, 4.1, 4.3, 4.6, 5.0, 5.1, 6.0, 7.5, 12.0, 13.0, 14.6, 15.4, 15.5, 15.6, 16.0, 17.0, 17.3, 18.0, 19.0, 19.2, 19.3, 20.2, 20.4, 21.0, 21.4, 22.0, 23.0, 23.5, 24.0, 25.0, 25.2, 25.6, 26.0, 26.1, 26.3, 27.3, 27.6, 28.0, 28.2, 30.0, 31.0, 32.0, 32.1, 33.0, 33.6, 34.0, 34.6, 35.5, 36.0, 36.5, 37.0, 39.0, 39.6, 40.0, 40.6, 41.0, 41.2, 41.6, 42.0, 42.1, 42.4, 43.0, 44.2, 45.0, 45.2, 45.3, 46.2, 46.6, 47.2, 47.5, 49.0, 50.1, 50.5, 50.6, 52.1, 53.0, 53.3, 54.0, 54.2, 54.6, 57.0, 57.1, 57.5, 58.0, 59.0, 61.0, 62.0, 63.0, 64.0 and 64.3.

藜
3877: appears 1 time in: 47.3.

禮
3886: appears 1 time in: 34.X.

履
3893: appears 12 times in: 2.1, 10.0, 10.1, 10.2, 10.3, 10.4, 10.5, 10.6, 10.X, 30.1, 34.X and 54.1.

離
3902: appears 6 times in: 12.4, 30.0, 30.2, 30.3, 30.X and 62.6.

厲
3906: appears 27 times in: 1.3, 6.3, 9.6, 10.5, 18.1, 21.5, 24.3, 26.1, 27.6, 33.1, 33.3, 34.3, 35.4, 35.6, 37.3, 38.4, 43.0, 44.3, 49.3, 51.2, 51.5, 52.3, 53.1, 56.3, 58.5, 62.4 and 63.6.

涖
3912: appears 1 time in: 36.X.

麗
3914: appears 1 time in: 58.X.

立
3921: appears 4 times in: 28.X, 32.X, 42.6 and 59.X.

歷
3931: appears 1 time in: 49.X.

良
3941: appears 2 times in: 26.3 and 54.5.

兩
3953: appears 1 time in: 30.X.

列
3984: appears 1 time in: 52.3.

洌
3987: appears 1 time in: 48.5.

連
4009: appears 1 time in: 39.4.

漣
4012: appears 1 time in: 3.6.

林
4022: appears 1 time in: 3.3.

臨
4027: appears 8 times in: 19.0, 19.1, 19.2, 19.3, 19.4, 19.5, 19.6 and 19.X.

鄰
4033: appears 5 times in: 9.5, 11.4, 15.5, 51.6 and 63.5.

吝
4040: appears 20 times in: 3.3, 4.1, 4.4, 11.6, 13.2, 18.4, 20.1, 21.3, 22.5, 28.4, 31.3, 32.3, 35.6, 37.3, 40.3, 44.6, 45.3, 47.4, 57.3 and 64.1.

陵
4067: appears 3 times in: 13.3, 51.2 and 53.5.

靈
4071: appears 1 time in: 27.1.

雷
4083: appears 1 time in: 56.X.

樂
4129: appears 2 times in: 5.X and 16.X.

漏
4152: appears 1 time in: 48.2.

廬
4158: appears 1 time in: 23.6.

陸
4191: appears 3 times in: 43.5, 53.3 and 53.6.

祿
4196: appears 2 times in: 12.X and 43.X.

鹿
4203: appears 1 time in: 3.3.

亂
4220: appears 2 times in: 45.1 and 63.0.

囍
4235: appears 1 time in: 47.6.

雷
4236: appears 15 times in: 3.X, 16.X, 17.X, 21.X, 24.X, 25.X, 27.X, 32.X, 34.X, 40.X, 42.X, 51.X, 54.X, 55.X and 62.X.

羸
4240: appears 4 times in: 34.3, 34.4, 44.1 and 48.0.

類
4244: appears 1 time in: 13.X.

綸
4252: appears 1 time in: 3.X.

輪
4254: appears 2 times in: 63.1 and 64.2.

隆
4255: appears 1 time in: 28.4.

龍
4258: appears 6 times in: 1.1, 1.2, 1.5, 1.6, 1.7 and 2.6.

旅
4286: appears 8 times in: 24.X, 56.0, 56.1, 56.2, 56.3, 56.4, 56.6 and 56.X.

律
4297: appears 1 time in: 7.1.

攣
4300: appears 2 times in: 9.5 and 61.5.

馬
4310: appears 11 times in: 2.0, 3.2, 3.4, 3.6, 22.4, 26.3, 35.0, 36.2, 38.1, 59.1 and 61.4.

莽
4354: appears 1 time in: 13.3.

茅
4364: appears 3 times in: 11.1, 12.1 and 28.1.

緻
4387: appears 1 time in: 29.6.

妹
4410: appears 7 times in: 11.5, 54.0, 54.1, 54.3, 54.4, 54.5 and 54.X.

沬
4412: appears 1 time in: 55.3.

門
4418: appears 4 times in: 13.1, 17.1, 36.4 and 60.2.

悶
4420: appears 1 time in: 28.X.

蒙
4437: appears 7 times in: 4.0, 4.1, 4.2, 4.4, 4.5, 4.6 and 4.X.

迷
4450: appears 2 times in: 2.0 and 24.6.

靡
4455: appears 1 time in: 61.2.

袂
4456: appears 1 time in: 54.5.

密
4464: appears 2 times in: 9.0 and 62.5.

廟
4473: appears 3 times in: 45.0, 59.0 and 59.X.

眇
4476: appears 2 times in: 10.3 and 54.2.

滅
4483: appears 5 times in: 21.1, 21.2, 21.6, 28.6 and 28.X.

蔑
4485: appears 2 times in: 23.1 and 23.2.

面
4497: appears 1 time in: 49.6.

民
4508: appears 7 times in: 7.X, 10.X, 11.X, 18.X, 19.X, 20.X and 48.X.

冥
4528: appears 2 times in: 16.6 and 46.6.

明
4534: appears 16 times in: 17.4, 21.X, 22.X, 30.X, 35.X, 36.0, 36.1, 36.2, 36.3, 36.4, 36.5, 36.6, 36.X, 48.3, 49.X and 56.X.

鳴
4535: appears 4 times in: 15.2, 15.6, 16.1 and 61.2.

命
4537: appears 12 times in: 6.4, 7.2, 7.6, 11.6, 12.4, 14.X, 44.X, 47.X, 49.4, 50.X, 56.5 and 57.X.

莫
4557: appears 4 times in: 33.2, 42.6, 43.2 and 53.5.

幕
4559: appears 1 time in: 48.6.

謀
4578: appears 1 time in: 6.X.

茂
4580: appears 1 time in: 25.X.

母
4582: appears 2 times in: 18.2 and 35.2.

拇
4584: appears 2 times in: 31.1 and 40.4.

木
4593: appears 7 times in: 28.X, 46.X, 47.1, 48.X, 50.X, 53.4 and 53.X.

目
4596: appears 1 time in: 9.3.

納
4607: appears 2 times in: 4.2 and 29.4.

乃
4612: appears 8 times in: 3.2, 17.6, 45.1, 45.2, 46.2, 47.5, 49.0 and 49.2.

南
4620: appears 5 times in: 2.0, 36.3, 39.0, 40.0 and 46.0.

難
4625: appears 1 time in: 12.X.

囊
4627: appears 1 time in: 2.4.

能
4648: appears 5 times in: 10.3, 34.6, 50.2, 54.1 and 54.2.

柅
4659: appears 1 time in: 44.1.

泥
4660: appears 3 times in: 5.3, 48.1 and 51.4.

鳥
4688: appears 4 times in: 56.6, 62.0, 62.1 and 62.6.

鮑
4700: appears 1 time in: 47.6.

年
4711: appears 5 times in: 3.2, 24.6, 27.3, 63.3 and 64.4.

寧
4725: appears 2 times in: 8.0 and 58.4.

凝
4732: appears 1 time in: 50.X.

牛
4737: appears 8 times in: 25.3, 26.4, 30.0, 33.2, 38.3, 49.1, 56.6 and 63.5.

內
4766: appears 1 time in: 8.2.

女
4776: appears 9 times in: 3.2, 4.3, 20.2, 28.2, 31.0, 37.0, 44.0, 53.0 and 54.6.

我
4778: appears 11 times in: 4.0, 9.0, 20.3, 20.5, 27.1, 42.5, 48.3, 50.2, 56.4, 61.2 and 62.5.

惡
4809: appears 3 times in: 14.X, 33.X and 38.1.

遏
4812: appears 1 time in: 14.X.

罷
4841: appears 1 time in: 61.3.

八
4845: appears 1 time in: 19.0.

拔
4848: appears 2 times in: 11.1 and 12.1.

敗
4866: appears 1 time in: 24.6.

班
4889: appears 3 times in: 3.2, 3.4 and 3.6.

磐
4904: appears 2 times in: 3.1 and 53.2.

包
4937: appears 7 times in: 4.2, 11.2, 12.2, 12.3, 44.2, 44.4 and 44.5.

Concordance

苞
4941: appears 1 time in: 12.5.

保
4946: appears 1 time in: 19.X.

豹
4954: appears 1 time in: 49.6.

北
4974: appears 2 times in: 2.0 and 39.0.

白
4975: appears 3 times in: 22.4, 22.6 and 28.1.

百
4976: appears 2 times in: 6.2 and 51.0.

帛
4979: appears 1 time in: 22.5.

背
4989: appears 1 time in: 52.0.

貝
5005: appears 1 time in: 51.2.

配
5019: appears 2 times in: 16.X and 55.1.

沛
5020: appears 1 time in: 55.3.

賁
5027: appears 8 times in: 22.0, 22.1, 22.2, 22.3, 22.4, 22.5, 22.6 and 22.X.

奔
5028: appears 1 time in: 59.2.

朋
5054: appears 10 times in: 2.0, 11.2, 16.4, 24.0, 31.4, 39.5, 40.4, 41.5, 42.2 and 58.X.

彭
5060: appears 1 time in: 14.4.

匕
5076: appears 1 time in: 51.0.

比
5077: appears 8 times in: 8.0, 8.1, 8.2, 8.3, 8.4, 8.5, 8.6 and 8.X.

妣
5082: appears 1 time in: 62.2.

閉
5092: appears 1 time in: 24.X.

彼
5093: appears 1 time in: 62.5.

鼻
5100: appears 1 time in: 21.2.

敝
5101: appears 2 times in: 48.2 and 54.X.

必
5109: appears 1 time in: 62.4.

匹
5170: appears 1 time in: 61.4.

辟
5172: appears 1 time in: 12.X.

辨
5240: appears 4 times in: 10.X, 13.X, 23.2 and 64.X.

變
5245: appears 2 times in: 49.5 and 49.6.

翩
5249: appears 1 time in: 11.4.

賓
5259: appears 2 times in: 20.4 and 44.2.

頻
5275: appears 2 times in: 24.3 and 57.3.

牝
5280: appears 2 times in: 2.0 and 30.0.

品
5281: appears 1 time in: 57.4.

冰
5283: appears 1 time in: 2.1.

並
5292: appears 1 time in: 48.3.

瓶
5301: appears 1 time in: 48.0.

平
5303: appears 3 times in: 11.3, 15.X and 29.5.

跛
5317: appears 2 times in: 10.3 and 54.1.

剝
5337: appears 8 times in: 23.0, 23.1, 23.2, 23.3, 23.4, 23.6, 23.X and 58.5.

陂
5345: appears 1 time in: 11.3.

嶓
5351: appears 1 time in: 22.4.

逋
5373: appears 1 time in: 6.2.

不
5379: appears 96 times in: 1.X, 2.2, 3.2, 3.3, 3.4, 4.0, 4.3, 4.6, 5.6, 6.0, 6.1, 6.2, 6.4, 8.0, 8.5, 9.0, 10.0, 11.2, 11.3, 11.4, 12.0, 12.X, 13.3, 14.6, 15.4, 15.5, 16.2, 16.5, 18.2, 18.6, 19.2, 20.0, 23.0, 23.5, 23.6, 24.1, 24.6, 24.X, 25.0, 25.2, 26.0, 27.5, 28.2, 28.X, 29.5, 29.6, 30.3, 32.3, 32.X, 33.6, 33.X, 34.4, 34.6, 35.5, 36.1, 36.3, 36.6, 39.0, 40.6, 43.0, 43.1, 43.4, 44.2, 45.1, 45.X, 46.6, 47.0, 47.1, 47.3, 48.0, 48.1, 48.3, 50.2, 50.3, 50.6, 51.0, 51.6, 52.0, 52.2, 52.X, 53.3, 53.5, 54.5, 55.6, 56.4, 56.X, 57.5, 60.0, 60.1, 60.2, 60.3, 61.1, 62.0, 62.2, 62.5 and 63.5.

僕
5401: appears 2 times in: 56.2 and 56.3.

三
5415: appears 21 times in: 4.0, 5.6, 6.2, 6.6, 7.2, 8.5, 13.3, 18.0, 29.6, 35.0, 36.1, 40.2, 41.3, 47.1, 49.3, 53.5, 55.6, 57.4, 57.5, 63.3 and 64.4.

桑
5424: appears 1 time in: 12.5.

喪
5429: appears 12 times in: 2.0, 34.5, 38.1, 48.0, 51.0, 51.2, 51.5, 56.3, 56.6, 57.6, 62.X and 63.2.

塞
5446: appears 1 time in: 50.3.

索
5459: appears 1 time in: 51.6.

所
5465: appears 4 times in: 6.1, 40.0, 56.1 and 59.4.

瑣
5466: appears 1 time in: 56.1.

蘇
5488: appears 1 time in: 51.3.

素
5490: appears 1 time in: 10.1.

愬
5494: appears 1 time in: 10.4.

俗
5497: appears 1 time in: 53.X.

夙
5502: appears 1 time in: 40.0.

速
5505: appears 1 time in: 5.6.

Concordance

棟
5506: appears 1 time in: 50.4.

雖
5519: appears 1 time in: 55.1.

隨
5523: appears 7 times in: 17.0, 17.3, 17.4, 17.X, 31.3, 52.2 and 57.X.

遂
5530: appears 4 times in: 34.6, 37.2, 47.X and 51.4.

歲
5538: appears 5 times in: 13.3, 29.6, 47.1, 53.5 and 55.6.

損
5548: appears 7 times in: 41.0, 41.1, 41.2, 41.3, 41.4, 41.6 and 41.X.

巽
5550: appears 5 times in: 57.0, 57.2, 57.3, 57.6 and 57.X.

訟
5558: appears 5 times in: 6.0, 6.2, 6.4, 6.5 and 6.X.

斯
5574: appears 2 times in: 40.4 and 56.1.

思
5580: appears 5 times in: 19.X, 31.4, 52.X, 59.4 and 63.X.

死
5589: appears 3 times in: 16.5, 30.4 and 61.X.

巳
5590: appears 3 times in: 41.1, 49.0 and 49.2.

祀
5592: appears 2 times in: 47.2 and 47.5.

四
5598: appears 2 times in: 30.X and 44.X.

沙
5606: appears 1 time in: 5.2.

殺
5615: appears 1 time in: 63.5.

山
5630: appears 17 times in: 4.X, 15.X, 17.6, 18.X, 22.X, 23.X, 26.X, 27.X, 31.X, 33.X, 39.X, 41.X, 46.4, 52.X, 53.X, 56.X and 62.X.

善
5657: appears 3 times in: 14.X, 42.X and 53.X.

上
5669: appears 29 times in: 5.X, 8.X, 9.X, 10.X, 14.X, 16.X, 19.X, 20.X, 23.X, 31.X, 34.X, 35.X, 38.X, 39.X, 40.6, 43.X, 45.X, 48.X, 50.X, 53.X, 54.X, 56.X, 59.X, 60.X, 61.X, 62.0, 62.X, 63.X and 64.X.

尚
5670: appears 6 times in: 9.6, 11.2, 18.6, 29.0, 55.1 and 60.5.

裳
5671: appears 1 time in: 2.5.

賞
5672: appears 1 time in: 64.4.

商
5673: appears 2 times in: 24.X and 58.4.

舍
5699: appears 3 times in: 3.3, 22.1 and 27.1.

赦
5702: appears 1 time in: 40.X.

射
5703: appears 3 times in: 40.6, 48.2 and 56.5.

舌
5705: appears 1 time in: 31.6.

涉
5707: appears 13 times in: 5.0, 6.0, 13.0, 15.1, 18.0, 26.0, 27.5, 27.6, 28.6, 42.0, 59.0, 61.0 and 64.3.

設
5711: appears 1 time in: 20.X.

申
5712: appears 1 time in: 57.X.

身
5718: appears 3 times in: 39.X, 52.0 and 52.4.

愼
5734: appears 3 times in: 27.X, 56.X and 64.X.

生
5738: appears 6 times in: 20.3, 20.5, 20.6, 28.2, 28.5 and 46.X.

牲
5739: appears 1 time in: 45.0.

眚
5741: appears 6 times in: 6.2, 24.6, 25.0, 25.6, 51.3 and 62.6.

省
5744: appears 3 times in: 20.X, 24.X and 51.X.

升
5745: appears 7 times in: 13.3, 46.0, 46.1, 46.3, 46.5, 46.6 and 46.X.

勝
5754: appears 3 times in: 33.2, 43.1 and 53.5.

尸
5756: appears 2 times in: 7.3 and 7.5.

師
5760: appears 12 times in: 7.0, 7.1, 7.2, 7.3, 7.4, 7.5, 7.X, 11.6, 13.5, 15.6, 16.0 and 24.6.

筮
5763: appears 2 times in: 4.0 and 8.0.

噬
5764: appears 7 times in: 21.0, 21.2, 21.3, 21.4, 21.5, 21.X and 38.5.

豕
5766: appears 3 times in: 26.5, 38.6 and 44.1.

施
5768: appears 3 times in: 15.X, 43.X and 44.X.

史
5769: appears 1 time in: 57.2.

使
5770: appears 1 time in: 41.4.

始
5772: appears 1 time in: 6.X.

士
5776: appears 2 times in: 28.5 and 54.6.

時
5780: appears 3 times in: 25.X, 49.X and 54.4.

矢
5784: appears 3 times in: 21.4, 40.2 and 56.5.

事
5787: appears 12 times in: 2.3, 6.1, 6.3, 6.X, 18.6, 29.X, 38.0, 41.1, 42.3, 51.5, 57.X and 62.0.

視
5789: appears 5 times in: 10.3, 10.6, 27.4, 51.6 and 54.2.

世
5790: appears 1 time in: 28.X.

CONCORDANCE

是
5794: appears 2 times in: 62.6 and 64.6.

勢
5799: appears 1 time in: 2.X.

失
5806: appears 5 times in: 8.5, 17.2, 17.3, 35.5 and 64.6.

十
5807: appears 5 times in: 3.2, 24.6, 27.3, 41.5 and 42.2.

食
5810: appears 14 times in: 5.5, 5.X, 6.3, 11.3, 23.6, 26.0, 27.X, 36.1, 47.2, 48.1, 48.3, 48.5, 50.3 and 53.2.

石
5813: appears 2 times in: 16.2 and 47.3.

碩
5815: appears 2 times in: 23.6 and 39.6.

鼫
5816: appears 1 time in: 35.4.

實
5821: appears 4 times in: 27.0, 50.2, 54.6 and 63.5.

識
5825: appears 1 time in: 26.X.

收
5837: appears 1 time in: 48.6.

首
5839: appears 6 times in: 1.7, 8.6, 30.6, 36.3, 63.6 and 64.6.

受
5840: appears 4 times in: 31.X, 35.2, 48.3 and 63.5.

狩
5845: appears 1 time in: 36.3.

數
5865: appears 1 time in: 60.X.

鼠
5871: appears 1 time in: 35.4.

庶
5874: appears 2 times in: 22.X and 35.0.

束
5891: appears 1 time in: 22.5.

衰
5908: appears 1 time in: 15.X.

帥
5909: appears 1 time in: 7.5.

霜
5919: appears 1 time in: 2.1.

水
5922: appears 11 times in: 6.X, 7.X, 8.X, 29.X, 39.X, 47.X, 48.X, 59.X, 60.X, 63.X and 64.X.

順
5935: appears 2 times in: 14.X and 46.X.

說
5939: appears 6 times in: 4.1, 9.3, 26.2, 33.2, 38.6 and 47.5.

大
5943: appears 57 times in: 1.2, 1.5, 2.2, 3.5, 5.0, 6.0, 7.6, 10.3, 11.0, 12.0, 12.2, 12.5, 13.0, 13.5, 14.0, 14.2, 14.X, 15.1, 16.4, 18.0, 18.3, 19.5, 24.6, 26.0, 26.X, 27.5, 27.6, 28.0, 28.X, 30.3, 30.X, 34.0, 34.4, 34.X, 36.3, 37.4, 39.0, 39.5, 39.6, 42.0, 42.1, 44.3, 45.0, 45.4, 46.0, 46.1, 46.X, 47.0, 49.5, 50.6, 57.0, 59.0, 59.5, 61.0, 62.0, 64.3 and 64.4.

他
5961: appears 1 time in: 61.1.

帶
6005: appears 1 time in: 6.6.

泰
6023: appears 2 times in: 11.0 and 11.X.

眈
6028: appears 1 time in: 27.4.

坦
6057: appears 1 time in: 10.2.

道
6136: appears 5 times in: 9.1, 10.2, 11.X, 17.4 and 24.0.

咷
6152: appears 2 times in: 13.5 and 56.6.

得
6161: appears 26 times in: 2.0, 11.2, 16.4, 17.3, 21.4, 21.5, 23.6, 25.3, 28.2, 28.5, 29.2, 29.6, 35.5, 36.3, 40.2, 41.3, 41.6, 48.0, 50.1, 51.2, 53.4, 55.2, 56.2, 56.4, 61.3 and 63.2.

德
6162: appears 19 times in: 2.X, 4.X, 6.3, 9.6, 9.X, 12.X, 16.X, 18.X, 26.X, 29.X, 32.3, 32.5, 35.X, 39.X, 42.5, 43.X, 46.X, 53.X and 60.X.

登
6167: appears 2 times in: 36.6 and 61.6.

羝
6195: appears 2 times in: 34.3 and 34.6.

地
6198: appears 16 times in: 2.X, 7.X, 8.X, 11.X, 12.X, 15.X, 16.X, 19.X, 20.X, 23.X, 24.X, 35.X, 36.6, 36.X, 45.X and 46.X.

弟
6201: appears 1 time in: 7.5.

娣
6202: appears 3 times in: 54.1, 54.3 and 54.5.

帝
6204: appears 5 times in: 11.5, 16.X, 42.2, 54.5 and 59.X.

敵
6221: appears 1 time in: 61.3.

覿
6230: appears 2 times in: 47.1 and 55.6.

涕
6250: appears 2 times in: 30.5 and 45.6.

稊
6252: appears 1 time in: 28.2.

惕
6263: appears 4 times in: 1.3, 6.0, 9.4 and 43.2.

逖
6265: appears 1 time in: 59.6.

臺
6314: appears 1 time in: 30.3.

渫
6318: appears 1 time in: 48.3.

顛
6337: appears 3 times in: 27.2, 27.4 and 50.1.

電
6358: appears 2 times in: 21.X and 55.X.

天
6361: appears 23 times in: 1.5, 1.X, 5.X, 6.X, 9.X, 10.X, 11.X, 12.X, 13.X, 14.3, 14.6, 14.X, 25.X, 26.6, 26.X, 33.X, 34.X, 36.6, 38.3, 43.X, 44.5, 44.X and 61.6.

田
6362: appears 5 times in: 1.2, 7.5, 32.4, 40.2 and 57.4.

CONCORDANCE

頂
6390: appears 1 time in: 28.6.

鼎
6392: appears 8 times in: 50.0, 50.1, 50.2, 50.3, 50.4, 50.5, 50.6 and 50.X.

定
6393: appears 1 time in: 10.X.

庭
6405: appears 5 times in: 36.4, 43.0, 52.0, 60.1 and 60.2.

多
6416: appears 2 times in: 15.X and 26.X.

朵
6419: appears 1 time in: 27.1.

它
6439: appears 2 times in: 8.1 and 28.4.

沱
6442: appears 1 time in: 30.5.

斗
6472: appears 2 times in: 55.2 and 55.4.

度
6504: appears 1 time in: 60.X.

毒
6509: appears 1 time in: 21.3.

獨
6512: appears 3 times in: 24.4, 28.X and 43.3.

瀆
6515: appears 1 time in: 4.0.

塗
6525: appears 1 time in: 38.6.

徒
6536: appears 1 time in: 22.1.

突
6540: appears 1 time in: 30.4.

兌
6560: appears 7 times in: 58.0, 58.1, 58.2, 58.3, 58.4, 58.6 and 58.X.

對
6562: appears 1 time in: 25.X.

退
6568: appears 3 times in: 20.3, 34.6 and 57.1.

敦
6571: appears 3 times in: 19.6, 24.5 and 52.6.

遯
6586: appears 8 times in: 28.X, 33.0, 33.1, 33.3, 33.4, 33.5, 33.6 and 33.X.

屯
6592: appears 4 times in: 3.0, 3.2, 3.5 and 3.X.

豚
6600: appears 1 time in: 61.0.

臀
6602: appears 3 times in: 43.4, 44.3 and 47.1.

東
6605: appears 3 times in: 2.0, 39.0 and 63.5.

棟
6607: appears 3 times in: 28.0, 28.3 and 28.4.

動
6611: appears 1 time in: 47.6.

同
6615: appears 7 times in: 13.0, 13.1, 13.2, 13.5, 13.6, 13.X and 38.X.

童
6626: appears 6 times in: 4.0, 4.5, 20.1, 26.4, 56.2 and 56.3.

災
6652: appears 4 times in: 24.6, 25.3, 56.1 and 62.6.

載
6653: appears 4 times in: 2.X, 9.6, 14.2 and 38.6.

在
6657: appears 16 times in: 1.2, 1.4, 1.5, 7.2, 14.X, 17.4, 24.X, 26.X, 34.X, 37.2, 57.2, 57.6, 61.2, 62.5, 63.X and 64.X.

再
6658: appears 1 time in: 4.0.

裁
6664: appears 1 time in: 11.X.

簪
6679: appears 1 time in: 16.4.

臧
6704: appears 1 time in: 7.1.

則
6746: appears 10 times in: 4.0, 14.1, 25.2, 30.3, 34.6, 38.6, 41.3, 42.X, 43.X and 60.3.

昃
6755: appears 1 time in: 30.3.

惻
6758: appears 1 time in: 48.3.

左
6774: appears 4 times in: 7.4, 11.X, 36.2 and 36.4.

作
6780: appears 5 times in: 6.X, 16.X, 30.X, 40.X and 42.1.

錯
6793: appears 1 time in: 30.1.

祖
6815: appears 2 times in: 16.X and 62.2.

足
6824: appears 2 times in: 23.1 and 50.4.

族
6830: appears 1 time in: 13.X.

罪
6860: appears 1 time in: 40.X.

摧
6866: appears 1 time in: 35.1.

萃
6880: appears 5 times in: 45.0, 45.1, 45.3, 45.5 and 45.X.

樽
6886: appears 1 time in: 29.4.

宗
6896: appears 3 times in: 13.2, 38.5 and 63.3.

從
6919: appears 6 times in: 2.3, 6.3, 17.6, 31.4, 42.4 and 62.3.

叢
6921: appears 1 time in: 29.6.

咨
6923: appears 1 time in: 45.6.

資
6927: appears 3 times in: 56.2, 56.4 and 57.6.

苗
6932: appears 1 time in: 25.2.

茲
6935: appears 1 time in: 35.2.

子
6939: appears 86 times in: 1.3, 1.X, 2.0, 2.X, 3.2, 3.3, 3.X, 4.2, 4.X, 5.X, 6.X, 7.5, 7.X, 9.6, 9.X, 10.X, 12.0, 12.X, 13.0, 13.X, 14.3, 14.X, 15.0, 15.1, 15.3, 15.X, 17.2, 17.3, 17.X, 18.1, 18.X, 19.X,

20.1, 20.5, 20.6, 22.X, 23.6, 26.X, 27.X, 28.X, 29.X, 31.X, 32.5, 32.X, 33.4, 33.X, 34.3, 34.X, 35.X, 36.1, 36.5, 36.X, 37.3, 37.X, 38.X, 39.X, 40.5, 40.X, 41.X, 42.X, 43.3, 43.X, 45.X, 46.X, 47.X, 48.X, 49.6, 49.X, 50.1, 50.X, 51.X, 52.X, 53.1, 53.X, 54.X, 55.X, 56.X, 57.X, 58.X, 60.X, 61.2, 61.X, 62.X, 63.X, 64.5 and 64.X.

字
6942: appears 1 time in: 3.2.

肺
6950: appears 1 time in: 21.4.

自
6960: appears 15 times in: 1.X, 5.4, 8.2, 9.0, 9.1, 11.6, 14.6, 27.0, 29.4, 35.X, 37.X, 38.1, 43.0, 44.5 and 62.5.

次
6980: appears 5 times in: 7.4, 43.4, 44.3, 56.2 and 56.3.

外
7001: appears 1 time in: 8.4.

萬
7030: appears 2 times in: 8.X and 25.X.

亡
7034: appears 23 times in: 11.2, 12.5, 31.4, 32.2, 34.4, 35.3, 35.5, 37.1, 38.1, 38.5, 43.4, 45.5, 49.0, 49.4, 52.5, 56.5, 57.4, 57.5, 58.2, 59.2, 60.6, 61.4 and 64.4.

妄
7035: appears 6 times in: 25.0, 25.1, 25.3, 25.5, 25.6 and 25.X.

王
7037: appears 26 times in: 2.3, 6.3, 7.2, 8.5, 8.X, 16.X, 17.6, 18.6, 20.4, 20.X, 21.X, 24.X, 25.X, 30.6, 35.2, 37.5, 39.2, 42.2, 43.0, 45.0, 46.4, 48.3, 55.0, 59.0, 59.5 and 59.X.

望
7043: appears 3 times in: 9.6, 54.5 and 61.4.

罔
7045: appears 2 times in: 34.3 and 35.1.

往
7050: appears 50 times in: 2.0, 3.0, 3.3, 3.4, 4.1, 10.1, 11.0, 11.3, 12.0, 14.2, 18.4, 22.0, 23.0, 24.0, 25.0, 25.1, 25.2, 26.3, 26.X, 28.0, 31.3, 31.4, 32.0, 33.1, 35.5, 36.1, 38.5, 38.6, 39.1, 39.3, 39.4, 39.6, 40.0, 41.0, 41.1, 41.6, 42.0, 43.0, 43.1, 44.1, 45.0, 45.1, 45.3, 48.0, 51.5, 55.1, 55.2, 57.0, 60.5 and 62.4.

威
7051: appears 2 times in: 14.5 and 37.6.

爲
7059: appears 8 times in: 4.6, 10.3, 42.1, 42.4, 43.1, 45.1, 48.3 and 53.6.

惟
7066: appears 1 time in: 3.3.

維
7067: appears 4 times in: 17.6, 29.0, 35.6 and 40.5.

謂
7079: appears 1 time in: 62.6.

衛
7089: appears 1 time in: 26.3.

違
7093: appears 3 times in: 6.X, 41.5 and 42.2.

尾
7109: appears 7 times in: 10.0, 10.3, 10.4, 33.1, 63.1, 64.0 and 64.1.

未
7114: appears 6 times in: 48.0, 49.5, 58.4, 64.0, 64.3 and 64.X.

位
7116: appears 3 times in: 45.5, 50.X and 52.X.

文
7129: appears 1 time in: 9.X.

問
7141: appears 1 time in: 42.5.

聞
7142: appears 1 time in: 43.4.

甕
7151: appears 1 time in: 48.2.

握
7161: appears 1 time in: 45.1.

渥
7162: appears 1 time in: 50.4.

巫
7164: appears 1 time in: 57.2.

无
7173: appears 150 times in: 1.3, 1.4, 1.7, 2.2, 2.3, 2.4, 3.3, 3.4, 4.3, 5.1, 6.2, 6.3, 7.0, 7.2, 7.4, 7.5, 8.0, 8.1, 8.6, 9.4, 10.1, 11.3, 12.4, 13.1, 13.6, 14.1, 14.2, 14.4, 14.6, 15.4, 15.5, 16.6, 17.0, 18.1, 18.3, 19.2, 19.3, 19.4, 19.6, 19.X, 20.1, 20.5, 20.6, 21.1, 21.2, 21.3, 21.5, 22.6, 22.X, 23.3, 23.5, 24.0, 24.1, 24.3, 24.5, 25.0, 25.1, 25.3, 25.4, 25.5, 25.6, 25.X, 27.3, 27.4, 28.1, 28.2, 28.5, 28.6, 28.X, 29.4, 29.5, 30.1, 30.6, 31.5, 32.0, 32.1, 32.4, 33.6, 34.5, 34.6, 35.1, 35.5, 35.6, 37.2, 38.1, 38.2, 38.3, 38.4, 40.0, 40.1, 40.6, 41.0, 41.1, 41.4, 41.6, 42.1, 42.3, 43.3, 43.4, 43.5, 43.6, 44.2, 44.3, 44.4, 44.6, 45.1, 45.2, 45.3, 45.4, 45.5, 45.6, 46.2, 46.4, 47.0, 47.2, 47.X, 48.0, 48.1, 48.4, 49.2, 50.1, 50.6, 51.3, 51.5, 51.6, 52.0, 52.1, 52.4, 53.1, 53.4, 54.0, 54.6, 55.1, 55.3, 55.6, 57.2, 57.5, 59.3, 59.5, 59.6, 60.1, 60.3, 61.4, 61.5, 62.2, 62.4, 63.1, 64.0, 64.5 and 64.6.

吾
7188: appears 1 time in: 61.2.

武
7195: appears 2 times in: 10.3 and 57.1.

勿
7208: appears 26 times in: 1.1, 3.0, 4.3, 7.6, 11.3, 11.6, 16.4, 25.5, 27.3, 29.3, 33.1, 35.5, 37.5, 38.1, 42.5, 42.6, 43.2, 44.0, 45.1, 46.0, 48.6, 51.2, 55.0, 62.4, 63.2 and 63.3.

物
7209: appears 6 times in: 2.X, 13.X, 15.X, 25.X, 37.X and 64.X.

甿
7211: appears 1 time in: 47.6.

屋
7212: appears 1 time in: 55.6.

牙
7214: appears 1 time in: 26.5.

啞
7226: appears 2 times in: 51.0 and 51.1.

羊
7247: appears 5 times in: 34.3, 34.5, 34.6, 43.4 and 54.6.

揚
7259: appears 2 times in: 14.X and 43.0.

楊
7261: appears 2 times in: 28.2 and 28.5.

Concordance

野
7314: appears 2 times in: 2.6 and 13.0.

夜
7315: appears 1 time in: 43.2.

言
7334: appears 15 times in: 5.2, 6.1, 7.5, 26.X, 27.X, 36.1, 37.X, 43.4, 47.0, 49.3, 51.0, 51.1, 51.6, 52.5 and 53.1.

嚴
7347: appears 1 time in: 33.X.

宴
7364: appears 2 times in: 5.X and 17.X.

燕
7399: appears 1 time in: 61.1.

音
7418: appears 2 times in: 61.6 and 62.0.

殷
7423: appears 1 time in: 16.X.

夤
7427: appears 1 time in: 52.3.

引
7429: appears 2 times in: 45.2 and 58.6.

陰
7444: appears 1 time in: 61.2.

飲
7454: appears 4 times in: 5.X, 27.X, 53.2 and 64.6.

盈
7474: appears 2 times in: 8.1 and 29.5.

約
7493: appears 1 time in: 29.4.

襘
7498: appears 3 times in: 45.2, 46.2 and 63.5.

藥
7501: appears 1 time in: 25.5.

躍
7504: appears 1 time in: 1.4.

幽
7505: appears 3 times in: 10.2, 47.1 and 54.2.

牖
7507: appears 1 time in: 29.4.

憂
7508: appears 2 times in: 19.3 and 55.0.

由
7513: appears 2 times in: 16.4 and 27.6.

攸
7519: appears 32 times in: 2.0, 3.0, 4.3, 14.2, 19.3, 22.0, 23.0, 24.0, 25.0, 25.2, 25.6, 26.3, 27.3, 28.0, 32.0, 32.1, 33.1, 34.6, 36.1, 37.2, 40.0, 41.0, 41.6, 42.0, 43.0, 44.1, 45.0, 45.3, 54.0, 54.6, 57.0 and 64.0.

有
7533: appears 129 times in: 1.6, 2.0, 2.3, 3.0, 4.3, 5.0, 5.2, 5.6, 6.0, 6.1, 7.5, 7.6, 7.X, 8.1, 8.X, 9.4, 9.5, 11.3, 12.4, 14.0, 14.2, 14.X, 15.0, 15.3, 15.X, 16.3, 16.4, 16.6, 17.1, 17.3, 17.4, 17.X, 18.1, 18.3, 18.X, 19.0, 19.X, 20.0, 22.0, 22.X, 23.0, 24.0, 24.6, 25.0, 25.2, 25.5, 25.6, 26.1, 26.3, 27.X, 28.0, 28.4, 29.0, 29.2, 30.6, 31.X, 32.0, 33.1, 33.3, 33.X, 34.1, 36.1, 37.1, 37.5, 37.6, 37.X, 38.3, 39.X, 40.0, 40.5, 41.0, 41.4, 41.6, 41.X, 42.0, 42.3, 42.5, 42.X, 43.0, 43.2, 43.3, 43.6, 44.1, 44.2, 44.5, 44.X, 45.0, 45.1, 45.5, 47.0, 47.4, 47.5, 47.6, 48.6, 48.X, 49.3, 49.4, 49.5, 49.X, 50.2, 50.X, 51.5, 51.6, 52.5, 53.1, 53.X, 54.4, 54.X, 55.1, 55.2, 55.5, 56.X,

57.0, 57.5, 58.4, 58.5, 59.0, 59.4, 60.5, 60.X, 61.1, 61.2, 61.5, 61.X, 62.X, 63.4, 64.4, 64.5 and 64.6.

宥
7536: appears 1 time in: 40.X.

友
7540: appears 2 times in: 41.3 and 58.X.

右
7541: appears 2 times in: 11.X and 55.3.

祐
7543: appears 1 time in: 14.6.

容
7560: appears 2 times in: 7.X and 19.X.

用
7567: appears 55 times in: 1.1, 3.0, 4.1, 4.3, 5.1, 7.6, 8.5, 11.2, 11.6, 14.3, 15.1, 15.5, 15.6, 17.6, 18.5, 20.4, 21.0, 24.6, 27.3, 28.1, 29.3, 29.4, 29.6, 30.6, 33.1, 33.2, 34.3, 35.0, 35.6, 36.2, 36.X, 40.6, 41.0, 42.1, 42.2, 42.3, 42.4, 44.0, 45.0, 45.2, 46.0, 46.2, 46.4, 47.2, 47.5, 48.3, 49.1, 53.6, 56.X, 57.2, 59.1, 62.4, 62.X, 63.3 and 64.4.

墉
7578: appears 2 times in: 13.4 and 40.6.

榮
7582: appears 1 time in: 12.X.

永
7589: appears 9 times in: 2.7, 6.1, 8.0, 22.3, 42.2, 45.5, 52.1, 54.X and 62.4.

于
7592: appears 71 times in: 2.6, 3.3, 5.1, 5.2, 5.3, 5.4, 5.5, 5.6, 10.3, 11.2, 11.3, 11.6, 12.5, 13.0, 13.1, 13.2, 13.3, 13.6, 14.3, 16.2, 17.5, 17.6, 19.0, 20.4, 22.5, 24.6, 27.2, 29.1, 29.3, 29.6, 30.X, 34.1, 34.4, 34.5, 35.2, 36.1, 36.2, 36.3, 36.4, 36.6, 38.2, 40.5, 40.6, 42.2, 43.0, 43.1, 43.3, 44.1, 46.4, 46.6, 47.1, 47.2, 47.3, 47.4, 47.5, 47.6, 51.2, 51.6, 53.1, 53.2, 53.3, 53.4, 53.5, 53.6, 56.4, 56.6, 58.5, 59.X, 61.6, 64.4 and 64.6.

豫
7603: appears 7 times in: 16.0, 16.1, 16.3, 16.4, 16.6, 16.X and 63.X.

畬
7606: appears 1 time in: 25.2.

與
7615: appears 4 times in: 6.X, 13.X, 25.X and 61.2.

譽
7617: appears 6 times in: 2.4, 18.5, 28.5, 39.1, 55.5 and 56.5.

輿
7618: appears 8 times in: 7.3, 7.5, 9.3, 23.6, 26.2, 26.3, 34.4 and 38.3.

遇
7625: appears 11 times in: 13.5, 21.3, 38.2, 38.4, 38.6, 43.3, 55.1, 55.4, 62.2, 62.4 and 62.6.

渝
7635: appears 3 times in: 6.4, 16.6 and 17.1.

於
7643: appears 4 times in: 5.X, 23.X, 43.X and 45.X.

虞
7648: appears 3 times in: 3.3, 45.X and 61.1.

語
7651: appears 1 time in: 27.X.

CONCORDANCE

羽
7658: appears 1 time in: 53.6.

雨
7662: appears 7 times in: 9.0, 9.6, 38.6, 40.X, 43.3, 50.3 and 62.5.

禦
7665: appears 2 times in: 4.6 and 53.3.

玉
7666: appears 1 time in: 50.6.

裕
7667: appears 2 times in: 18.4 and 35.1.

魚
7668: appears 4 times in: 23.5, 44.2, 44.4 and 61.0.

欲
7671: appears 2 times in: 27.4 and 41.X.

獄
7685: appears 5 times in: 21.0, 22.X, 55.X, 56.X and 61.X.

育
7687: appears 4 times in: 4.X, 18.X, 25.X and 53.3.

曰
7694: appears 2 times in: 26.3 and 47.6.

月
7696: appears 4 times in: 9.6, 19.0, 54.5 and 61.4.

刖
7697: appears 1 time in: 47.5.

元
7707: appears 27 times in: 1.0, 2.0, 2.5, 3.0, 6.5, 8.0, 10.6, 11.5, 14.0, 17.0, 18.0, 19.0, 24.1, 25.0, 26.4, 30.2, 38.4, 41.0, 41.5, 42.1, 42.5, 45.5, 46.0, 48.6, 49.0, 50.0 and 59.4.

淵
7723: appears 1 time in: 1.4.

原
7725: appears 1 time in: 8.0.

園
7731: appears 1 time in: 22.5.

遠
7734: appears 2 times in: 24.1 and 33.X.

雲
7750: appears 4 times in: 3.X, 5.X, 9.0 and 62.5.

隕
7756: appears 1 time in: 44.5.

允
7759: appears 2 times in: 35.3 and 46.1.

孕
7765: appears 2 times in: 53.3 and 53.5.

慍
7766: appears 1 time in: 43.3.

蹢
8000: appears 1 time in: 44.1.

蔀
8001: appears 3 times in: 55.2, 55.4 and 55.6.

窨
8002: appears 2 times in: 29.1 and 29.3.

牿
8003: appears 1 time in: 26.4.

脢
8004: appears 1 time in: 31.5.

肇
8005: appears 1 time in: 6.6.

汔
8006: appears 2 times in: 48.0 and 64.0.

頄
8007: appears 1 time in: 43.3.

顒
8008: appears 1 time in: 20.0.

繘
8009: appears 1 time in: 48.0.

邅
8010: appears 1 time in: 3.2.

嬬
8011: appears 1 time in: 54.3.

PinYin Pronunciation

Pinyin	English	Explanation
b	spit	Unaspirated p, as in spit.
p	pay	Strongly aspirated p, as in pit.
m	may	As in English mummy.
f	fair	As in English fun.
d	stop	Unaspirated t, as in stop.
t	take	Strongly aspirated t, as in top.
n	nay	As in English nit.
l	lay	As in English love.
g	skill	Unaspirated k, as in skill.
k	kay	Strongly aspirated k, as in kill.
h	hay	Like the English h if followed by "a". It is pronounced roughly like the Scots ch and Russian x (Cyrillic "kha").
j	hatch	No equivalent in English. Like q, but unaspirated. Not the s in Asia, despite the common English pronunciation of "Beijing".
q	cheek	No equivalent in English. Like cheek, with the lips spread wide with ee. Curl the tip of the tongue downwards to stick it at the back of the teeth and strongly aspirate.
x	she	No equivalent in English. Like she, with the lips spread and the tip of your tongue curled downwards and stuck to the back of teeth when you say ee.

Pinyin	English	Explanation
zh	junk	Rather like ch (a sound between choke, joke, true, and drew, tongue tip curled more upwards). Voiced in a toneless syllable.
ch	church	As in chin, but with the tongue curled upwards; very similar to nurture in American English, but strongly aspirated.
sh	shirt	As in shoe, but with the tongue curled upwards; very similar to marsh in American English.
r	ray	Similar to the English z in azure and r in reduce, but with the tongue curled upwards, like a cross between English "r" and French "j".
z	reads	Unaspirated c, similar to something between suds and cats; as in suds in a toneless syllable.
c	hats	Like the English ts in cats, but strongly aspirated, very similar to the Polish c.
s	say	As in sun.
w	way	As in water.
y	yea	As in yes. Before a u, pronounce it with rounded lips.

Contents

Preface.. 5

THE 64 HEXAGRAMS

1	The Creative...	9
2	The Receptive	14
3	Difficulties at the Beginning	20
4	Youthful Folly	27
5	Waiting	33
6	Conflict...	38
7	The Army...	44
8	Union..	49
9	Little Domestication	54
10	Treading	59
11	Harmony	64
12	Standstill..	71
13	Fellowship..	76
14	Great Possession	81
15	Modesty..	86
16	Enthusiasm	91
17	Following	96
18	Correcting Decay	102
19	Approach	108
20	Contemplation...	113

21 Biting Through..	118
22 Elegance.	122
23 Splitting Apart	126
24 Return.	130
25 Innocence	136
26 Great Accumulation..	142
27 Nourishment..	147
28 Great Excess..	153
29 The Pit	158
30 Clinging Light	164
31 Influence	169
32 Duration.	173
33 Retreat	177
34 Great Power...	182
35 Progress..	188
36 Suppressed Light...	194
37 The Family.	201
38 Antagonism	205
39 Hampered..	211
40 Liberation...	215
41 Decrease.	220
42 Increase..	226
43 Breakthrough.	232
44 Close Encounter	238
45 Gathering Together...	243
46 Ascending...	249
47 Oppression	254
48 The Well.	261
49 Revolution..	266
50 The Caldron...	272
51 The Arousing.	278

Contents

52	Restraint	284
53	Gradual Development	289
54	The Marrying Maiden	295
55	Abundance	301
56	The Wanderer	307
57	Gentle Influence	313
58	Joyousness	319
59	Dispersion	322
60	Limitation	327
61	Inner Truth	331
62	Excess of the Small	336
63	Already Across	343
64	Before Crossing	348

Concordance	355
PinYin Pronunciation	391
Chart of Trigrams and Hexagrams	396

Chart of Trigrams and Hexagrams

Upper ▶ Lower ▼	Quian	Zhen	Kan	Gen	Kun	Xun	Li	Dui
Quian	1	34	5	26	11	9	14	43
Zhen	25	51	3	27	24	42	21	17
Kan	6	40	29	4	7	59	64	47
Gen	33	62	39	52	15	53	56	31
Kun	12	16	8	23	2	20	35	45
Xun	44	32	48	18	46	57	50	28
Li	13	55	63	22	36	37	30	49
Dui	10	54	60	41	19	61	38	58

www.ingramcontent.com/pod-product-compliance
Lightning Source LLC
Chambersburg PA
CBHW042321090526
44585CB00025BA/2789